47 20
A

Alan Russell
1985

Building Expert Systems

generating partial molecular structures consistent with the data and then elaborating them in all plausible ways. By rapidly eliminating implausible substructures, it avoids an otherwise exponential search. By systematically generating all plausible structures, it finds even those candidates that human experts occasionally overlook.

META-DENDRAL adds analysis knowledge to DENDRAL by proposing and selecting fragmentation rules for organic structures. It generates and tests possible fragmentations by examining experimental data, retaining those hypothetical rules that prove sufficiently valuable. A rule is valuable if it will apply frequently but predict incorrect fragmentations very rarely. DENDRAL surpasses all humans at its task and, as a consequence, has caused a redefinition of the roles of humans and machines in chemical research.

Another line of development, beginning with SAINT (Slagle 1961), culminates in MACSYMA (Martin and Fateman 1971), an expert system developed at Massachusetts Institute of Technology for symbolic mathematics. Like DENDRAL, MACSYMA surpasses most human experts. It performs differential and integral calculus symbolically and excels at simplifying symbolic expressions. Used daily by mathematical researchers and physicists worldwide, MACSYMA incorporates hundreds of rules garnered from experts in applied mathematics. Each rule expresses one way to transform an expression into an equivalent; the solution to a problem requires finding a chain of rules that transforms the original expression into one that is suitably simplified.

EXPERT (Weiss, Kulikowski, and Safir 1978a, b; Weiss and Kulikowski 1979) is an expert-system-building language that evolved from CASNET, an expert system for consultation in the diagnosis and treatment of glaucoma. EXPERT has been used primarily for building consultation models in ophthalmology, endocrinology, and rheumatology.

CADUCEUS at Carnegie-Mellon University in Pittsburgh (Pople, Myers, and Miller 1975; Pople 1981) and MYCIN at Stanford (Shortliffe 1976) each address different medical diagnosis problems. CADUCEUS consists of an extremely large semantic network of relationships between diseases and symptoms in internal medicine. In 1982 the system possessed approximately 100,000 associations representing nearly 85 percent of all relevant knowledge. It also employs some sophisticated strategies that attempt to distinguish multiple diseases. Field evaluations now underway with guidance from the National Institutes of Health will determine its suitability for deployment.

MYCIN addresses the problem of diagnosing and treating infectious blood diseases. Its knowledge comprises approximately 400 rules relating possible conditions to associated interpretations. In its problem-solving, MYCIN tests a rule's conditions against available data or requests data from the physician. If appropriate, it tries to infer the truth or falsity of a condition from other rules. When a panel of experts evaluated the performance of several different agents, including medical experts, interns, and MYCIN, MYCIN's performance was judged as good as or superior to that of all others.

An offshoot of MYCIN is TEIRESIAS, a program that assists in the construction of large knowledge bases by helping transfer expertise from the human expert to the knowledge base (Davis, Buchanan, and Shortliffe 1977; Davis and Lenat 1980). Here the expert carries on a dialogue with TEIRESIAS in a subset of natural language.

MYCIN's use of independent rules of a simple IF—THEN form stimulated a variety of related systems. PROSPECTOR at SRI (Duda, Gaschnig, and Hart 1979; Duda and Gaschnig 1981) used an analogous form of knowledge representation for mineral deposit relationships. PROSPECTOR now includes about a dozen knowledge bases for different kinds of deposits. Like MYCIN, it determines the most plausible diagnosis by assessing the degree of support for each antecedent condition. This process applies recursively until data on all relevant conditions are requested and combined heuristically. At Stanford a domain-independent version of MYCIN was produced, called EMYCIN (van Melle 1979). EMYCIN contains all of MYCIN except its knowledge of infectious blood disease. EMYCIN facilitated the development of related diagnostic applications, such as PUFF (Freiherr 1980). ROSIE,* developed at Rand, provides a general-purpose programming system for building expert systems (Fain et al. 1981, 1982; F. Hayes-Roth et al. 1981). ROSIE evolved from an earlier programming system named RITA, for Rand Intelligent Terminal Agent (R. Anderson and Gillogly 1976a, b), both deriving their motivation from the success of MYCIN's rule-oriented style of knowledge representation and the appeal that its English-oriented explanation facility has for users. ROSIE extends these qualities and incorporates numerous additional facilities, such as knowledge representation techniques, interactive communications with users and systems, general and stylized English programming, and an interactive programming environment. ROSIE is the first system designed to support a wide class of new expert systems applications.

Early work at Carnegie-Mellon University with PSG (Newell 1973; Newell and McDermott 1976), a production system language for studying and modeling human cognition, led to the development of the OPS series of production system languages (Forgy and McDermott 1977; Forgy 1981) and R1 (McDermott 1980a, b), an expert sys-

---

*A registered trademark of the Rand Corporation.

tem for configuring DEC VAX computer systems. R1 represents the most successful application of the OPS languages to expert-system-building tasks.

The last line emanates from the speech-understanding systems, especially the HEARSAY-II system (Erman et al. 1980). HEARSAY-II, developed at Carnegie-Mellon University, was one of the first two systems capable of understanding connected discourse from a 1,000-word vocabulary. Although this skill rivals that of a ten-year-old child, it does not meet the high performance criterion previously established for expert systems. Nevertheless, the speech-understanding task is probably the most difficult yet undertaken with considerable success by AI researchers. Many researchers believe that the general ideas incorporated in HEARSAY-II will play a role in future expert systems (Erman et al. 1980; Chapter 4 in this book; Nii and Feigenbaum 1978). The principal features of HEARSAY-II include multiple, cooperating specialists; problem-solving at different levels of abstraction, varying from abstract and aggregate to precise and localized; and an incremental development of partial solutions that opportunistically exploits key data or powerful knowledge. Two projects aim to develop general-purpose frameworks for building expert systems based on these properties of HEARSAY-II. These are AGE at Stanford (Nii and Aiello 1979) and HEARSAY-III at ISI (Balzer, Erman, and London 1980).

This completes the historical survey of expert systems and expert system languages. The bibliography cites background reports for several additional systems (Clancey 1979; Clancey, Shortliffe, and Buchanan 1979; Davis and Lenat 1980; Barr and Feigenbaum 1981; Barstow 1979; Bennett and Engelmore 1979; Bobrow and Collins 1975; Bundy 1979; Carbonell 1970; Davis, Buchanan, and Shortliffe 1977; Davis 1977; Davis 1980; Gelernter et al. 1977; Reboh 1979; Stefik 1978a; Waterman and Hayes-Roth 1978; Waterman 1979; Waterman and Jenkins 1979; Winston and Horn 1981). Although this survey does not fully describe all these systems, it should accomplish its primary objectives. First, it explicates and provides the motive for the central precept of the area: that knowledge is power. Thus any general principles propounded for the expert systems area should be rooted in knowledge-intensive applications. Second, this survey documents the breadth and significance the area has attained in less than two decades, supporting the impression that, while maturing rapidly, it can expect considerably more progress in the years to come. Finally, this survey has introduced many of the technical ideas and mechanisms that play roles in expert systems. The next section generalizes from experience to date and explains these underlying ideas in greater depth.

1.2   Fundamentals of Knowledge Engineering

To describe their discipline, researchers in the field of expert systems have adopted the term *knowledge engineering*, which combines scientific, technological, and methodological elements. A principle of knowledge engineering holds that expert performance rarely conforms to some rigorous algorithmic process, yet that such performance does lend itself to computerization. Extracting, articulating, and computerizing the expert's knowledge constitute the essential tasks in this area.

1.2.1   Knowledge and Skill

What is knowledge in a given domain? Speaking abstractly, knowledge consists of descriptions, relationships, and procedures in some domain of interest (Bernstein 1977). The descriptions in a knowledge base, which identify and differentiate objects and classes, are sentences in some language whose elementary components consist of primitive features or concepts. A description system generally includes rules or procedures for applying and interpreting descriptions in specific applications. A knowledge base also contains particular kinds of descriptions, known as *relationships*. These express dependencies and associations between items in the knowledge base. Typically such relationships describe taxonomic, definitional, and empirical associations. Procedures, on the other hand, specify operations to perform when attempting to reason or solve a problem.

   In practice, knowledge does not appear in some precipitated form that neatly fits such abstract categories. Lying like an unmined and unrefined substance, knowledge somehow enables the human expert to solve hard problems. It takes many forms. A form frequently encountered consists of empirical associations. Doctors and geologists, for example, have knowledge of many such associations in the form of likely causes for observed data. Concomitant with that knowledge, experts employ heuristic methods for combining probabilistic, errorful, and uncertain data and inferences. Many experts possess other knowledge forms as well, in the form of concepts, constraints, and regulations that govern operations in their field (Waterman and Peterson 1980, 1981). They may also utilize causal models of the systems they study, as well as reasoning schemes that use these models to predict, diagnose, plan, or analyze situations (Fagan et al. 1979; Brown, Burton, and Bell 1974; Brown and Burton 1975; Borning 1979; Director et al. 1981; de Kleer et al. 1979b; Rieger and Grinberg 1977;

Sussman and Steele 1980; Wipke 1976). In short, knowledge consists of (1) the symbolic descriptions that characterize the definitional and empirical relationships in a domain and (2) the procedures for manipulating these descriptions.

To understand expert performance, it helps to consider the difference between knowledge and skill. The skilled performance of some task often involves many features not present in a well-informed but unskilled performance. These include great speed or other efficiencies, reduced error, reduced cognitive load (attentional requirements), and increased adaptability and robustness. Such features reflect both knowledge and engineering. Skill means having the right knowledge and using it effectively (Lenat, Hayes-Roth, and Klahr 1979a).

Knowledge engineering addresses the problem of building skilled computer systems, aiming first at extracting the expert's knowledge and then organizing it in an effective implementation. The several generic types of expert systems that exist have certain components in common.

1.2.2 Types of Expert Systems

Most knowledge-engineering applications fall into a few distinct types. Table 1.1 summarizes these.

Interpretation systems infer situation descriptions from observables. This category includes surveillance, speech understanding, image analysis, chemical structure elucidation, signal interpretation, and many kinds of intelligence analysis. An interpretation system explains observed data by assigning to them symbolic meanings describing the situation or system state accounting for the data.

Prediction systems infer likely consequences from given situations. This category includes weather forecasting, demographic predictions, traffic predictions, crop estimations, and military forecasting. A prediction system typically employs a parametric dynamic model with parameter values fitted to the given situation. Consequences inferable from the model form the basis of the predictions. By ignoring probability estimates, prediction systems can generate large numbers of possible scenarios.

Diagnosis systems infer system malfunctions from observables. This category includes medical, electronic, mechanical, and software diagnosis, among others. Diagnosis systems typically relate observed behavioral irregularities with underlying causes, using one of two techniques. One method essentially uses a table of associations between behaviors and diagnoses. The other method combines knowledge of system design with knowledge of potential flaws in

TABLE 1.1   Generic categories of knowledge engineering applications.

Category	Problem Addressed
Interpretation	Inferring situation descriptions from sensor data
Prediction	Inferring likely consequences of given situations
Diagnosis	Inferring system malfunctions from observables
Design	Configuring objects under constraints
Planning	Designing actions
Monitoring	Comparing observations to plan vulnerabilities
Debugging	Prescribing remedies for malfunctions
Repair	Executing a plan to administer a prescribed remedy
Instruction	Diagnosing, debugging, and repairing student behavior
Control	Interpreting, predicting, repairing, and monitoring system behaviors

design, implementation, or components to generate candidate malfunctions consistent with observations.

Design systems develop configurations of objects that satisfy the constraints of the design problem. Such problems include circuit layout, building design, and budgeting. Design systems construct descriptions of objects in various relationships with one another and verify that these configurations conform to stated constraints (Eastman 1981; Fenves and Norabhoompipat 1978; Freeman and Newell 1979; Grinberg 1980). In addition, many design systems attempt to minimize an objective function that measures costs and other undesirable properties of potential designs. This view of the design problem can subsume goal-seeking behavior as well, with the objective function incorporating measures of goal attainment.

Planning systems design actions. These systems specialize in problems of design concerned with objects that perform functions. They include automatic programming as well as robot, project, route, communication, experiment, and military planning problems (Stefik 1981a, b; B. Hayes-Roth and F. Hayes-Roth 1978; Sacerdoti 1973, 1975). Planning systems employ models of agent behavior to infer the effects of the planned agent activities.

Monitoring systems compare observations of system behavior to features that seem crucial to successful plan outcomes. These crucial features, or vulnerabilities, correspond to potential flaws in the plan. Generally, monitoring systems identify vulnerabilities in two ways. One type of vulnerability corresponds to an assumed condition whose violation would nullify the plan's rationale. Another kind of vulnerability arises when some potential effect of the plan violates a planning constraint. These correspond to malfunctions in predicted states. Many computer-aided monitoring systems exist for nuclear power plant, air traffic, disease, regulatory, and fiscal management tasks, although no expert systems for these problems have left the laboratory.

Debugging systems prescribe remedies for malfunctions. These systems rely on planning, design, and prediction capabilities to create specifications or recommendations for correcting a diagnosed problem. Computer-aided debugging systems exist for computer programming in the form of intelligent knowledge base and text editors (see Chapter 5), but none qualifies as an expert system.

Repair systems develop and execute plans to administer a remedy for some diagnosed problem. Such systems incorporate debugging, planning, and execution capabilities. Computer-aided systems occur in the domains of automotive, network, avionic, and computer maintenance, as well as others, but expert systems are just entering this field.

Instruction systems diagnose and debug student behaviors (Brown, Burton, and Bell 1974; Brown and Burton 1975; Clancey 1979; Clancey, Shortliffe, and Buchanan 1979; Sleeman and Brown 1982). They incorporate diagnosis and debugging subsystems that specifically address the student as the system of interest. Typically these systems begin by constructing a hypothetical description of the student's knowledge that interprets the student's behavior. Then they diagnose weaknesses in the student's knowledge and identify an appropriate remedy. Finally they plan a tutorial interaction intended to convey the remedial knowledge to the student.

The last type of system to be considered is called control. An expert control system adaptively governs the overall behavior of a system. To do this, the control system must repeatedly interpret the current situation, predict the future, diagnose the causes of anticipated problems, formulate a remedial plan, and monitor its execution to ensure success. Problems addressed by control systems include air traffic control, business management, battle management, and mission control. The technology of knowledge engineering should handle many control problems that resist treatment by more traditional mathematical approaches.

1.2.3   Components of Expert Systems

Figure 1.2 shows an idealized representation of an expert system. No existing expert system contains all the components shown, but one or more components occur in every expert system. Each component of this ideal system is described briefly in turn.

The ideal expert system contains a language processor for problem-oriented communications between the user and the expert system; a "blackboard" for recording intermediate results; a knowledge base comprising facts as well as heuristic planning and problem-solving rules; an interpreter that applies these rules; a scheduler to control the order of rule processing; a consistency enforcer that adjusts previous conclusions when new data (or knowledge) alter their bases of support; and a justifier that rationalizes and explains the system's behavior.

The user interacts with the expert system in problem-oriented language, usually some restricted variant of English and in some cases via means of a graphics or structure editor. The language processor mediates information exchanges between the expert system and the human user. Typically the language processor parses and interprets user questions, commands, and volunteered information. Conversely the language processor formats information generated by the system, including answers to questions, explanations and justifications for its behavior, and requests for data. Existing expert systems generally employ natural language parsers written in INTER-LISP (Teitelman and Masinter 1981) to interpret user inputs, and use less sophisticated techniques exploiting canned text to generate messages to the user.

The blackboard records intermediate hypotheses and decisions that the expert system manipulates. Every expert system uses some type of intermediate decision representation, but only a few explicitly employ a blackboard for the various types of decisions shown in Figure 1.2. The figure identifies three types of decisions recorded on the blackboard: plan, agenda, and solution elements. Plan elements describe the overall or general attack the system will pursue against the current problem, including current plans, goals, problem states, and contexts. For example, a plan may recommend processing all low-level sensor data first, then formulating a small number of the most promising hypotheses, refining and elaborating each of these hypotheses until one best hypothesis emerges, and finally focusing

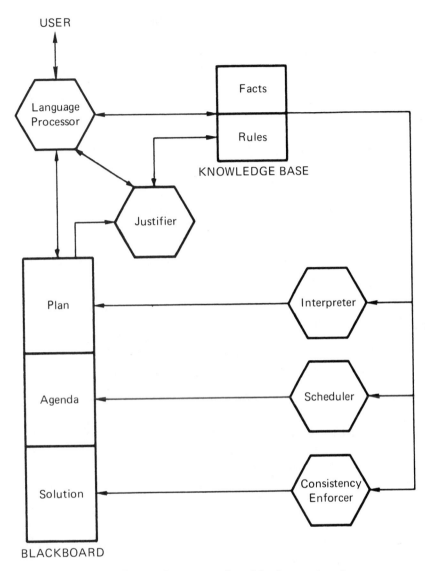

USER

Language Processor

Facts

Rules

KNOWLEDGE BASE

Justifier

Plan

Agenda

Solution

BLACKBOARD

Interpreter

Scheduler

Consistency Enforcer

FIGURE 1.2   Anatomy of an ideal expert system.

exclusively on that hypothesis until the complete solution is found. This kind of plan has been incorporated in several expert systems. The agenda elements record the potential actions awaiting execution, which generally correspond to knowledge base rules that seem relevant to some decision placed on the blackboard previously. The solution elements represent the candidate hypotheses and decisions the system has generated thus far, along with the dependencies that relate decisions to one another. Often these dependencies are called *links*.

The scheduler maintains control of the agenda and determines which pending action should be executed next. Schedulers may embody considerable knowledge, such as "Do the most profitable thing next" and "Avoid redundant effort." To apply such knowledge, the scheduler needs to give each agenda item priority according to its relationship to the plan and other extant solution elements. To do this, the scheduler generally needs to estimate the effects of applying the potential rule.

The interpreter executes the chosen agenda item by applying the corresponding knowledge base rule. Generally the interpreter validates the relevance conditions of the rule, binds variables in these conditions to particular solution blackboard elements, and then makes those changes to the blackboard that the rule prescribes. Interpreters of this sort are generally written in LISP because of its facility for manipulating and evaluating programs. Other languages are also suitable.

The consistency enforcer attempts to maintain a consistent representation of the emerging solution. This may take the form of likelihood revisions when the solution elements represent hypothetical diagnoses and some new data are introduced (Shortliffe 1976; Duda and Gaschnig 1981; Erman et al. 1980). Alternatively the enforcer might implement truth-maintenance procedures when the solution elements represent logical deductions and their truth-value relationships (McDermott and Doyle 1980). Most expert systems use some kind of numerical adjustment scheme to determine the degree of belief in each potential decision. This scheme attempts to ensure that plausible conclusions are reached and inconsistent ones are avoided.

The justifier explains the actions of the system to the user. In general, it answers questions about why some conclusion was reached or why some alternative was rejected. To do this, the justifier uses a few general types of question-answering plans. These typically require the justifier to trace backward along blackboard solution elements from the questioned conclusion to the intermediate hypotheses or data that support it. Each step backward corresponds to the inference of one knowledge base rule. The justifier collects these intermediate inferences and translates them into English for presentation to the user. To answer "Why not...?" questions, the system uses a heuristic variant of this technique. Supposedly it can identify a possible chain of rules that would reach the questioned conclusion but that did not apply because the relevance condition of some rule failed. The justifier explains the system's decision to reject a possible conclusion by claiming that such failed conditions impede all reasoning chains that can support the conclusion.

Finally the knowledge base records rules, facts, and information about the current problem that may be useful in formulating a solution. Whereas the rules of the knowledge base have procedural interpretations, the facts play only passive roles.

1.2.4 The Basic Ideas of Intelligent Problem-solving

The ideas that underlie an approach to intelligent problem-solving, listed in Table 1.2, motivate and help explain the primacy of knowledge in expert systems. Since, in most cases, experts face problems that do not have easily formalized or algorithmic solutions, heuristic methods must be used; and effective solutions depend on the timely

TABLE 1.2   The basic ideas.

1. Knowledge = Facts + Beliefs + Heuristics

2. Success = Finding a good-enough answer with the resources available

3. Search efficiency directly affects success

4. Aids to efficiency:
    a. Applicable, correct, and discriminating knowledge
    b. Rapid elimination of "blind alleys"
    c. Elimination of redundant computation
    d. Increased speed of computer operation
    e. Multiple, cooperative sources of knowledge
    f. Reasoning at varying levels of abstraction

5. Sources of increased problem difficulty:
    a. Errorful data or knowledge
    b. Dynamically changing data
    c. The number of possibilities to evaluate
    d. Complex procedures for ruling out possibilities

use of knowledge to identify potential decisions that are promising and to rule out unpromising ones.

The central notion of intelligent problem-solving is that a system must construct its solution selectively and efficiently from a space of alternatives. When resource-limited, the expert needs to search this space selectively, with as little unfruitful activity as possible. An expert's knowledge helps spot useful data early, suggests promising ways to exploit them, and helps avoid low-payoff efforts by pruning blind alleys as early as possible. An expert system achieves high performance by using knowledge to make the best use of its time.

1.2.5   Architecture

Although the basic ideas of intelligent problem-solving allow for a wide diversity of implementations, a few principles of architecture have begun to emerge. In this context the term *architecture* refers to the science and method of design that determine the structure of the expert system. The emergent principles reflect current understanding of the best way to design structures that support intelligent problem-solving.

The MYCIN (Shortliffe 1976) and HEARSAY-II (Erman et al. 1980) systems provide an excellent contrast that illustrates many of these principles. The basic approach to diagnosis taken in MYCIN employs an exhaustive, backward-chaining search augmented by a numerical, heuristic combining function to rank competing hypotheses. MYCIN's exhaustive search considers all possible antecedents of all possible conclusions, except where previous data obviate testing some conditions. MYCIN's backward-chaining method collects data by regressing from possible conclusions to related antecedent conditions and from these conditions to their required data, recursively if necessary. MYCIN's algorithm for determining *certainty factors*, numeric judgments of plausibility, provides a heuristic technique for combining uncertain and incomplete data with experts' rules of inference.

MYCIN's methods can cope effectively with diagnostic and interpretation problems of limited complexity. Problems characterized by small search spaces, reliable data, and reliable knowledge permit correspondingly simple system architectures. Systems of this sort employ exhaustive search. They need pursue only one line of reasoning at a time. They can reason monotonically because they can avoid making erroneous intermediate decisions that eventually require retractions.

HEARSAY-II, on the other hand, has many design features that support more sophisticated reasoning schemes. The problem complexities of speech understanding originally motivated these design features, but many other applications since have demanded similar capabilities. In contrast with MYCIN, HEARSAY-II addresses an intrinsically hard problem with characteristics that require particular architectural prescriptions. These characteristics include unreliable data or knowledge, a large search space of possible solutions, inadequate methods for evaluating partial solutions accurately, lack of a fixed sequence of actions that solves the problem effectively, interactions among decisions that address separate subproblems of the task, the need to guess likely subsolutions to further the analysis, absence of a strong problem-solving model that could determine effectively which line of reasoning to pursue, the need for integrating diverse bodies of knowledge in the same problem-solving system, and the need for specialized knowledge representations to improve the efficiency of knowledge application.

Because the HEARSAY-II speech-understanding system addressed all of these problems to some extent, its organization as a collection of cooperating, independent specialists provides a framework for a wide variety of related problem-solving tasks. In fact this kind of design has been adopted for a variety of applications, including: protein crystallography (Nii and Feigenbaum 1978), task planning and scheduling (B. Hayes-Roth and F. Hayes-Roth 1978), experiment planning (Stefik 1981a, b), automatic programming (Balzer, Erman, and London 1980; Barstow 1977), text comprehension (Nii and Aiello 1979), and image understanding (Hanson and Riseman 1978).

Figure 1.3 represents some of the relationships between problem characteristics and associated design features, ideas developed more fully in Chapter 4. The chart prescribes the kinds of architectural embellishments to adopt as problem complexity increases in various ways. Problem complexities are characterized in terms of nonexclusive disjunctions. The simplest type of problem and associated architecture is shown in box 1. The first kinds of possible complexities lead to boxes 2, 3, or 4. These include less reliable data and knowledge, data that vary over time, and of course larger search spaces. In addition to the technique of hierarchical generate-and-test suggested in box 4 for dealing with a big search space, three other lines of design elaboration are pursued in boxes 5, 9, and 11. The line emanating from box 5 considers a sequence of increasingly harder problems that have no evaluator for partial solutions. The line starting at box 9 addresses problem difficulties arising from the lack of a single strong model. Box 11 reflects the forefront of current expert systems architecture in its prescription for data structure compilation and other practices of cognitive economy (Lenat, Hayes-Roth, and Klahr 1979a; see also Chapter 7).

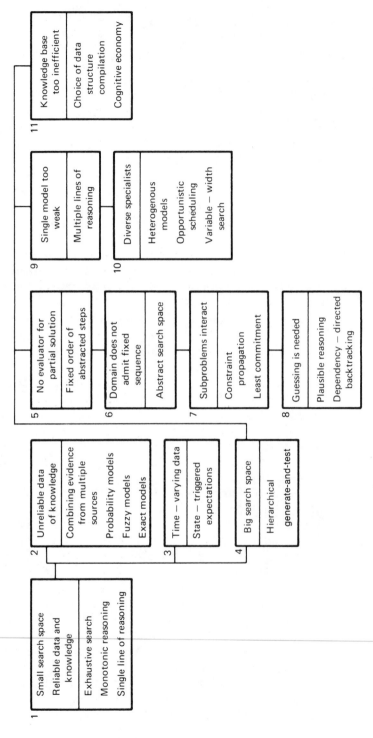

FIGURE 1.3 Successive architectural embellishments appropriate to increasingly complex problems.

These architectural prescriptions reflect a distillation of experience from a few dozen systems. Undoubtedly, they provide an early and somewhat uncertain set of rules for system designers; but, as in other expert system application areas, these heuristic rules represent the current state of expert knowledge. They merely provide a basis for solving hard problems and can offer no guarantee of success in all new undertakings.

1.3   The Construction of Expert Systems

Workers in expert systems conduct principally empirical research to determine how to solve a problem requiring extensive knowledge and skill. To fashion a solution, they must build a working system by exploiting two types of assets, a methodology and a set of tools.

1.3.1   A Methodology for Building Expert Systems

Because it takes experimentation to achieve high performance, an expert system evolves gradually. This evolutionary or incremental development technique has emerged as the dominant methodology in the expert systems area. The procedure of extracting knowledge from an expert and encoding it in program form is called *knowledge acquisition*. This transfer and transformation of problem-solving expertise from a knowledge source to a program is the heart of the expert-system development process.

The burden of uncovering and formalizing the expert's knowledge falls on the shoulders of the knowledge engineer. Through an extended series of interactions, the knowledge engineering team (the knowledge engineer and the expert) defines the problem to be attacked, discovers the basic concepts involved, and develops rules that express the relationships existing between concepts. Although work is progressing on automating the expert system development process (see Chapter 5, Sec. 5.4), at present knowledge engineers must rely on their own skill and insight to guide the knowledge-acquisition activity.

Table 1.3 summarizes the major stages in the evolution of an expert system (see Chapter 5). During *identification*, the knowledge engineer and expert work together to identify the problem area and define its scope. They also identify the participants in the development process (additional experts), determine the resources needed

TABLE 1.3   Stages in the evolution of an expert system.

Identification:	Determining problem characteristics
Conceptualization:	Finding concepts to represent knowledge
Formalization:	Designing structures to organize knowledge
Implementation:	Formulating rules that embody knowledge
Testing:	Validating rules that embody knowledge

(time, computing facilities), and decide upon the goals or objectives of building the expert system. A small but interesting subproblem may be identified and used to focus the knowledge-acquisition process.

During *conceptualization*, the expert and knowledge engineer explicate the key concepts, relations, and information-flow characteristics needed to describe the problem-solving process in the given domain. They also specify subtasks, strategies, and constraints related to the problem-solving activity.

Formalization involves mapping the key concepts and relations into a formal representation suggested by some expert-system-building tool or language. The knowledge engineer must select the language and, with the help of the expert, represent the basic concepts and relations within the language framework.

During *implementation*, the knowledge engineer combines and reorganizes the formalized knowledge to make it compatible with the information flow characteristics of the problem. The resulting set of rules and associated control structure define a prototype program capable of being executed and tested.

Finally, *testing* involves evaluating the performance of the prototype program and revising it to conform to standards of excellence defined by experts in the problem domain. Typically the expert evaluates the program's performance and assists the knowledge engineer in the forthcoming revisions.

These stages of expert system development are not clear-cut, well-defined, or even independent. At best they characterize roughly the complex process we call knowledge acquisition. For example, formalization and implementation are closely related, and failures to provide adequate rules and control during implementation may lead to immediate reformalizations. Also, during testing the knowledge engineering team may find that prototype correction requires partially revising the result of some earlier stage. This could involve reformulating rules and control processes, redesigning knowledge structures, discovering new concepts or abandoning old ones, and even redefining the problem's scope and goals.

Eventually the prototype will solve the initial subproblem and provide the desired interface features. From this point on, the team enters a new, more expansive type of iterative cycle. The team specifies additional desired capabilities, assigns priorities to them, and step by step implements and evaluates them. New test cases continually suggest extensions and features the current system should have. Often these extensions correspond to refinements of current knowledge needed to make distinctions previously overlooked. More generally, new features require new domain knowledge.

The knowledge base may reach an unmanageable size and shape. If it does, the knowledge engineer and expert reassess the initial categorizations and representations selected in an attempt to rethink the basic foundations of their approach or to reconceptualize the expertise. If successful, they select a new way to organize the knowledge and a more suitable architecture for the needed reasoning process. Thus the existing system gives way to a new one, created in the new image. Few extant systems have ever undergone more than one rebirth of this sort. One should expect, however, that a very long term development effort might see more of these major paradigm shifts.

In sum, an expert system evolves by proceeding from simple to increasingly hard tasks, improving incrementally the organization and representation of knowledge. Occasional knowledge reorganizations and architectural remodelings also occur when additional desired capabilities exceed the capacity of the existing system.

1.3.2   Tools for Building Expert Systems

Table 1.4 lists the primary tools presently available for knowledge engineering tasks. Except for OPS, they operate in the INTERLISP environment. ROSIE is an excellent general-purpose tool for building prototype expert systems. EMYCIN, KS300, and KAS are very useful general tools for diagnostic tasks. KAS provides facilities akin to those of EMYCIN but has not yet been used in the variety of ways EMYCIN has. KS300 is an industrial system based on the EMYCIN methodology. OPS is the most powerful pure production-system interpreter available. AGE provides the best extant tool for developing a variety of different architectures. INTERLISP provides a LISP programming environment preferred by most workers in the field.

Despite the wealth of knowledge accumulated about constructing

TABLE 1.4   Programming systems for building expert systems.

Tool	Developer	Features
ROSIE	Rand Corporation	Rule-based, Procedure-oriented, General purpose
OPS5	Carnegie Mellon University	Production-system formalism, General purpose
EMYCIN	Stanford University	Rule-based, Diagnosis and explanation
KAS	Stanford Research Institute	Rule-based, Diagnosis and explanation
AGE	Stanford University	LISP-based, Builds various PS architectures
INTERLISP	Xerox Corporation	LISP programming environment

expert systems, choosing an appropriate tool for building a particular system remains a difficult yet crucial task. A tool that in some sense well suits a particular problem area can facilitate the development process, shorten the development time, and lead to a finished product that performs with a high degree of efficiency.

Table 1.5 summarizes guidelines for choosing an appropriate expert-system-building tool. (See Chapter 6 for a more complete discussion of this topic.) The predominant consideration involves matching the problem characteristics to necessary tool features and hence particular tools.

Figure 1.4 outlines a basis for this selection process. The problem characteristics suggest certain solution features, and these together with the desired expert system features suggest tool features that would facilitate development. The desired tool features then form the basis for choosing a particular tool.

Suppose, as a very simple example, that one problem characteristic is uncertain and errorful data and one desired system feature is self-modification (the system will augment or change its own knowledge). The problem characteristic suggests using certainty combining and truth maintenance as solution features, which in turn suggest

TABLE 1.5   Choosing an appropriate tool for building an expert system.

Issues	Maxims
Generality:	Pick a tool with only the generality necessary to solve the problem.
Selection:	Let the problem characteristics determine the tool selected.
Speed:	When time is critical, choose a tool with built-in explanation/interaction facilities.
Testing:	Test the tool early on by building a very small prototype system.

picking a tool with certainty factors and a truth-maintenance facility. The desired system feature of self-modification suggests the tool should also contain rule and control modification facilities.

1.4   Conclusions and Outlook

This chapter has surveyed the rapid development of the expert systems area to reveal its underlying techniques and concepts. Clearly expert knowledge provides a rich source of opportunities for intelligent systems.

Some points worthy of discussion have thus far been overlooked. First, workers in this field speculate that *the most significant by-*

FIGURE 1.4   Basis for selection of an expert system tool.

product of expert systems work will be the codification of knowledge. Human culture derives value from knowledge codification, and the opportunity to automate knowledge increases the incentive. Equally important, however, the technology of expert systems provides an opportunity for feedback and knowledge evaluation. This will stimulate development of new knowledge, especially knowledge related to performing tasks expertly. In many areas of human endeavor, this will signal a transition from a personal to a public basis for thought. This transition will revolutionize human culture.

Characteristics of an expert system that set it apart from a conventional program have already been mentioned. However, *the most potentially significant and innovative characteristic of an expert system is believed to be that of self-knowledge, knowledge about its own operation and structure.* Although currently the use of self-knowledge is somewhat simplistic, providing basic explanation and justification capabilities, the potential for its application is remarkable. Expert systems are expected to become quite adept at rationalization, at examining and analyzing their own chains of reasoning during problem-solving (see Chapter 2). Future systems will do more than just display the rules that produced their conclusions. To explain their operation, they will reconstruct rational lines of argument from fundamental principles of the domain, tailored to fit the perceived audience. This self-knowledge will also provide the basis for various types of self-modification capabilities, including rule correction, knowledge base reorganization, and system reconfiguration (see Chapter 7 and F. Hayes-Roth 1983).

The last point to be made concerns the commercial exploitation of this new technology. *The next generation of expert systems can be expected to fare well in the commercial marketplace.* Numerous applications readily suggest themselves in which a computerized expert can play some important role. Currently, however, only a small number of experienced practitioners have the talent required to develop expert systems. Considerable economic competition exists for these people. The field should be expected to develop rapidly in areas of great commercial interest, such as energy and minerals, home entertainment, office automation, and military systems.

QUESTIONS

1. What makes knowledge valuable? What does it take to exploit this value?
2. Identify a contemporary human system that uses knowledge to

simplify work but that would resist knowledge engineering techniques. Why would it resist?

3. Identify all the knowledge required to water house plants effectively. What kind of expert system could perform this task?

4. Suppose Thomas Edison had worked with knowledge, rather than electricity, as the new source of power. What kinds of appliances might have evolved rather than items such as hot plates, toasters, radios, and televisions?

5. Identify a contemporary industry that cannot use knowledge effectively because of technical limitations. What is the knowledge and what must be done to engineer an effective system?

2

What Are Expert Systems?

Ronald J. Brachman, Saul Amarel,
Carl Engelman, Robert S. Engelmore,
Edward A. Feigenbaum, and David E. Wilkins

This chapter tackles the issue of definitions and boundaries to explain what an expert system is and why. Several traits characterize an expert system, including the symbolic nature of the task it performs, a broad and robust intelligence, an ability to rationalize and justify its behavior, a capacity to expand its range of capabilities and refine its skills, and an ability to solve important problems involving complexity and uncertainty. Existing expert systems demonstrate clearly both what has been achieved and what remains to be done.

Since the DENDRAL project began in the late 1960s, some of the most productive work in artificial intelligence has been in the subdiscipline whose main goal is producing expert-level performance in programs. DENDRAL's aim was the kind of performance that might rival that of human experts in elucidating the structure of complex molecules from mass spectrograms. With heuristic DENDRAL's success at a tough interpretation problem normally reserved for experienced human chemists, a new methodology became viable: building systems in limited domains of expertise with knowledge elicited from human experts.

Many other projects that used methodology developed at Stanford followed, forming the active area of research that came to be known as expert systems. The aim of this chapter is to determine in somewhat precise terms just what work in expert systems means.

A brief description of a working program in action serves as an introduction to the concept of the expert system. From the state of this art, the chapter moves back in time, with a discussion of when and how the most important current ideas entered the mainstream of research. The principal contribution of this chapter is embodied in its definition of *expert system*. This definition uses seven semi-independent dimensions:

- Expertise. High-level rules, the avoidance of blind search, and high performance
- Reasoning by symbol manipulation
- Intelligence. Fundamental domain principles and weak reasoning methods
- Difficulty or complexity
- Reformulation. Conversion from a description in lay terms to a form suitable for expert-rule application
- Reasoning about self in various forms, especially for explanation
- Type of task

After these fundamental properties of expert systems are presented, several specific systems are assessed.

2.1 History

2.1.1 A Real Expert System

Imagine for a moment that you are a pulmonary physiologist, working in a pulmonary function laboratory. You have just completed a series of measurements on a patient you suspect has some sort of obstructive airway disease (OAD). Under normal circumstances you would study the results of your tests and include your interpretation of the data in a manually prepared report. But this occasion is different. Instead of dictating or writing, today you will stand by and watch PUFF, an expert system, do the work for you.

A typist at a computer terminal starts PUFF and enters the laboratory data describing the amount of gas in the lungs and the flow of gases into and out of them in the following exchange. Information supplied by the typist is preceded by a double asterisk (**) and is printed in **boldface**; PUFF's questions and responses are in TYPE-WRITER font; explanations are *italicized* and placed in parentheses.[1]

19-Nov-79 14:41:28

PUFF

(PUFF asks the user for pulmonary function test results and patient data and then executes rules to reach conclusions in interpreting the tests.)

PATIENT-7
  1) Patient's identifying number:
     ** **7446**
  2) Referral diagnosis:
     ** **ASTHMA**

(RV, TLC, FVC, etc. are the lung test measurements.)

  3) RV/RV-predicted:
     ** **261**
  4) TLC(body box)observed/predicted:
     ** **139**
  5) TLC(DLCO)observed/predicted:
     ** **111**
  6) FVC/FVC-predicted:
     ** **81**
  7) FEV1/FVC ratio:
     ** **40**
  8) The slope F5025:
     ** **9**
  9) The FEV1/FVC threshold:
     ** **77**
 10) MMF/MMF-predicted:
     ** **12**
 11) The DLCO/DLCO-predicted:
     ** **117**
 12) Change in FEV1 (after dilation):
     ** **31**
 13) The change in resistance (after dilation):
     ** **2.0**
 14) The severity of coughing:
     ** **NONE**
 15) The number of pack-years of smoking:
     ** **17**

(Pack-years = Number of packs per day × Number of years patient has smoked.)

16) The degree of dyspnea:
    ** **NONE**

At the conclusion of the dialogue, PUFF first types a summary of some of the most important pulmonary function data:

SUMMARY OF DATA

The degree of dyspnea: NONE
The severity of coughing: NONE
The number of pack-years of smoking: 17
Referral diagnosis: ASTHMA
RV/RV-predicted: 261
FVC/FVC-predicted: 81
TLC(body box)observed/predicted: 139
FEV1/FVC ratio: 40
MMF/MMF-predicted: 12
The DLCO/DLCO-predicted: 117
The slope F5025:   9

Finally, PUFF gives its interpretation of the data and its pulmonary disease diagnosis:

INTERPRETATION

Obstruction is indicated by curvature of the flow-volume loop.
Forced vital capacity is normal but the FEV1/FVC ratio is reduced, suggesting airway obstruction.
Low mid-expiratory flow is consistent with severe airway obstruction.
Change in expired flow rates following bronchodilation shows that there is reversibility of airway obstruction.
Improvement in expired flow rates following dilation indicates reversibility of airway obstruction, and this is confirmed by improvement in airway resistance.
Good response to bronchodilators is consistent with an asthmatic condition, and their continued use is indicated.
The high diffusing capacity is consistent with asthma.
Elevated lung volumes indicate overinflation.
Airway obstruction is consistent with the patient's smoking history.
The pulmonary diffusing capacity for carbon monoxide is normal.
Obstructive airways disease of the asthmatic type.

After you look over the interpretation produced by PUFF and are satisfied that its diagnosis matches your own, you might wish to add a simple comment, such as "These test results are consistent with those of previous visits" or "These test results show considerable improvement over those in the previous visit."

The foregoing is an actual case taken from the patient files of the pulmonary function laboratory at the Pacific Medical Center in San Francisco, with the patient's identifying number changed. This case was chosen because it is a fairly typical case of OAD and thus representative of those in the patient library. PUFF, an expert system developed at Stanford's Heuristic Programming Project (Kunz et al. 1978), is in routine use in the laboratory; approximately 95 percent of its reports are accepted without modification. When comments are added, they are usually similar to the two examples in the preceding paragraph.

To illustrate the similarity between reports produced by PUFF and those produced without the computer, by pulmonary physiologists, two sets of measurements and interpretations of roughly the same situation are presented below. First, an actual set of measurements and interpretation statements, shown in Figure 2.1, is given. The test measurements listed in the top half of the figure are collected by the laboratory equipment. The pulmonary physiologist then dictates the interpretation statements to be included in a manually prepared report. One sample measurement is the patient's total lung capacity (TLC), the volume of air in the lungs at maximum inspiration, shown on the fourth line of measurements. This patient's TLC is 129 percent of that predicted in a normal patient of the same sex, height, and weight, whose TLC value is established at 100 percent. The high value of 129 percent indicates the presence of obstructive airways disease. The interpretation and final diagnosis is a summary of this kind of reasoning about the combinations of measurements taken in the lung tests.

The form of the interpretations generated by PUFF is shown in Figure 2.2. This report is for the same patient, seen four years later. The pulmonary function test data are set forth, followed by the interpretation statements and a pulmonary function diagnosis, as in the earlier typed report. The pulmonary physiologist checks the PUFF report and requests that a typist make changes, when necessary, in the interpretation or diagnosis statements.

2.1.2 Seminal Developments in the History of Expert Systems

The culmination of fifteen years of developmental work in expert systems, PUFF, like several other recent systems, was built simply by applying existing technology to new domains of expertise. In this sec-

PRESBYTERIAN HOSPITAL OF PMC
CLAY AND BUCHANAN, BOX 7999
SAN FRANCISCO, CA 94120
PULMONARY FUNCTION LAB

WT 40.8 KG, HT 161 CM, AGE 65, SEX F
REFERRAL DX–   TEST DATE 5-13-76

			PREDICTED (+/-SD)		OBSER	(%PRED)	POST DILATION OBSER	(%PRED)
INSPIR VITAL CAP	(IVC)	L	2.7	(0.6)	2.3	(83)		
RESIDUAL VOL	(RV)	L	2.0	(0.1)	3.8	(193)	3.1	(154)
FUNC RESID CAP	(FRC)	L	2.9	(0.3)	4.6	(158)	3.9	(136)
TOTAL LUNG CAP	(TLC)	L	4.7	(0.7)	6.1	(129)	5.5	(116)
RV/TLC		%	42.		62.		55.	
FORCED EXPIR VOL	(FEV1)	L	2.3	(0.5)	1.5	(66)	1.6	(71)
FORCED VITAL CAP	(FVC)	L	2.7	(0.6)	2.3	(85)	2.4	(88)
FEV1/FVC		%	82.		64.		66.	
FORCE EXP FLOW 200-1200		L/S	3.6	(0.8)	1.8		1.9	
FORCED EXP FLOW 25-75%		L/S	2.6	(0.5)	0.7		0.7	
FORCED INS FLOW 200-1200		L/S	2.5	(0.5)	2.5		3.4	
AIRWAY RESISTANCE (RAW)								
(TLC = 6.1)			2.5		1.5		2.2	
DF CAP-HGB = 14.5 (DSBCO)								
(TLC = 4.8)			23.		17.4	(72)	....	

INTERPRETATION

The vital CAPACITY is low, the residual volume is high as is the total lung capacity, indicating air trapping and overinflation. This is consistent with a moderately severe degree of airway obstruction as indicated by the low FEV1, low peak flow rates, and curvature to the flow volume loop. Following isoproterenol aerosol there is virtually no change.

The diffusing capacity is low indicating loss of alveolar capillary surface.

Conclusion: Overinflation, fixed airway obstruction and low diffusing capacity would all indicate moderately severe obstructive airway disease of the emphysematous type. Although there is no response to bronchodilators on this one occasion, more prolonged use may prove to be more helpful.

PULMONARY FUNCTION DIAGNOSIS: OBSTRUCTIVE AIRWAYS DISEASE, MODERATELY
SEVERE, EMPHYSEMATOUS TYPE

FIGURE 2.1   Verbatim copy of pulmonary function report
dictated by physician.

PRESBYTERIAN HOSPITAL OF PMC
CLAY AND BUCHANAN, BOX 7999
SAN FRANCISCO, CA 94120
PULMONARY FUNCTION LAB

WT 40.8 KG, HT 161 CM, AGE 69, SEX F
REFERRAL DX–   TEST DATE 05/13/80

			PREDICTED (+/-SD)	OBSER	(%PRED)	POST DILATION OBSER	(%PRED)
INSPIR VITAL CAP	(IVC)	L	2.7	2.3	(86)	2.4	(90)
RESIDUAL VOL	(RV)	L	2.0	3.8	(188)	3.0	(148)
TOTAL LUNG CAP	(TLC)	L	4.7	6.1	(130)	5.4	(115)
RV/TLC		%	43.	62.		56.	
FORCED EXPIR VOL	(FEV1)	L	2.2	1.5	(68)	1.6	(73)
FORCED VITAL CAP	(FVC)	L	2.7	2.3	(86)	2.4	(90)
FEV1/FVC		%	73.	65.		67.	
PEAK EXPIR FLOW	(PEF)	L/S	7.1	1.8	(25)	1.9	(26)
FORCED EXP FLOW 25-75%		L/S	1.8	0.7	(39)	0.7	(39)
AIRWAY RESIST (RAW)							
(TLC = 6.1)			0.0 (0.0)	1.5		2.2	
DF CAP-HGB = 14.5							
(TLC = 4.8)			24.	17.4	(72)	(74%IF TLC = 4.7)	

INTERPRETATION

Elevated lung volumes indicate overinflation. In addition, the RV/TLC ratio is increased, suggesting a moderately severe degree of air trapping. The forced vital capacity is normal. The FEV1/FVC ratio and mid-expiratory flow are reduced and the airway resistance is increased, suggesting moderately severe airway obstruction. Following bronchodilation, the expired flows show moderate improvement. However, the resistance did not improve. The low diffusing capacity indicates a loss of alveolar capillary surface, which is mild.

Conclusions: The low diffusing capacity, in combination with obstruction and a high total lung capacity is consistent with a diagnosis of emphysema. Although bronchodilators were only slightly useful in this one case, prolonged use may prove to be beneficial to the patient.

PULMONARY FUNCTION DIAGNOSIS: 1. MODERATELY SEVERE OBSTRUCTIVE
                                   AIRWAYS DISEASE. EMPHYSEMATOUS TYPE.

FIGURE 2.2 Pulmonary function report generated by PDP-11 version of PUFF.

tion, the roots of this technology are illustrated by surveying briefly some milestones in the history of the field and by illuminating the sources of the most important ideas that currently direct expert systems work, as well as by concentrating on a few efforts that introduced seminal ideas and techniques.

The **DENDRAL** project (Buchanan 1969a, b, 1978a), which began in 1965, originated the fundamental idea of expert systems—knowledge engineering—manipulating large amounts of expert, heuristic knowledge into a form that a program can use to help solve difficult problems. The program inferred molecular structure from mass spectrographic information. Although an algorithm for generating all possible molecular structures existed, an exhaustive search would have been extremely expensive. The DENDRAL program encoded the heuristic knowledge of expert chemists into rules that controlled such a search, making it possible to obtain a satisfactory answer with a fraction of effort. The idea of using rules to represent expert knowledge has permeated expert systems work ever since. DENDRAL also introduced the concept of data-directed search control. Heuristic rules could infer constraints on the molecular structure from the mass spectrographic data, which greatly pruned the search. The DENDRAL project has produced significant results for chemists, and one paper (Smith et al. 1973) shows that the program does better than experts on certain problems.

The Causal Associational Network program—**CASNET**—was developed during the early and midseventies (Weiss, Kulikowski, and Safir 1977, 1978a). Its primary use has been in the diagnosis and therapy of glaucoma, and ophthalmologists have rated its performance close to expert. The program provides a general framework for modeling diseases instead of merely modeling glaucoma. This program was one of the first attempts to provide a general framework for building expert systems, and it led to the development of EXPERT (Weiss and Kulikowski 1979), a general tool that has been applied to rheumatology and endocrinology as well as to glaucoma.

Instead of using static rules like MYCIN and DENDRAL, the CASNET program introduced a causal network to model diseases. Within this network the program reasons to determine the effects of a therapy or disease. Thus the system represents the disease as a dynamic process about which it reasons and can explain to the user. The program also accommodates probabilistic rules and incorporates differing expert opinions that it can use to give alternative diagnoses.

The **MACSYMA** program (Martin and Fateman 1971) has achieved high competence in the symbolic computations associated with applied analysis. Dozens of mathematicians seek its assistance in algebraic computation daily. The roots of MACSYMA can be traced back to early algebraic manipulation programs for general mathematical simplification (T. Hart 1961; Wooldridge 1963; Korsvold 1965), and in one case, Slagle's SAINT, for symbolic integration (Slagle 1961).

An important contribution of **SAINT**, much improved upon in Moses's later symbolic integration program, **SIN** (Moses 1967), was the introduction of a "semantic" pattern matcher. Two concepts are actually involved here. One is that the basic control structure of an expert program could be that of pattern-invoked procedures. The other is that specializing the pattern matcher to the specific problem domain greatly simplifies the representation of expert rules. For example, if X^2 can be recognized as matching $A*X^2 + B*X + C$ (try to formulate what is involved here), fewer rules may be needed. One of the major differences between SIN and SAINT was the greater knowledge built into SIN, which allowed it to classify problems with such completeness that, at each step, only one transformation needed to be tried—win or lose. It was expert in the sense of substituting knowledge for search.

The next event in the development of symbolic integration programs was the provision of a program by the emergent **MATHLAB** system (Engelman 1971) for the integration of rational functions (Manove, Bloom, and Engelman 1968), a seminumeric computation. In this case the expert system uses pattern-directed heuristic transformations to reduce its problem to one for which an algorithm exists. In a similar way another computationally effective algorithm proved essential to DENDRAL. That algorithm enumerated all possible chemical structures, that is, it computed the size of the solution space rather than the solution.

MYCIN (Shortliffe 1976) gives consultative advice on diagnosis and therapy for infectious diseases that, studies indicate, compares favorably with advice given by experts in infectious disease. The program was developed about the same time as CASNET. MYCIN's medical knowledge is represented in terms of production rules involving certainty factors, which help accommodate probabilistic reasoning. The rules are invoked using a backward-chaining control strategy that effectively makes MYCIN hypothesis-driven, since it works backward from its conclusions.

MYCIN also developed the idea of making many uses of one data base. Using backward-chaining of rules, MYCIN can give the reasons for its decisions in terms of its rules and can carry on a dialogue by asking the user for information needed to continue the backward-chaining. The rules also provide the structure that the TEIRESIAS system (Davis 1977b) uses to assist in acquiring, correcting, and using new knowledge. As in CASNET, the clear structure of MYCIN has led to a more general framework for expert systems (embodied in EMY-CIN (van Melle 1979) and to applications in other domains such as pulmonary function and control of a medical instrument called a ventilator.

TEIRESIAS (Davis 1977b) facilitates automatic acquisition of new knowledge in the MYCIN system. Concerned with use of metalevel knowledge that is not specific to MYCIN or its domain, TEIRESIAS does assume that rulelike units of knowledge are used and that a chain of such rules suffices as an explanation of system behavior. Metaknowledge is knowledge about how MYCIN knowledge is represented and used. For example, TEIRESIAS has rule models and rules about the structure of rules. One such metarule dictates that rules mentioning the culture site of an organism should also mention the organism's portal of entry. Such a rule enables TEIRESIAS to detect faulty rules as they enter the system. Using the context of the dialogue and its own knowledge of what a rule should look like, TEIRESIAS can fill in much of a new rule for an expert. Metalevel knowledge provides for better explanatory abilities, since the program can present its understanding of a rule at various levels of detail instead of just replacing the rule verbatim.

Several **speech-understanding systems** were developed during the 1970s. Though none of them achieved the quality performance expected of an expert system, some of them, most notably **HEARSAY-II** (Erman et al. 1980), strongly influenced later work on expert systems. HEARSAY-II used a global working memory (the "blackboard"), in which different types and levels of information were all integrated into a uniform structure. This eliminated unnecessary recalculation, made modification easier, and made it simpler to obtain a global view of the current state of the solution for use in a control strategy. This blackboard was used by various knowledge sources (KSs). Each KS contained a different type of knowledge that could be applied to the problem. HEARSAY-II provided ways of focusing, so the system could shift its attention appropriately from one area of the interpretation problem to another. This idea of independent knowledge modules has been used frequently in expert systems and contributes to the ability to modify and acquire knowledge.

CADUCEUS (originally called INTERNIST) (Pople 1977) is a medical consultation system that attempts to make a diagnosis in the domain of internal medicine. The program displays expert performance in about 85 percent of internal medicine, so its knowledge base is one of the largest in any expert system. The diagnosis problem is complicated because a patient can have more than one disease, which makes the number of possible combinations enormous. Like CASNET, CADUCEUS represents its medical knowledge in a structure, the disease tree, about which the program reasons dynamically.

CADUCEUS employs special tactics in order to reason with its huge disease tree and produce results in a reasonable amount of time.

The program builds up disease models as it goes, and dynamically partitions its disease tree into disease areas corresponding to the patient's symptoms. CADUCEUS combines data-directed and hypothesis-directed reasoning in the same framework. The patient data are used first to predict hypotheses, and these are then used to predict other manifestations that must either be confirmed or used to change the hypotheses.

SOPHIE (Brown and Burton 1975) acts as an electronics laboratory instructor that interacts with a student who attempts to debug a piece of malfunctioning equipment. Responding quickly in restricted English, it is expert enough for actual instruction. SOPHIE employs a simulation model of electronics. It also has declarative knowledge of a particular circuit, encoded in a semantic net, and routines that reason with this form of knowledge. When the situation in the circuit changes (for example, a fault is inserted), SOPHIE moves from the explicit, declarative realm into the simulator, determines the details of voltages and currents at various points, and in the end updates its semantic net with the new values. In this way it can avoid calculating all of the values by means of elaborate symbolic reasoning using Kirchhoff's laws and so on. Thus the program embodies techniques for combining the results of running simulations with information obtained by reasoning from declarative knowledge in order to answer many types of questions.

PROSPECTOR (Duda, Gaschnig, and Hart 1979), structured similarly to MYCIN, gives expert advice on finding ore deposits from geological data. Networks are used to express the knowledge in PROSPECTOR, both judgmental knowledge which is expressed as rules and static knowledge about domain objects. The program contains a knowledge acquisition system (KAS) that facilitates the acquisition of all types of knowledge in PROSPECTOR. KAS continually prompts the user until all missing parts of a new structure are filled in. This process is driven by an external grammar that can be changed without difficulty, making it easy to modify KAS as PROSPECTOR evolves. The core of KAS is a network editor that understands various mechanisms in PROSPECTOR and gives the user a limited ability to edit new knowledge in terms of content rather than form.

2.2   Fundamental Qualities of Expert Systems

In the expert systems literature, the word *expert* is taken seriously. The various projects, however, have apparently taken for granted that the important characteristics of an expert can, in fact, be identified.

For example, while high-quality performance is certainly a necessary qualification of an expert, it alone is not enough. AI researchers, for example, tend not to identify fast Fourier transform programs as expert systems, despite the fact that these programs are better at Fourier transforms than, say, DENDRAL is at molecular structure elucidation. What are the presumptions, therefore, about experts and expertise that are unspoken but central to expert systems work?

Some of the intuitive features of being an expert bear examination here. First, of course, is the *quality* of the behavior to be addressed. No matter how fast one performs a task, hardly anyone will be satisfied if the result is a bad performance or an inaccurate judgment. On the other hand the *speed* at which a decision is reached *is* an important factor: even the most accurate of diagnoses slowly arrived at may not be useful, for instance, if in the meantime the patient dies. The principal contribution to relative speed in expert decision-making, according to the expert system literature, seems to be the level at which the rules of decision-making and patterns of symptoms to be recognized are expressed. High-level patterns correspond to highly aggregated, abstracted, or condensed descriptions of what are actually highly detailed phenomena. The belief is that the higher the level of structure that can be matched or recognized, the more conceptual ground can be covered in one inferential leap. One interesting feature of the kind of rules that have been embodied in expert systems is their sketchiness. They are often admitted to be merely rules of thumb, or *heuristics*. The heuristic factor, however, is probably not as important as the reduction of the search area provided by such high-level rules.

One feature of expertness is that it usually comes in *narrow, specialized domains*. For example, it is easy to imagine an expert in almost any technical field (say, mass spectrometry or protein crystallography), but not in such everyday activities as understanding natural language or visual scenes. Specialization in expertness seems to reflect a trade-off between depth and breadth of knowledge: one can know a great deal about only a small number of things. Specialization and expertness go hand in hand.

Although the explicit emphasis in expert systems work has of course been on expertise, these systems also reflect general erudition. For example, spectrogram-reading experts may appear to use only the rules of chemistry and physics, but no doubt they must rely from time to time on general mathematical knowledge and simple common sense. This gives rise to an emphasis on *explanation*. Some researchers believe a capability for explanation is one of the most important features that an expert system can have. Explanation serves several purposes, among these to reassure a human observer of the validity of a chain of inference steps. Yet simply tracing the expert rules invoked during a problem-solving session is the least satisfactory type of explanation a system can generate. The human's intuition that a system understands the problem it is trying to solve is fostered more by an explanation in terms of the *basic principles* of a domain. The direction implied by this factor is the construction of expert systems firmly based in the fundamentals of their domains of expertise.

2.2.1   The Nature of the Present Definition

Any attempt to clarify the meaning of the term *expert system* is bound to be complex. Seven features are analyzed in the following paragraphs that seem to be truly fundamental to the goals of work in the field.[2]

The seven defining dimensions will be presented as if they were simple linear axes along which systems could vary continuously. On the far end of each imaginary continuum is an ideal quality; it will be obvious at the end of this analysis that no existing system is close to the goal on a single axis, let alone on all of them. However, it is submitted that these criteria for expertness are a useful metric for understanding and assessing expert systems. They can be used to characterize a given system's emphasis, since no system really pushes very far on more than one dimension; they can also be used as a comparison metric for various systems, both in coverage of criteria and in closeness to accomplishing goals.

Finally, it will be noted that not all of the dimensions of artificial expertness are independent. Nevertheless, it seemed best to discuss these as if they were independent criteria, because at this point it is difficult to determine the details of any single axis, not to mention interactions among several. Note that discussion throughout concerns expertness as embodied in expert systems, not necessarily as it is in humans. It is not yet clear how artificial and natural expertness relate, even though, throughout their history, expert systems have been loosely modeled after both externally and introspectively observed behavior of human experts.

2.2.2   Expertise

The most important goal in expert system work is to attain the high level of performance that a human expert achieves in some task. Acting like an expert in this regard means producing high-quality results in minimal time, usually by taking advantage of tricks of the trade and high-level inference patterns (hunches) that come from years of experience at a given task.

2.2.2.1   High Performance

The first and most obvious criterion for expert systems is that they successfully solve the problems to which they are applied. This is a difficult dimension along which to assess systems, since in some areas there is no single right answer to a problem. Some systems handle a very limited range of problems extremely well and then degrade rapidly when presented problems even slightly outside the set that the system was built to handle. It may not even be possible to tell where the range of appropriate problems ends. Hence this factor in expert system behavior, while so obviously important, is difficult to quantify. It is only in the strongly technical domains that systems may easily be compared in terms of their success or failure on particular problems.

2.2.2.2   Finding Solutions Efficiently

Although successful performance of a task is part and parcel of expert behavior, it is not sufficient in itself to determine that a system is expert. The way in which such successful behavior is arrived at is what counts. In particular the quality true experts seem to possess that laymen do not is an ability to recognize large-scale patterns and jump quickly to reasonable hypotheses. Expert behavior seems to demand that blind search through large numbers of hypotheses be avoided in favor of quick elimination of many possibilities in each inferential move.

High-level macromoves that allow large amounts of ground to be covered in each step are a key feature of all the expert systems that have been built to date. Each seems to rely fundamentally on some technique, trick, or nonintrospectable algorithm to give it leverage on the particular kinds of problems that experts solve easily but that amateurs can handle only with much elaborate longhand calculation. For example, in the DENDRAL system, there is a structure-proposing program whose internal reasonings are not available to the system as a whole. The algorithm produces quickly and even more accurately than human chemists complete and nonredundant lists of candidate structures.

It should be noted that in the DENDRAL case, as well as in others, relative speed in producing structures or diagnosing syndromes has been attained at the expense of an ability to explain how a result was derived. Systems that use expert-leverage rules and algorithms like DENDRAL cannot in general tell which basic principles and inference steps were used to produce a result. In a sense, the expert knowledge in these systems is "compiled" in a way that cannot be unraveled by whatever interpreters are available to the system.[3]

In addition to sacrificing explicability, expert-leverage rules can trade off robustness for power. The more basic inference steps that are crowded into a single large-scale pattern-match, the more fragile that large match step becomes. When patterns for substeps begin to just miss, step-by-step analysis can detect small differences. In the large-scale case, most often a near miss is as bad as a complete mismatch.

2.2.2.3   On Artificial Expertness

Quality and adroitness of performance seem to be the crux of the ordinary English use of the word *expert*. The dictionary says that an expert is someone who is skilled. However, this sense misses the mark within the context of expert systems. It takes more than good performance to make an expert system. For example, numerical analysis programs for solving differential equations perform well but fall short of the mark as AI expert systems. In particular these programs do not achieve expertise by the right means, which is why the definition of artificial expertness, as embodied in expert systems, does not end here.

2.2.3   Symbol Manipulation

A central premise of expert systems work concerns the kind of information with which the systems reason. Specifically, expert systems employ symbolic reasoning. At least one prominent member of the AI community believes that "the most fundamental contribution so far of artificial intelligence and computer science to the joint enterprise of cognitive science has been the notion of a *physical symbol system*, i.e., the concept of a broad class of systems capable of having and manipulating symbols, yet realizable in the physical universe" (Newell 1980).

A consequence of the prominence of the physical symbol system hypothesis is the recent emergence of the *representation of knowledge* as one of the most central enterprises in the field. Almost every AI project of recent vintage—from natural language understanding to visual perception to planning to expert systems—has employed an explicit symbolic representation of the information in its domain of concern. General languages for representing arbitrary knowledge are becoming a focus in this preoccupation with using symbols for facts and metainformation for a given domain. A survey of knowledge representation work (Brachman and Smith 1980) identified more than eighty projects addressing these issues.

One of the working hypotheses in this field is that knowledge is representational; that is, "knowing" consists in large part in representing symbolically facts about the world. This lends support to Newell's physical symbol system hypothesis, at least as a central assumption in the field at large and in expert systems work in particular. Attention in this area focuses increasingly on basic issues of representation, especially on logical foundations and on first-order predicate calculus as a representation medium.[4] In sum, the first important factor that distinguishes work on expert systems from simply high-quality special-purpose programming is its relation to AI in general and to symbolic, representational reasoning in particular.

2.2.4   General Problem-Solving Ability in a Domain

It follows from the emphasis on symbolic reasoning that expert systems should exhibit a sort of generally intelligent behavior. An expert system can be more or less intelligent, depending on the scope of its basic principles and the quality of its general-purpose reasoning processes. The former emphasizes the breadth of coverage of the domain by the system. Roughly speaking, this is a product of the number of principles the system knows and the detail in which it knows them. The latter is an expression of the simple fact that having all of the knowledge in the world is worthless if one cannot apply it effectively. The quality of reasoning is based on the accessibility of relevant facts and principles as well as on completeness of the inference procedure and efficacy of its implementation.

The principal quality that general knowledge and inferential ability produces, over and above what expert rules do, is *robustness*. As new, unanticipated patterns crop up, inflexible, compiled solutions fail. General problem-solving abilities allow a more graceful degradation at the outer edges of domain knowledge—a kind of conceptual extrapolation—as well as permit interpolation between high-level rules that are not complete within the domain. A generally competent expert might also plan experiments to help fill in gaps in his or her knowledge.

It should be noted that this type of knowledge is essentially the antithesis of high-level macro-move expertise. It is knowledge that is explicitly *not* compiled, so that it may support general inferential procedures. Applying knowledge with general methods, however, is inevitably slower than using multistep inferential rules. If this were the only type of knowledge available to it, a system might eventually reach the same conclusions as a bona fide expert but certainly not with the same efficiency. A system strong on only this dimension would be an inexpert scholarly system, a system with extensive academic knowledge of a domain and complete, weak methods for problem-solving within it, but with no "feel" for the domain or skill at handling its common high-level patterns.

The ability to fall back on reasoning from first principles is clearly one quality that sets expert systems apart from Fourier transform programs. Work in this field to date, however, has emphasized finding the macromoves of expert-level inference, so that most fundamental knowledge has been ignored (Hart 1980). Yet the intent of expert systems work is to produce systems that are as robust in their fields as human experts are. Thus, while not yet a common property, general problem-solving ability in the domain of expertise, coupled with extensive knowledge of basic principles, is an important axis along which to measure expert systems.

2.2.5 Complexity and Difficulty

To try to quantify the next intrinsic feature of expert systems is exasperating. Workers in this field believe that certain domains do not qualify as potential arenas for expertise because they are somehow not complex enough. The reasoning required to solve problems in such a domain may not involve enough steps or enough alternatives at any branch point. Problems have to be complicated enough to require an expert.

This point parallels in a sense the notion of expert rules. It is exactly the longer, tortuous search paths that are to be avoided by such rules. As a result it seems that the more complicated the domain, the more expertise one can attain. Quantifying the complexity of a given domain or type of problem, however, is not something that is much discussed.

2.2.6 Reformulation

One of the critical tasks that real experts do and that expert systems are just beginning to approach is to take a problem stated in some arbitrary initial form and convert it into the form appropriate for processing by expert rules. The problem, of course, should be one that it is reasonable to expect an expert to handle. Its form may be simply a collection of data with the demand to find appropriate patterns and act accordingly in the specific domain covered by the expert. This might be called the *reformulation* dimension of expertise.

A good reformulation system is one that also knows its limits.

Overzealous reformulation should be avoided; expert systems should not be forcing problems into models that are really inappropriate for their solution.

Reformulation can range from simple translation from one surface form to another (as in MACSYMA) to complete reconceptualization of a problem or situation description. (For a detailed discussion of the reformulation problem see Mark 1976 and Mostow 1983.)

2.2.7   Abilities Requiring Reasoning about Self

Another set of abilities required in an expert system allows it to reason about its own processes. The several uses for this type of cognitive capability are given an entire chapter in this book. Here only the *explanation* aspect of self-knowledge is briefly touched on; the discussion of "strategic, descriptive, and system knowledge" is left for Chapter 7.

Expert systems need the ability to rationalize their own decisions. Rationalization is the ability for the system to look at its own chain of reasoning and understand it as if it were another task domain requiring expertise. It seems that explanation, so commonly cited as a central feature of expert systems, is really only a by-product of the more fundamental ability to reconstruct the inference paths that the system must have taken to arrive at its conclusion.

Explanation in expert systems is usually associated with some form of tracing of rules that fire during the course of a problem-solving session. This is about the closest to real explanation that today's systems can come, given the fact that their knowledge is represented almost exclusively as high-level rules. However, a satisfactory explanation of how a conclusion was derived demands an ability to connect the inference steps with fundamental domain principles as justifications. (Therefore, this dimension of our definition of expert systems is immediately not independent of the one about reasoning from first principles. Real explanation, of course, is impossible in terms of basic principles without knowing those principles.) Each high-level macromove can be justified only by recourse to the basic principles that make it sound—the rule cannot be its own justification. (A crude approximation to this might be achieved by associating with each high-level rule some English text to be used in explanation; this obviates generating an explanation automatically from basic principles that make it sound—the rule cannot be its own justification. (A crude approximation to this might be achieved by associ- benefits.) The important point here is that this kind of explanation requires an ability to reconstruct a rational line of argument. This reconstruction must be built out of the fundamental principles of the domain and must be able to satisfy another expert as to the soundness of the reasoning sequence. This rational reconstruction is sophisticated behavior more akin to general perception than to rule-tracing. The system either needs to observe its own reasoning, as if it were an outsider, or to associate appropriate fundamental principles with each expert rule. One of the interesting consequences of this sort of rationalization is that it is a construction of a *likely* path by which the expert arrived at its conclusion, not necessarily the one that the system actually used. Thus explanation is generally a fallible process.

Explanations by human experts, in general, are tailored to their audiences. The details of reasoning as related to another expert in the same domain will be different from those related to a layman. This requires a kind of intelligent behavior not apparent in the explanation facilities of current expert systems.

The ability to explain a line of reasoning may not be a necessary part of some kinds of systems. Rigorously scientific systems may reach conclusions that are self-explanatory to other experts and thus may stand as explanation in themselves. Or imagine the case of an intelligent Mars rover. With a low bandwidth and long-delay communication line, extensive explanation may prove undesirable. In this case, a simple sort of rule-tracing might be appropriate. On the other hand, more judgmental, subjective domains demand more elaborate explanations. A satisfactory explanation of how a geological determination was reached may involve much more than simply a trace of rules. In fact an interactive explanation scenario, wherein another expert can probe in depth the reasoning behind a judgment, may be more appropriate. This sort of explanation becomes more critical as the cost of a wrong decision and the frequency of unexpected results increase.

2.2.8   Task

The final defining dimension of expert systems is the generic task that the system is built to do. Different tasks may substantially change the picture of a system's architecture. This is certainly not a continuous dimension, given the fact that expert systems have been built to do all of the following: interpretation, diagnosis, monitoring, prediction, instruction, planning, and design.

The architectural implications of the task requirements are treated in depth in Chapters 3 and 4. What is raised here is simply the point that the intended task is another dimension of expert systems that affects their comparison and that measurement of success (see Chapter 8) depends on the type of task.

2.2.9   Other Considerations

Some features whose effects on the concept of an artificial expert system are currently unclear should be pointed out. These are features that human experts have, perhaps by virtue of their being either human or generally intelligent rather than expert.

In particular, it is noted without comment that human experts:

- Learn from further experience (become more expert)
- Reconceptualize
- Acquire general knowledge
- Have common sense—across all domains
- Can reason by analogy

2.2.10   Summary

An expert system is one that has expert rules and avoids blind search, performs well, reasons by manipulating symbols, grasps fundamental domain principles, and has complete weaker reasoning methods to fall back on when expert rules fail and to use in producing explanations. It deals with difficult problems in a complex domain, can take a problem description in lay terms and convert it to an internal representation appropriate for processing with its expert rules, and it can reason about its own knowledge (or lack thereof), especially to reconstruct inference paths rationally for explanation and self-justification. An expert system works on (generally at least) one of these types of task: interpretation, diagnosis, prediction, instruction, monitoring, planning, and design.

2.3   Review of Characteristics of Current Expert Systems

The following assessment of selected expert systems is intended to illustrate further the main defining dimensions used to characterize an expert system. The systems are compared with regard to the following dimensions: task, performance, expertise, extendability, explanation, utility, reasoning under uncertainty, solution method, knowledge representation, knowledge acquisition, user interface and special features.

2.3.1 DENDRAL

The task of DENDRAL is interpretation and hypothesis formation; it identifies candidate molecular structures from mass spectral and nuclear magnetic response data. DENDRAL's performance is characterized by accurate, high-quality results for limited classes of problems. Each class is characterized by a set of molecular structures with certain characteristics. DENDRAL's performance is extremely efficient and is improving steadily as the system moves from a research setting to commercial environments.

DENDRAL's expertise derives from compiled, hand-crafted knowledge in forms directly usable by the system. It does not reason from or directly manipulate basic principles of chemistry, thus its range of expertise is narrow. In addition, its explanation facilities are minimal. DENDRAL can be extended or improved only through a reprogramming effort involving designers working together with domain experts.

DENDRAL is widely used; parts of the system are used regularly by research chemists throughout the United States. The system has demonstrated the usefulness of AI methods and tools in a real scientific inference task and has focused attention on both technical and social issues in knowledge engineering.

With regard to reasoning under uncertainty, fragmentation rules in the system operate with certainty but deliberately overlook small stochastic and statistical errors between the rules and actual empirical results. The solution method incorporates a complete hypothesis generator, constrained by data-driven rules and filtered by a strong evaluator that can rapidly prune possible substructures from consideration.

In DENDRAL knowledge is represented as a special piece of code for the molecular structure generator, and as production rules for the data-driven component and evaluator. Knowledge acquisition requires reprogramming or production-rule editing. DENDRAL contained no special user-interface facilities in the early stages of development, but such facilities were developed for the commercial version of the system.

2.3.2 CASNET/GLAUCOMA

The task of CASNET/GLAUCOMA is diagnosis, interpretation, and therapy of glaucoma by hypothesis-driven data elicitation and question selection. The system's performance is comparable to that of human experts in the field; it is highly efficient since speed of response was a design requirement from the start.

The system's expertise derives from compiled, hand-crafted

knowledge in a limited area, and is used to fashion a high-level model of how the disease evolves. However, the system has no understanding of the basic physiological processes involved. The system can be extended or improved by including new causal and associational rules in the disease model (or network) and then compiling the new model. Testing and improvement is performed by domain experts accessing the system via computer networks.

Explanation facilities in the system are fairly good and include extensive references to medical literature. The system's utility is high; it is used for research by a community of ophthalmologists in the United States and Japan.

Reasoning under uncertainty is a crucial part of the system; all inferential links have weights, and the system's conclusions depend on the degree of corroboration obtained from different inferential links.

The solution method used by the system incorporates data-directed interpretation under the constraints of a causal model of disease. Knowledge in the casual model has a semantic-net-style representation. Knowledge acquisition requires editing the causal model and then recompiling it.

The user interface in the CASNET/GLAUCOMA model is well engineered and incorporates restricted dialogue formats. Special features include multiple modes of processing. These modes reflect knowledge base differences that encode differences in schools of thought in the field and hence different medical opinions.

2.3.3 MACSYMA

The task of MACSYMA is the solution of a variety of mathematical problems, such as algebraic simplification and integration. It achieves high quality and very efficient performance in this domain.

The system's expertise derives from a collection of hand-crafted knowledge sources in specific areas of mathematics. Sophisticated patterns guide choices of routines appropriate for a given problem. However, MACSYMA cannot reason from basic principles, and thus has limited breadth. Furthermore, it has no explanation facilities and no reasoning under uncertainty. Members of the user community can extend or augment the system only by reprogramming or adding specialized routines.

MACSYMA is used extensively by scientists (many plasma physicists) and engineers, who access it via nets on a dedicated computer at the Massachusetts Institute of Technology. The system has had a significant impact on the development and application of symbolic manipulation processes in mathematics.

The solution method used by MACSYMA involves no search. Instead the results of a problem recognition phase establish an association with a specific solution method. Programmed routines are used for knowledge representation, and there are good mathematical interface facilities for the users.

2.3.4   MYCIN

The task of MYCIN is diagnosis and therapy in certain classes of infectious blood diseases. MYCIN produces high-quality results with performance comparable to experts in the field.

The system's expertise derives from hand-crafted knowledge in a limited application area. MYCIN has no understanding of basic medical principles involved in its decisions. The major emphasis is on explanation, mainly tracing the system's inferential processes and providing literature sources relevant to the rules that are used in these processes. TEIRESIAS, an ancillary system built to provide improved explanation capabilities, provides flexible knowledge acquisition and better user-interface facilities for the MYCIN system.

MYCIN can be extended by the inclusion of new production rules that represent increments of medical reasoning. Testing and improvement is done by knowledge engineers in collaboration with domain experts.

Although the MYCIN system is not currently used for research or clinical work, it is used in medical teaching. The system has been useful for spawning the development of the EMYCIN and KS300 systems, which provide a framework for building consultation systems. It has had a strong methodological impact, as well, on AI in areas such as rule-based programming and reasoning under uncertainty.

Reasoning under uncertainty is a crucial part of the MYCIN system. It assesses propositions on a scale from -1 (certainly wrong) to $+1$ (certainly right), requires intermediate results below a positive threshold, and combines multiple sources of evidence and uncertain rules to evaluate a measure of belief in hypotheses.

The solution method used by MYCIN is backward-chaining from diagnostic hypotheses to data, under the guidance of inferential rules. Knowledge is represented as production rules and knowledge acquisition involves adding new rules to the system.

MYCIN incorporates good human engineering in a convenient user interface. Especially helpful to users are the restricted natural language and tabular presentation of medical data. Special features include systematic validation experiments conducted for the system (Buchanan 1982). Work on MYCIN led to the development of a variety of special systems where MYCIN techniques and methodology are being used, such as PUFF.

2.3.5   CADUCEUS

The task of CADUCEUS is diagnosis. It uses hypothesis-driven data elicitation (question selection) to form several hypotheses (several possible diagnoses of diseases) from a set of data. Experiments indicate that this still developing system provides high-quality performance in internal medicine. The response is relatively slow on time-shared systems but is acceptable in a dedicated machine environment.

The system's expertise derives from a broad spectrum of hand-crafted knowledge, including about 500 diseases, 350 disease manifestations, and 100,000 symptomatic associations. The system has no understanding of the basic pathophysiological processes involved that would permit it to handle problems at the periphery of its area of expertise. Its explanation facilities are minimal.

The system can be extended by adding disease and symptom entities and by adding inferential links (evocation or manifestation links). Expertise has been conveyed to (encoded within) the system by a distinguished expert in internal medicine.

The system has some educational usage at present by medical students. It is also being used in current clinical trials sponsored by the National Institutes of Health. Its potential utility in medicine is enormous, as the system embodies expertise about nearly all of internal medicine. CADUCEUS has clearly made a significant contribution to AI research with regard to hypothesis formation in expert systems.

Reasoning under uncertainty is an important part of the approach used by CADUCEUS. The solution method combines data-directed and hypothesis-directed data interpretation under constraints of disease taxonomy and causality relationships. Knowledge in the system is represented as a network of findings and diseases via varied LISP programs. Knowledge acquisition involves editing the links between disease entities and the findings or symptoms.

The user interface facilities in CADUCEUS are being improved and refined. The unique feature of this highly complex system is that it has the largest knowledge base of the current generation of expert systems. While the knowledge base of the first version of the system is being augmented to achieve high performance in a wide domain of medicine, the second version provides a framework for continuing the research on hypothesis-formation methodologies.

2.3.6   PROSPECTOR

The task of PROSPECTOR is probabilistic interpretation of soil and geological deposit data. High-quality results have been achieved in specific domains of mineral exploration; PROSPECTOR's performance is comparable to that of expert geologists.

The system's expertise derives from limited hand-crafted knowledge. It has no understanding of the basic principles embodied in its knowledge base, but does considerable explanation of its reasoning processes, and reasoning under uncertainty is an integral part of the system.

The major thrust in improving the system's extendability has been the development of a knowledge acquisition system (KAS) to facilitate changes.

PROSPECTOR has proved extremely useful. It predicted a molybdenum deposit would be found in a certain location; the prediction was confirmed with a finding worth $100 million. The system has spurred the development of numerous ore deposit models. It has influenced AI research by its use of semantic-net models and its studies of the probabilistic basis for reasoning under uncertainty.

The solution method used by PROSPECTOR is bottom-up data interpretation. Knowledge is represented in semantic nets and is acquired through the KAS knowledge acquisition system. User interface facilities in PROSPECTOR are convenient and well engineered.

2.4 Summary Observations

The crop of expert systems in use today is well within the limits of what expert systems should be expected to do. As P. E. Hart (1980) puts it in "What's Preventing the Widespread Use of Expert Systems?"

Today's expert systems typically show up badly when measured along a number of dimensions:

- They are unable to recognize or deal with problems for which their own knowledge is inapplicable or insufficient.
- They have no independent means of checking whether their conclusions are reasonable.
- Explication of their reasoning processes is frequently silent on fundamental issues.

In other words, today's expert systems fall well short on dimensions requiring general intelligent behavior. They are more akin to *idiots savants* than to real human experts. Another characterization of the state of the art (Buchanan 1982) lists these shortcomings:

- Narrow domain of expertise
- Limited language for expressing facts and relations

- Limited assumptions about problem and solution methods (help required from a knowledge engineer)
- Stylized input/output languages
- Stylized explanations of line of reasoning
- Little knowledge of their own scope and limitations
- Knowledge bases extensible but little help available for initial design decisions
- Single expert as "knowledge czar"

In spite of these shortcomings, today's expert systems provide concrete examples of the maxim "Knowledge is power." Many directions can be followed to broaden or deepen the knowledge in these systems.

NOTES

1. A significant portion of this section is taken verbatim from Aikins 1980. We wish to thank Janice S. Aikins for permission to quote at length from her work.
2. The dimensions of this definition will be noted to contrast markedly with Buchanan's (1981) simpler characterization, which cites only utility, performance, and transparency. By the end of this chapter, how those criteria fit into a more detailed picture should be clear. In particular, utility is seen to be an incidental methodological influence, and not a defining criterion; performance is treated in the next subsection, on expertise; and transparency is an intuitive attempt to cover several other dimensions.
3. This is probably as far as the compiled/interpreted analogy should be taken. There is no indication that there must be, or ever was in the existing systems, any more explicitly stated description that actually gets compiled into opaque code. It is simply the nature of the macromoves of expert knowledge that their origins in more fundamental knowledge cannot be discerned.
4. Brachman (1979) discusses a series of levels of representational primitives—levels of abstraction of data used in reasoning—that places much of the work on representation languages in perspective.

QUESTIONS

1. Identify three tasks humans perform today that qualify them as "experts" but that will cease to require "expertise" fifty years

from now. What ordinary tasks do people perform today that required experts fifty years ago?

2. As knowledge expands, the capacity to absorb it is stretched beyond human limits. What happens to the knowledge, and how does it become reallocated?

3. What makes an expert system robust? How can this capacity be provided?

4. What kind of knowledge is needed to make a fast problem-solver? A thoughtful problem-solver? An instructive problem-solver? An expert problem-solver?

5. What design criteria would ensure that the knowledge bases in several individual expert systems could be combined? What behavioral characteristics would the combined system be likely to exhibit?

3

Basic Concepts for Building Expert Systems

**Mark Stefik, Janice Aikins, Robert Balzer,
John Benoit, Lawrence Birnbaum,
Frederick Hayes-Roth, and Earl Sacerdoti**

*This chapter summarizes the concepts involved in the general
field of artificial intelligence in order to present several ideas
that are central to knowledge engineering. Knowledge typically derives its value from its potential to pare down to
manageable size problems that appear impossibly complex.
This power comes from its capacity to shrink large search
spaces. Search techniques that cannot apply knowledge will
not succeed at difficult tasks. To utilize knowledge, many
new types of search structures and techniques have evolved.
A large number of potential applications can make use of
similar approaches.*

In 1962 Allen Newell surveyed several organizational alternatives for problem-solving programs. Since then many techniques have
been developed in artificial intelligence research, and several types
of expert systems have been built. Expert systems are problem-solving
programs that solve difficult problems requiring expertise. They are
termed knowledge-based because their performance depends critically

on utilizing facts and heuristics used by experts. Expert systems have been used as a vehicle for AI research with the rationale that they provide a forcing function for research issues in problem-solving and a reality test for their workability.

Some textbooks discuss principles of artificial intelligence (see, for example, Nilsson 1980) and give examples of advanced programming techniques (as does Charniak, Riesback, and McDermott 1979). However, there is no guidebook to direct aspiring expert systems architects through the issues and choices faced in designing a system. And an unguided sampling of expert systems in the literature can be quite confusing. Examples are scattered in diverse journals, conference proceedings, and technical reports. Systems with seemingly similar tasks sometimes have radically different organizations, and seemingly different tasks are sometimes performed with only minor variations on a single organization. Variations often reflect the immaturity of a field in which most of the systems are experimental. With the diversity of experiments, it is necessary to extract alternatives and principles that guide a designer, as this chapter does. This presentation is intended for readers with a computer science, but not necessarily an AI, background.

3.1   Vocabulary and Basic Concepts

In their 1975 Turing Award lecture Allen Newell and Herbert Simon emphasized two basic concepts: symbols and search. They were concerned with "physical symbol systems" that manipulate collections of symbolic structures and perform problem-solving tasks using heuristic search, their central hypothesis being that physical symbol systems have all of the necessary and sufficient means for intelligent action. Since expert systems are intended to embody the knowledge and intelligence of experts, the concepts of symbols and search are central. Emphasis, in this chapter, however, will be on the pragmatics of building expert systems rather than on the theoretical requirements for intelligence.

In this section symbol structures that can be used to represent facts are discussed, terminology from predicate calculus is reviewed, and several approaches to search compared for their effectiveness in inferring new facts from old ones. Some characteristics of common-sense reasoning that affect the computational organization of a problem-solver are considered. Also presented are several concepts that are not covered in introductory AI textbooks but that are important in expert systems.

3.1.1   Symbols

In their discussion of physical symbol systems, Newell and Simon
(1976) define a symbol as a physical pattern that can occur as a component of a symbol structure composed of a number of symbols
related in some physical way, as by being next to each other. It is sufficient to think of symbols as strings of characters and of symbol
structures as a type of data structure called list structures containing
symbols. The following are examples of symbols:

> Apple
> Transistor-13
> Running
> Five
> 3.14159.

And the following are examples of symbol structures:

> (On   Block1   Block2)
> (Plus   5   X)
> (Same-as   (Father-of Pete)   (Father-of   (Brother-of Pete))).

One of the early contributions of AI research to computer science
was the invention of list-processing languages for symbolic computation. These languages provided primitives for manipulating lists and
facilities for managing their storage (Charniak, Riesback, and McDermott 1979).

3.1.1.1   Predicate Calculus

Predicate calculus is a widely studied formal language of symbol
structures that can be used for representation in a computer. Let us
begin with simple examples of the use of flexible symbol structures
for representing facts and examine an illustration of why inference
methods must be knowledge-intensive to be effective. Although the
issues for reasoning in expert systems go beyond those of classical
logic, a knowledge of predicate calculus is an essential foundation for
understanding issues of representation and inference (Kleene 1967;
Suppes 1957).

Figure 3.1 is a picture of a table with some blocks on it. Some
symbol structures represent the information in the picture. Written
in a syntactic variation (prefix format) of predicate calculus, these
symbol structures are made up of terms and predicate symbols.
Terms are used for the names of things and predicates represent rela-

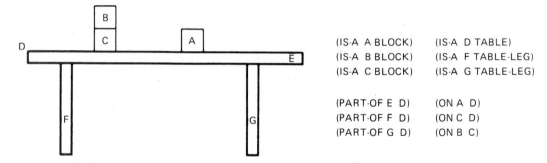

FIGURE 3.1   A table with blocks on it and a predicate calculus representation for the information.

tions between things. In this example, A, B, C, D, E, F, G, BLOCK, TABLE, TABLE-TOP, and TABLE-LEG are terms and IS-A, PART-OF, and ON are predicate names. In books on logic, simple predicates like those in Figure 3.1 are called propositions or atomic formulas.

In addition to using symbols for constants and predicates, predicate calculus allows for functions and logical connectives. Functions denote mappings between entities. For example, if TOP-OF is a function symbol, then

$$(\text{TOP-OF D})$$

denotes the top of table D. (The present syntax differs from the usual predicate calculus only in the placement of the predicate symbol. The prefix syntax was chosen to resemble list structures convenient in symbol processing languages such as LISP.) Connectives are used to combine formulas. These include "$\wedge$" (and), "$\vee$" (or), and "$\rightarrow$" (implies). For example, the formula "Either Block A is on table D or it is on Block B" might be represented in functional notation as

$$\text{ON (A D)} \vee \text{ON (A B)}.$$

In the present notation it would be represented as

$$(\text{OR   (ON A D) (ON A B)}).$$

The symbol "~" (not) is sometimes called a connective, although it is used to negate a formula and not to connect two formulas.

Predicate calculus can also express sentences involving quantifiers like "All blocks are small." In traditional notation this would be expressed as

$$(\forall x) \ [\text{BLOCK}(x) \rightarrow \text{SMALL}(x)].$$

A list structure notation for this could be

$$(\text{ALL } (x) \ (\text{IF } (\text{IS-A } x \text{ BLOCK}) \ (\text{SMALL } x)))$$

or

$$(\text{ALL } (x) \ (\ (\text{IS-A } x \text{ BLOCK}) \rightarrow (\text{SMALL } x))).$$

These formulas use "∀" (all), the universal quantifier, to indicate that the formula is true for all assignments of the variable x to entities in the domain of discourse. We say that the formula is quantified over x. The second important quantifier in predicate calculus is the existential quantifier "∃" (exists). This quantifier is used to indicate that the formula is true for some assignment of the variable to entities in a domain. A calculus is said to be first order if it allows quantification over terms, but not over predicate or function symbols.

Formulas that have been built out of terms and atomic formulas by using connectives and quantifiers are called well-formed formulas (wffs). Predicate calculus provides a number of well-defined rules for combining formulas.

In predicate calculus, a wff can be given an interpretation by assigning a correspondence between the elements of the language and the entities and relations of the domain of discourse. To each constant symbol must be assigned a corresponding entity in the domain, and to each predicate a relation in the domain. When a computer data base is composed of symbolic representations, the designer of the data base selects a vocabulary of predicates and terms to be used and decides what they will mean. Use of the data base follows an interpretation of the formulas as assertions in the domain of discourse. For example, the formulas in Figure 3.1 are meant to be interpreted as facts about the blocks and table in the illustration. The formula (PART-OF E D) is intended to represent the fact that E (the table top) is part of D (the table).

The strength of predicate calculus is that the language has well-understood interpretations to express many involved sentences. De Morgan's laws provide an example of manipulations that preserve standard interpretations. For example,

$$(\text{NOT } (\text{AND } A \ B))$$

is equivalent to

$$(\text{OR } (\text{NOT } A) \ (\text{NOT } B))$$

in predicate calculus. Another example is the use of parentheses for indicating scoping in quantification. The two formulas

$$(ALL\ (x)\ (SOME\ (y)\ (Loves\ x\ y)))$$
$$(SOME\ (x)\ (ALL\ (y)\ (Loves\ x\ y)))$$

mean respectively "Everyone has someone that he loves" and "There is someone who loves everybody."

3.1.1.2   Inference

In order for a system to reason, it must be able to infer new facts from what it has already been told. This involves dynamically creating new symbol structures from old ones. In predicate calculus, new wffs are produced by applying rules of inference to sets of wffs. In the situation in Figure 3.1, for example, we might have the following rules about the predicate ABOVE:

$(ALL\ (x)\ (ALL\ (y)\ ((ON\ x\ y) \rightarrow (ABOVE\ x\ y))))$
"If x is on y, then x is above y."
$(ALL\ (x)\ (ALL\ (y)\ (ALL\ (z)\ (AND\ (ABOVE\ x\ y)\ (ABOVE\ y\ z)) \rightarrow (ABOVE\ x\ z))))$
"If x is above y and y is above z, then x is above z."

Given the wffs in Figure 3.1, we can use the first rule to infer that the blocks are above everything that they are on; that is,

$$(ABOVE\ A\ D)$$
$$(ABOVE\ C\ D)$$
$$(ABOVE\ B\ C).$$

The second rule allows us to utilize the transitivity of the ABOVE relation to infer

$$(ABOVE\ B\ D).$$

This account is logically incomplete. The only rules described were domain rules, that is, wffs from the domain of discourse in Figure 3.1. Logical rules of inference—the rules about logic that take given wffs to yield derived wffs—were not mentioned. The foregoing reasoning implicitly used two rules of inference known as modus ponens and universal specialization. In standard notation, these are written:

Modus ponens: A, A→B q B
Universal specialization: A, ($\forall$x), W(x) q W(A)

where the symbol "q" is used to mean "yields." Modus ponens states that from the wffs A and A $\rightarrow$ B we can infer the wff B. Universal specification is similar except that it involves a universal quantifier. Universal specialization produces the wff W(A) from the wff $(\forall x)$ W(x), where A is any constant symbol. An often cited example of universal specialization is the inference that "Socrates is mortal" produced from the wffs "Socrates is a man" and "All men are mortal."

The direct application of this to expert systems is to represent "what is believed so far" by wffs stored in computer memory and to use inference rules to derive new facts and beliefs. This is a good idea, but it falls short as a means of representing knowledge in expert systems. One of the difficulties is that it is not enough simply to have the "facts at hand"; one must know how to use them. Consider, for example, the inference rule or-introduction

$$A \text{ q } A \vee B.$$

Or-introduction captures the idea that we can infer "A or B" either by proving A or by proving B. Given constants D, E, and F, we can use this rule to infer

$$D \vee E$$
$$D \vee F$$
$$E \vee F$$

as well as such wonders as

$$D \vee D$$
$$D \vee E \vee E$$
$$D \vee E \vee D \vee E$$
$$D \vee E \vee E \vee E \vee E \vee E \vee E \vee E$$

and so on without limit. This example shows that the unguided application of inference rules can be combinatorially explosive. The inferences are perfectly correct; they are just not particularly interesting. (The next section considers combinatorial explosions that arise in large search problems.)

Much work has been directed toward controlling combinatorial explosions. For example, some mechanical theorem-proving techniques avoid nonsense applications of or-introduction. Methods that use many rules of inference need to incorporate knowledge to control their use. An alternative but equally troubled approach is to use a single rule of inference such as resolution. (The interested reader is referred to Nilsson 1980 for examples of resolution and resolution strategies, as well as a bibliography.) Resolution has the important property of completeness, which means that any wff that follows from a set of wffs can eventually be derived.

Unfortunately the effort that it takes to derive a theorem with resolution is often quite impractical for even simple problems. Human problem-solvers can often solve problems using much more direct methods. *The reason is that the knowledge about problem-solving is much more encompassing than the knowledge about the application of inference rules.* In other words the speed and directness of human experts have little to do with their expertise about the semantics of AND, OR, and NOT and more to do with their expertise in the domain and in solving domain problems. It is possible to incorporate some problem-solving expertise in theorem-proving systems. Problem-solvers require such knowledge to be effective. The next section approaches this issue by considering the concept of search.

3.1.2   Search

Many problem-solving systems in AI are based on the formulation of problem-solving as search (Gardner 1981; Nilsson 1980). In this formulation a description of a desired solution is called a goal and the set of possible steps leading from initial conditions to a goal is viewed as a search space. Problem-solving is carried out by searching through the space of possible solutions for ones that satisfy a goal. These concepts are illustrated in the example that follows.

3.1.2.1   An Example of a State-space Search Problem

The simplest search formulation of problem-solving is state-space search. This representation of problem-solving uses states and operators. A state is a data structure that is like a snapshot of the problem at one stage of the solution; operators change one state into another. The idea is to find a sequence of operators that can be applied to a starting state until a goal state is reached.

A simple example of a state-space search, which has been used in many introductions to AI, is the eight-puzzle. An eight-puzzle is a tray containing eight square tiles numbered from 1 to 8. The space for a ninth tile is vacant, leaving an empty square in the tray, as shown in Figure 3.2. The goal is to put the tray of tiles into a specified configuration by sliding tiles.

A tile may be moved by sliding it vertically or horizontally into the empty square. This movement can be formalized concisely in terms of operators by viewing the empty square as an object that can be moved in any of the four directions. This provides four operators—up, down, left, and right—which can be applied to a state of the tray to yield another state. Figure 3.2 shows the effects of

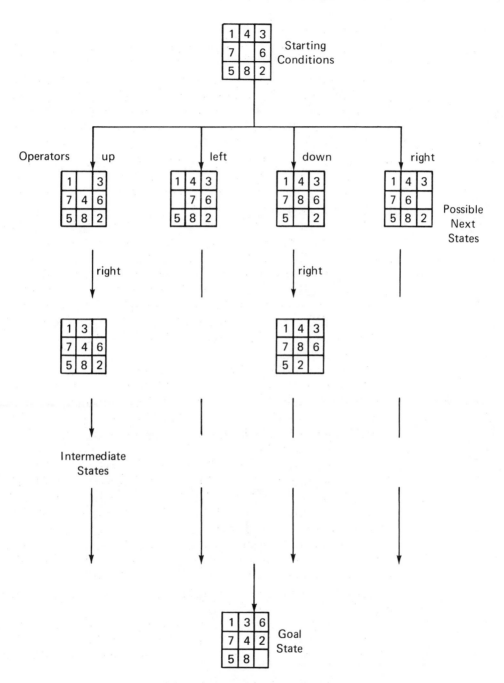

FIGURE 3.2   State-space representation of the eight-puzzle. Each board configuration is a "state" and operators are applied to move between states in the space to a goal.

applying these operators to the starting state of the eight-puzzle. Under some circumstances, particular operators may be inapplicable. In the eight-puzzle, operators are inapplicable when the empty square is on the edge of the figure and the proposed operator would move it off the tray. A state-space is the directed graph whose nodes are states and whose arcs are the operators that lead from one state to another. There are various ways to carry out the search for a solution. Blind search techniques systematically explore branches of the graph one step at a time.

3.1.2.2   Blind Search

Blind search methods can be goal-directed, data-directed, or bidirectional. In the eight-puzzle a goal-directed approach would involve searching backward from the desired end state to the initial conditions by applying the "inverse" operators. Data-directed search, which starts from the given initial conditions, is also called searching forward. Bidirectional search involves searching from both ends of a space in order to meet somewhere in the middle.

Given an orientation for a search, there are several different systematic orders in which the nodes of the solution space may be considered. Depth-first search is a search process that considers successive nodes in the space before considering alternatives at the same level. In the eight-puzzle case, a forward depth-first search would expand the graph of the state-space, starting with one of the states in the first row and then considering a successor to that state and then a successor of that successor and so on. A breadth-first search would expand the graph differently. First it would consider all four initial operators, and then it would consider all of the successors of those operators and then all of the successors of the successors and so on. To summarize, depth-first search dives deeply into the search tree, and breadth-first search descends uniformly across all possibilities. In a complete search depth-first and breadth-first approaches examine the same number of nodes. However, breadth-first search places a substantially greater demand on memory usage because it carries so many parallel paths.

3.1.2.3   Heuristic Search

Practical limits on the amount of time and storage available to spend on search problems always exist. Although in principle blind search methods can eventually find a solution to search problems, they are not practical for large problems because too many nodes are visited before a solution is found. This illustrates the phenomenon of combinatorial explosion that arises when problem-solvers lack sufficient knowledge to guide an inferential process.

For many applications it is possible to find domain-specific information to guide the search process and to reduce the amount of computation. This is called heuristic information, and search procedures that use it are called heuristic search methods. Heuristic searches can stop as soon as any satisfactory solution is found.

One form of heuristic search is to direct the search in a "best-first" order. To determine which branch of the search tree to expand, a domain-dependent evaluation function is used to estimate the closeness of the path to the goal. For example, Nilsson (1980) suggests the following evaluation function for the eight-puzzle:

$$f(n) = d(n) + W(n)$$

where $d(n)$ is the depth of node n in the tree and $W(n)$ counts the number of misplaced tiles. An evaluation function is supposed to give an estimate of the computational effort of pursuing a path. Nodes are tried in increasing order of their f values. In Figure 3.2, the f values of the branches in the first row (left to right) are 5, 7, 7, and 6, so the first move in the eight-puzzle state-space would be up.

Much attention has been given to characterizing evaluation functions formally, especially for games. Functions are said to be well behaved if they reliably and monotonically indicate an optimal path to a goal. The monotone restriction, for example, requires that an evaluation function must infallibly decrease as a goal is approached. Various theorems have been proved about search methods utilizing well-behaved evaluation functions (Nilsson 1980).

In many real problems well-behaved evaluation functions are elusive. Sometimes a strategic retreat is necessary; that is, one must seem to move away from a goal (overriding some evaluation function) in order to achieve it. For example, to enter a room it is worth detouring to an unlocked door even though a locked door is closer—if there is no key. In organic synthesis problems, it is sometimes helpful to add elaborate extra chemical structures to a molecule in order to provide a rigid framework for a later step in a series of reactions. If an evaluation function measures only chemical similarity, such reactions appear to be a retreat from the goal.

This illustrates a basic fact about evaluation functions: *To be useful, evaluation functions must characterize the solution space adequately, which generally requires a substantial amount of knowledge.* It is misleading to consider only simple arithmetic functions and weighted coefficients as the basic style for representing this knowledge. In expert systems, substantial amounts of symbolic computing may be appropriate for guiding a search.

3.1.2.4   Abstracting the Solution Space

One of the important skills in problem-solving is the ability to focus on the most important considerations in a problem. Search methods get bogged down when they can't see the forest for the trees. The following example illustrates the idea.

Consider the problem of driving from the San Diego Hilton Hotel to the New York Hilton. Assume the driver wants to take the fastest route and that other considerations (such as scenery or weather) are unimportant. Trip planning could be formalized as a search process that starts at the San Diego Hilton and fans out through the streets of San Diego, enumerating noncyclic paths until the fastest route to the New York Hilton is found. There are hundreds of roads in San Diego and hundreds of towns (with many roads) between San Diego and New York. Some heuristics about heading to the north and east and not doubling back too much could be applied, but the driver must be careful not to miss the fastest route, which is not likely to be along a straight line. Using these ideas and the fastest computer available, a driver would never manage to find a route to New York.

Computer problem-solvers need not be so simplemindedly methodical. In planning the trip without a computer, a driver would not be busy with street maps for all of the towns in the continental United States but might start instead with a reduced-scale map and consider only the main highways that cross the country. Street maps would be used only for incidentals of food and lodging along the way. The use of a reduced-scale map, an abstraction of a detailed continental map that leaves out the details, is essential to an efficient solution to the problem (or, often, to *any* solution).

This illustrates a general idea for reducing search in many kinds of problem-solving. *By searching an abstracted representation of a space, the combinatorics can be reduced.* The search of the abstract space is quicker because it is smaller; single steps in the abstract space correspond to big steps in the ground search space. For example, the driver may first decide to take Route 40 across the country. This breaks the original problem down into smaller problems, which can be tackled using intermediate levels of abstraction. In the driving example using a state map, one can plan to use Highway 15 to meet Route 40 at Los Angeles and, using a city map, plan a route out of San Diego. This amounts to *hierarchical problem-solving* through various levels of abstraction.

The importance of hierarchical methods for taming large search problems has been recognized for many years. In 1963, Minsky argued that, by introducing "planning islands," these methods reduce search by what he called a "fractional exponent":

> In a graph with 10 branches descending from each node, a 20-step search might involve 10^{20} trials, which is out of the question, while the insertion of just four lemmas or sequential subgoals might reduce the search to only 5×10^4 trials, which is within reason for machine exploration. Thus it will be worth a relatively enormous effort to find such "islands" in the solution of complex problems. Note that even if one encountered, say 10^6 failures of such procedures before success, one would still have gained a factor of perhaps 10^{10} in over-all trial reduction! Thus practically any ability at all to "plan" or "analyze" a problem will be profitable, if the problem is difficult. It is safe to say that all simple, unitary, notions of how to build an intelligent machine will fail, rather sharply, for some modest level of problem difficulty. Only schemes which actively pursue an analysis toward obtaining a set of sequential goals can be expected to extend smoothly into increasingly complex problem domains. (1963:441−442)

Hierarchical methods have been used in several expert systems. As in the road map example, it is not necessary to introduce fully described intermediate islands in order to achieve hierarchical reasoning; abstract descriptions can be used instead.

3.1.2.5 Generate-and-Test

State-space search is sometimes formulated as generate-and-test. This formulation divides the search process into two parts: a generator of possible solutions and a tester, which prunes solutions that fail to meet some constraints. A generator is said to be *complete* if it is capable of producing every possible solution; it is said to be nonredundant if in the course of generation it produces each solution only once. In most applications the generating and testing processes overlap in time.

An important issue is the distribution of knowledge between the generator and the tester. Putting as much knowledge as possible in the generator often leads to a more efficient search. An important form of generate-and-test that does this is hierarchical generate-and-test. This formulation permits pruning of candidate solutions that are only partially specified (only the first half may need to be specified, say). When a partial description is pruned, an entire class of solutions corresponding to the description is eliminated from the generation process (see Figure 3.3). Hierarchical generate-and-test applies powerful pruning rules early in the generation process.

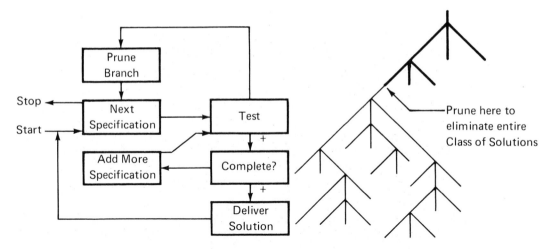

FIGURE 3.3   Hierarchical generate and test eliminates whole classes of solutions by early pruning of partial descriptions.

In summary, a search process navigating in a large space can exploit:

- The ability to follow plausible paths (by using an evaluation function to guide an incomplete search, for example)
- The ability to search abstract spaces and refine the solutions to the detailed space (as in hierarchical planning)
- Or, the ability to prune effectively (reasoning by class elimination in hierarchical generate-and-test)

The first and second methods are most applicable for problems where the goal is to "satisfice" (to satisfy without sacrificing too much). The third method is appropriate for optimizing because it admits a complete search if the pruning rules are sufficiently powerful.

3.1.3   Symbolic Reasoning

An expert systems architect must understand representation and search, traditional topics in sources on AI. The architect must also understand the organization of systems for symbolic computation. To begin with, expert reasoning is often nonmonotonic. That is, it requires the making and retraction of assumptions. This leads to consideration of how to account for justifications in problem-solving and how a program can treat beliefs as tentative. Such dynamic reasoning requires substantial problem-solving knowledge. One way to organize this knowledge is to view problem-solvers as working on several related metalevels.

3.1.3.1   Assumptions and Commitments

Experts, like other people, face the need to act in spite of the lack of time, facts, and knowledge. When experts solve problems, they use methods different from those of formal mathematical reasoning. In mathematical reasoning every conclusion must follow from previous information. In contrast, commonsense reasoning needs to draw conclusions from partial information, and people tentatively accept plausible conclusions for which they have no proof.

The need for commonsense reasoning can be illustrated by the trip-planning example. Suppose one wants to drive a car to a restaurant. Many things are required for the car to operate correctly. To be ready for use, a car must have gasoline, have a charge in its battery, have air in its tires, have no leaks in its tires, and so on. It would not be surprising to see a person who was about to drive to the restaurant glance at the fuel gauge. The glance would be explained by saying that the person knew the car needed gasoline. If the driver opened the hood to check the battery (or flashed the lights on and off), the behavior would be unusual, because batteries are rarely broken. And if the person walked around the car to check the tires, an observer might be surprised. If the person dismounted the tires to check for leaks, some questions would arise. After all, if the tires are full of air, they probably do not have any leaks.

In each of these examples, common sense leads to certain assumptions. One way to think about assumptions is in terms of *default values*. For example, assume that batteries are charged. Sometimes a person knows that assumptions pertain only to certain conditions. Such assumptions can be contingent on certain conditions. For example, if the battery is not brand new and the lights were not left on and the generator has been working, assume that the battery is charged. Both cases depend on a style of reasoning for making assumptions in the absence of contrary information. Another rationale for making assumptions is based on a view of reasoning as a resource-limited process. An example of this would be: If you cannot prove otherwise (without taking the wheels off the car), assume that the tires have no leaks. This heuristic assumes that a fact is true unless the contrary can be proved using limited resources.

In these cases assumptions and further inferences based on them must be regarded as tentative—subject to revision given new information. This aspect of reasoning is called nonmonotonic. Formal mathematical logic is monotonic in the sense that inferences are additive; no belief need ever be retracted (Winograd 1980).

Assumptions are also used in reasoning by means of *reductio ad absurdum*, as in the sequence:

> Assume A
> Prove B
> Prove ~B
> Retract A
> Conclude ~A.

Nonmonotonic reasoning is also important in design and planning problems. In these problems the space of possible solutions is sometimes very large, and it is usually not possible to anticipate the consequences of a preliminary design choice. A designer knows generally what is wanted but not how to create it. In design, assumption takes the form of a tentative decision. For example, the following might be the interior dialogue of a designer thinking through options:

- Suppose we use serial transmission on the data bus.
- Then the bus will fit through the wiring channel.
- And the maximum data rate will be 6 MHz.
- But that's too slow.
- So we'd better use a parallel scheme for the bus.

The designer conjectures a serial implementation, then checks to see whether some design constraints are satisfied. Since the bus would be too slow, the designer adopts a parallel implementation instead. In this example the new information was obtained by exploring the consequences of the design assumption.

In summary, commonsense reasoning requires that a system be able to revise its beliefs in light of new knowledge received or derived. This suggests a view of reasoning in which beliefs are transient and subject to change.

3.1.3.2   Dependencies and Justifications

To revise its beliefs in response to new knowledge, a problem-solver must reason about dependencies among its current set of beliefs. New beliefs can be the consequences of new information received or derived. This section considers the recording and use of dependency information for belief revision, first by showing how the techniques are an extension of backtracking in search.

Chronological backtracking is an approach for implementing search. In this approach search failure results in backtracking, that is, first retracting all of the actions and inferences since the most recent choice point and then continuing with the next alternative for that choice. Because of the last-in, first-out order of the backtracking, the memory for storing the set of active beliefs can be implemented by a push-down stack. Chronological backtracking is often needlessly inefficient because all failures arising on the search path are forgotten when the path is abandoned. The general reason for failures that are independent of the search will be rediscovered subsequently on other search paths. The following story about a hypothetical robot illustrates the difficulty:

> Robie wants to pick up the block. It reaches to pick it up with its right hand. But the block is hot and Robie burns its hand! Robie drops the block and backtracks. Robie reaches to pick it up with his left hand ...

Chronological backtracking discards too much information. A much better idea is to trace errors and inconsistencies back to the inferential steps that created them. This requires recording the inferential steps. Such records are called dependency records. A search method that analyzes dependencies and decides what to invalidate is called nonchronological or dependency-directed.

The fundamental objects in dependency records are beliefs, inference rules, and justifications. Justifications represent inferences. The simplest sort of justification is a record of immediate antecedents. For example, suppose the given reasoning system has the statements:

Belief 1:   My car has no gasoline.
Belief 2:   If a car has no gasoline, it will not start.
Rule 3:   Modus ponens

From these data it might infer the new statement:

Belief 4:   My car will not start.

Justification for this belief identifies the logical support for this inference. It could be represented as a data-base record like the following:

Justification 1
    Support for: Belief 4
    Inference rule: Rule 3
    Premises: (Belief 1, Belief 2)

Justifications can help maintain an active set of beliefs called a theory. This process is called belief revision (Doyle 1980a) or "truth maintenance'' (the latter is somewhat of a misnomer). All beliefs in the current theory must have valid justifications and the theory is updated whenever justifications are added or modified. A justification is valid if each of the beliefs it mentions is currently active, and some beliefs (called premises) are always active.

Belief revision can be used for reasoning with assumptions and defaults. The following scenario drawn from the earlier rules about starting a car shows how a belief revision system could act:

1. Robie the robot has the goal to drive to the restaurant.
2. It forms a subgoal to start the car.
3. Robie checks the fuel gauge.
4. It turns on the ignition.
5. The engine turns over vigorously but will not start.
6. Robie tries many things but cannot figure out what is wrong.
7. Finally, Robie taps the fuel gauge with its finger, and the needle swings to empty.

This scenario illustrates several points about nonmonotonic reasoning. First, there are many things that Robie could check. For example, the following statements are not in the story:

- Robie checks the tires for air.
- Robie checks the battery for charge by turning on the lights.

Robie does not check these things because it assumes that they are satisfactory. There are many possible reasons for making these assumptions. For example, Robie may know: Unless you have evidence for flat tires, assume that they have air. Robie may omit the test of the battery charge either because it assumes that the battery is charged, or because it knows that turning on the ignition will effectively test this anyway. When the car does not start, Robie needs to reconsider its assumptions. For example, it could try the step: Turn on the lights to check the battery. Alternatively Robie might use the rule: If the starter turns the engine vigorously, the battery is charged. This rule saves Robie the effort of testing the assumption that the battery has a charge and provides a new justification for that belief. In the last steps in the scenario, Robie has eliminated many possible causes for the problem. Before it can identify the real problem—lack of gasoline—Robie must suspect that the needle in the fuel gauge has become stuck. This scenario shows that Robie's beliefs are working hypotheses that are subject to change pending further information. This style of reasoning amounts to reasoning about justifications.

A critical issue in this style of reasoning is well-founded support, and there are some pitfalls involving cyclical support structures for the unwary. An important question is "What mechanisms should be used to resolve ambiguities when there are several possible revisions?" It is clear that this choice needs to be controlled, but the process is fundamentally heuristic. In the examples, knowledge about justifications to reason about choices was used. Doyle (1980) has proposed a style of dialectical argumentation in which the primary step is to argue about the kinds of support for beliefs. In such systems the complexity of knowledge about belief revision would itself require a substantial knowledge base. Every approach relies critically on the kinds of dependency records that are created and saved. This work is at the frontier of current AI research (see especially Quinlan 1982 and F. Hayes-Roth 1983).

It is clear that the technique of storing dependency information can be important in a variety of applications. This is not to suggest that the techniques for revising beliefs are well understood but that basic algorithms are needed for making changes to the set of beliefs (or their justifications) when their support is changed. Doyle (1979) and McAllester (1980) present alternative approaches, but much more work can be done.

3.1.3.3   Constraints and Goals

Programming languages are usually organized around unidirectional computations. Programs produce desired outputs using predetermined operations on their inputs. In contrast, constraint systems are nondirectional. A constraint such as

(EQUALS Voltage (TIMES Current Resistance))

says no more about how to compute voltage than how to compute current. Rather, it defines a relationship between referents of symbols. Given the knowledge of how to solve linear equations, this constraint enables us to compute a numerical value for any of the arguments given values for the other two.

Constraints need not be numerical. For example, the following constraint describes a relationship between variables bearing on material selection in a storage battery:

(Resists Wall-Material Battery-Fluid).

If the variable Battery-Fluid is bound to a strong acid, this constraint restricts the choice of values for the variable Wall-Material. If the

wall material were already determined, the constraint could be used
to limit the choices of a battery fluid. As in the preceding electrical
constraint, some means of finding solutions that satisfy the constraint
must be provided. For different kinds of problems, the solution process may range from a heuristic search to matrix methods for the solution of mathematical equations.

Constraints can be viewed as partial descriptions of entities. For
example, in a circuit design system we could start with a partial
description of some circuit element and then collect constraints on
its implementation that are implied by the interfaces with other circuit elements. In this way the constraints effectively augment the partial description of the circuit element.

Constraints can be used to represent goals in hierarchical search
methods. For example, Figure 3.4 shows two representations of an
"inverter" in an integrated circuit design system. The upper figure
shows the symbol for an inverter at the switch level of abstraction.

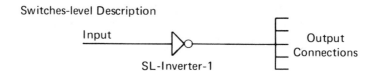

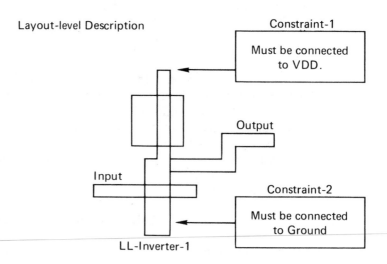

**FIGURE 3.4   Introducing constraints in a hierarchical
design.**

This level describes a circuit in terms of digital signal levels and leaves out most layout information, such as geometry, as well as some device details, such as power and ground connections. The lower part of Figure 3.4 shows a representation of an inverter at the layout abstraction level. This inverter is an implementation of the switch level inverter, and it includes many decisions about geometry. In addition, two constraints have been introduced that specify that parts of the layout inverter should be connected to power and ground. In this figure, the layout level description is an implementation of the switch-level description. The designer chooses to introduce constraints about connections to power and ground and to defer decisions about how exactly to route the wires to make the connections.

These constraints can be satisfied by routing appropriate wires to other parts of the circuit. If the constraints cannot be satisfied, the inverter will not function and the design will need to be changed, at least at the switch level. The advantage of introducing the two constraints instead of wiring the layout inverter immediately is that this allows decisions about the wiring route to be deferred until later. For example, there may not be enough information yet to determine the location of power and ground. Also, other considerations in the design of the circuit may be more important than this inverter as regards the location of power and ground.

The second point illustrates an important phenomenon in problem-solving: Subproblems interact. Subproblems are said to be nearly independent when they can be solved with little (but not negligible) coordination of the solution process. Typically these subproblems are locally underconstrained, meaning that they permit more than one solution when only local constraints are considered. In this circumstance it is tempting to act as if the subproblems are independent and to try to solve them separately. In some lucky cases this works fine, but often the difficulties show up when the subproblem solutions are combined. By introducing constraints instead of choosing particular values, the problem-solver is able to pursue a least-commitment style of problem-solving. It moves its attention opportunistically between subproblems and avoids overspecifying local decisions.

It is instructive to compare this tentative posting of constraints to the making of tentative assertions in belief-revision systems. Just as belief-revision systems can retract beliefs, constraint systems can withdraw or relax constraints. In hypothetical reasoning, assumptions are introduced so that their consequences can be explored. In constraint systems constraints can be introduced as goals in order to see whether they can be satisfied. For example, a circuit design system may introduce a constraint that the layout area of a component should fit within a given rectangle. Introducing the constraint does not assert that there is a design that will satisfy the constraint. The constraint may even turn out to be provably unsatisfiable. Rather, the constraint indicates a tentative subgoal in the search for a satisfactory design. In a belief-revision system the status of an assertion is either in, out, or unknown. In a constraint system the status may be either satisfied, unsatisfiable, withdrawn, or proposed. A constraint is satisfied if values for its arguments have been assigned that make the predicate true. A constraint is unsatisfiable if no set of assignments can be found to satisfy the constraint. A constraint is proposed if it has been formulated, but whether it can be satisfied is not yet known. A constraint is withdrawn if it is removed from consideration. These characterizations of the possible statuses of a constraint are exemplary; particular constraint systems may employ somewhat different distinctions.

Problem-solving systems that incorporate constraint satisfaction methods have been discussed in the literature for several years (Fikes 1975). For the most part AI has focused on systems that manipulate algebraic constraints and propagate values (Sussman and Steele 1980). A formulation of tentative hierarchical reasoning with constraints was demonstrated in an experiment planning system by Stefik (1981a).

3.1.3.4   Factoring into Metaproblems

Problem-solvers repeatedly decide what to do next. In the simplest organization, the selection of what to do next is made by a fixed search method. Recently there has been increased interest in systems that can reason about their own reasoning processes. In this formulation a metalevel problem-solver chooses, at the initial problem-solving, among several potential methods for deciding what to do next.

The idea of factoring decisions into metaproblems is illustrated by the following travel planning example. One useful piece of knowledge about automobiles is

A car needs gasoline before it can be driven.

In a state-space formulation, the requirement for gasoline would be called a precondition for the driving operator. Given this fact, one might expect a driver to check the gasoline supply before starting a trip and to plan first to get gasoline as needed. One approach to representing this behavior would be to add the rules:

Always check for gasoline before starting a trip.
If there is no gasoline, get some.

Because there are many similar facts about driving and cars (rules for battery water, brake fluid, transmission fluid, and oil) and writing such rules for every fact seems redundant, it would be better for a planner to use more general rules for all of the facts. For example:

If a precondition is not satisfied, create a subgoal to satisfy it.

This rule about testing preconditions is not specific to cars and trips. It is a rule about planning with facts and can be used as part of the planning task. Thus it is a statement about a metaproblem. It contributes indirectly to the decision about what the driver should do next. This organization suggests an economy of representation by separating problem-solving knowledge from knowledge about the ground domain. Many similar rules about planning are possible, for example:

If there are conflicting goals, give them priorities and achieve the important ones first.

If there are subgoals that are part of several major goals, plan to satisfy those subgoals before other subgoals.

There is no reason to limit consideration to only one metalevel. Rules can be formulated about selecting these planning rules; for example: keep options open; avoid planning-rules that limit choices.

The word *metaplanning* has been used to describe systems that plan about their own planning processes (B. Hayes-Roth and F. Hayes-Roth 1978). Stefik (1981b) used a layered metaplanning organization in an expert system for designing experiments in molecular genetics (MOLGEN), suggesting that the organization of a problem-solver into layers is an important technique for partitioning control considerations. Without this factoring, metalevel interactions can surface as confusing interactions between ground-level tasks. To reduce the apparent complexity of a system, Stefik advocates the use of separate layers for metaproblems until the information in the topmost layer is trivial. Wilensky (1981) has observed that there is a significant overlap between the knowledge needed for planning and for metaplanning.

Factoring into metaproblems seems to be a useful method for organizing knowledge in expert problem-solvers, but not much experience with it has been accumulated yet. General proposals for expressing control knowledge in terms of metaproblems have been advanced by de Kleer et al. (1979) and Weyhrauch (1980). But much more experience in creating such organizations is necessary before general versions of them will be well-understood.

3.1.4   Summary of Basic Concepts

The basic concepts for building expert systems began with symbols and symbol structures. Predicate calculus was reviewed as a formal language for symbol structures, and computers were seen as active devices that can use symbolic inference to infer new facts from what is known already. Some well-known syntactic rules of inference were also reviewed. Simply having a set of rules of inference is not enough; also needed is knowledge about problem-solving to guide the application of these rules, without which a combinatorial explosion occurs, resulting in the derivation of many correct but irrelevant inferences.

Search was discussed as a formulation of problem-solving with provisions for containing combinatorial explosions. The search concepts, goals, search spaces, and operators for moving between states were introduced. Heuristic search incorporates knowledge about the solution space to guide the search for solutions. This is a general approach to containing combinatorial explosions. The simplest example of a heuristic method is the use of evaluation functions to estimate distance to a goal, but this approach is usually infeasible in expert systems. Heuristics can involve large amounts of symbolic computation. A powerful approach involves abstractions of the solution space. Hierarchical generate-and-test depends on the early use of pruning rules to eliminate classes of solutions.

Practical problem-solving requires the making and retraction of assumptions. Examples of this in diagnostic and design problems were given. Belief revision systems keep track of assumptions and inferences by recording justifications for them in a dependency network. Dependency-directed backtracking is an approach to search that is superior to chronological backtracking. Dependency-directed reasoning can be extended to include reasoning about the problem-solving process itself by introducing justifications about goals and constraints. Such reasoning can be organized as a metalevel problem by dividing the goals, actions, and states of the problem-solver into metalevels.

3.2   A Characterization of Expert Tasks

Experts perform several generic tasks. Examining these tasks aids in understanding what makes expert reasoning difficult. The difficulties provide a guide to architectural relevance; they make it possible to focus on issues that relate to critical steps in reasoning.

Interpretation is the analysis of data to determine their meaning. In the case of interpretation of mass spectrometer data, for example, (Buchanan 1978a), the data are measurements of the masses of molecular fragments, and interpretation means the determination of one or more chemical structures. The main requirement of the task is to find consistent and correct interpretations of the data. It is often important that analysis systems be rigorously complete, that is, that they consider the possible interpretations systematically and discard candidates only when there is enough evidence to rule them out. The key problem is that data are often noisy and errorful; that is, data values may be missing, erroneous, or extraneous. (1) This means that interpreters must cope with partial information. (2) For any given problem the data may seem contradictory, so the interpreter must be able to hypothesize which data are believable. (3) When the data are unreliable, the interpretation will also be unreliable. Thus for credibility it is important to identify where information is uncertain or incomplete and where assumptions have been made. (4) Since reasoning chains can be long and complicated, it is helpful to be able to explain how the interpretation is supported by the evidence.

Diagnosis is the process of fault-finding in a system (or determination of a disease state in a living system), based on interpretation of potentially noisy data. (For an example of diagnosis of infectious diseases see Shortliffe 1976.) Requirements include those of interpretation. A diagnostician must understand the system organization (its anatomy) and the relations and interactions between subsystems. Key problems areas follow: (1) Faults can sometimes be masked by the symptoms of other faults; some diagnostic systems ignore this problem by making a single fault assumption. (2) Faults can also be intermittent; a diagnostician sometimes has to stress a system in order to reveal faults. (3) Diagnostic equipment can itself fail; a diagnostician has to do the best possible with faulty sensors. (4) Some data about a system can be inaccessible, expensive, or dangerous to retrieve; a diagnostician must decide which measurements to take. (5) Because the anatomy of natural systems such as the human body is not fully understood, a diagnostician may need to combine several (somewhat inconsistent) partial models.

Monitoring means interpreting signals continuously and setting off alarms when intervention is required. An example is monitoring a patient using a mechanical breathing device after surgery (Fagan 1980). A monitoring system is a partial diagnostic system with the requirement that the recognition of alarm conditions be carried out in real time. For credibility it must avoid false alarms. What constitutes an alarm condition is often context-dependent. To account for this key problem, monitoring systems have to vary signal expectations with time and situation.

Prediction means to forecast the course of the future from a model of the past and present. Predicting the effects of a change in economic policy is an example. (Some planning programs have a predictive component. There is currently much interest in developing expert systems for prediction and forecasting in a variety of areas.) Prediction requires reasoning about time. Predictors must be able to refer to things that change over time and to events that are ordered in time. They must have adequate models of the ways that various actions change the state of the modeled environment over time. There are four key problems: (1) Prediction requires the integration of incomplete information. When information is complete, prediction is not an AI problem (for example, "Where will Jupiter be two years from next Thursday?" is not a question for AI prediction. (2) Predictions should account for multiple possible futures (use hypothetical reasoning) and should indicate sensitivity to variations in the input data. (3) Predictors must be able to make use of diverse data, since indicators of the future can be found in many places. (4) The predictive theory may need to be contingent; the likelihood of distant futures may depend on nearer but unpredictable events.

Planning is preparing a program of actions to be carried out to achieve goals. An example is experiment planning in molecular genetics (Stefik 1981a, b). A planner is required to construct a plan that achieves goals without consuming excessive resources or violating constraints. If goals conflict, a planner establishes priorities. If planning requirements or decision data are not fully known or change with time, a planner must be flexible and opportunistic. Since planning always involves a certain amount of prediction, it has the requirements of that task as well. Key problems are as follows: (1) Planning problems are sufficiently large and complicated that a planner does not immediately understand all of the consequences of the planned actions, which means that the planner must be able to act tentatively, so as to explore possible plans. (2) If the details are overwhelming, the planner must be able to focus on the most important considerations. (3) In large, complex problems interactions often occur between plans for different subgoals. A planner must attend to these relationships and cope with goal interactions. (4) Often the planning context is only approximately known, so that a planner must operate in the face of uncertainty. This requires preparing for contingencies. (5) If the plan is to be carried out by multiple actors, coordination (choreography) is required.

Design is the making of specifications to create objects that satisfy particular requirements. Designing a digital circuit, one example, is an area of increased interest and activity in expert systems (Stefik et al. 1982; Lenat, Sutherland, and Gibbons 1982). Design has many of the same requirements as planning. Key problems are several: (1) In large assignments, a designer cannot immediately assess the consequences of design decisions but must be able to explore design possibilities tentatively. (2) Constraints on a design come from many sources, and usually there is no comprehensive theory that integrates constraints with design choices. (3) In very large systems a designer must cope with system complexity by factoring the design into subproblems. The designer must also cope with interactions between the subproblems, since they are seldom independent. (4) When a design is large, it is easy to forget the reasons for some design decisions and hard to assess the impact of a change in part of a design. This suggests that a design system should record justifications for design decisions and be able to use these justifications to explain decisions later. This is especially apparent when decisions about subsystems are made by different designers. (5) When designs are being modified it is important to be able to reconsider the design possibilities. During redesign designers need to be able to see the big picture in order to escape from points in the design space that are only locally optimal. (6) Many design problems require reasoning about spatial relations. Reasoning about distance, shapes, and contours demands considerable computational resources. Good methods of reasoning approximately or qualitatively about shape and spatial relationships do not yet exist.

Several issues appear repeatedly across this catalog of expert tasks: large solution spaces, tentative reasoning, time-varying data, and noisy data. Large solution spaces are typical in interpretation, planning, and design tasks. In the mass spectrometery example (Buchanan amd Feigenbaum 1978), some problems require that millions of possible chemical structures be considered. In planning and design tasks the number of reasonable solutions is usually a very small fraction of a very large number of possible solutions. In each of these tasks the size and characterization of the solution space is an important organizational parameter. Tentative reasoning is needed in diagnostic, design, and planning tasks. Many diagnostic procedures profitably employ assumptions about the number of faults or about the reliability of sensors. Partway through diagnosis, it may be discovered that these assumptions are unwarranted. This places a premium on the ability to undo the effects of assumptions. Similarly, to employ simplifying assumptions (abstractions) in design and planning tasks is often appropriate because of scale. In any given design some of the assumptions will fail, so there is an incentive to employ methods that facilitate the reworking of assumptions and trade-offs during iterations of the design process. Patient monitoring and diagnosis tasks are concerned with situations that evolve over time—as diseases follow their natural course or as treatments are administered. Finally sensors often yield noisy data. This is a factor for any task involving reasoning from measurements, such as interpretation, diagnostic, and monitoring tasks. The next chapter considers organizational prescriptions for each of these concerns.

QUESTIONS

1. Identify five typical ways to obviate search in problem-solving. Identify five properties of tasks that make searching unavoidable.
2. What is wrong with simply employing logic to produce expert behavior?
3. In striving for implementation efficiency, is it better to test, first of all, conditions that are likely to fail or those that are likely to succeed? Why?
4. Which mathematical programming techniques, such as linear and dynamic programming, help solve search tasks?
5. What makes an abstraction useful? How can we engineer new abstractions that simplify problem-solving?

ACKNOWLEDGMENTS

We thank Daniel Bobrow, John Seeley Brown, Johan de Kleer, Richard Fikes, Adele Goldberg, Richard Lyon, John McDermott, Allen Newell, and Christopher Tong for reading early versions of this text and providing many helpful suggestions. Thanks also to Terri Doughty for help in preparing the figures and manuscript and to Lynn Conway for encouraging this work, as well as to the Xerox Corporation for providing the intellectual and computational environment in which it could be done.

PART II

Building an Expert System

4

The Architecture of Expert Systems

**Mark Stefik, Janice Aikins, Robert Balzer,
John Benoit, Lawrence Birnbaum,
Frederick Hayes-Roth, and Earl Sacerdoti**

*This chapter summarizes what is known about expert system
design and architecture. The many different approaches evident in previous applications reflect a few basic choices.
Together, the complexity of the application task and the type
of knowledge available determine the most appropriate
overall organization. System designs as different as MYCIN
and HEARSAY-II adhere to common principles of knowledge
systems architecture but vary tremendously due to differences in their tasks and their knowledge bases.*

Edward A. Feigenbaum defines the activity of knowledge engineering
as follows:

> The knowledge engineer practices the art of bringing the principles
> and tools of AI research to bear on difficult applications problems
> requiring experts' knowledge for their solution. The technical issues of
> acquiring this knowledge, representing it, and using it appropriately to
> construct and explain lines-of-reasoning, are important problems in
> the design of knowledge-based systems . . . . The art of constructing
> intelligent agents is both part of and an extension of the programming
> art. It is the art of building complex computer programs that represent
> and reason with knowledge of the world. (1977)

This chapter is intended as a prescriptive guide to building expert systems. To illustrate the strengths and limitations of architectural alternatives, a number of contemporary systems are cited. These examples are presented at a level of detail adequate for making the ideas clear, yet removed from the particulars of the task and the programming implementation. The reader seeking a more detailed discussion of implementation is encouraged to consult a textbook on artificial intelligence programming (such as Charniak et al. 1979).

One of the most variable characteristics of expert systems is the way they search for solutions. The choice of search method is affected by many characteristics of a domain, such as the size of the solution space, errors in the data, and the availability of abstractions. Inference is at the heart of a reasoning system, and failure to organize it properly can result in problem-solvers that are hopelessly inefficient, naive, or unreliable. As a consequence of this, search is one of the most studied topics in AI.

We will start with a very restricted class of problems that admits a very simple search process. The domain restrictions under which this organization is applicable will be articulated, and its limitations thereby exposed. Then the requirements on the task domain will be relaxed and ameliorating techniques introduced as architectural prescriptions. Figure 4.1 is a chart of the cases that will be considered. Each box in the figure corresponds to one of the cases and the numbering indicates the order in which the cases are discussed. The lines connecting the boxes organize the cases into a tree structure such that a sequence of cases along a branch corresponds to increasingly elaborate considerations of a basic idea. The first three branches consider the complications of unreliable data or knowledge, time-varying data, and a large search space. Any given problem may require combining ideas from any of these topics. The problem of a large search space is then considered along three major branches. The first branch (cases 5−8) considers organizations for abstracting a search space. The second branch focuses on methods for incomplete search. The third branch considers only ways to make the knowledge base itself more efficient. This breakdown is mainly pedagogical. Real systems may combine these ideas.

4.1 Small Search Space with Reliable Knowledge and Data

Systems for complex tasks are generally more complicated than systems for simple tasks. A very simple architecture that has been used

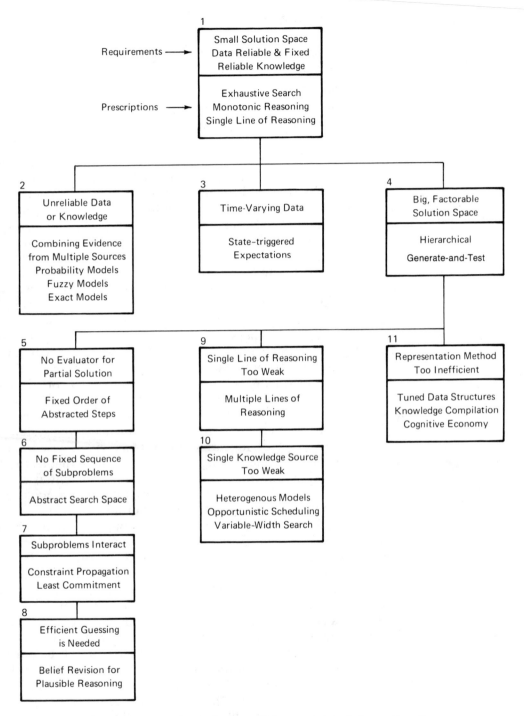

FIGURE 4.1 Case 1 begins with a restricted class of problems that admits a very simple organization. These assumptions are relaxed one at a time in the other cases.

for relatively simple applications is described here. The requirements for task simplicity are threefold:

1. The data and knowledge should be reliable.

2. The data and knowledge should be static.

3. The space of possible solutions should be small.

On the surface these requirements seem quite mild. Indeed people
who have not looked closely into problem-solving widely believe that
most problems satisfy these requirements. After all, for many problems the facts seem straightforward, and there are not many solutions
to consider. Under closer examination, however, most real tasks fail
to meet these requirements (the examples of expert tasks listed in
Chapter 3 do not).

The first requirement is that the data and knowledge be
reliable—that is, neither noisy nor errorful. There can be no extraneous signals and no missed signals (due to poor sampling for example).
In real applications few sources of data meet these requirements.
Besides data reliability, there must be knowledge reliability. Reliable
knowledge is applicable without concern about consistency or
correctness. Systematic application of reliable knowledge should not
lead to false, approximate, or tentative conclusions. The main advantage of reliability for both data and knowledge is the monotonicity of
the system. In the simplest architecture the memory is a monotonic
data base to which conclusions are added by the reasoning system. No
provisions need be made for retraction of facts, given new information. It is enough to develop a single line of reasoning; that is, there is
no need to develop multiple arguments to support potential conclusions. If more than one inference rule is applicable at a given time,
the order in which they are applied is unimportant.

The second requirement is intended to avoid the problem of reasoning with time-dependent data. This means that the system need
not be concerned with invalidating facts as time passes.

The requirement that the search space be small implies that no
provisions need be made to cope with the limitations of computational resources. There is to be no concern about computationally
efficient data structures or avoidance of combinatorial explosions. It
does not matter whether the search is for one solution or for all possible solutions as long as the space is small. If the search is exhaustive,
the maximum size of the solution space depends on the time it takes
to consider a single solution. A useful number to keep in mind for this
maximum is ten factorial (10!). If 25 milliseconds are required to
consider a solution, then 10! solutions can be considered sequentially during a full 24-hour day. This provides a practical upper limit
for exhaustive search. The surprise is that the ceiling is so low.

An organization for solving these problems has two main parts: a memory and an inference method. The simplest organization of the memory would be a list of inferred facts (beliefs). For many problems the beliefs can be limited to the predicate calculus such as

(On Block1 Block2)
(NOT (On Block2 Table-1)) .

Some systems optimize the storage format of the data. For example, in frame systems (Bobrow 1977) the indexing of the well-formed formulas (wffs) is organized to make the commonest access paths more efficient. Data that are used together are stored together in frames. In the following sections, these restrictions on the problems are relaxed.

4.2   Unreliable Data or Knowledge

Experts sometimes make judgments in a hurry, under the press of a deadline. All of the data may not be available, some may be suspect, and some of the knowledge for interpreting the data may be unreliable. These difficulties are part of the normal state of affairs in many interpretation and diagnostic tasks. The problem of drawing inferences from uncertain or incomplete data has invited a variety of technical approaches.

One of the earliest and simplest approaches to reasoning with uncertainty was incorporated in the MYCIN expert system (Davis 1977c; Shortliffe 1976) for selecting antibiotic therapy for bacteremia. One of the requirements for MYCIN was to represent judgmental reasoning such as "A suggests B" or "C and D tend to rule out E." To this end MYCIN introduced a model of approximate implication, using numbers called certainty factors to indicate the strength of a heuristic rule. The following is an example of a rule from MYCIN's knowledge base:

If   the infection is primary-bacteremia, and
       the site of the culture is one of the sterile sites, and
       the suspected portal of entry of the organism is the gastro-intestinal tract,
then   there is suggestive evidence (0.7) that the identity of the organism is bacteroids.

The number 0.7 in this rule indicates that the evidence is strongly indicative (0.7 of 1) but not absolutely certain. Evidence confirming a hypothesis is collected separately from that which disconfirms it, and the "truth" of the hypothesis at any time is the algebraic sum of the evidence. This admits the combination of evidence favoring and opposing the same hypothesis.

The introduction of these numbers is a departure from the exactness of predicate calculus. In MYCIN things are not just true or false; reasoning is inexact and that inexactness is numerically characterized in the rules by an expert physician. Facts about the world are represented as 4-tuples with numeric truth values. For example:

(IDENTITY ORGANISM-2 KLEBSIELLA .25)

means "The identity of organism-2 is Klebsiella with certainty 0.25." In predicate calculus the rules of inference tell us how to combine wffs and truth values. MYCIN has its own method of combining formulas. When the premise of a rule is evaluated, each predicate returns a number between 1 and -1 (-1 means "definitely false"). MYCIN's version of AND performs a minimization of its arguments; OR performs a maximization of its arguments. This results in a numerical value between -1 and 1 for the premise of a rule. For rules whose premise values surpass an empirical threshold of 0.2, a conclusion is made with a certainty that is the product of the premise value and the certainty factor of the rule. These rules of combination can be shown to have certain properties, such as insensitivity to the order in which the rules are applied. MYCIN's certainty factors are derived from probabilities but have some distinct differences (Shortliffe 1976).

A reasonable question about such approaches is whether they are unnecessarily ad hoc. A criticism commonly voiced is that MYCIN introduces its own formalism for reasoning with uncertainty when there are thoroughly studied probabilistic approaches available. For example, Bayes' Rule could be used to calculate the probability (of a disease) in light of specified evidence from the a priori probability of the disease and the conditional probabilities relating the observations to the diseases. The main difficulty with Bayes' Rule is the large number of data needed to determine the conditional probabilities used in the formula. The amount of data is so unwieldy that conditional independence of observations is often assumed. It can be argued that such independence assumptions undermine the rigorous statistical model. A middle ground that replaces observations with subjective estimates of prior probabilities has been proposed by Duda, Hart, and Nilsson (1976) and analyzed for its limitations by Pednault, Zucker, and Muresan (1981).

Another approach to inexact reasoning that diverges from classical logic is fuzzy logic as discussed by Zadeh (1979a) and others. In fuzzy logic, a statement like "X is a large number" is interpreted as having an imprecise denotation characterized by a fuzzy set. A fuzzy set is a set of values with corresponding possibility values as follows:

Fuzzy Proposition: X is a large number.
Corresponding Fuzzy Set: $(X \in (0, 10), .1)$
                            $(X \in (10, 1{,}000), .2)$
                            $(\{X > 1{,}000\}, .7)$

The interpretation of the proposition "X is large" is that "X might be less than 10" with possibility 0.1, or between 10 and 1,000 with possibility 0.2, and so on. The fuzzy values are intended to characterize an imprecise denotation of the proposition.

Fuzzy logic deals with the laws of inference for fuzzy sets. Its utility in reasoning about unreliable data depends on the appropriateness of interpreting soft data (Zadeh 1979b) as fuzzy propositions. Little agreement exists among AI researchers on the utility of these modified logics for intelligent systems or even on their advantages for reasoning with incomplete data.

Pseudoprobability and fuzzy approaches for reasoning with partial and unreliable data depart from predicate calculus by introducing a notion of inexactness. Other approaches are possible. For example, the belief-revision work cited in the previous chapter attempts to cope with partial information while preserving the exactness of predicate calculus. Belief-revision systems admit precise statements about incomplete information. Any fuzziness enters only as non-monotonicity when the system as a whole is considered.

The use of exact inference methods on unreliable data in an expert system is illustrated by the GA1 program (Stefik 1978a). GA1 is a data-interpretation system that copes with errorful data by exploiting the redundancy of experimental data in order to correct errors.

GA1 infers DNA structures from segmentation data. The system's task is to assemble models of complete DNA structures, given data about pieces (called segments) of the structures. The segment data are produced by chemical processes involving enzymes that break DNA apart in predictable ways. In a typical problem, several independent breaking processes called digestions are performed and the resulting segments are measured. These digestions give independent measurements of the DNA molecule. For example, independent estimates of molecular weight can be computed by summing the weights of the segments in any of the complete digestions. A digestion is termed complete if all of the molecules have been cleaved in all possible places by the enzymes.

An example of a rule for correcting missing data is: If a segment appears in a complete digestion for an enzyme that fails to appear in the incomplete digestion for that enzyme, it may be added to the list of segments for the incomplete digestion. This rule is based on the observation that segments are easier to overlook in incomplete digestions than in complete digestions. It places more confidence in data from complete digestions than from incomplete ones. Other data-correction rules incorporate more elaborate reasoning by modeling predictable instrument error, such as failure to resolve measurements that are too close together. These rules enable GA1 to look to the data for evidence of instrument failure.

All of the data correction in GA1 could have been modeled by a belief-revision system. Rules like the one just mentioned could be used to justify beliefs about which data are correct. GA1 could then have begun its interpretation task and withdrawn any of its interpretations when data were invalidated. GA1 used a much simpler approach, since all of the data correction could be done at once by running the correction rules in a fixed order. Then GA1 interpreted the data by searching a large space of possible solutions (using a method to be described subsequently). Since it was possible to correct all of the data before interpretation, it was not necessary to be able to retract interpretations of the data, and the machinery for recording and revising justifications was not needed.

Several methods for reasoning with unreliable data and knowledge have been proposed. The probability-related and possibility methods use modified logics to handle approximations and numerical measures for combining evidence. In contrast, data-correction rules can reason with partial information without compromising the exactness of predicate calculus. If it is necessary to reason from the data before correcting it, such rules can be incorporated into belief-revision systems. All of these methods depend on the formalization of extra metaknowledge in order to correct the data, take back assumptions, or combine evidence. The availability of this metaknowledge is a critical factor in the viability of these approaches to particular applications. A special method for contending with both fallible knowledge and limited computational resources will be considered later.

4.3   Time-Varying Data

Some expert tasks involve reasoning about situations that change over time. One of the earliest approaches in AI to take this into account was the situational calculus introduced by McCarthy and Hayes (1969) for representing sequences of actions and their effects.

The central idea is to include "situations" along with the other objects modeled in the domain. For example, the formula

(ON Block-1 Table-2 Situation-2)

could represent the fact that in Situation-2, Block-1 is on Table-2. A key feature of this formulation is that situations are discrete. This discreteness reflects the intended use of this calculus in robot planning problems. A robot starts in an initial situation and performs a sequence of actions. After each action the state of the robot's world is modeled by another situation. In this representation a situation variable can take situations as values. In some implementations, the actual situation variable is left implicit by indexing the formulas according to situations.

Actions in situational calculus are represented by functions whose domains and ranges are situations. For each action a set of frame axioms characterizes the set of assertions (the frame) that remains fixed while an action takes place within it. In planning a robot's actions, an example of an action would be the Move action for moving an object to a new location. A frame axiom for Move would be that all objects not explicitly moved are left in their original location.

While several issues can be raised about this approach to representing changing situations, AI systems have used it for a variety of tasks with only minor variations. Sometimes the changes of situation are signaled by time-varying data, rather than by the autonomous actions of a robot. An example of this is the Ventilator Manager (VM) system (reported by Fagan et al. 1979 and Fagan 1980), a program that interprets the clinical significance of patient data from a physiological monitoring system. VM monitors the postsurgical progress of a patient requiring mechanical breathing assistance. A device called a mechanical ventilator provides breathing assistance for seriously ill patients, the type and settings of the ventilator being adjusted to match the patient's needs. As the patient's status improves, various adjustments and changes are made, such as replacing the mechanical ventilator with a "T-piece" to supply oxygen to the patient. In VM's application, a patient's situation is affected by the progression of disease and the response to therapeutic interventions. For such applications the model of clinical reasoning must account for information received from tests and observations over time.

VM illustrates knowledge suitable for coping with time-varying data. This knowledge in VM is organized in terms of several kinds of rules: transition rules, initialization rules, status rules, and therapy rules. Periodically VM receives a new set of instrument measurements and then reruns all of its rules. Transition rules are used to detect when the patient's state has changed, as when the patient starts to breathe on the T-piece. The following is an example of a transition rule:

If   the current context "Assist," and
the respiration rate has been stable for 20 minutes, and
the I/EW ratio has been stable for 20 minutes,
then   the patient is on CMV [controlled mandatory ventilation].

This rule governs the transition between an Assist context and a CMV context. When the premise of a transition rule is satisfied in VM, a new context is entered. These contexts correspond to specific states or situations. When a context is changed, VM uses initialization rules to update its information for the new context (expectations and unacceptable limits for the measurements). These rules refer to the recent history of the patient in order to establish new expectations and information for the new context. Part of one such rule follows:

If   the patient transitioned from "Assist" to "T-piece" or
the patient transitioned from "CMV" to "T-piece"
then   expect the following:

	Acceptable				Ideal	
	Very low	Low	Min	Max	High	Very high
SYS		110			150	
DIA		60			95	
MAP	60	75			110	120
Pulse rate		60			120	
ECO2	22	28	30	40	45	50

VM's reasoning about time is limited to adjacent time intervals, being concerned only with the previous state and the next state. Its mechanisms for dealing with this are state-triggered expectations and rules for dynamic belief-revision. The transition rules in VM govern changes of context. Data arrive periodically, but context is changed only when it is adequately supported by the evidence. The initialization rules are essentially like the frame axioms—establishing what changes and what stays the same in the new context. Once a context is set, the expectations are used to govern VM's behavior until the context is changed again.

Programs that need to reason about more distant events require more elaborate representations of events and time. For example, planning and prediction require reasoning about possible futures. For these applications the situational calculus must be extended to allow for multiple possible futures with undetermined operations, unordered sets of possible future events, and the possible actions of uncontrolled multiple actors. Although AI systems capable of these kinds of reasoning seem within reach, their construction is still a research enterprise.

4.4 Large but Factorable Solution Space

In the restricted class of problems, the first case (Section 4.1), it was stipulated that the data and knowledge must be reliable, that the data must be static, and that the search space must be small. Some techniques for relaxing the first two requirements have already been discussed. With this section we begin consideration of techniques for coping with very large search spaces.

In many data-analysis tasks it is desirable to find every interpretation that is consistent with the data. This conservative attitude is standard in high-risk applications, such as the analysis of poisonous substances or medical diagnosis. A systematic approach would be to consider all possible cases and to rule out those inconsistent with the data. Reasoning by elimination has been familiar to philosophers for years, but it has often been regarded as impractical. The difficulty is that there is often no practical way to consider all the possible solutions.

The DENDRAL program (Buchanan and Feigenbaum 1978) is probably the best-known AI program that reasons by elimination (using generate-and-test). The reason it works is that pruning is incorporated early in the generate-and-test cycle. This method is examined here in more detail, some of the characteristics of problems on which it will work are stated, and examples are given of the kinds of knowledge that can be incorporated to make this method practical. Since the problem area for the DENDRAL program is rather complicated for tutorial purposes, the simpler expert system, GA1 (Stefik 1978a), is considered.

Like DENDRAL, GA1 is a data-interpretation program that infers a complete molecular structure from measurements of molecular pieces. Figure 4.2 gives a simple example of the kind of data that GA1 would have about a molecule. The top part of the figure shows that a molecule is made up of segments of measurable length. The lines labeled A and B that cut across the circle indicate the sites where the molecule is cleaved by enzymes (named A and B, respectively). All of the molecules that concern GA1 are linear or circular, which means that all of the molecular segments are linear pieces that can be arranged end to end. When a sample of molecules is completely digested by an enzyme, pieces are released whose sizes can be measured. The goal is to infer the structure of the original molecule from the digest data, and sometimes more than one molecular structure is consistent with the available data.

A primary task in problems like this is to create a workable generator of all of the possible solutions (all of the possible molecules). In GA1 the first step is to apply data-correction rules as shown in case 2 (Section 4.2.) Then GA1 determines an initial set of generator constraints, a set of segments and enzyme sites for building candidate molecules. The rules for deriving the list will not be elaborated here, but they make conservative use of molecular weight estimates and redundant data from several digests. The generation process then begins by combining these segments and sites and testing whether the combinations fit the evidence. For example, the following lists (among others) correspond to the complete molecule in Figure 4.2.

$$(1 \; A \; 2 \; B \; 3 \; A \; 4 \; B)$$
$$(2 \; B \; 3 \; A \; 4 \; B \; 1 \; A)$$
$$(1 \; B \; 4 \; A \; 3 \; B \; 2 \; A)$$

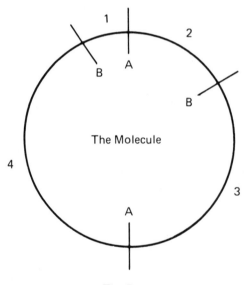

The Data

Complete A Digest: 5 5
Complete B Digest: 3 7
Complete A&B Digest: 1 2 3 4

FIGURE 4.2   Enzyme A cleaves the circular molecule at the points labeled A. Enzyme B cleaves it at the points labeled B. The table lists the fragments that would be observed under ideal digestion experiments.

These equivalent representations can be generated by starting with any of the four segments in the picture of the molecule in Figure 4.2 and reading off the sites and segments around the circle either clockwise or counterclockwise. This provides eight equivalent representations for the same molecule. The situation is analogous to the case where English sentences have different syntax but the same meaning. A generator is said to be nonredundant if it produces exactly one of the equivalent representations of a solution (the canonical form) during the generation process. GA1 does this by incorporating rules for pruning noncanonical structures during the generation process. An example of such a rule follows:

If   circular structures are being generated,
then   only the smallest segment in the list of initial segments should be used for the first segment.

The key to effective use of generate-and-test is to prune classes of inconsistent candidates as early as possible. For example, consider the following structure from the generation process for the sample problem:

(1 B 2 B).

GA1 treats this as a description of all the molecules that match the pattern,

(1 B 2 B <Segment> <Site> <Segment> <Site>)

where any of the remaining segments and sites may be filled in the template. It is easy to see that no molecule matching this template is consistent with the data in Figure 4.2 because all such molecules would yield a segment of length 2 in the complete digest for B. Other pruning considerations are more global. When such pruning rules exist, the solution space is said to be factorable.

GA1 has been run on problems where the number of possible candidates is several billion. The pruning rules are so effective at eliminating classes of solutions, however, that most problems require only a few seconds of computer time.

After the generator is finished, usually twenty or thirty candidates make it through all of the pruning rules. Only one or two of these will be consistent with all of the data. In principle it is possible to add more pruning rules to GA1 so that only the consistent solutions remain. The rules needed to do this become increasingly complex and specialized, however. It then becomes difficult to prove the correctness of such rules (so that solutions will not be missed) and to ensure that the rules are faithfully represented in the program. Also a point of diminishing returns is reached when each new specialized rule covers a smaller number of cases. In GA1 this problem is addressed by applying a digestion-process model to the final candidates and comparing its predictions with the observed data. A simple scoring function then penalizes candidates that predict extra or missing segments. Because the number of disagreements between the idealized digests of two different molecules diverges rapidly for small molecular differences, it was not necessary to tune the scoring function to recognize wrong solutions.

In summary generate-and-test is an appropriate method to consider when it is important to find all of the solutions to a problem. For the method to be workable, however, the generator must partition the solution space in ways that allow for early pruning. These criteria are often satisfied in data interpretation and diagnostic problems.

4.5   No Evaluator for Partial Solutions

Generate-and-test is a method of last resort for many problems involving large search spaces. The most common difficulty is that no generator of solutions can be found for which early pruning is viable. Design and planning problems are of this nature. One usually cannot tell from a fragment of a plan or design whether that fragment is part of a satisfactory complete solution; there is no reliable evaluator of partial solutions expressed as solution fragments.

This section considers the first of several approaches to problem-solving without early pruning. These approaches have in common the idea of abstracting the search space (see Chapter 3) but differ in their assumptions about the nature of that space. Abstraction emphasizes the important considerations of a problem and enables its partitioning into subproblems. The simplest case is a fixed partitioning in the abstract space that is appropriate for all of the problems in an application.

This case is illustrated by the R1 program reported by McDermott (1980b). R1's area of expertise is the configuring of Digital Equipment Corporation's VAX computer systems. Its input is a customer's order and its output is a set of diagrams displaying the spatial relations among the components on the order. This task includes a substantial element of design. In order to determine whether a customer's order is satisfactory (that is, whether it can be filled and is complete and consistent), R1 must determine a spatial configuration for the components and add any necessary components that are missing.

The configuration task can be viewed as a hierarchy of subtasks with strong temporal interdependencies. R1 partitions the configuration task into six ordered subtasks as follows:

1. Determine whether there is anything grossly wrong with the customer's purchase order (mismatched items, major prerequisites missing, etc.).
2. Put the appropriate components in the central processing unit and its expansion cabinets.
3. Put boxes in the UNIBUS expansion cabinet and put the appropriate components in those boxes.
4. Put panels in the UNIBUS expansion cabinets.
5. Lay out the system on the floor.
6. Do the cabling.

The actions within each subtask are highly variable: they depend on the particular combination of components in an order and on the way these components have been configured so far. Associated with each subtask in R1 is a set of rules for carrying out the subtask. An example of a rule for the third subtask follows:

If   the most current active context is assigning a power supply, and
      a UNIBUS adaptor has been put in a cabinet, and
      the position it occupies in the cabinet (its nexus) is known, and
      there is space available in the cabinet for a power supply for that nexus, and
      there is an available power supply, and
      there is no H7101 regulator available,
then   add an H7101 regulator to the order.

R1 has approximately 800 rules about configuring VAX systems. Most of the rules are similar to those in the example. They define situations in which some partial configuration should be extended in particular ways. These rules enable R1 to combine partial configurations to form an acceptable configuration, indicating what components can (or must) be combined and what constraints must be satisfied in order for the combinations to be acceptable. They make use of a data base describing properties of about 400 VAX components. Other rules describe the temporal relationships between subtasks by determining their ordering. (These rules are analogous to the transition rules described for VM except that the rules monitor the state of R1's problem-solving instead of data from external sensors.) The approach that R1 uses is called Match. It is one of what Newell (1973) calls "weak methods" for search. Match enables R1 to explore the space of possible configurations with the basic operations of creating and extending partial configurations. Match explores this space by starting in an initial state, going through intermediate states, and stopping in a final state without any backtracking. Each state in the space is a partially instantiated configuration. R1 proceeds through its six major tasks in the same order for each problem; it never varies the order and it never backs up in any problem. The benefit of the abstraction space is that R1 needs to do very little search.

The conditions that make Match viable are both its source of power and its weakness. The key requirement is that there can be no backtracking. This means that at any intermediate state R1 must be able to determine whether the state is on a solution path. This requires existence of a partial ordering of decisions for the task such that the consequences of applying an operator bear only on later parts of the solution.

Match is insufficient for the complete task in R1. The subtask of placing modules on the UNIBUS is formulated essentially as a bin-packing problem—namely, how to find an optimal sequence that fits within spatial and power constraints. No way of solving this problem without search is known. Consequently R1 uses a different method for this part of the problem.

In summary, abstraction should be considered for applications where there is a large search space but no method for early pruning. R1 is an example of a system that uses a fixed abstract solution. Within this framework it uses the Match method to search for a solution. Whether Match is practical for an application depends on how difficult it is to order the intermediate states. They must be ordered so that no state can be reached before all the required information for deciding whether that state is on a solution path has been determined.

4.6 No Fixed Partitioning of Subproblems

When every example problem in an application can be partitioned into the same subproblems, the organization described in the previous section should be considered. In applications with more varied problems, no fixed set of subproblems can provide a useful abstraction. For example, planning domains such as errand-running (B. Hayes-Roth and F. Hayes-Roth 1978) require plans rich with structure. To be useful, abstractions must embody the variable structure of the plans.

Top-down refinement tailors an abstraction to fit each problem.

The following aspects of the approach are important:

- Abstractions for each problem are composed from terms (selected from a space of terms) to fit the structure of the problem.
- During the problem-solving process, these concepts represent partial solutions that are combined and evaluated.
- The concepts are assigned fixed and predetermined abstraction levels.
- The problem solution proceeds from the top downward, that is, from the most abstract to the most specific.
- Solutions to the problem are completed at one level before moving down to the next more specific level.
- Within each level subproblems are solved in a problem-independent order. (This creates a partial ordering of the intermediate abstract states.)

The best-known example of a program using this approach is the ABSTRIPS program (Sacerdoti 1974). ABSTRIPS was an early robot planning program that made plans for a robot to move objects (boxes) between rooms. A design goal for ABSTRIPS was to provide abstractions sufficiently different from the detailed ground space to achieve a significant improvement in problem-solving efficiency but sufficiently similar so that the mapping down from abstractions would not be complex or time-consuming. This led to an interesting and simple approach for representing abstractions.

Abstractions in ABSTRIPS are plans that differ from ground-level plans only in the amount of detail used to specify the preconditions of operators. This level of detail is indicated by associating a number (termed a *criticality value*) with all of the literals used in preconditions. For example, Sacerdoti suggested the following criticality assignments in a robot planning domain:

Type and Color	4
InRoom	3
PluggedIn and Unplugged	2
NextTo	1

In this example the predicates for Type and Color of objects are given high criticalities, since the robot has no operator for changing them. These predicates, together with the set of robot actions, are combined to form plans for solving particular problems; the space of possible plans is the set of all of the plans that can be built up from these pieces. The most abstract plans are the ones that include only the higher criticality concepts.

Planning in ABSTRIPS starts by setting criticality to a maximum. Planning within each level proceeds backward from goals. Preconditions whose criticality is below the current level are invisible to the planner, since it is presumed that they will be accounted for during a later pass. After a plan is completed at one level, the criticality level is decremented and planning is started on the next lower level. The previous abstract version of the plan is used to guide the elaboration of the plan. For example, an early version of a plan may determine the route that the robot takes through the rooms. In more detailed versions steps for opening and closing doors are included. In this way the abstract plans converge to the specific plan, the sequence of abstract plans being created differently for each problem.

ABSTRIPS was a great advance over its predecessor STRIPS, which lacked the hierarchical planning ability. Generally when hierarchical and nonhierarchical approaches have been systematically compared, the former have dominated. ABSTRIPS was substantially more efficient than STRIPS, and the effect increased dramatically as longer plans were tried. Since then many other hierarchical planning programs have been created. In most of the later programs the abstraction concepts have been arranged in a hierarchy, without actually assigning them criticality numbers.

In summary, the interesting feature of top-down refinement is the flexibility of the abstractions. Abstraction states are individually constructed to fit each problem in the domain. In contrast to Match, top-down refinement places only a partial ordering on the intermediate states of the problem-solver. Still, there are some important conditions about problem-solving in the domain of application that are inherent in the method. The basic assumption is that a small fixed amount of problem-solving knowledge about criticality levels and top-down generation is sufficient. Furthermore, it must be possible to assign a partial criticality ordering to the domain concepts. What is important for one problem must be important for all of the problems.

4.7 Interacting Subproblems

One basic difficulty with top-down refinement is the lack of feedback from the problem-solving process. It is presumed that the same kinds of decisions should be made at the same point (the criticality level) for each problem in the domain. An approach called the *least-commitment principle* is based on a different principle for guiding the reasoning process. The basic idea is that decisions should not be made arbitrarily or prematurely but postponed until there is enough information.

Reasoning based on the least-commitment principle requires the following abilities:

- The ability to know when there is enough information to make a decision
- The ability to suspend problem-solving activity on a subproblem when the information is not available
- The ability to move between subproblems, restarting work as information becomes available
- The ability to combine information from different subproblems

Figure 4.3 shows an example of this style of reasoning from the NOAH system reported by Sacerdoti (1977). NOAH was a robot plan-

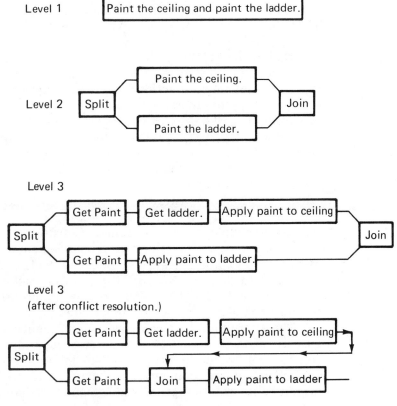

FIGURE 4.3 Example of planning in NOAH. NOAH analyzes the interactions between the steps in order to assign them an ordering in time. In this example, the 'painting the ladder' is seen to be in conflict with using it. To complete both goals, NOAH decides to paint the ceiling first. Later processing will factor out common subplans like 'get paint'.

ning system that used a least-commitment approach to assign a time-ordering to operators in a plan. Earlier planning programs inserted operators into a plan as they worked backward from goals. In contrast, NOAH assigned the operators only a partial ordering and added specifications for a complete ordering of the operators only as required.

In Figure 4.3 NOAH starts with two subgoals: paint the ceiling and paint the ladder. Plans for the two subgoals are expanded in parallel and a conflict is found. If the ladder is painted first, it will be wet and the ceiling cannot be painted. In other words the step to paint the ladder violates a precondition (that the ladder be usable) for the step to paint the ceiling. This interference between the subgoals provides NOAH with enough information to order the tasks. If it had arbitrarily ordered the steps and painted the ladder first, it would have had to plan around the wet ladder, perhaps waiting for it to dry. The resulting plan would not have been optimal.

Another example of this style of reasoning was used in MOLGEN reported by Stefik (1981a). MOLGEN is an expert system for designing molecular genetics experiments. MOLGEN's architecture involves representation of interactions between subproblems as constraints and discovery of interactions between subproblems via constraint propagation. MOLGEN uses explicit metalevel problem-solving operators (as opposed to domain-specific operations) to reason with constraints (see Figure 4.4); it alternates between least-commitment and heuristic strategies in problem-solving.

In the least-commitment strategy, MOLGEN makes a choice only when its available constraints have sufficiently narrowed its alternatives. Its problem-solving operators are capable of being suspended so that a decision can be postponed. Constraint propagation is the mechanism for moving information between subproblems. It enables MOLGEN to exploit the synergy between decisions in different subproblems. In contrast to ABSTRIPS' strict backward expansion of plans within levels, MOLGEN expands plans opportunistically in response to the propagation of constraints.

The alternation between least-commitment and heuristic strategies in MOLGEN illustrates an interesting limitation of the least-commitment principle. Every problem-solver has only partial knowledge about solving problems in a domain. With the least-commitment principle, the solution process must come to a halt whenever choices must be made but no compelling reason exists for deciding on any of them. This situation is called a least-commitment deadlock because operations in all of the subproblems go into a "waiting for more constraints" state. When MOLGEN recognizes this situation, it switches to its heuristic approach and makes a guess (see Figure 4.5). In many cases a guess will be workable, and the solution process can continue

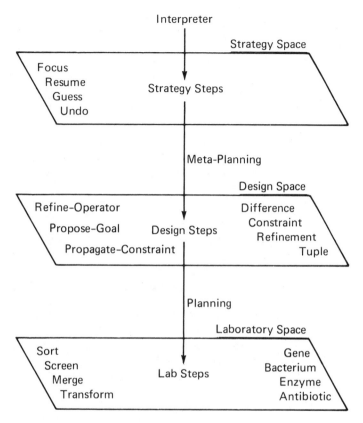

FIGURE 4.4 MOLGEN's planning spaces. The design space *plans* by selecting and executing laboratory steps; the strategy space *meta-plans* by selecting and executing design steps.

to completion. In other cases a bad guess can lead to conflicts. The number of conflicts caused by (inaccurate) guessing is a measure of the incompleteness of the problem-solving knowledge. Conflicts can also arise from the least-commitment process in cases where the goals are fundamentally unattainable.

In summary, the least-commitment principle coordinates decision-making with the availability of information and moves the focus of problem-solving activity among the available subproblems. The least-commitment principle is of no help when there are many options and no compelling reasons for choices. In these cases some form of plausible reasoning is necessary. In general this approach uses more information to control the problem-solving process than the top-down refinement approach.

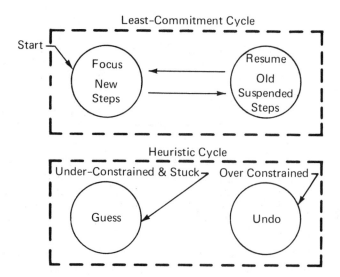

FIGURE 4.5   Least-commitment and heuristic cycles. This diagram shows how the strategy operators are controlled by MOLGEN's interpreter. The least-commitment cycle makes conservative changes in the plan, depending on synergy between subproblems (and constraint propagation) to keep going. When MOLGEN runs out of least-commitment steps, it resorts to guessing, using the heuristic cycle.

4.8   Guessing Is Needed

Guessing, or plausible reasoning, is an inherent part of heuristic search. For example, the generator in a generate-and-test system guesses about partial solutions so that they can be tested. Another example is problem-solvers based on top-down refinement, which implicitly assume that they will be able to refine higher abstractions to specific solutions. Some examples follow of generic situations where guessing is important:

1. Many problem-solvers need to cope with incomplete knowledge and may be unable to determine the best choice at some stage in problem-solving. In such cases a problem-solver is unable to finish without making a guess. Examples of this are assumptions introduced as a first step in hypothetical reasoning and assumptions introduced to break a least-commitment deadlock.

2. A search space may be quite dense in solutions. If solutions are plentiful and equally desirable and there is no need to get them all, guessing can be efficient.

3. Sometimes there is an effective way to converge to solutions by systematically improving approximations. (Top-down refinement is an example of this.) In cases where convergence is rapid, it may be appropriate to guess even when solutions are rare.

The difficulty with guessing is in identifying wrong guesses and recovering from them efficiently. Plausible reasoning can benefit from particular architectural features, as in the system called EL (Sussman 1977). Forward reasoning with electrical laws is used by that system to compute electrical parameters (voltage or current) at one node of a circuit from parameters at other nodes. EL uses only a few laws, such as Ohm's Law, which defines a linear relation between voltage and current for a resistor, and Kirchoff's Law for current, which states that the current flowing out of a node equals the current flowing into it. Much of EL's power derives from the exhaustive application of these laws and the ability to reason with these laws symbolically as shown in Figure 4.6.

Figure 4.6 illustrates a circuit in which resistors are connected in a ladder arrangement. The analysis task is to determine the voltages and resistances at all of the nodes of the circuit. Symbolic reasoning about the circuit is much simpler than writing and solving equations for the series and parallel resistor network. Analysis begins with the introduction of a variable e to represent the unknown node voltage at the end of the ladder. This yields a current $e/5$ through resistor R6. Then, by Kirchoff's Law, the result is the same current through R5, which gives a voltage $2e$ on the left of the resistor. This voltage across R4 allows computation of the current through it using Ohm's Law. The application of electrical laws in terms of symbolic unknowns continues until all of the voltages are defined in terms of e. Finally, we have $8e = 10$ volts, and thus $e = 5/4$ volts.

Sometimes circuit analysis requires the introduction of more than one variable to represent unknown circuit parameters. In general the analysis involves two processes: one-step deductions and coincidence. The one-step deductions are direct applications (sometimes symbolic) of the electrical laws. A coincidence occurs when a one-step deduction is made that assigns a value to a circuit parameter that already has a value, either symbolic or numeric. At the time of a coincidence, it is often possible to solve the resulting equation for one variable in terms of the others. This allows EL to eliminate unknowns.

The propagation method can be extended to any devices where the electrical laws are invertible and where the algebra required for the symbolic reasoning is tractable. Unfortunately, many simple and important electrical devices, such as inverters and transistors, are too complicated for this approach. For example, a diode is approximately represented by exponential equations. Electrical engineering has an

BEFORE ANALYSIS

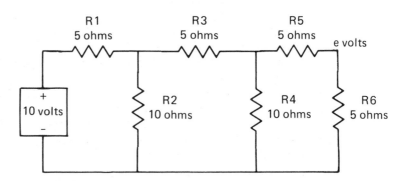

AFTER ANALYSIS

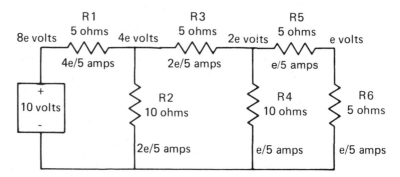

FIGURE 4.6   Symbolic propagation of electrical parameters. Analysis begins by assigning the symbol e to the unknown voltage at the upper right corner of the ladder. Other values are derived by stepwise application of Ohm's and Kirchhoff's laws.

approach for these devices called "the method of assumed states." It is here that guessing enters into EL's problem-solving.

The method of assumed states uses a piecewise linear approximation for complicated devices. The method requires assuming in which linear region a device is operating. EL has two possible states for diodes (on or off) and three states for transistors (active, cutoff, and saturated). Once a state is assumed, EL can use tractable linear expressions for the propagation analysis, as before.

After making an assumption, EL must check whether the assumed states are consistent with the voltages and currents predicted for the devices. It detects incorrect assumptions by means of a contradiction, an event in which chosen assumptions are seen to be inconsistent. When this happens some of the assumptions need to be changed. Intelligent processing of contradictions involves determining which assumptions to revise. Implementing this idea in the problem-solver led to the architectural features of queue-based control and dependency-directed backtracking.

The operators in EL that perform the propagation analysis are called "demons." They are placed in queues and run sequentially by a scheduler. When they run, demons make assertions in the data base and then return to the scheduler. This data-base activity results in other demons whose triggers match the assertions to be added to the queue.

EL has three queues for direct current (DC) analysis with different priorities. The lowest-priority queue is used for device-state assumptions. These demons are given a low priority so that the immediate consequences of an assumption will be explored before more assumptions are made. The middle queue is used for most of the electrical laws. The high-priority queue is used for demons that detect contradictions. These demons are given a high priority so that invalid assumptions will be detected before too much computational work is done. These demons trigger the dependency-directed backtracking.

EL keeps dependency records of all of its deductions and assumptions. In EL an assertion is believed (or "in") if it has well-founded support from atomic assumptions. An assertion without such support is said to be "out." If an out assertion returns to favor, it is said to be "unouted." Figure 4.7 gives an example of this process in a data base. A1, B1, and C1 are atomic data that are currently in. Suppose that A1 and A2 are mutually exclusive device-state assumptions. The top of Figure 4.7 shows which facts are in when A1 is in. Assertions following from A2 are indicated in dotted lines to show that they are in the data base, but that they are out. Arrows indicate support. The bottom figure shows what happens if A1 is outed and A2 is unouted. These ideas are the precursors of those used in subsequent work on belief-revision systems.

An important aspect of EL's problem-solving is its ability to recover from tentative assumptions. But details of implementation and knowledge will not be covered here, since there are many ways to approach this problem. The main points are as follows:

1. In the event of a contradiction, EL needs to decide what to withdraw. It is ineffective simply to withdraw all of the assumptions that are antecedents of the contradictory assertion. Therefore EL must decide which of the assumptions are most unlikely to change and this requires domain-specific knowledge.

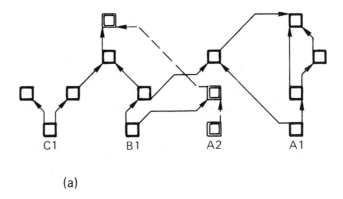

(a)

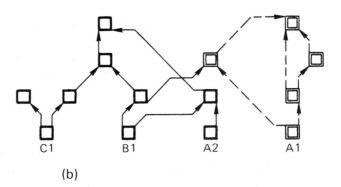

(b)

FIGURE 4.7   Example of belief revision in EL. The dark
boxes are in and the lighter ones are out. In (a), A1 is in
and so all of its consequences are also in. In (b), A1 is out
but A2 is in.

2. EL must redo some of the propagation analysis. At times it is possible to salvage some of the symbolic manipulation that has been
   done (elimination of variables). EL has special demons that carefully decide what to forget.

3. Contradictions are remembered so that combinations of choices
   found to be inconsistent are not tried again.

In summary, EL is an example of a program with organizational
provisions for plausible reasoning. It uses symbolic forward reasoning for analyzing circuits. To analyze complicated devices EL has to
assume linear operating regions. Dependency-directed backtracking
enables it to recover from incorrect assumptions. It also uses a
priority-oriented queue to schedule tasks so that contradictions will

be found quickly and the immediate consequences of assumptions will be considered before further assumptions are made.

4.9   Single Line of Reasoning Is Too Weak

In an explanation of how a problem has been solved, 20–20 hindsight is often invoked and mistakes along the way omitted, making it appear that a very direct and reasonable route was followed from beginning to end. In developing intuitions about problem-solving behavior, this impression is misleading. Actually, there are important and somewhat subtle reasons for being able to use multiple lines of reasoning in problem-solving, and several of the systems just described gain power from this ability. These systems use multiple lines of reasoning to broaden the coverage of an incomplete search or to combine the strengths of separate models.

The HEARSAY-II system (Erman et al. 1980), provides the best example of the first purpose. In coping with the conflicting demands of searching a large space with limited computational resources, HEARSAY-II performs a heuristic and incomplete search. In general, programs that have fallible evaluators can decrease the chances of discarding a good solution from weak evidence by carrying a limited number of solutions in parallel.

A good example of combining the strengths of multiple models is given by the SYN program (Sussman and Steele 1980; de Kleer and Sussman 1980). SYN is a program for circuit synthesis, that is, for determining values for components in electrical circuits. The EL program determined circuit parameters, such as voltage, given fully specified components in a circuit. SYN determines values for the components (such as the resistance of resistors), given the form of the circuit and some constraints on its behavior.

SYN uses many of the propagation analysis ideas developed for EL. What is interesting, however, is its new organizational idea of slices or multiple views of a circuit, which corresponds to the idea of equivalent circuits in electrical engineering practice. The idea that a voltage divider made from two resistors in series can be viewed as a single resistor is a simple example of a slice; one slice of the circuit describes it as two resistors, and another slice describes it as one. To analyze the voltage divider, SYN uses the second slice to compute the current through the divider. Then, by reverting back to the first slice, SYN can compute the voltage at the midpoint. In general the idea is to switch among equivalent representations of circuits to overcome blockages in the propagation of constraints. The power of slices is that they provide redundant paths for information to travel in propagation analysis.

By exploiting electrically equivalent forms of circuits involving resistors, capacitors, and inductances, SYN is capable of analyzing rather complex circuits without extensive algebraic manipulation. Furthermore, the idea of slices is not limited to electrical circuits. For example, algebraic transformations of equations can be viewed as means for shifting perspectives. Sussman and Steele also give an example of understanding a mechanical watch by using structural and functional decompositions.

In summary, slices are used to combine the strengths of different models. Combined with forward reasoning, they provide redundant paths for information to propagate. A problem-solver based on this idea must know how to create and combine multiple views.

4.10   Single Source of Knowledge Is Too Weak

An important adjunct to the use of multiple lines of reasoning in problem-solving is the use of multiple sources of knowledge. The HEARSAY-II system, for example, coordinates diverse sources of knowledge, using an opportunistic scheduler. A system for speech understanding, HEARSAY-II interprets spoken requests for information from a data base. Production of speech involves a series of transformations, starting with the speaker's intentions, through choice of semantic and syntactic structures, and ending with sound generation. To understand speech, HEARSAY-II must reverse this process.

In HEARSAY-II the knowledge for understanding speech is organized as a set of interacting modules called knowledge sources (KSs) illustrated by the arrows in Figure 4.8. The KSs cooperate in searching a multilevel space of partial solutions, extracting acoustic parameters, classifying acoustic segments into phonetic classes, recognizing words, parsing phrases, and generating and evaluating hypotheses about undetected words and syllables. The knowledge sources are as follows:

Semantics	Generates interpretation for the information retrieval system
SEG	Digitizes the signal, measures parameters, produces labeled segmentation

POM	Creates syllable-class hypotheses from segments
MOW	Creates word hypotheses from syllable classes
Word-Ctl	Controls the number of hypotheses made by MOW
Word-Seq	Creates word-sequence hypotheses for potential phrases
Word-Seq-Ctl	Controls the number of hypotheses made by Word-Seq
Predict	Predicts words that follow phrases
Verify	Rates consistency between segment hypotheses and contiguous word-phrase pair
Concat	Creates a phrase hypothesis from a verified contiguous word-phrase pair
RPOL	Rates the credibility of hypotheses

As indicated in Figure 4.8, the KSs communicate through a global data base called a blackboard, with seven information levels, which are HEARSAY-II's heterogeneous abstraction spaces. The primary relationships between levels is compositional: word sequences are composed of words, words are composed of syllables, and so on. Entities on the blackboard are hypotheses. When KSs are activated, they create and modify these hypotheses on the blackboard, record the evidential support between levels, and assign credibility ratings. For example, a sequence of acoustic segments can be evidence for identifying a syllable in a specific interval of the utterance; the identification of a word as an adjective can be evidence that the following word will be an adjective or noun.

HEARSAY-II's use of abstraction differs from the systems considered in Sections 4.5–4.8. Those systems all make use of uniform abstraction spaces. The abstractions are uniform in that they use the same vocabulary as the final solutions and differ only in the amount of detail. For example, in the planning systems, abstract plans have the same structure and vocabulary as final plans. In HEARSAY-II the diversity of knowledge needed to solve problems justifies the use of heterogeneous abstraction spaces.

A computational system for understanding speech is caught between three conflicting requirements: a large space of possible messages to understand, variability in the signal, and the need to finish in a limited amount of time. The number of possible ideal messages is a function of the vocabulary, the language constraints, and the semantics of the application. The number of actual messages that a system encounters is much larger than this because speech is affected by many sources of variability and noise. At the semantic level errors correspond to peculiarities of conceptualization; at the

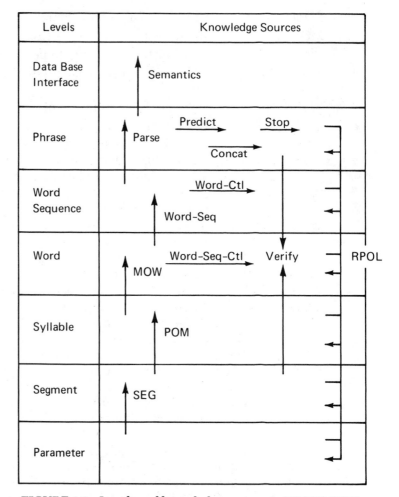

Levels	Knowledge Sources

(figure content)

Data Base Interface — Semantics

Phrase — Parse, Predict, Stop, Concat

Word Sequence — Word-Ctl, Word-Seq

Word — MOW, Word-Seq-Ctl, Verify, RPOL

Syllable — POM

Segment — SEG

Parameter

FIGURE 4.8   Levels and knowledge sources in HEARSAY-II.

syntactic level, to peculiarities of grammar. At the lexical and phonemic levels the variance is in word choice and articulation. Errors at the lower levels compound difficulties at the high levels. For example, the inability to distinguish between the four phrases

till Bob rings
tell Bob rings
till Bob brings
tell Bob brings

may derive from ambiguities in the acoustic levels. HEARSAY-II copes with this by getting the KSs at different levels to cooperate in the solution process. In doing this, HEARSAY-II combines both top-down and bottom-up processing and reasons about resource allocation with a process called opportunistic scheduling.

Examples of top-down processing include the reduction of a general sentential concept into alternate sentence forms, each sentence form into specific alternative word sequences, specific words into alternative phone sequences and so on, until a best interpretation is identified. Bottom-up processing tries to synthesize interpretations from the data. For example, temporally adjacent word hypotheses might be combined into syntactic or conceptual units. In HEARSAY-II some KSs use top-down processing and other KSs use bottom-up processing.

All KSs compete to be scheduled and HEARSAY-II tries to choose the most promising KSs at any given moment, using opportunistic scheduling. Such scheduling combines the idea of least commitment with strategies for managing limited computational resources. The opportunistic scheduler adapts automatically to changing conditions of uncertainty by changing the breadth of search, using as a basic mechanism the interaction between KS-assigned credibility ratings on hypotheses and scheduler-assigned priorities of pending KS activations. When hypotheses have been rated equally, KS activations for their extension are scheduled together. In this way ambiguity between competing hypotheses causes HEARSAY-II to search with more breadth and to delay the choice among competing hypotheses until more information is brought to bear. On the other hand, when inconsistent hypotheses compete, HEARSAY-II executes first KSs that intend to operate upon the more credible hypothesis.

HEARSAY-II's approach to data interpretation differs from that of GA1 discussed in Section 4.4. Both programs contend with very large search spaces. Both programs need to have effective ways to rule out large classes of solutions. GA1 does this with early pruning. In the absence of constraints, it would expand every solution in the space. HEARSAY-II constructs a complete solution by extending and combining partial candidates. Because of its opportunistic scheduler, it heuristically selects a limited number of partial candidates to pursue. To avoid missing solutions, HEARSAY-II must not focus the search too narrowly on the most promising subspaces.

In summary, HEARSAY-II provides an example of an architecture created to meet several conflicting requirements. Multiple levels provide the necessary abstractions for searching a large space, and levels are heterogeneous to match the diversity of the interpretation knowledge. Opportunistic scheduling combines the least-commitment idea with the ability to manage computational resources by varying the breadth of search and by combining top-down and bottom-up processing.

4.11 General Representation Methods Are Too Inefficient

Research on expert systems has benefited from the simplicity of using uniform representation systems. As knowledge bases become larger, however, the efficiency penalty incurred by using declarative and uniform representations can become significant. Attention to these matters will become increasingly important in ambitiously conceived future expert systems with increasingly large knowledge bases.

Changes in the representation of knowledge are considered in this section as architectural approaches for tuning the performance of expert systems. These changes include the use of specialized data structures, knowledge compilation, and knowledge transformations.

The organization of data structures has consequences for the efficiency of retrieving information. Selection and creation of efficient data structures is a principal part of most computer science curriculums and many textbooks are available (such as Knuth 1973). Consequently, several of the programs discussed in previous cases (DENDRAL, GA1, and HEARSAY-II) use specialized data structures. In general, these data structures are designed so that facts that are used together are stored together and facts that are used frequently can be retrieved efficiently.

Choice of data structure depends on assumptions about how the data will be used. A common assumption about special data structures is that they are complete with regard to specific relationships. For example, in GA1's data structure for molecular hypotheses, molecular segments are connected if and only if they are linked in the data structure. This sort of assumption is commonplace in representations like maps, which are assumed to show all of the streets and street intersections. Representations whose structure in the medium is analogous to the structure of the world being modeled are sometimes called analogical representations.

The use and selection of data structures in systems where many kinds of information are used is not as well understood. Not much experience has been accumulated with systems that mix a variety of different representations. One step in this direction is tagging relations with information that describes the chosen representation so that specialized information can be accessed and manipulated using uniform mechanisms. Ideas along this line appeared in Davis's thesis (1976), where schemata were used to describe some formatting and computational choices, but the work has not been extended to describe general dimensions of representation (Bobrow 1975) for use by a problem-solver.

Another important idea for knowledge bases is compiling knowledge. Compilation refers to any process that transforms one representation of knowledge into another representation that can be used more efficiently. Transformation can include optimization as well as the tailoring of representations for particular instruction sets. Space does not permit a detailed discussion of techniques here, but some examples are listed below to suggest the breadth of the idea.

1. Burton (1976) reported a system for taking augmented transition network (ATN) grammars and compiling them into executable code. These compiled grammars could be executed to parse sentences much more rapidly than previous interpreter-based approaches.

2. Production-system languages have been studied and experimented with for several years (Davis and King 1976). A basic difficulty with many production systems, however, is that large production system programs execute more slowly than small ones. The extra instructions do not need to execute to slow down the system; their mere presence interferes with the matching process that selects productions to run. An example of one such language is OPS2 reported by Forgy and McDermott (1977). Forgy conducted a study of ways to make such production systems more efficient by compiling them into a network of "node programs" (Forgy 1979b, 1982). The compiler exploits two properties of production systems: structural similarity and temporal redundancy. Structural similarity refers to the fact that many productions contain similar conditions; temporal redundancy refers to the fact that individual productions change only a few facts in the memory so that most of the data are unchanged from cycle to cycle. Forgy's RETE matching process exploits this by looking only at the changes in the memory. Forgy's analysis shows how several orders of magnitude of speed-up can be achieved by compiling the productions and by making some simple changes to computing hardware. Hayes-Roth et al. implemented a similar scheme to enhance the performance of their rule-based speech analysis modules but eventually rejected all production rule architectures as a feasible basis for the HEARSAY-II system (Hayes-Roth, Mostow, and Fox 1978).

3. Another system that compiles a knowledge base of production rules, EMYCIN, was reported by van Melle (1980). EMYCIN is not considered a pure production system since it is not strictly data-driven; the order in which the rules are tried in EMYCIN is controlled by the indexing of parameters. This means that EMYCIN's interpreter does not repeatedly check elements in the working memory, so that some of the optimizations used by Forgy would provide much less of an improvement for EMYCIN. EMYCIN's rule compiler

concentrates on eliminating redundancy in the testing of similar patterns in rules and compiles them into decision trees represented as LISP code.

4. The HARPY system for speech recognition reported by Lowerre (1976) illustrates several issues about compilation. HARPY represents the knowledge for recognizing speech in a unified data structure (context-free production rules), which represents the set of all possible utterances in HARPY's domain. This data structure represents essentially the same information that was used in HEARSAY-II except for parameterization and segmentation information. HARPY'S knowledge compiler combines the syntax, lexical, and juncture knowledge into a single large transition network. First it compiles the grammar into a word network; then it replaces each word with a copy of its pronunciation graph and inserts word-juncture rules at the word boundaries. In the final network each path from a start node to an end node represents a sequence of segments for some sentence. With the knowledge in its compiled form, HARPY is capable of performing a rapid search that attempts to find the best match between an utterance and a set of interpretations. This special variant of dynamic programming with pruning was dubbed "beam search." Major concerns about the extensibility of this idea are that the highly stylized form of the input that HARPY can accept makes it difficult to add new knowledge and that the compilation is expensive for a large knowledge base (13 hours of PDP-10 time for a 1,000-word grammar).

The promise of knowledge compilation ideas is to make it possible to use very general means for representing knowledge while an expert system is being built and debugged. Then a compiler can be applied to make the knowledge base efficient enough to compete with hand coding. Given a compiler, there is no need to sacrifice flexibility for efficiency. The knowledge base can be changed at any time and recompiled as needed. The compiler can also be modified to rerepresent the knowledge efficiently as hardware is changed or as the trade-offs of representation become better understood. Techniques for doing this are just beginning to be explored and will become increasingly important in the next few years.

So far in this discussion of efficiency, it has been assumed that the designers of a knowledge base must anticipate how knowledge will be used and arrange for it to be represented efficiently. Lenat, Hayes-Roth, and Klahr (1979a) coined the term "cognitive economy" to refer to the issues faced by systems that automatically improve their performance by changing representations, changing access (caching), and compiling knowledge bases. Systems like this need to be able to predict how representations should be changed, perhaps by measurements on representative problems. The ideas of cognitive economy and knowledge compilation are more speculative than other ideas that have been considered, and many theoretical and pragmatic issues have to be resolved before they will become generally practical.

4.12   Summary of Knowledge-Engineering Cases

This pedagogical tour of cases began with the consideration of a very simple architecture suitable for problems with a small solution space and reliable, constant data and knowledge. Few real problems satisfy all of these requirements.

In the second case (Section 4.2) ways to cope with unreliable data or knowledge were considered. Probabilistic, fuzzy, and exact methods were discussed. All of these methods are based on the idea of increasing reliability by combining evidence, and each method requires the use of metaknowledge about how to combine evidence. Probabilistic (and pseudoprobabilistic) approaches use various a priori and conditional probability estimates; fuzzy approaches use fuzzy set descriptions; exact approaches use nonmonotonic data-correction rules. Errorful data and knowledge seem to be ubiquitous in real applications. In Section 4.10, the tenth case, this issue was taken up again to discuss how an opportunistic scheduler can be used to cope with the conflicting requirements of errorful data, limited computational resources, and a large search space by varying the breadth of a heuristic search.

In the third case time-varying data were considered, starting with the situational calculus and then discussing a program that used transition rules to trigger expectations in a monitoring task. More sophisticated ways to reason with time seem to require more research.

The remaining cases dealt with ways to cope with large search spaces, beginning with the hierarchical generate-and-test approach in the fourth case. This requires a solution space to be factorable in order to allow early pruning, an approach that explores the space of solutions systematically and can be quite effective for returning all consistent solutions.

Generate-and-test is a weak method, applicable only when early pruning is feasible. It requires the ability to generate candidates in a way that allows large classes to be pruned from very sparse partial solutions. In many applications solutions must be instantiated in substantial detail before they can be ruled out. Fortunately it is not necessary in all applications to consider all possible solutions and to choose the best; satisficing is sufficient. The next few cases described reasoning with abstractions to reduce the combinatorics without early pruning. The methods presented are usually applicable in satisficing tasks.

In case 5, in Section 4.5, a form of reasoning based on fixed abstractions was considered. This approach requires that all of the information needed for testing partial solutions be available before a subproblem is generated. This requirement exposes the weakness of this approach: some problems cannot be solved from the available information without backtracking. While the abstractions make the problem-solver efficient, their use is too rigid for some applications.

Top-down refinement is more flexible. Abstractions are composed from a set of concepts in a hierarchical space. The simplest version of top-down refinement (Section 4.6) uses a fixed criticality ordering on the concepts and a fixed partial order for solving subproblems.

Top-down refinement does not allow for variability in the readiness to make decisions. The seventh case involved the least-commitment principle, which says that decisions should be postponed until there is enough information. This approach tends to exploit the synergy of interactions between subproblems. It requires the ability to suspend activity in subproblems, move information between subproblems, and then restart them as information becomes available. In this case the problem-solving knowledge is much richer than in the previous methods, and it was suggested that principles like least-commitment should be incorporated as part of metalevel problem-solving.

An inherent difficulty with pure least-commitment approaches is the phenomenon of a least-commitment deadlock. When a problem-solver runs out of decisions that it can make immediately, it must make a guess in order to continue. The amount of guessing is a measure of its missing knowledge, and knowledge bases are usually incomplete. This theme was continued in Section 4.8, the eighth case, where dependency-directed backtracking was discussed as an approach supporting efficient retraction of beliefs in plausible reasoning.

Cases 9 and 10 illustrated the use of multiple lines of reasoning to enhance the power of a problem-solver and the use of heterogeneous abstraction models to capture the variety of knowledge in some applications. An opportunistic scheduler uses knowledge sources as soon as they become applicable (either top-down or bottom-up) and controls the breadth of search.

Finally, some methods for speeding up processing and information retrieval were considered: specialized data structures and knowledge compilers. These techniques do not attack the basic combinatorics of search, but they do reduce the cycle time of problem-solvers and will become increasingly important in future expert systems with large knowledge bases.

Articulating these ideas about expert systems forces a decision about what is essential and important in previous systems. In some cases the same points could have been made about other expert systems. Recent critical work in expert systems has focused on the mechanisms of problem-solving; research has been most fruitful when it has been directed toward substantial applications. In these applications both knowledge bases and methods were tested and revised.

Any system is a product of its time. System builders necessarily operate against a background of competing ideas and controversies and must also confront the limitations of their resources. Summarizing experiments and formulating a simplified theory necessarily involves stepping outside of this rich historical context and being inescapably bound to a current vantage point. The ferment of activity in expert systems indicates that the theory of building intelligent systems is far from complete.

QUESTIONS

1. What kind of architecture would be most appropriate for an automated automobile driver? For an automated knowledge engineer?
2. What determines the complexity of a problem? How can this be measured?
3. What determines the power of knowledge? Can this be measured?
4. Consider a system for intelligent computer-aided design. Would the same architecture be best for generating circuit designs and analyzing (interpreting) other people's designs?
5. When knowledge is compiled, it requires new application schemes. How does this affect the appropriate architecture? Can the initial architecture be eliminated completely?

ACKNOWLEDGMENTS

We thank Daniel Bobrow, John Seeley Brown, Johan de Kleer, Richard Fikes, Adele Goldberg, Richard Lyon, John McDermott, Allen Newell, and Christopher Tong for reading early versions of this chapter and providing many helpful suggestions. Thanks also to Terri Doughty for help in preparing the figures and manuscript and to Lynn Conway for encouraging this work, as well as to the Xerox Corporation for providing the intellectual and computational environment in which it could be done.

5

Constructing an Expert System

**Bruce G. Buchanan, David Barstow,
Robert Bechtal, James Bennett,
William Clancey, Casimir Kulikowski,
Tom Mitchell, Donald A. Waterman**

*The evolutionary development of an expert system is
explained in this chapter. The key task, acquiring knowledge
from experts, resists linear, one-pass techniques. Instead,
knowledge acquisition and system-building interact insepar-
ably. Choices regarding the desired initial capabilities determine what knowledge to acquire first and how to engineer it
for use. Over time, the knowledge base expands to support
additional capabilities, and this expansion often strains the
capacity of the initial knowledge formulation. Thus the
knowledge engineer frequently reaches a point where future
progress depends on improved conceptualization and related
reformulation of that knowledge.*

Knowledge of a domain takes many forms. When that knowledge
is firm, fixed, and formalized, algorithmic computer programs that
solve problems in the domain are more appropriate than heuristic
ones. However, when the knowledge is subjective, ill-codified and

partly judgmental, expert systems embodying a heuristic approach are more appropriate. This type of knowledge is rarely formulated in a fashion that permits simple translation into a program. Thus the process of extracting knowledge from an expert (or source of expertise) and transferring it to a program (expert system) is an important and difficult problem. This process is termed *knowledge acquisition*. It involves problem definition, implementation, and refinement, as well as representing facts and relations acquired from an expert.

The knowledge-acquisition process is illustrated here by tracing the life cycle of an expert system from conception to adolescence. Such systems are typically constructed through a process of iterative development. After initial design and implementation, the system grows incrementally both in breadth and depth. While other large software systems may also grow by accretion, for expert systems this style of construction seems inescapable.

One distinguishing characteristic of expert systems is *transparency*. This means that the system is understandable, both to the system developer and the system user. Expert systems often separate domain-specific knowledge from general problem-solving knowledge to improve transparency. This allows the examination and modification of the knowledge base containing the domain-specific knowledge. Expert systems can further enhance transparency by using the domain-specific concepts commonly referred to and used by domain experts.

Another distinguishing characteristic of expert systems is *performance*. Skillful performance depends on the quantity and quality of the knowledge incorporated into the program. It follows that expert systems must acquire highly detailed and refined domain-specific knowledge. Maintaining the transparency and performance of an expert system is a poorly understood and difficult problem.

Only tentative generalizations can be made about the maturation of expert systems because only two examples of mature systems exist, DENDRAL and MACSYMA. The discussion of building an expert system should sound familiar to systems analysts and others who have designed complex software, for the process is much the same: considerable knowledge about a specific problem has to be encoded for later interpretation by (or within) a program.

This chapter presents alternative models for knowledge acquisition and a scenario of the knowledge-acquisition process in the context of the chemical spill problem of Chapter 10. The second section generalizes from that scenario to identify major stages in the process. Knowledge facilities available for aiding knowledge engineers and the prospects of automated knowledge acquisition are examined next. Finally maxims for knowledge engineering are stated.

5.1   The Knowledge-Acquisition Process

Knowledge acquisition is the transfer and transformation of problem-solving expertise from some knowledge source to a program. Potential sources of knowledge include human experts, textbooks, data bases, and one's own experience. In this chapter the focus is primarily on acquiring knowledge from human experts. These are specialists, although not necessarily the very best practitioners, in a narrow area of knowledge about the world. The expertise to be elucidated is a collection of specialized facts, procedures, and judgmental rules about the narrow domain area rather than general knowledge about the domain or commonsense knowledge about the world.

The transfer and transformation required to represent expertise for a program may be automated or partially automated in some special cases. Most of the time a second person, called an analyst or knowledge engineer, is required to communicate with the expert and the program.

5.1.1   Modes of Knowledge Acquisition

Knowledge acquisition is a bottleneck in the construction of expert systems. The knowledge engineer's job is to act as a go-between to help an expert build a system. Since the knowledge engineer has far less knowledge of the domain than the expert, however, communication problems impede the process of transferring expertise into a program. The vocabulary initially used by the expert to talk about the domain with a novice is often inadequate for problem-solving; thus the knowledge engineer and expert must work together to extend and refine it. One of the most difficult aspects of the knowledge engineer's task is helping the expert to structure the domain knowledge, to identify and formalize the domain concepts.

Knowledge for an expert system can be acquired in several ways, all of which involve transferring the expertise needed for high-performance problem-solving in a domain from a source to a program. The source is generally a human expert but could also be the empirical data, case studies, or other sources from which a human expert's own knowledge has been acquired. The process of translating the knowledge from the source to the program may be performed by a knowledge engineer or by a program.

In the 1950s and 1960s the knowledge used in many of the early AI programs was hand-crafted. A programmer would transform an expert's knowledge into code without separating the knowledge from the reasoning mechanism. Hand-crafting knowledge requires that the programmer learn enough about the domain to converse effectively with the expert, but it does not assume the expert has any knowledge of computing or of the specific implementation involved. The programmer already is an expert or quickly becomes one. It takes a great deal of effort to build and debug such a program, and it is nearly impossible to keep the problem-solving knowledge consistent when frequent updating occurs.

More recently knowledge engineering has become the method of knowledge acquisition. The expert interacts with a knowledge engineer or program to build the system. Figure 5.1 illustrates this interaction.

The knowledge engineer converses with the expert, as in hand-crafting, but the domain knowledge is separated from the rest of the program in conceptually simple data structures called the knowledge base. Its main advantages are transparency and flexibility: yesterday's knowledge base can be more easily extended and modified in light of today's changes than can knowledge embedded in hand-crafted code.

The expert conversant with computer technology can interact more directly with the expert system via an intelligent editing program, as is illustrated in Figure 5.2. Here the expert converses with the editing program rather than with a knowledge engineer. The editing program must have sophisticated dialogue capabilities and considerable knowledge about the structure of knowledge bases. This method replaces one set of communication problems (expert to programmer) with another (expert to program). Its idea is at least as old as McCarthy's Advice Taker (McCarthy 1968); it is probably best developed in the work on TEIRESIAS (Davis 1976).

Since the expert builds the knowledge base partly from past experience and textbook cases, there is reason to hope that an induc-

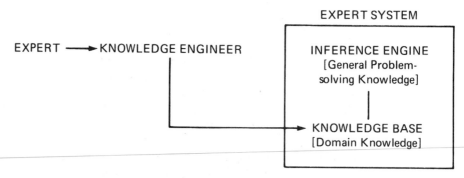

FIGURE 5.1 Knowledge engineering—Expert to knowledge base via a knowledge engineer.

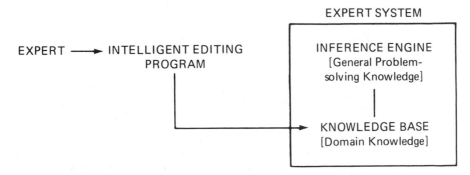

FIGURE 5.2   Knowledge engineering—expert to knowledge base via an intelligent editing program.

tion program could build a knowledge base for an expert system in a
similar way, as illustrated in Figure 5.3.

Finding meaningful, causal associations in a large data base requires considerable basic knowledge of the domain overlaid on statistical routines. Although prototype machine learning programs
exist, no induction programs are in general use for automatic knowledge acquisition in expert systems.

A final knowledge-acquisition method that may become feasible
in the future, acquiring the knowledge directly from textbooks (Badre
1973), is illustrated in Figure 5.4. An expert's education comes
partly from textbooks. A technical vocabulary results in fewer problems of understanding than does open-ended, everyday vocabulary.
Nevertheless, having a program read a textbook and extract knowledge in a useful form requires more sophistication than language-
understanding programs possess today and the ability to view and
understand diagrams.

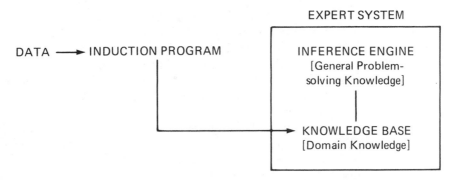

FIGURE 5.3   Induction—data to knowledge base via an
induction program.

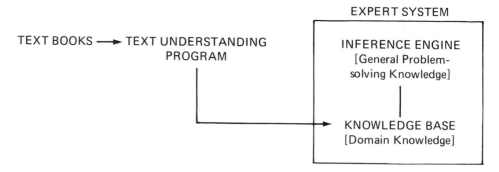

FIGURE 5.4   Text understanding—text to knowledge base via a text understanding program.

5.1.2   Composite Scenario for Knowledge Acquisition

The following idealized scenario presents some of the important steps a knowledge engineer typically takes during the evolutionary development of an expert system. The problem, identifying chemical spills and their sources at the Oak Ridge National Laboratory (ORNL), is detailed in Chapter 10.

The director of ORNL faces a problem. EPA regulations forbid the discharge of quantities of oil or hazardous chemicals into or upon waters of the United States, when this discharge violates specified quality standards. ORNL has approximately 200 buildings on a 200-square-mile government reservation, with 93 discharge sites entering White Oak Creek. Oil and hazardous chemicals are stored and used extensively at ORNL. The problem is to detect, monitor, and contain spills of these materials.

The ORNL director assigns the task of dealing with this problem to the head of the Chemistry Division, who decides that what is needed is a computer system that incorporates the expertise of people familiar with spill detection and containment. A person who has some experience constructing systems of this type is found in the Computer Sciences Division, and the task of building an expert system for dealing with oil and chemical spills is assigned to this knowledge engineer.

The knowledge engineer's first step is to become familiar with the problem and the domain. This includes locating sources of expertise (books, people) through on-site visits and learning from them as much as possible about the problem. The knowledge engineer talks to a number of people familiar with oil spills, then obtains and reads reports and articles dealing with past spills. Finally, in the Chemistry

Division, the knowledge engineer finds an expert on the subject who agrees to collaborate in the building of the system.

In the process of becoming familiar with the problem, the knowledge engineer also characterizes tentatively the types of general reasoning tasks the system is likely to perform (see Chapter 3). For the spill problem, the primary task might initially seem to be identification of the spill material and location of its source. Alternatively the system could be called on to monitor the progress of the spill through the laboratory and manage the assignment of cleanup crews and containment methods. The character of the system's basic tasks is a major factor determining which language or system to use when formalizing the domain knowledge.

After a few weeks of informal study the knowledge engineer feels comfortable enough with the problem domain and the associated subject matter to converse intelligently with the expert. The knowledge engineer then sets up a series of meetings with the expert to identify the problem and characterize it informally. During these meetings the expert and the knowledge engineer decide to restrict the scope of the system's expertise in order to keep the problem tractable. Guided by the following passage from a government report (fictitious, for illustrative purposes only), they decide to concentrate on identifying, locating, and containing the spill:

> When an accidental inland spill of an oil or chemical occurs, an emergency situation may exist, depending on the properties and quantity of the substance released, the location of the substance, and whether or not the substance enters a body of water. The observer of a spill should 1) characterize the spill and the probable hazards, 2) contain the spilled material, 3) locate the source of the spill and stop any further release, and 4) notify the Department of Environmental Management.

When the problem has been adequately constrained, the knowledge engineer begins to determine the major domain concepts that will be required to perform each of these tasks. The knowledge engineer schedules numerous meetings with the expert over a period of a few months to uncover the basic concepts, primitive relations, and definitions needed to talk about the problem and its solutions. During these meetings the knowledge engineer attempts to understand what concepts are important and relevant to the problem by asking the expert to explain and justify reasoning used to deal with specific types of spill problems. One of the early interactions between the expert and knowledge engineer during these meetings is shown below. (This and other interactions used in this scenario were abstracted from interviews conducted during the Workshop on Expert Systems, described in the Preface of this book.)

KNOWLEDGE ENGINEER: Suppose you were told that a spill had been detected in White Oak Creek one mile before it enters White Oak Lake. What would you do to contain the spill?

EXPERT: That depends on a number of factors. I would need to find the source in order to prevent the possibility of further contamination, probably by checking drains and manholes for signs of the spill material. And it helps to know what the spilled material is.

KNOWLEDGE ENGINEER: How can you tell what it is?

EXPERT: Sometimes you can tell what the substance is by its smell. Sometimes you can tell by its color, but that's not always reliable since dyes are used a lot nowadays. Oil, however, floats on the surface and forms a silvery film, while acids dissolve completely in the water. Once you discover the type of material spilled, you can eliminate any buildings that either don't store the material at all or don't store enough of it to account for the spill.

The knowledge engineer listens to the expert in order to characterize the expertise in terms of a few broad kinds of knowledge that have been encountered when developing expert systems. In addition to recording terms that the expert uses in a well-defined, technical manner (such as odor and color), the knowledge engineer also notes other organizational mechanisms that the expert seems to use. For example, clearly classes of compounds exist with generic properties that readily distinguish them in the field. Such classes help organize the hundreds of actual compounds that are stored on-site. Another example of this classification expertise might be evident in the way the expert groups locations of spills (which sites are more prone to a spill, which are potentially more hazardous). These constructs form the basis for certain types of inferences the expert makes during problem-solving. This identification of terms used in a technical way and the description of any additional organizational mechanisms constitute the structural expertise about the domain.

A second kind of knowledge the knowledge engineer listens for are the basic strategies the expert uses when performing the task. What facts does the expert try to establish first? What kinds of questions does the expert ask first? Does the expert make initial guesses about anything based on tentative information? How does the expert then determine which questions to use to refine the guess? In what order does the expert pursue each of the important subtasks, and does this order vary according to the case?

When these two forms of knowledge are coupled, they constitute what is called the expert system's *inference structure*. The structural knowledge indicates (1) what tasks and terms the consultant is to determine, and the strategic knowledge indicates (2) how and when the expert system is to establish them.

In addition the knowledge engineer also listens for justifications of the associations, terms, and strategical methods the expert uses when solving a problem. These are important to record not only for the knowledge engineer's own clarification but also for maintaining adequate system documentation and allowing accurate system explanations. These kinds of knowledge ease the task of designing, constructing, and later modifying the expert system.

Thus, to return to the last explanation of spill identification, the knowledge engineer follows up on the expert's comments with additional questions to help develop and clarify the basic concepts upon which the explanation is based. The result is a set of concepts, some basic, some not, which the knowledge engineer feels are relevant to the explanation. This set includes:

- Task: Identification of spill material
- Attributes of spill
  Type of spill: Oil, acid
  Location of spill: <A set of drains and manholes>
  Volume of spill: <A number of liters>
- Attributes of material
  Color: Silvery, clear, etc.
  Odor: Pungent/choking, etc.
  Does it dissolve?
  Possible locations: <A set of buildings>
  Amount stored: <A number of liters>

The knowledge engineer purposely ignores some of the terms (such as reliability and dyes) at this point to simplify the task.

During this conceptualization stage the knowledge engineer has also been thinking about how to formalize the knowledge being gathered—that is, what architectures would best organize the knowledge. This task involves picking the organization and tool or programming environment to use for this particular application. From his discussions with the expert, the knowledge engineer has determined that the data are well-structured and fairly reliable and that the decision processes involve feedback and parallel decisions. Together with the other characteristics of the problem, this suggests to the knowledge engineer the use of a rule-based language. The knowledge engineer has also determined that tree-searching and asynchronous input/output are integral parts of the problem. Thus the use of either EMYCIN, KAS, or EXPERT is ruled out, lest their restrictive control structures be insufficient for these tasks. After much thought the knowledge engineer decides that both ROSIE and OPS5 are suitable for the problem, but picks ROSIE (F. Hayes-Roth et al. 1981; Fain et al. 1981, 1982) in the belief that its English-like syntax will speed system development.

As a first step in testing the adequacy of using ROSIE for this type of application, the knowledge engineer attempts to represent the concepts in ROSIE formalism, as shown below. (Both the assertions and the rules shown are actual ROSIE code. The square brackets, ordinarily used for comments in ROSIE, here indicate the range of choices available in the assertions.)

Assert each of BUILDING 3023 and BUILDING 3024
      is a building.
Assert s6-1 is a source in BUILDING 3023.
Assert s6-2 is a source in BUILDING 3024.
Assert s6-1 does hold 2000 gallons of gasoline.
Assert s6-2 does hold 50 gallons of acetic acid.

Assert each of d6-1 and d6-2 is a drain.
Assert each of m6-1 and m6-2 is a manhole.
Assert any drain is a location
      and any manhole is a location.
Assert each of diesel oil, hydraulic oil, transformer oil
      and gasoline is an oil.
Assert each of sulfuric aid, hydrochloric acid
      and acetic acid is an acid.
Assert every oil is a possible-material of the spill
      and every acid is a possible-material of the spill.

Assert the spill does smell of [some material, e.g., gasoline,
      vinegar, diesel oil].
Assert the spill does have [some odor, e.g., a pungent/choking,
      no] odor.
Assert the odor of the spill [is, is not] known.
Assert the spill does form [some appearance, e.g., a silvery
      film, no film].
Assert the spill [does, does not] dissolve in water.

The knowledge engineer now uses these primitive concepts to represent the knowledge as a set of ROSIE rules that capture the meaning of the expert's method of identifying the spill material. This representation is a first step toward prototype implementation. The result is the following:

To determine-spill-material:

[1] If the spill does not dissolve in water
     and the spill does form a silvery film,
   let the spill be oil.

[2] If the spill does dissolve in water
 and the spill does form no film,
 let the spill be acid.

[3] If the spill = oil
 and the odor of the spill is known,
 choose situation:
 if the spill does smell of gasoline,
 let the material of the spill be
 gasoline with certainty .9;
 if the spill does smell of diesel oil,
 let the material of the spill be
 diesel oil with certainty .8.

[4] If the spill = acid
 and the odor of the spill is known,
 choose situation:
 if the spill does have a pungent/choking odor,
 let the material of the spill be
 hydrochloric acid with certainty .7;
 if the spill does smell of vinegar,
 let the material of the spill be
 acetic acid with certainty .8.
 End.

At this point the knowledge engineer has a set of rules and concepts that reflect several assumptions about the representations that are related to the kinds of knowledge gathered earlier. One assumption is that a rule-based formalism can be used to capture the concepts and inference processes of the expert. A second assumption is that these particular ROSIE constructs accurately capture the important structural aspects of the concepts the expert has used. A third assumption is that the control structure that ROSIE uses to apply the rules reflects the expert's basic problem-solving strategy. And, finally, a fourth assumption is that the rules reflect associations and methods that either are used by the expert when solving the problem or are understandable rationalizations of such methods.

The knowledge engineer validates all of these assumptions through extended testing of these prototype rules and concepts. The knowledge engineer shows the rules to the expert and asks for reactions. Sometimes, alternatively, the knowledge engineer executes the rules and shows the results to the expert.

KNOWLEDGE ENGINEER: Here are some rules I think capture your explanation about determining the type of material spilled and eliminating possible spill sources. What do you think?

EXPERT: Uh-huh (long pause). Yes, that begins to capture it. Of course if the material is silver nitrate it will dissolve only partially in the water.

KNOWLEDGE ENGINEER: I see. Well, let's add that information to the knowledge base and see what it looks like.

The knowledge engineer may now revise the knowledge base by refining the rules in the prototype, redesigning the knowledge structures, or reformulating basic domain concepts. In this case the knowledge engineer refines rules and reformulates concepts to handle the additional information supplied by the expert. A new rule must be added to the set of example rules to handle silver nitrate. After discussion with the expert, the knowledge engineer decides to replace the concept of a material "dissolving" by the more general concept of "solubility" of the material. The following additions, deletions, and modifications (which are in ROSIE code) must be made to the knowledge base:

Add: Assert the solubility of the spill is
              [some level—high, moderate, low].

Delete: Assert the spill [does, does not] dissolve in water.

Modify: [1] If the solubility of the spill is low
                   and the spill does form a silvery film,
                   let the spill be oil.

Add: [1.5] If the solubility of the spill is moderate,
                   let the material of the spill be silver-nitrate with
                   certainty .6.

Modify: [2] If the solubility of the spill is high
                   and the spill does form no film,
                   let the spill be acid.

After several months of interacting with the expert to define the basic concepts, extract rules, and modify the consultant's problem-solving strategy, the knowledge engineer will have constructed a knowledge base with a few hundred rules and parameters. The knowledge engineer continues to refine and extend the prototype model for several more months, perhaps using additional experts to check the accuracy and consistency of the consultant's predictions or collecting a data base of actual spills and using these to test system performance. At this point the knowledge engineer decides the current prototype has become unwieldy as a result of ad hoc incremental improvement. The knowledge engineer discards it and quickly implements a new, more efficient system, which now must be extended and refined. Thus after more than a year of concentrated

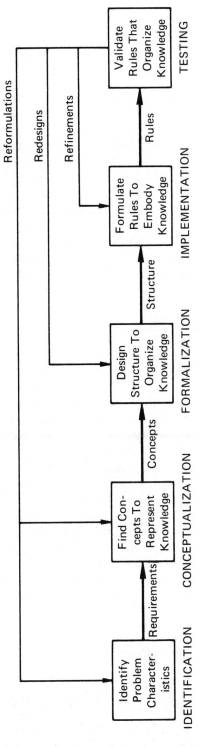

FIGURE 5.5 Stages of knowledge acquisition.

139

effort, the knowledge engineer has completed the development of a credible expert system. Several more months will be spent testing the new system in the field, effectively changing it from a prototype model to a working expert system.

In summary, developing the system comprises two main phases (see Figure 5.5). The first phase involves identifying and conceptualizing the problem. Identification includes selecting and acquiring an expert, knowledge sources, and resources, and clearly defining the problem. Conceptualization includes uncovering the key concepts and relations needed to characterize the problem. The second phase then deals with the formalization, implementation, and testing of an appropriate architecture for the system, including constant reformulation of concepts, redesign of representations, and refinement of the implemented system. Revision results from the expert's criticisms and suggestions for improving the system's behavior and competence. Much time is spent in the latter phase as the system evolves. But accurately scoping the problem and carefully attending to the task types and strategies in the initial phase can dramatically affect the outcome.

5.2   Major Stages of Knowledge Acquisition

In acquiring knowledge from various sources, such as from experts or books, the knowledge engineer proceeds through several stages before producing an expert system. These stages can be characterized as problem identification, conceptualization, formalization, implementation, and testing, as shown in Figure 5.5. However, the process is not as neat and well-defined as the figure might suggest. These stages are simply a rough characterization of the complex and ill-structured activity that takes place during knowledge acquisition. They will vary from one individual situation to another, and the acquisition process is not understood well enough to outline a standard sequence of steps that will optimize the expert-system-building process. Nevertheless a significant body of experience has been gained by various groups designing knowledge bases for diverse domains over the past fifteen years.

5.2.1   Identification Stage

The first step in acquiring knowledge for an expert system is to characterize the important aspects of the problem. This involves identifying the participants, problem characteristics, resources, and goals. Each of these categories will now be discussed in detail.

5.2.1.1 Participant Identification and Roles

Before the knowledge-acquisition process can begin, the participants must be selected and their roles defined. The most common scenario involves interaction between a single domain expert and a single knowledge engineer. Domain experts act as informants who tell the knowledge engineers about their knowledge or expertise. The domain expert does so without necessarily having a carefully conceived teaching strategy in mind. Nor does the domain expert reformulate previous statements spontaneously. The knowledge engineer is an "acquirer" who restates what has been understood of the problem and confirms it using test cases and other experts.

The knowledge-acquisition process can also include other participants. There may be multiple domain experts, multiple knowledge engineers, and even interdisciplinary experts. The domain expert may act as a teacher rather than an informant, imparting knowledge in an organized fashion and at a level that is adjusted to the apparent knowledge of the recipient. Since this knowledge focuses primarily on problem-solving tasks, the master–apprentice analogy may be more appropriate. In any case, the knowledge engineer must be willing and able to learn a great deal about the specifics of the domain.

5.2.1.2 Problem Identification

Once the participants are chosen, the knowledge engineer and domain expert can proceed toward identifying the problem under consideration. This involves an informal exchange of views on various aspects of the problem, its definition, characteristics, and subproblems. The objective is to characterize the problem and its supporting knowledge structures so that the development of the knowledge base may begin. Several iterations of problem definition may be necessary since the knowledge engineer or domain expert may find that the initial problem considered is too large or unwieldy for the resources available.

For problem identification, it is important to answer the following questions:

- What class of problems will the expert system be expected to solve?
- How can these problems be characterized or defined?

- What are important subproblems and partitioning of tasks?
- What are the data?
- What are important terms and their interrelations?
- What does a solution look like and what concepts are used in it?
- What aspects of human expertise are essential in solving these problems?
- What is the nature and extent of "relevant knowledge" that under-lies the human solutions?
- What situations are likely to impede solutions?
- How will these impediments affect an expert system?

The knowledge engineer and domain expert work closely together to define the problem. An initial informal characterization of the prob-lem by the domain expert leads to questions by the knowledge engineer and clarification of terms and key concepts. The domain expert gives narrative descriptions of prototypical problems, explain-ing how to solve these problems and the reasoning that underlies their solutions. After several cycles of restatement, the knowledge engineer and domain expert arrive at a final informal description they can agree on for the problem formulation. In short, the participants isolate and verbalize the knowledge relevant to solving the problem and identify the key elements of the problem description.

5.2.1.3 Resource Identification

Resources are needed for acquiring the knowledge, implementing the system, and testing it. Typical resources are knowledge sources, time, computing facilities, and money.

The domain expert and knowledge engineer must use various sources to obtain knowledge relevant to building the expert system. For the domain expert these include past problem-solving experi-ence, textbooks, and examples of problems and solutions. For the knowledge engineer the sources include experience on analogous problems and knowledge about methods, representations, and tools for building expert systems.

Time is a critical resource. Both the knowledge engineer and domain expert must be able to devote many months of intensive activity just to get the first prototype running. Additional time and effort will also be required if either one has difficulty understanding the other's concepts and methods.

Computing and financial resources are obviously critical. Both must be present over a period of two years or more. It must be remembered, too, that software resources, such as appropriate knowledge engineering tools, are as important as hardware.

5.2.1.4   Goal Identification

It is likely that the domain expert will identify the goals or objectives of building the expert system in the course of identifying the problem. It is helpful, however, to separate the goals from the specific tasks of the problem, since they constitute additional constraints that can be useful in characterizing the desirability or feasibility of certain approaches. Examples of possible goals are formalizing an otherwise informal set of practices, distributing scarce expertise, helping experts solve problems better, and automating routine aspects of the expert's job.

The knowledge engineer should also determine any external constraints that could affect the success of the enterprise. For example, identifying the source of a chemical spill has different implications depending on whether the program's output will be used by a troubleshooter or by the Environmental Protection Agency.

5.2.2   Conceptualization Stage

The key concepts and relations, already mentioned during the identification stage, are made explicit during the conceptualization stage. The knowledge engineer may find it useful to diagram these concepts and relations to make permanent the conceptual base for the prototype system.

The following questions need to be answered before proceeding with the conceptualization process:

- What types of data are available?
- What is given and what is inferred?
- Do the subtasks have names?
- Do the strategies have names?
- Are there identifiable partial hypotheses that are commonly used? What are they?
- How are the objects in the domain related?
- Can you diagram a hierarchy and label causal relations, set inclusion, part−whole relations, etc.? What does it look like?
- What processes are involved in problem solution?
- What are the constraints on these processes?

- What is the information flow?
- Can you identify and separate the knowledge needed for solving a problem from the knowledge used to justify a solution?

This stage, like the previous one, involves repeated interactions between the knowledge engineer and the domain expert that are important and difficult and that can consume considerable time. It will be tempting to try to analyze the problem correctly and completely before implementing a trial system, but experience has shown that to be a mistake. Once the key concepts and relations are written down, much can be gained from formalizing them and working toward an initial implementation.

The knowledge engineer will bring to bear some ideas of representations and tools in helping to direct the conceptualization but must not select a particular one prematurely. The knowledge engineer may try to apply these ideas in building a prototype for a subproblem. The knowledge engineer may decide against showing this to the domain expert to prevent it from contaminating the formalization process, the next stage of acquisition.

As in the identification stage, conceptualization must be challenged by specific examples of problem-solving activity, and the concepts must be modified so that they cover and are consistent with this activity.

5.2.3   Formalization Stage

The formalization process involves mapping the key concepts, subproblems, and information flow characteristics isolated during conceptualization into more formal representations based on various knowledge-engineering tools or frameworks. The knowledge engineer now takes a more active role, telling the domain expert about the existing tools, representations, and problem types that seem to match the problem at hand. If, as a result of informal experimentation with a preliminary prototype, the knowledge engineer believes there is a close fit to an existing tool or framework, the two may proceed directly to fill in the requirements of the framework. The output of this stage is a set of partial specifications describing how the problem can be represented within the chosen tool or framework.

Three important factors in the formalization process are the hypothesis space, the underlying model of the process, and the characteristics of the data. To understand the structure of the hypothesis space, one must formalize the concepts and determine how they link to form hypotheses. The granularity and structure of concepts must also be decided: Is it useful to describe concepts as structured objects, for example, or are they best treated as primitive entities? Are causal or spatiotemporal relations among the concepts important and should they be represented explicitly? The concepts provide clues about the nature of the hypothesis space—whether or not it is finite, whether it consists of prespecified classes or must be generated from concepts by some procedure, whether or not it is useful to consider hypotheses hierarchically, whether or not there will be uncertainty or other judgmental elements related to the final and intermediate hypotheses, and whether or not diverse levels of abstraction would be useful.

Uncovering an underlying model of the process used to generate solutions in the domain can be an important step in formalizing knowledge. The types one can look for include both behavioral and mathematical models. If the expert uses a simplistic behavioral model when reasoning or justifying reasoning, analyzing it may yield numerous important concepts and relations. If there is a mathematical (analytical or statistical) model underlying part of the conceptual structure, it may provide enough additional problem-solving information to be included directly in the expert system. Or it may serve merely to justify the consistency of the causal relations in the expert system's knowledge base.

Understanding the nature of the data in the problem domain is also important in formalizing knowledge. If the data can be explained directly in terms of certain hypotheses, it is useful to know if the nature of this relation is causal, definitional, or merely correlational, because this may help explain how hypotheses that directly explain data can be related to other, high-level hypotheses and how these hypotheses relate to the structure of goals in the problem-solving process. Answers to the following pertinent questions will provide additional insight into the nature of the data in the domain.

- Are the data sparse and insufficient or plentiful and redundant?
- Is there uncertainty attached to the data?
- Does the logical interpretation of data depend on their order of occurrence over time?
- What is the cost of data acquisition?
- How are data acquired or elicited? What classes of questions need to be asked to obtain data?
- How can certain data characteristics be recognized when sampled or extracted from a continuous data stream; how can features be extracted from waveforms or pictures, or from parsing natural language input?
- Are the data reliable, accurate, precise (hard); or are they unreliable, inaccurate or imprecise (soft)?
- Are the data consistent and complete for the problems to be solved?

The result of formalizing the conceptual information flow and subproblem elements is a partial specification for building a prototype knowledge base. This specification follows from the choice of organizing framework and the explicit sketch of the concepts and relations essential to the problem.

It is possible that different expert-system-building languages or tools will be most appropriate for different subproblems. Insofar as a single tool or representational framework is most useful and easy to work with, the knowledge engineer must evaluate the disadvantages of mismatches that will occur when a single tool is chosen and select the one with the least overall disadvantage. Often a few important subproblems dictate this choice; the knowledge engineer chooses a tool that minimizes the representational mismatch for these subproblems (see Chapter 6).

5.2.4   Implementation Stage

Implementation involves mapping the formalized knowledge from the previous stage into the representational framework associated with the tool chosen for the problem. As the knowledge in this framework is made consistent and compatible and organized to define a particular control and information flow, it becomes an executable program. The knowledge engineer evolves a useful representation for the knowledge and uses it to develop a prototype expert system.

The domain knowledge made explicit during the formalization stage specifies the contents of the data structures, the inference rules, and the control strategies. The tool or representation framework specifies their form. Local consistency of the problem-solving primitives will already have been worked out in previous stages but does not guarantee an executable program, since there may be global mismatches between data structures and some rule or control specifications. Such inconsistencies must be eliminated to ensure rapid development of the prototype expert system.

The development of the prototype system is an extremely important step in the expert system construction process. Some code may be salvaged from this throw-away program for later versions, but the most important part of the exercise is testing the adequacy of the formalization and of the basic underlying ideas.

The prototype knowledge base is implemented by using whatever knowledge-engineering aids are available for the chosen representation (editors, intelligent editors, or acquisition programs). When existing aids are inadequate, the knowledge engineer must develop new ones. It may even be necessary to develop a new expert-system-building tool or language, if no available existing tools seem appropriate for the problem under consideration.

5.2.5   Testing Stage

The testing stage involves evaluating the prototype system and the representational forms used to implement it. Once the prototype system runs from start to finish on two or three examples, it should be tested with a variety of examples to determine weaknesses in the knowledge base and inference structure. The experienced knowledge engineer will elicit from the domain expert those problems likely to challenge the system's performance and reveal serious weaknesses or errors. The elements usually found to cause poor performance because of faulty adjustment are input/output characteristics, inference rules, control strategies, and test examples, all of which are discussed briefly in each of the following paragraphs.

The primary *input/output* (I/O) characteristics are data acquisition and conclusion presentation. The method of acquiring data may be faulty or inadequate due to the fact that wrong questions are being asked or not enough information is being gathered. For example, questions may be difficult to understand, ambiguous, or poorly stated for the user of the expert system. Human engineering may be poor, or there may not be enough opportunity for the user to interrupt the problem-solving flow in order to enter data according to a preferred form and sequence.

The physical mode of data entry is clumsy for most systems and most users. Few persons find typing on a terminal keyboard efficient. Eventually touch and voice input will provide a significant improvement in this area. Understanding technical subsets of natural languages in connected sentences of text (or spoken input) will also mark a significant advance in I/O.

The conclusions output by the program may either be adequate or inadequate. There may be too few or too many conclusions, with not enough or too many intermediate hypotheses specified. The conclusions may not be appropriately organized or ordered, and the output may be at an inappropriate level of detail, either too verbose or too sparse.

The most obvious place to look for errors in reasoning is in the set of *inference rules.* Such rules are seldom independent of one another, although it is convenient at first to assume that they are. Among other things, rules may be incorrect, inconsistent, incomplete, or entirely missing. If a rule's premises are incorrect, they may lead to an inappropriate context of application, thus invalidating its logic. Here the problem is often failure to note subcases. Similarly, the conclusion of a rule may be incorrect, often in scope or in failure to separate subcases. And even if both premises and conclusions are correct, they may be linked via incorrect measures of association.

Since rules are not independent, their effect on other rules must be considered. Qualifications, degrees, and weights on links are all important, but they cannot be assigned independently of how whole blocks of rules will be used in the context of actual cases. Care must be taken to avoid producing hypotheses and intermediate conclusions that are separately plausible but combine in semantically nonsensical ways. Blocks of rules, then, must be augmented to reject such combinations.

Errors in a prototype system often occur in the *control strategies* used. When the system considers items in an order that differs from the "natural order" the expert prefers, the knowledge engineer must look to the control structure for problems. Sequencing is more than cosmetic: there are often good reasons why data are considered in a particular way. For example, considering X before Y may sometimes allow Y to be ignored altogether. Manifestations of inefficiency may also point to problems in the control structure: DENDRAL, for example, would exhaust available space in a breadth-first search of a large hypothesis space. The use of a depth-first exploration not only prevented that problem but provided the first few hypotheses to the user quickly after the problem analysis began. Additional control knowledge can also keep the program from printing overly complex conclusions or explanations.

Finally, problems with a prototype system may arise from selecting poor *test examples*. Sometimes failures can be traced to peculiarities of the test problem that were outside the intended scope of the system. More often, however, the set of test cases is too homogeneous and fails to test the program adequately. To ensure against such homogeneity, the test problem examples must be organized so that they cover the subproblems, probe the boundaries of expected "hard" cases, deal with the "classical" or prototypical cases of a problem, exhibit ambiguity (overlap with other problems), and provide for situations involving both hard and soft data.

Other aspects of evaluating knowledge bases and the performance of the expert programs using them can be found in Chapter 8.

5.2.6 Prototype Revision

In the course of building an expert system, there is almost constant revision, which may involve reformulation of concepts, redesign of representations, or refinement of the implemented system (see Figure

5.5). Refinement of the prototype normally involves recycling through the implementation and testing stages in order to tune or adjust the rules and their control structures until the expected behavior is obtained. What specific changes are to be made in the course of the refinement process depends heavily on the representational scheme used in building the prototype knowledge base and on the class of problem-solving activity that predominates (interpretation versus planning, for instance).

The result of revision should be a convergence of performance, once the expert system's scope of reasoning has been stabilized. If this does not occur, the knowledge engineer must undertake more drastic modifications of the architecture or knowledge base. For example, if the performance appears to suffer from some intractable deficiencies that hinge critically on the choice of representation, this choice may have to be changed. This is called redesign, a recycling back through the formalization stage with the new representation.

If the difficulties are even more serious, they may involve mistakes of conceptualization or identification that will necessitate a reformulation of some of the concepts (objects, relations, or processes) used in the program. It may be necessary either to include additional sources of data or to augment the set of conclusions in order to enrich the knowledge base. Additional subproblems may also have to be addressed if their solutions substantially enhance performance.

5.3   Aids for Knowledge Acquisition

Knowledge acquisition for expert systems consists of three primary tasks: entering data or knowledge into the system, avoiding erroneous data and knowledge, and debugging or augmenting the knowledge to make the system perform as desired. Experience with these tasks has led to the development of techniques and computer aids to assist in the knowledge-acquisition process. Such aids have been developed in connection with specific systems, but they embody techniques that are of general value. Computer aids and techniques for knowledge acquisition can be divided into three categories: knowledge-base editors and interfaces, explanation facilities, and knowledge-base revision.

5.3.1   Knowledge-Base Editors and Interfaces

A text editor is one kind of knowledge-acquisition tool. Using an editor facilitates the task of entering knowledge into the system and decreases the chance of error. No systems developed to date can avoid all errors that might occur when constructing or modifying a knowledge base. But increasingly sophisticated editors are being developed that (1) provide a well-engineered user interface and automate certain bookkeeping functions, (2) help the user avoid typographic and syntactic errors, and (3) check for semantic inconsistencies between the newly introduced fact and the current information in the knowledge base. Interfaces and editors affect the expert's attitude toward the developing system, and a good editor can make the difference between success and failure in knowledge acquisition. Most knowledge-base editors (and many text editors) provide smooth user interfaces that facilitate instruction and display information conveniently.

Editing a knowledge base efficiently requires a method for routine bookkeeping. For example, editors in systems such as EMYCIN and INTERLISP have important bookkeeping functions such as keeping track of unfinished editing or noticing permanent changes to the knowledge base and requesting information relevant to them. When a rule is created or modified in EMYCIN, the date, time, and user are recorded and stored along with the new rule, making it possible to determine later which user of the system is responsible for which facts in the knowledge base.

Specialized editors developed for specific expert system frameworks (EMYCIN, STAMMER, ROSIE) also help the user avoid typographic and syntactic errors. These systems typically understand the syntax of the expert-system-building language and can thus provide syntax-directed prompting and type checking. For example, when entering a production rule in such a system the user might expect the editor to prompt for the various fields in the rule, supply default options, check syntax, and perhaps check the spelling of keywords.

Certain very sophisticated editors (UNITS, KAS, AIMDS, ACE, ONCOCIN, RLL) check not only the syntax of the input knowledge but the semantics as well. They check the completeness and consistency of input data to reveal errors in the "meanings" of input facts that would not be obvious from a syntactic check alone. For example, suppose we define a new unit (a schema or a frame) in the UNITS system to describe an instance of a brick house. Assuming the appropriate relations among buildings, houses, and brick houses have been defined, any fact concerning this brick house will be checked automatically for consistency with other facts stored in the knowledge base about brick houses in general, about houses in general, and about buildings in general. If a conflict occurs between facts concerning this brick house and other facts in the knowledge base associated with generalizations about brick houses, the knowledge-base editor signals a conflict. Such semantic checking helps avoid inconsistencies in the knowledge base that would be difficult to observe or track down at later stages of system development. Semantic checking is generally more difficult to implement than syntactic checking; it requires having a precisely defined semantics for the representation language. Hierarchically organized representation systems such as UNITS are especially well-suited to this kind of checking, since they make explicit certain interdependencies among facts in the knowledge base.

5.3.2   Explanation Facilities

Expert systems need the ability to explain the reasoning that led to solutions of problems, if only to help the expert and knowledge engineer refine and improve the system. Such explanations suggest appropriate changes in the knowledge base by clarifying the steps in the problem solution that led to an incorrect answer and the facts in the knowledge base that led to the incorrect steps.

Debugging and trace mechanisms are a primitive, though useful form of explanation in well-engineered interactive programming systems. In INTERLISP, for instance, a programmer can trace particular functions and set prearranged break-points in the computation. Such facilities help a system developer examine, follow, and understand the performance of a running system.

Just as specialized editors can provide more useful services than general editors by exploiting information about the system framework, specialized explanation facilities can provide more useful information than general-purpose trace facilities. Specialized explanation systems have been constructed for several expert system tools (among them EMYCIN, KAS, and EXPERT).

One common extension over simple tracing facilities is the ability to reconstruct a chain of reasoning after it has been completed, rather than merely listing steps during execution. Constructing a history of the inference process and then using it to explain system behavior after the fact usually involves displaying one or more of the rules used to reach the conclusion in question. This technique has proven valuable in the refinement stage of knowledge acquisition: by analyzing the explanations provided by the system, the expert can focus on the key assumptions and inferences involved in solving a problem. In EMYCIN this type of explanation facility, along with an editor for revising and adding rules, produces an interactive system for analysis and refinement of the knowledge base.

Another type of explanation is useful in systems that ask users for information from which to draw conclusions. The user might wish to check the system's reasoning by asking, "Why do you want to know?"

An appropriate answer usually involves the rule currently being considered, as in "So that the value of Y can be determined." Sometimes this explanation will be extended to include other related rules.

Hypothetical information is also useful as an explanation aid. For example, a user may find it informative to know "What would have happened if X?" or "Why was Y not among the conclusions?"

5.3.3   Knowledge-Base Revision

Once the explanation aids have helped to focus on the reason the system failed and a set of possible revisions to the knowledge base has been isolated, it is necessary to select an appropriate one. Doing this without introducing new bugs or direct inconsistencies can be assisted by semantic consistency checks or automated testing.

Semantic consistency checking (see the previous discussion on knowledge-base editors) helps detect inconsistencies between the new revisions and existing knowledge in the knowledge base. For example, to help correct bugs, TEIRESIAS (Davis 1977b, 1978) first suggests what kind of rule will correct the perceived problem and then offers to write a specific form of the rule, if it can, on the assumption that the new rule must apply to the case in which the problem was noticed. It next checks with the user to see if that specific rule makes good sense and offers the user an opportunity to change it. If the user edits the rule, TEIRESIAS matches the new rule against its internally derived model of other similar rules to check for consistency and completeness, finally recommending the new rule in the correct syntax and with values associated with all the parameters. As a check, after all modifications have been made to correct perceived problems, TEIRESIAS reruns the current case with the new rules to see if the problems have been fixed. Correctness is judged by the user at the terminal.

Automated testing, another method for choosing an appropriate knowledge-base revision, involves testing the system on a large number of problems to determine the general impact of the revision. The revision resulting in the best overall performance may then be implemented. EXPERT and EMYCIN provide such facilities. The EXPERT system, for example, allows for efficient testing of changed results may change due to a particular knowledge base-revision are derives from storing and indexing the cases so that only cases whose results may change due to a particular knowledge-base revision are considered.

Automated testing can also indicate which parts of the knowledge base are the weakest and thus the most likely candidates for revision. For example, a program developed as part of the EXPERT system (Politakis and Weiss 1981) evaluates the current rules according to how many correct and incorrect problem solutions they are involved in over a large set of test cases. This program finds weak rules in the knowledge base. Furthermore, it may be possible for the system to suggest the kind of change to be made to a rule (generalize its precondition, increase its certainty weight, and so on) on the basis of global statistics regarding its performance.

5.3.4   Difficulties in Knowledge Acquisition

Several major difficulties are involved in acquiring knowledge for an expert system. One of the most troublesome is representation mismatch, the difference between the way a human expert normally states knowledge and the way it must be represented in the program. Others include the human's inability to express knowledge possessed, limits on expert system technology, and the complexity of testing and refining the expert system.

Research on knowledge-acquisition tools has recently begun to focus on ways to decrease the representation mismatch between the human expert and the program under development. One form of this research might be characterized as research on learning by being told. This is an extension of the research on advice-taking, a notion originally introduced by McCarthy (1968). The attempt here is to develop programs capable of accepting advice as it would often be given to a human novice. For example, in teaching a novice how to play the card game Hearts, an expert might advise the novice to "avoid taking the queen of spades." A human novice would be able to internalize or *operationalize* this advice by translating it into specific techniques or procedures that would result in not acquiring the queen of spades ("Don't lead the ace of spades"). A computer program capable of operationalizing advice in a few domains (including Hearts) has been developed by Mostow (1981, 1983). This work is part of a larger research effort (F. Hayes-Roth, Klahr, and Mostow 1980a, b) for studying automated methods for advice-taking and knowledge refinement.

Another method of easing the representation mismatch between expert and program is to allow the expert to converse with the system in natural language. One step in this direction is to develop computer representations for knowledge that are easily represented in their English-language equivalent. This approach has been taken in developing the ROSIE system (Fain et al. 1981a, b; F. Hayes-Roth et al. 1981). Another system being designed to converse in English, KLAUS (Haas and Hendrix 1980), attempts to acquire knowledge about the English vocabulary the human expert uses at the same time that it is trying to acquire domain knowledge for problem-solving.

Another major difficulty in knowledge acquisition is verbalization by the expert. It is almost always difficult for the human expert to describe knowledge in terms that are precise, complete, and consistent enough for use in a computer program. This difficulty stems from the inherent nature of the knowledge that constitutes human expertise: it is often subconscious and may be approximate, incomplete, and inconsistent.

The human expert's inability to express knowledge even with the help of the knowledge engineer leads to difficulties in all phases of knowledge acquisition. During conceptualization, problems in expression often make it difficult to isolate the appropriate set of basic concepts that characterize the task domain. In the formalization, representation, and implementation phases, this problem leads to incompletely and incorrectly stated knowledge in the program. Watching the human expert at work, which can be structured into protocol analysis (Waterman and Newell 1971), can be a very useful tool in avoiding or reducing problems of expression. For instance, in the conceptualization phase, it is often productive to ask the expert to work through a few problems, then to go back through each solution in detail to determine the apparent reasoning strategy, the justification for each problem-solving step, and the knowledge brought to bear on the problem.

Other major difficulties in knowledge acquisition arise because of limits on the current technology for developing expert systems. Representation languages used by current systems are limited in their expressive capabilities. It is often difficult or impossible to characterize all of the relevant domain knowledge in a given representation system, even when the expert is able to communicate the knowledge to the knowledge engineer. Furthermore, even the knowledge that can be captured must sometimes be stated in a way that seems foreign to the human expert.

Still other difficulties in knowledge acquisition stem from the need to understand the operation of the expert system during the testing and refinement phase of knowledge acquisition. During this phase a complex computer program is being developed incrementally via a cycle of testing and debugging. In order to isolate the specific bug that caused an incorrect problem solution, it may be necessary to trace through dozens of inferences involving hundreds of facts. The interactions between the stored factual knowledge and the control strategy used by the system must be thoroughly understood in order to associate the observed bug with its true cause. Furthermore, unless the interdependencies among pieces of knowledge are well understood, revisions in the knowledge base can introduce subtle but far-reaching errors that may decrease overall performance while correcting one observed bug. In response to this difficulty several systems have been proposed for aiding in the acquisition, tuning, and consistency checking of knowledge in rule-based systems (Davis 1976; Politakis 1981), frame-based systems (Sridharan 1980; Stefik 1981a), and reasoning systems in general (F. Hayes-Roth 1983).

5.4 Automating Knowledge Acquisition

The various knowledge-acquisition aids represent attempts to shift responsibility for parts of the knowledge-acquisition task from human to computer. Only a small number of systems currently exist that automate portions of the knowledge-acquisition task. Although knowledge-acquistion by automated learning is still very much in the experimental stage, a significant amount of research is being conducted in this area. This research involves many difficulties. One important difficulty with most existing methods is that they work with a fixed representation language developed by the designer. Such systems thus automate only parts of the implementation, testing, and refinement phases of knowledge acquisition, leaving earlier phases (including the selection of a representation) to manual methods. Since the representation language determines the range of describable, and hence learnable knowledge, and since current learning systems are unable to refine their representation languages, the initial choice of representation is especially critical. Methods are needed that will allow these systems to refine their representations as they are learning. The EURISKO system (Lenat 1982), written in RLL, has achieved high performance in very large system integration (VLSI) circuit design solely because of its ability to induce new kinds of useful slots. Other major difficulties in machine learning include dealing with unexpected errors in the training data, utilizing domain knowledge to guide learning, and learning from self-generated practice problems.

Programs have been constructed that learn both *factual knowledge in a domain*, and *strategic knowledge*, or heuristics for problem-solving. The META-DENDRAL program (Buchanan and Feigenbaum 1978), for example, learns rules that predict how classes of compounds fragment in a mass spectrometer. These rules represent factual knowledge about mass spectrometry. META-DENDRAL has formulated rules for classes of compounds that had not been previously characterized by chemists (Buchanan et al. 1976). Another program, called AQ11 (Michalski 1980), has been used to formulate factual knowledge in the form of rules for diagnosing plant diseases. These rules have proved more effective than those generated manually by an expert (although the expert could still analyze test cases more effectively than the program using its automatically formulated rules).

Programs such as META-DENDRAL and AQ11 are based upon methods for inferring general classification rules from training examples. These methods search for common features of the positive training examples (members of the class) that distinguish them from the negative training examples (nonmembers). For instance, in forming rules to diagnose plant diseases, AQ11 searches for features common to plants known to have a particular disease that distinguishes them from healthy plants. This general inductive inference problem has received considerable attention in AI, philosophy, and psychology (Bruner, Goodnow, and Austin 1956; Plotkin 1971; Waterman and Newell 1971; Winston 1970; F. Hayes-Roth 1974, 1983; Vere 1975; Mitchell 1978; Lenat 1976).

Learning methods for acquiring strategic knowledge have also been used. Whereas factual knowledge captures what is true in a problem domain, strategic or control knowledge captures strategies for how to solve problems in the domain. In many domains it is more difficult for human experts to elucidate their control knowledge than their factual knowledge of the domain. Thus automated methods for acquiring control knowledge may be particularly useful.

One early program that acquired control knowledge was designed to learn good strategies for playing draw poker (Waterman 1970). The control knowledge is represented by heuristics that recommend specific actions (drop, bluff, call) in appropriate classes of game situations. This program faces the same general inductive inference problem as the programs that learn factual knowledge. The training examples for this program are situations in which it is appropriate or inappropriate to take the specified action. Training data are obtained from finding what an expert poker player would do in specific instances. Several research groups are studying the problem of learning control knowledge for expert problem-solving (Anderson 1980; Lenat 1980a; Mitchell 1982; Mitchell, Uthoff, and Banerji 1983; Mostow 1983).

Although various programs demonstrate the feasibility of using inductive inference methods, several issues stand in the way of using machine learning as a cost-effective method for knowledge acquisition. First, because the inference methods are too weak to select the appropriate generalizations of the data from the many that are plausible, meaningless or trivial generalizations sometimes result. Second, the most successful systems tend to be those specially tuned to a problem domain through a long iterative process of trial and error. For such systems, it may require more effort to develop a learning program for acquiring knowledge in a particular domain than it would to acquire the knowledge using manual methods.

Three routes exist by which learning techniques may become cost-effective for knowledge acquisition in expert systems. First, these methods might reach a level of sophistication where they can outperform manual knowledge-acquisition methods and would therefore become worth the large cost. Second, if general learning systems can be developed (at the same level of generality as systems such as KAS, EXPERT, and EMYCIN, for example), the cost of knowledge acquisition by learning may decrease dramatically. Third, learning may become cost-effective when the domain has no human experts because of its complexity or novelty or both (as in three-dimensional VLSI design (Lenat 1982b).

An intriguing possibility (whose feasibility has not yet been convincingly demonstrated) is that the development of automated learning methods may present a breakthrough in the knowledge-acquisition bottleneck familiar in the construction of expert systems. A program might analyze and monitor its own performance at a level of detail and breadth of scope that surpass human abilities and might therefore be more effective at acquiring and refining particular kinds of knowledge. On the other hand the unconvincing performance of learning systems to date, coupled with the high cost of developing learning programs for specific applications, has led some (Simon 1980) to question whether learning programs can be a cost-effective route to developing expert systems.

Possible benefits of automating knowledge acquisition are (1) automated methods might prove more competent than humans for acquiring or fine-tuning certain kinds of knowledge, thus producing systems with greater expertise; and (2) automated methods might significantly reduce the high cost in human resources involved in constructing expert systems. Costs of automated knowledge acquisition include the cost in human resources of constructing the knowledge-acquisition system and the cost in computer resources of executing the knowledge-acquisition system.

5.4.1   Maximizing the Benefits of Automated Knowledge Acquisition

To maximize the benefits of automated knowledge acquisition, focus should be on acquiring the kinds of knowledge that are difficult to acquire manually but for which automated methods are feasible. Areas where manual knowledge acquisition is limited by human cognitive abilities should be considered. Human experts typically have less difficulty stating factual domain knowledge than in stating control knowledge (knowledge about when and how to use the facts). A chemist, for instance, would find it much easier to state a factual rule about mass spectroscopy (say, the fact that double bonds rarely fragment in a mass spectrometer) than to state when and how to use that knowledge for structure elucidation. There appear to be at least two reasons for the varying difficulty: (1) experts tend to be less conscious of problem-solving strategies in their domain than they are of factual knowledge in the domain, and (2) in order to express strategy knowledge that will be useful to a particular expert system, one must understand in considerable detail the problem-solving framework and control knowledge currently embodied in the system. As the complexity of expert systems continues to grow, the second of these reasons becomes extremely significant: humans find it very difficult to deal with the morass of detail involved in understanding the effects of even a small change to control knowledge. Hence since manual methods for acquiring strategic knowledge push the limits of human cognitive abilities, automated methods for acquiring strategic knowledge will be particularly important to expert systems development.

5.4.2   Reducing the Costs of Automated Knowledge Acquisition

The cost of computer resources is falling rapidly with recent progress in hardware technology, while the cost of human labor (especially of knowledge engineers) is increasing. Thus the benefit of reducing human resource costs far outweighs the cost in computer resources for automated knowledge acquisition. This fact results in the following guideline for research: *Efficiency of machine learning programs is unimportant, except when inefficiency interferes with the competence of the learning program itself.*

As an illustration, suppose one has a program able to improve the performance of a medical diagnosis system beyond the level of performance that can be reached by any manual knowledge-acquisition methods. It would be unimportant whether this learning program required one second or one year of central-processing-unit time to acquire this knowledge, since the benefits would far outweigh the cost in either case. This idea holds true even in domains where improvement in performance is only an increase in execution efficiency without a qualitative change in problem-solving expertise. A very inefficient one-time run of the learning program can be worth the cost when amortized by the number of times the expert system performs.

While costs of computer resources involved in automated knowledge acquisition are relatively unimportant, the cost of human resources to develop such systems can be overwhelming. For instance, one automated knowledge-acquisition system, the META-DENDRAL program (Buchanan and Feigenbaum 1978), took many person-years to develop. And fewer person-years might have been required for a chemist to analyze the input data by hand in order to learn what META-DENDRAL learned. Although META-DENDRAL was a success as a research project for other reasons, it was certainly a more costly method of knowledge acquisition for DENDRAL than manual knowledge acquisition would have been. This case illustrates an important point: *If automated knowledge-acquisition methods are to be cost-effective, concern with the human costs of producing automated knowledge-acquisition systems for individual expert systems is important.* An obvious solution is to stress generality in research on automated knowledge-acquisition methods, so that such systems will not have to be built from scratch for each new expert system constructed. The guideline for research is that *generality of learning programs is a critical issue in making automated knowledge acquisition cost-effective.*

This guideline does not mean that machine learning methods must be ignorant of knowledge of the domain. Recent work in machine learning suggests the opposite—that domain knowledge provides an essential constraint for controlling learning. Generality in learning methods that provide for the use of domain knowledge must therefore be sought. To accomplish this, learning methods must be clearly separated from the domain knowledge that they utilize.

In summary, knowledge acquisition lies at the heart of the design and construction of expert systems. Current tools are primitive by comparison with designers' visions but are adequate for constructing some systems. If machine learning methods are to become cost-effective in the construction of expert systems, then research efforts must be focused by analyzing the likely costs and benefits of automating knowledge acquisition.

5.5   Maxims for Constructing Expert Systems

This chapter has mentioned or alluded to many maxims for knowledge engineering that represent intuitions or heuristics knowledge engineers have developed about how best to proceed when building an expert system. In many ways these maxims are similar to well-known guidelines for building other types of software.

They are summarized here with the hope that they will be helpful to future knowledge engineers.

5.5.1   Task Suitability

Focus on a narrow specialty area that does not involve a lot of common-sense knowledge.

Artificial intelligence techniques have not yet progressed to the point where computers are adept at commonsense reasoning. And to build a system with expertise in several domains is extremely difficult, since this is likely to involve different paradigms and formalisms.

Select a task that is neither too easy nor too difficult for human experts.

Based on current techniques, "too easy" might be defined as "taking a few minutes" and "too hard" might be defined as "requiring a few months." The ability to build expert systems will grow, but at the present these rules of thumb are probably right. Rather than aiming for a program that is an expert in domain D, aim for an expert performing task T within domain D. The number of relevant concepts should be bounded and of the order of several hundreds.

Define the task very clearly.

This is both obvious and crucial. At the outset one should be able to describe the nature of the inputs and outputs rather precisely, and the expert should be able to specify many of the important concepts and relations. One should have access to many specific examples of problems and solutions.

Commitment from an articulate expert is essential.

After all, knowledge engineering today is a process of rendering human expertise into machine-usable form. You cannot hope to do this without a long-term commitment from such an expert.

5.5.2   Building the Mark-I, or Prototype, System

Become familiar with the problem before beginning extensive interaction with the expert.

Read relevant reports and talk to other experts to learn as much about the problem domain as possible. Otherwise the process of identifying the problem and explicating key concepts and relations will be exceptionally difficult.

Clearly identify and characterize the important aspects of the problem.

The first set of intensive interactions with the expert should identify the roles of the participants in the knowledge-acquisition process, define the problem to be attacked, determine the resources available for the project, and characterize the goals or objectives of building the expert system.

Record a detailed protocol of the expert solving at least one prototypical case.

Many questions can be answered later from the protocol. It provides a list of vocabulary terms and hints about strategies.

Choose a knowledge-engineering tool or architecture that minimizes the representational mismatch between subproblems.

Different expert-system-building languages or tools may be most appropriate for different subproblems. Nonetheless, it will be easier and more productive to choose a single tool for the job. Pick the one with the least overall disadvantages for the subproblems under consideration.

Start building the prototype version of the expert system as soon as the first example is well understood.

A common error is waiting until the knowledge base is close to complete before programming. Make an initial commitment to a simple representation and a simple control structure. Work with those as vehicles for discovering what new knowledge needs to be added. As a rough guideline, one should plan to have the Mark-I version running within months, rather than years, of the start of a project.

Work intensively with a core set of representative problems.

Pick a half-dozen or so target problems, including both the input and the desired output. Pick several simple ones that focus on different aspects of the task, so that the resulting system will not be too special-purpose. Get the rules right for these problems before looking at other problems. These target problems can also be used as milestones for the implementation effort.

> Identify and separate the parts of the problem that have caused trouble for AI programs in the past.

Do not avoid working on them, but try to keep them out of the Mark-I version. Some such problems are English understanding and generation, geometric or spatial models, complex temporal or causal relations, modal logic, understanding human intentions, reasoning with imprecise concepts, mass nouns, and counterfactual conditionals.

> Build in mechanisms for indirect reference.

Even though it takes more thought, the benefits of increased flexibility will pay off. For example, refer to members of a class by naming the class concept rather than by listing the members explicitly.

> Separate domain-specific knowledge from general problem-solving knowledge.

This supports transparency and the incremental development of the system.

> Aim for simplicity in the "inference engine."

Simple inference engines are more easily built, permitting experimentation with the rules quite soon. Besides, the point of knowledge engineering is to make as much knowledge accessible as possible. Knowledge encoded in a complex inference engine is not very accessible.

> Don't worry about time and space efficiency in the beginning.

The primary concern should be building a knowledge base and an inference engine that can solve the task. With success, one can start to worry about efficiency.

> Find or build computerized tools to assist in the rule-writing process.

For example, a rule editor can be immensely valuable. Especially with LISP-based systems, such tools are not overly complex and generally pay off quickly.

Pay attention to documentation.

Even the Mark-I version needs a one- or two-page description, so that collaborators can run the program on their own.

Don't wait until the informal rules are perfect before starting to build the system.

This is just another way of saying that one should start implementing early. It is repeated because it is such a common error. Remember: one does not have much hope of getting the initial informal rules exactly right anyway, and trying to implement them is a powerful aid to shaping them in necessary directions.

When testing the system, consider the possibility of errors in input/output characteristics, inference rules, control strategies, and test examples.

Be sure the user has the opportunity to enter data according to particular preferences and that conclusions presented are appropriately organized. Check for incorrect, inconsistent, incomplete, or missing rules. The control strategy should cause the system to consider items in an order "natural" to the user. See that the test examples cover all the subproblems and probe the boundaries of expected "hard" cases.

5.5.3   Extending the Mark-I Version

Build a friendly interface to the system soon after the Mark-I is finished.

Once the Mark-I version has demonstrated the feasibility of the approach, one will want to let other people experiment with it before building the Mark-II version, the second prototype. A friendly interface will maximize the benefit derived from that experimentation.

Provide some capabilities for examining the knowledge base and the line of reasoning soon after the Mark-I version is finished.

This is another important way to permit useful experimentation. Keeping the system transparent and understandable facilitates system development and debugging.

Provide a "gripe" facility.

Give users a way to record complaints when the builder is not present. Don't make them learn everything about the operating system's mail facility or text editor.

Keep a library of cases presented to the system.

With each set of modifications, run the system on all the library cases to see if old problems are fixed or if new problems are introduced. After the Mark-I version is running, automate the storage, retrieval, and use of library cases.

5.5.4   Finding and Writing Rules

Don't just talk with the expert, watch him or her doing examples.

The details of the expertise are not always apparent when discussing the task and domain in the abstract. The expert's actual rules are much more visible while he or she is solving concrete problems, and examples provide opportunities to ask specific questions about why some action was (or was not) taken.

Use the terms and methods that the experts use.

The knowledge base will be impossible to modify otherwise.

Look for intermediate-level abstractions.

Intermediate-level concepts are perhaps the most important tool available for organizing the knowledge base, both conceptually and computationally. In many cases these concepts may not be explicitly mentioned by the expert; instead, they must be identified by looking for similarities in the ways that the expert describes different concepts.

If a rule looks big, it is.

The printed version of a formal rule is a good indicator of whether the rule actually encodes a single "chunk" of the expert's knowledge. If it "feels big," it probably is and should be broken into several smaller rules.

If several rules are very similar, look for an underlying domain concept.

Often, similarities among rules indicate an important domain concept that has not been explicated fully. Although it may not have a name and the expert might not even be aware of it, it may be useful to make it explicit and have the expert name it.

> If tempted to escape from knowledge representation formalism into pure code, resist the temptation for at least a little while.

The goal of the enterprise is to have an explicit machine-usable encoding of an expert's knowledge. "Pure" code is not usually explicit or machine-understandable enough. On the other hand, if using a little code avoids a problem temporarily, do not be too dogmatic about formalism.

5.5.5 Maintaining Your Expert's Interest

> Engage the expert in the challenge of designing a useful tool.

There will be problems and delays. If one has described the system-building enterprise as an intellectual challenge, the expert will be more tolerant and helpful than if unrealistic expectations have been created about how easy it will be.

> Give the expert something useful on the way to building a large system.

As the system is being built, there will be opportunities both to clarify concepts for the expert and to provide computational tools that are of immediate benefit. Develop these opportunities.

> Insulate the expert, as well as the user, from technical problems.

They should never have to worry about operating systems, terminal modems, programming languages, and so on.

> Be careful about feeling expert.

It is very easy to be deluded into thinking one knows a great deal about the domain. Remember: the expert became one only after years of training and experience.

5.5.6 Building the Mark-II System

> Throw away the Mark-I system.

The goal for the Mark-I system should be to have a machine-usable knowledge base and a much clearer understanding of the task. The

Mark-II system can reflect the clearer understanding and one may be able to build computerized tools to help translate the knowledge base into the new formalism.

In the Mark-II (and later) versions, begin to consider generality.

Will the system always be limited to small problems? When the knowledge base grows, will the system bog down? Can the system be generalized to work on large classes of problems? Can the system be made robust enough to be completely fail safe and idiot proof?

Identify the intended users of the final system.

What kind of help do they want? How do they describe the bottlenecks in their work? What is the context in which the expert system will be used?

Make system I/O appear natural to the users.

Stylized pseudo-English can be easy to understand and also easy to parse and generate. The form in which answers are displayed should be close to standard textbook forms.

5.5.7   Evaluating the System

Ask early about how you will evaluate the success of your efforts.

Will testimonials be collected? Will correct solutions for new problems be required? Is Nobel prize-winning performance expected?

Ask early about how the expert would evaluate the performance of the system.

Does its success depend on solving the problem attempted? If not, then the task is not clear enough or the expert may have false expectations. The expert may expect not only the right answer but also the right way of getting the answer.

The user interface is crucial to the ultimate acceptance of the system.

A system that does a superb job may not be accepted if it is too hard to use or too brittle in the hands of an inexperienced user. A little human engineering may make the difference between success and failure.

5.5.8 General Advice

Exploit redundancy.

Redundant data, hypothesis structures, and inference rules can be useful in avoiding problems caused by erroneous or missing information. No conclusion should rely too strongly on a single piece of evidence.

Be familiar with the architecture of several expert systems.

One major problem will be matching the task with an appropriate paradigm. The wrong architecture can make a task quite hard; the right one can make it much easier.

The process of building an expert system is inherently experimental.

One is experimenting with both the total system framework and the individual knowledge chunks. There is really little chance everything can be figured out beforehand. The only way the rest can be learned is by trying to build a high-performance system.

QUESTIONS

1. Why can't all the knowledge be acquired for an expert system without iterative and evolutionary development today? What advances would change this?
2. Which of the steps in knowledge acquisition can be automated easily? Which cannot?
3. Identify three specific knowledge-acquisition functions of general utility.
4. Identify three knowledge-acquisition strategies that experts use. What knowledge makes them better than the average person?
5. Give an example of knowledge reformulation in science or industry. Show how this alters what trainees need to learn.

ACKNOWLEDGMENTS

Thanks are due to Peter Hart and Allan Terry for contributing to the workshop discussions.

6

An Investigation of Tools for Building Expert Systems

**Donald A. Waterman
and Frederick Hayes-Roth**

In this chapter are reported the results of attempting to use eight different knowledge-engineering tools on a single problem, managing the emergency that arises when oil or hazardous chemicals spill into a public waterway. Although no single application effort ever reached maturity as an expert system, each approach manifests distinctive features of style, formulation, conceptualization, and implementation— differences that reveal the power of today's knowledge-engineering tools and related methodologies to determine the shape of an artificial expert.

Expert systems are fast becoming the leading edge of artificial intelligence technology because of the need for such systems in commercial and scientific enterprises and also because AI technology has evolved to the point where expert systems development has become well understood and feasible in many domains. An expert system is a computer program that embodies the expertise of one or more experts in some domain and applies this knowledge to make useful inferences for the user of the system. More specifically, an expert system has a number of basic characteristics that distinguish it from conventional programs (see Chapter 2). First, it must perform well. It does this by applying expert rules in a relatively efficient manner in order to reach acceptable solutions. Second, it bases its reasoning process on symbol manipulation. This approach implies that "knowing" something involves a symbolic representation of facts or world knowledge. Third, an expert system must have some knowledge of the basic principles in its domain of interest. These can be used both to provide additional help when expert rules fail and to produce intelligent explanations of the reasoning process. The expert system must be capable of reasoning about its own knowledge and also of reconstructing inference paths for explanation and justification. Fourth, it must be able to reformulate the problem—that is, to convert a problem description in lay terms into an internal representation convenient for processing with its expert rules. Finally, the expert system must handle formidable problems in a real-world domain.

The types of tasks addressed include interpretation, diagnosis, prediction, instruction, monitoring, planning, and design. Although current expert systems tend to have each of the characteristics mentioned, the extent to which each characteristic is present varies with different systems. Very few expert systems contain all of the characteristics listed.

The complex and arduous process of building an expert system can require years of effort. Much of the work is knowledge acquisition, extracting knowledge from human experts and representing it in machine-usable form (Waterman 1981). The magnitude of the effort depends in part on the tool used to build the expert system. In fact the choice of tool affects not only the speed but also the feasibility of constructing such a system.

A number of tools or languages exist for constructing expert systems (see Chapter 9). These range from general-purpose programming languages such as LISP (as described in Winston and Horn 1981) to highly specialized systems such as EMYCIN (van Melle, Shortliffe, and Buchanan 1981) that aid in the construction and testing of expert systems for diagnosis and consultation. Although these tools have been used in numerous knowledge-engineering applications, it has been difficult to compare them because the domains under consideration have always been quite different.

This chapter describes an investigation into the comparative merits of eight different knowledge-engineering tools: EMYCIN, KAS, EXPERT, OPS5, ROSIE, RLL, HEARSAY-III, and AGE. To avoid the difficulties inherent in comparing systems geared to different domains, all eight tools were applied to the same subtask within a crisis-management problem (described in detail in Chapter 10). The results of this investigation, presented in this chapter, are organized as follows: Section 6.1 describes the structure of the investigation, including its motivation, organization, and limitations. Section 6.2 consists of eight case studies, one for each of the tools under investigation. Each study briefly describes the tool, the subproblem considered, the design of the resulting system, and the strengths and weaknesses of the tool in this regard. Section 6.3 compares the case studies in relation both to the given crisis-management problem and to the general topic of building expert systems. Finally, Section 6.4 describes the lessons learned from this investigation.

6.1   The Investigation

The primary purpose of the investigation was to gain a more complete understanding of the issues and problems involved in the development and use of different tools for building expert systems (see also Ennis 1982). To uncover common issues and difficulties, a representative set of tools was applied to a particular problem area. Thus two major decisions had to be made: (1) the problem had to be both constrained enough to be accomplished in a reasonable time period and realistic enough to provide interesting issues and difficulties; and (2) a method for applying the representative set of tools to the chosen problem had to be selected.

An environmental crisis-management problem was chosen as the focus of the investigation. This problem involved creating an on-line assistant to aid a crisis manager in locating and containing an oil or hazardous chemical spill at the Oak Ridge National Laboratory (ORNL). Rapid location and containment of spills are difficult at the ORNL complex because its 200-square-mile grounds contain over 200 buildings, many of which store oil and hazardous chemicals. The containers for these potential contaminants range in size all the way from small, one-gallon bottles to huge storage tanks that hold thousands of gallons. A tree-structured drainage system that connects the buildings collects all spills, eventually discharging them into nearby White Oak Creek. As soon as observers detect discharges in the creek, an emergency response program is initiated. This response includes characterizing the spill and its probable hazards, warning others in the area, containing the spilled material, locating the source of the spill in order to stop any further release, and notifying the appropriate governmental authorities.

The method for applying knowledge-engineering tools to this crisis-management problem was to have two-person teams who were familiar with eight of the most successful tools spend three days of intense interaction with experts in hazardous chemical spills. Until the workshop began, the nature of the application task was a mystery to all participants except Hayes-Roth. Using its own high-level language, each team attempted to design and implement an initial, rudimentary expert system within the hazardous spill domain. A preliminary report on hazardous chemical spills (Chapter 10) provided an additional source of knowledge for the teams.

Upon evaluation the structure of this investigation reveals both inherent strengths and weaknesses. On the positive side, applying eight different tools to the same problem provides a means for tool comparison that could not be made any other way. This comparison included design techniques, knowledge representation, and performance features. On the negative side, the artificiality of the time-stressed situation seemed to cause the most concern. Giving the knowledge engineers only three days with highly prepared experts rather than the usual several months with unprepared experts did not permit extensive design or development of the expert system and provided little chance for interaction through a development and testing cycle in which the experts could have helped test the evolving expert system.

The time limit seriously affected the analysis of the various knowledge-engineering groups, causing them to focus on a somewhat simplified version of the actual crisis-management problem. Yet the problem they addressed was complex enough to uncover most of the issues involved in the design and implementation of a typical expert system; and, since all groups operated under the same constraints, comparison of their activities and results should shed light on the relative merits of the various tools that were used.

One team that would have proved useful—composed of LISP experts programming the expert system directly in LISP—was unable to attend the workshop. The LISP application would have been a helpful benchmark against which to evaluate other tools. It also would have been interesting to see how a team of C programmers or even FORTRAN programmers would have handled the problem.

6.2   Case Studies

The following case studies describe each of the eight knowledge-engineering tools applied to the ORNL chemical spill problem. Although these case studies include ideas taken from reports written by the expert system teams at the end of the workshop, space limitations allow only a brief overview of each tool at the beginning of each case study. A more comprehensive discussion of each of these tools is provided in Chapter 9; detailed descriptions, in the references cited within each case study.

After the overview in each case study is a description of the actual problem considered by the team, most of them concentrating on locating the source of the spill, which seemed the most straightforward problem. Next is a description of the team's expert system design, based on the team's own high-level language. A short review of the design process then explains the strategies and motivations of the teams during the development of the design. Each case study concludes with reflections on the strengths and weaknesses of the tool used and on any new perceptions generated through this particular application of the tool.

This spill-management problem has certain features that imply the need for particular problem-solving and control techniques. For example, many of the decisions are based on the current state of the crisis situation, which changes rapidly over time, implying the need for event-driven rules. Reports from observers in the field must be read and processed when they are made rather than at the problem-solver's convenience. Thus methods are needed for temporary interruption of current processing in order to attack more immediate problems. During this crisis situation many independent subproblems are presented that need to be solved simultaneously, for example determining the spill material and locating its source. A solution involving multiple parallel and asynchronous goals would be useful therefore, implying the need of a high-level executive to control and monitor lower-level goal applications. The eight languages studied were developed for different types of applications; and the fact that some are more suited to handling the spill problem than others should be considered when comparing performances. In particular, EMYCIN, EXPERT, and KAS, designed for diagnosis-type applications, tend to match the problem domain less well than the other tools.

6.2.1   EMYCIN

6.2.1.1   Overview of EMYCIN

EMYCIN (van Melle 1981b) is a domain-independent version of MYCIN (Shortliffe 1976), a production-rule-oriented system for medical consultation. Since the MYCIN framework was developed for diagnosis and consultation, EMYCIN is most appropriate for deductive problems involving diagnosis. Problem-specific knowledge in EMYCIN is represented as production rules of the form: IF <antecedent> THEN <action>, where the antecedent is a Boolean expression composed of predicates of object-attribute-value triples. A "context tree" organizes domain entities into a simple hierarchy and provides some of the inheritance characteristics of a frame mechanism. EMYCIN associates a certainty value ranging from -1 (false) to $+1$ (true) with every attribute-object-value triple. An antecedent is then considered to be "true" if its certainty is greater than some given threshold (say, 0.2) and "false" if it is below some other threshold (say, -0.2). Rule execution includes an updating of the certainty of the consequent. This involves combining the certainty of the antecedent, the consequent, and the rule itself, in accordance with selected evidence-combining formulas (Shortliffe 1975).

EMYCIN uses a backward-chaining control strategy. This means that after it chooses a goal, or proposition (for example, "The spilled material is oil"), it selects rules whose consequents deal with that goal and recursively attempts to prove the subgoals suggested by the rules' antecedents. When it reaches computational dead ends, EMYCIN queries the user for information needed.

6.2.1.2   The Problem Considered

The EMYCIN team decided that only a few subproblems were tractable within the somewhat restrictive EMYCIN framework. These included assessing the hazard associated with the spill, identifying the spill material, and locating the spill source. Since searching for the spill appeared to be a straightforward task, the team concentrated almost exclusively on the source-location problem. To limit its task the EMYCIN team assumed the following:

- A single pollutant source
- Continuous flow of the pollutant
- A single observer available for inspection
- A documented pollutant source

These are the standard assumptions made by the workshop teams, and they provide the most constraint or simplification. Six of the seven other teams adopted only minor variations of these assumptions.

All the teams, including EMYCIN, ignored the issue of how to provide their system with a useful sense of time; they did not try to predetermine, for example, how long it should take the observers to complete particular tasks and when activities should be initiated or abandoned due to time.

6.2.1.3   Design of the Resulting System

The primary goal in the EMYCIN model was to determine the location of the spill source. The team considered two methods for doing this: tracing the spill back through the drainage network; and narrowing the search to areas that could conceivably drain into the spot where the spill material was found. The second method requires the use of known pollutant characteristics, such as identity or volume, together with the ORNL inventory showing the location of all chemicals and oils. The EMYCIN team therefore designed and implemented the first method, incorporating only a portion of the second.

The team first attempted to implement the backtracking entirely with EMYCIN rules, which proved so awkward that the members redesigned their model to use a single rule invoking a special-purpose LISP function to perform the search. This design required LISP programming ability but was more intuitively satisfying and clearly more efficient than the original design.

Data in the model are represented as LISP predicates like (LOCATION ALONG-CREEK), which stands for the location where the spill was first reported. Procedural knowledge is represented in rule form. The English equivalent of a typical rule is given below.

If   1) the location where the spill was first reported is one of {parking-area, road, railroad, construction-site} and
        2) the liquid is not flowing,
then   it is definite (1.0) that the following is one of the suggestions for discovering the source of the spill:
        Consider possible mobile sources. Request chemical analysis to assist in identification.

As in all EMYCIN models, control involves backward-chaining from a top-level goal, querying the user when computational deadends occur. The following rule from the model illustrates the EMYCIN control structure:

If   1) the location where the spill was first reported is not the source,
        2) the liquid is flowing, and
        3) the spill basin is known,
then   determine suggestions for discovering the source of the spill by backtracking from the spill basin,
        or, failing that, determine the node farthest back in the drainage network to which the spill has been traced.

The goal to be satisfied is "determine suggestions for discovering the source of the spill." The model attempts this by trying to satisfy conditions 1−3. If these conditions are satisfied, the model activates the special-purpose LISP rule to backtrack through the drainage basin. If not, or if backtracking fails, the model makes suggestions about how to use the inventory lists to determine the approximate location of the spill. Appendix 1.1 shows a trace of the operation of the model, which contains nineteen EMYCIN rules. (Five of the eight teams produced executable models during the three-day design-and-development effort. Although these models are understandably simple, they do provide additional information on the strengths and limitations of the various tools. Appendix 1 includes transcripts illustrating the operation of these models.)

6.2.1.4   Evaluation of EMYCIN

The EMYCIN model incorporates a sophisticated front end that elicits information from the user simply and effectively and has the facility of explaining how conclusions are reached. The model does not handle the drainage basin search with economy, however, nor does it attempt to provide an interrupt facility to handle new data on arrival or to process multiple goals in parallel.

EMYCIN's greatest strength lies in the realm of human engineering, since it provides a very convenient environment and user interface for building an expert diagnostic system. The knowledge-acquisition facility permits rapid construction of a knowledge base, and the consultation interpreter uses that knowledge to support a smooth interaction with the user. In addition the consultation facility provides explanations, with no effort required on the part of the knowledge engineer, though explanation was not particularly critical for the simple EMYCIN model.

A major weakness of EMYCIN derives from its constrained control structure. Backward-chaining is the principal method of control, with limited provision for forward-chaining (antecedent-driven rules). As a result, the EMYCIN team had difficulty implementing the drainage basin search. The team could not express the search algorithm as a small, simple set of network-independent rules because of the lack of support for iteration in the language. This would be no problem in a data-driven system with even a simple recognize-act cycle. Furthermore, the team could not conveniently represent the static drainage network connections in a way that EMYCIN rules could access, even assuming that iteration were possible. Neither could the team embody the drainage network topology in EMYCIN's context tree, since the drainage network tree had a nontrivial hierarchy. The only workable pure EMYCIN formulation involved coding the topology of the drainage network directly into EMYCIN rules, one for each possible path through the network. The team tried this method, but the representation was neither natural nor appealing.

The constrained control structure also inhibited the team from providing any sort of interrupt facility or technique for simultaneously processing multiple goals, such as locating the spill source and identifying the spill material.

6.2.2 KAS

6.2.2.1 Overview of KAS

KAS is the knowledge-acquisition system for PROSPECTOR, a consultation program developed for diagnosis problems in mineral exploration (Duda 1979b). KAS bears the same relationship to PROSPECTOR as EMYCIN does to MYCIN: it permits the use of the PROSPECTOR inference engine on problems outside the geology domain.

KAS is not a programming language but, rather, a skeleton system for constructing rule-based diagnostic systems. It contains two basic methods of representing knowledge for such tasks: (1) probabilistic inference rules of the form: IF <antecedent> THEN <rule-strength> <rule-strength> <consequent>, and (2) partitioned semantic networks (Hendrix 1979). In addition, the system builder can designate any antecedents or consequents as contexts states that must be sufficiently established before rules can be enabled, and can attach procedures to consequents that are invoked when the consequent becomes sufficiently well established.

The inference rules in KAS represent plausible knowledge, where observation of the antecedent situation changes belief in the consequent situation. KAS rules incorporate two rule strengths (likelihood ratios); the first changes the probability of the consequent when the antecedent is known to be present, and the second changes the probability when the antecedent is known to be absent. Partitioned semantic networks represent the antecedent and consequent situations. For example, the situation of having oil in White Oak Creek could be represented by

$$\left.\begin{array}{l} \text{COMPOSED-OF E1 OIL} \\ \text{LOCATION-OF E1 WHITE-OAK-CREEK} \end{array}\right\} P$$

Here the entity E1 corresponds to the oil. The brace indicates that the presence of oil in White Oak Creek is hypothetical, currently believed with probability P. The constants OIL and WHITE-OAK-CREEK would appear in a taxonomy of materials and locations. Statements can be composed of logical combinations of other statements. Thus, the statement "A large oil spill or a strong acid spill strongly suggests an emergency" could be represented as follows:

$$\left.\begin{array}{l}\text{LARGE}\quad\text{STRONG}\\ \text{OIL}\quad\text{OR}\quad\text{ACID}\xrightarrow{\text{Ls, Ln}}\text{EMERGENCY}\\ \text{SPILL}\quad\text{SPILL}\end{array}\right\}P$$

Here Ls and Ln are the likelihood ratios that measure the degree of sufficiency and necessity of the rule, while P is the probability that the antecedents do indeed suggest the consequents.

6.2.2.2   The Problem Considered

Since KAS is a diagnosis program intended for interactive consultation, the KAS team addressed the problem of giving advice to a possibly inexperienced on-scene coordinator about the best strategy for locating the spill source. Related to the important general problem of setting priorities in a crisis situation, this process would be a significant component of a more comprehensive expert system. The team did not address the problem of actually searching the drainage system to locate the spill source.

The KAS team did not have to make simplifying assumptions concerning the number of pollutant sources, type of flow, number of observers available, or pollutant source documentation, since its members addressed the problem of determining a good strategy for locating the spill source, rather than applying that strategy.

6.2.2.3   Design of the Resulting System

The KAS model has one top-level goal: to determine the best strategy for locating the spill source. This requires examining four hypotheses about the best strategy: (1) backtrack through the storm drains; (2) call the building supervisor; (3) check the recorded sources; (4) hunt for undocumented sources. Each of these hypotheses is further elaborated in a similar way. For example, three major factors are considered in order to determine the favorability of the backtracking strategy: (1) Is the spill flowing continuously? (2) Is the basin known? (3) Are maps of the storm drains available? The model determines the best strategy based on information obtained from the user concerning the current spill. It also provides warnings and recommendations for observers.

As in all KAS models, data are represented in semantic net form, and procedural knowledge is represented as probabilistic inference rules. Control in the model is via both forward- and backward-chaining and leads to querying the user when additional information is needed.

Because of time constraints at the workshop, the semantic net constructs were representative rather than complete; simple representations were constructed for nodes involving the identity of the pollutants. A transcript of the KAS model working on the spill problem is shown in Appendix 1.2. This model contains approximately thirty-five KAS rules.

6.2.2.4   Evaluation of KAS

Like the EMYCIN model, the KAS model incorporates useful facilities for input/output, data-base construction, and explanation. However, because of the design criterion, it does not address the drainage basin search problem. The model also does not attempt to provide mechanisms for handling new data on arrival or for parallel processing of multiple goals.

One obvious strength of KAS is its sophisticated knowledge-entry environment. This feature permitted the KAS team to build a simple model quickly that could respond to volunteered information, seek additional information efficiently, weigh and balance competing factors in reaching conclusions, and explain its conclusions. Even with a small and somewhat inadequate knowledge base, plausible behavior was obtained from this model in a very short time. In addition, KAS has facilities for augmenting the model's knowledge base as well as for recognizing synonyms, revising answers, summarizing, and tracing.

KAS is not a general-purpose knowledge-engineering tool, however. Although it does have the ability to invoke itself recursively on subclassification problems, it does not permit the binding of antecedent variables to be used in consequent actions. Thus KAS could not be used naturally to solve the problem of searching the drainage basin, monitoring the activities of two or more agents, or optimizing the allocation of resources.

Even the computationally simple problem of retrieving a list of buildings and filtering it by the identity and volume of the pollutant is beyond the capabilities of KAS. This could be accomplished only by writing a LISP function and calling it from KAS. Although KAS could be modified to make it more like a programming language, this would compromise important features of the system, such as explanation, that depend on its simple, uniform, declarative representation of knowledge.

Systems like EMYCIN, KAS, and EXPERT, which have efficient but restrictive methods for plausible or probabilistic inference, have sacrificed other aspects of knowledge representation. This may be the price paid for efficiency. Nevertheless, these restrictive special-purpose systems have a very useful role to play in specialized problems.

6.2.3 EXPERT

6.2.3.1 Overview of EXPERT

EXPERT is a programming system developed for building consultation models based on classification problems (Weiss and Kulikowski 1979, 1981). It has been used primarily to develop diagnostic models in medicine, specifically in ophthalmology, endocrinology, and rheumatology.

An EXPERT model selects appropriate hypotheses by interpreting given facts or observations. Such a model consists of hypotheses, findings, and decision rules. The hypotheses are the conclusions the model may infer. Structured into a taxonomic classification, they may include diagnostic and prognostic categories. They may also include intermediate hypotheses representing higher level abstractions of the other categories and usually associated with certainty measures. The findings are the facts or observations elicited during a consultation, which are recorded as true, false, numerical, or unavailable responses to queries posed by EXPERT. The decision rules describe logical relationships among findings and hypotheses. EXPERT uses three types of rules: FF, FH, and HH. FF rules relate findings to other findings, for example,

If $FACT_1$ is false, $FACT_2$ is true.

FH rules relate facts to hypotheses; for example,

If $FACT_1$ is false and $FACT_2$ is true,
affirm $HYPOTHESIS_1$ with a confidence of 0.8.

HH rules relate hypotheses to other hypotheses, as in

If $HYPOTHESIS_1$ has a confidence of 0.4 to 1 and
$HYPOTHESIS_2$ has a confidence of 0.6 to 1,
affirm $HYPOTHESIS_3$ with a confidence of 1.

EXPERT evaluates its rules in an ordered manner, rather than relying on backward-chaining as EMYCIN does. When more than one rule is applicable to the same hypothesis, the rule with the highest confidence is used.

6.2.3.2   The Problem Considered

The EXPERT team concentrated on building a fairly general consultant for the spill problem. The users of the consultant system were viewed as intelligent but inexpert people who would need advice during a spill crisis. The major problems considered by the team were spill discovery, spill characterization (including material, location, flow, volume, and hazards), regulation violation analysis, agency notification, and spill countermeasures.

In order to constrain the task, the EXPERT team assumed a single pollutant source, possible sporadic flow of pollutant, a single observer available for inspection, and a documented pollutant source. The only difference between these assumptions and those of the EMYCIN team concerns pollutant flow: The EXPERT team did not assume the pollutant flow had to be continuous.

6.2.3.3   Design of the Resulting System

The EXPERT model has three primary goals: to recommend spill notification and containment procedures, to locate the spill source, and to identify the spill material. The model uses a typical EXPERT representation consisting of hypotheses (the set of potential interpretations), findings (the set of possible queries), and rules (the set of decision rules relating hypotheses and findings). Examples of these types of representations are shown below, along with their English interpretations.

```
**hypothesis
VIOL   ORO-DOE should be notified of the spill.

**findings
OIL    The spill material type is oil—film or sheen.
CHEM The spill material type is chemical.
ORO    The agency ORO-DOE has been notified·of the spill.

**rules
```

If   (the spill material is oil—film or sheen
       or the spill material is chemical)
       and the agency ORO-DOE has not been notified of the spill
then ORO-DOE should be notified of the spill
       with probability .9.

Control in the model occurs via forward-chaining through the rules. Rule and fact ordering provide a natural sequencing through the user queries and the entire deduction process. In addition, the model permits the user to see the current status of the deduction (called an *interpretation*) in the middle of questioning and to revise responses to previous questions. For example, the user may report that the ORNL Department of Environmental Management (DEM) has not been notified and then at some later time (after notifying DEM) interject the information that DEM has been notified.

Previous EXPERT medical models were somewhat different from the spill model in that responses in the medical models were changed only if they were reported erroneously, and the models did not require such dynamically varying sets of sequential interpretations. Also, confidence measures, often used to reason in an uncertain environment, play a relatively unimportant role in the EXPERT spill model. A transcript of a sample session with the model is shown in Appendix 1.3. This model contains approximately thirty-five EXPERT rules.

6.2.3.4   Evaluation of EXPERT

Like the EMYCIN and KAS models, the EXPERT model employs useful user-interface facilities that ease and expedite interaction. This interaction takes place primarily via menus, and at any point the user can direct the model to summarize the current state of its processing. However, the model does not handle the drainage basin search directly within EXPERT and does not address the problem of parallel processing multiple goals. But it does permit the user to interrupt processing to input new data or to change previous answers to questions.

The major strength of EXPERT is its human engineering. The system is easy to use and permits the rapid development of a prototype model. As a result EXPERT is a very convenient tool for those problems that can be cast as classification problems, that is, composed of prespecified lists of conclusions and observations. EXPERT can also be applied to problems that are not simply classification problems, as the development of the spill model demonstrates. A mechanism for suspending EXPERT in midexecution and calling another program that can supply results to it helps to make it a more generally applicable system.

The control structure of EXPERT does not permit a simple solution to the spill source location problem within the EXPERT formalism. Consequently the EXPERT team implemented a backtracking procedure in FORTRAN, to be called by the EXPERT model. The problem of processing simultaneous goals cannot be easily handled within the EXPERT control structure and was not addressed by the EXPERT team.

6.2.4 OPS5

6.2.4.1 Overview of OPS5

OPS5 is a rule-based programming language (Forgy 1981) descended from earlier OPS languages designed for AI and cognitive psychology applications (Forgy and McDermott 1977). Data elements in OPS5 are either vectors or objects with associated attribute-value pairs. For example, the assertion that a spill management system should locate the source of the spill before trying to contain it could be represented as the vector:

(TASK-ORDER   SOURCE-LOCATION   CONTAINMENT),

while the statement that sulfuric acid is a colorless acid could be represented by the attribute-value element:

(MATERIAL ^NAME H2SO4 ^COLOR COLORLESS ^CLASS ACID).

The carat, "^", is an operator that distinguishes attributes. Rules in OPS5 are data-driven and operate on a single global data base. The rules have the form <antecedent> → <consequent>, where the antecedent is a partial description of data elements and the consequent is one or more action to be taken if the antecedent matches the data base. A rule for notifying appropriate agencies when there is an active goal of coordination and notification has not been made could be represented as

```
(P CO-ORDINATE-6
   (GOAL ^STATUS ACTIVE ^WANT CO-ORDINATE)
 -(NOTIFICATION)   →(MAKE NOTIFICATION)).
```

Control in OPS5 is governed by the recognize-act cycle, a simple loop in which rules with satisfied antecedents are found, one is selected (conflict resolution), and its actions are performed. Most OPS5 programs make heavy use of goals to direct the processing, putting them into the data base and deleting them when appropriate for the current problem-solving strategy. The collection of rules that are sensitive to the goal for a given task compose the "method" for that task. Methods and goals are not features of the OPS5 language; they are simply convenient organizing principles. The rules associated with a method can perform tasks directly, or they can create goals that ask other rules to perform the tasks. Creating a goal is analogous to calling a subroutine or evoking a knowledge source. Thus the specificity of the goals and methods determines the granularity of the resulting model.

6.2.4.2   The Problem Considered

The OPS5 team focused both on the overall organization of the spill crisis management system and on locating the spill source. The overall organization was of interest because it presented control issues that the team had not faced before, including coordinating a number of asynchronous subtasks where the coordinator has only limited control over when the needed information will become available. Here the subtasks included having human agents search the drainage system for the spill source.

The OPS5 team made the following basic assumptions to constrain the task: a single pollutant source, continuous flow of pollutant, multiple observers available for inspection, and a possible undocumented pollutant source. Variations from the standard assumptions involve the availability of multiple observers and the existence of undocumented sources.

6.2.4.3   Design of the Resulting System

The OPS5 model has three primary goals: to locate the spill source, to contain the spill, and to identify the spill material. The model consists of sixty-two rules distributed among twelve methods. When the system begins, it enters the "interview" method to learn from the user all it can about the spill. Then it enters the "coordinate" method, assigning human agents to gather information and locate the spill. The methods (for characterizing the source, for example) guide the agents in their respective tasks. After the model requests information from an agent, it continues with other tasks, temporarily suspending the current task, until the information becomes available. The model attempts to contain the spill by directing an agent to find the spill source. The agent is then told to contain it or, if containment is not possible, to warn downstream communities. The model attempts to identify and locate the spill by assigning agents to analyze samples of the spilled material and to search the drainage basin for the spill source.

The OPS5 model uses a topological map of the appropriate drainage basin to direct the agent's search of the basin's manholes.

The agent is told to follow chains of contaminated manholes up the basin, looking for the most contaminated manhole. The system also uses information concerning the spilled material (name, type, or volume) to narrow the search area.

Data in the model are vectors or objects with attribute-value pairs, while procedural knowledge takes the form of rules controlled by goals, as illustrated in the OPS5 overview. A transcript of the OPS5 model being applied to the spill problem is given in Appendix 1.4.

6.2.4.4   Evaluation of OPS5

Unlike the EMYCIN, KAS, and EXPERT models, the OPS5 model does not have sophisticated front-end facilities for expanding the data base or explaining its reasoning processes. However, the model does perform the drainage basin search effectively and does process multiple goals (locate spill source, determine spill material) in parallel. But it does not provide an interrupt facility to handle new data on arrival.

One of the strengths of OPS5 is language generality, which makes it easy to tailor the design of an expert system to fit the characteristics of its domain. This generality also facilitates diverse data representations and control structures within a single program and permits different organizing principles in different sections of a program. Thus the model easily handles the drainage basin search and multiple goals, and it can interrupt work on one goal to process another. But OPS5 does not have built-in problem-solving strategies or system organizations, features its designers felt may hinder the refinement process, particularly if the OPS5 program is to discover new ways to organize its methods, perform old tasks, and represent information.

Another strength of OPS5, not particularly apparent in the OPS5 model, is its powerful pattern-matching capability. In a general-purpose production-system language, pattern matching is crucial: it affects all aspects of the design, from control constructs to data representations. OPS5 permits quite complex patterns that are processed by a very efficient pattern matcher. Thus the user can place much of the burden of solving his problem on the pattern-matcher. The R1 system for configuring VAX-11 computers (McDermott 1980a−c) illustrates this point, since it solves a difficult problem, using complex patterns and almost no search.

A major weakness of OPS5 is its lack of a sophisticated programming environment. Although the language does have some debugging aids, the overall programming environment lacks the power of a typical LISP system. The ideal programming environment would permit an unsophisticated user to communicate with OPS5 in a subset of natural language, enter rules, test the system's performance, and then add or modify rules as required. Unfortunately the general-purpose nature of the language complicates the human-engineering problem. How to preserve the language's generality while at the same-time making it a suitable tool for a typical user remains an unsolved problem.

6.2.5   ROSIE

6.2.5.1   Overview of ROSIE

ROSIE is a general-purpose rule-based programming system suitable for a broad range of knowledge-engineering applications (Fain et al. 1981a, b; F. Hayes-Roth et al. 1981). Its most striking feature is its English-like syntax, which facilitates the creation and manipulation of the ROSIE data base. This data base contains general n-ary relations with English correspondences in the ROSIE language. To test relations in the data base, the user writes conditions in English that correspond to the relational forms. Five basic types of English relationships are modeled by the language:

1. Class membership	S11 is a source.
	The spill is an oil.
2. Predication	S11 is accessible.
	The spill is dangerous.
3. Intransitive verbs	S11 does leak.
	The spill does smell.
4. Transitive verbs	S11 does hold hydraulic oil.
	The spill does form a film.
5. Predicate complements	S11 is clearly marked.
	The spill is partially contained.

These relationships can be further refined by the use of prepositional phrases:

6. Prepositional phrases	S11 does appear in the inventory.
	The spill does float on the water.

These forms can be composed in the language in most natural ways. For example:

1, 2	The spill is a dangerous oil.
1, 2, 3	S11 is an accessible source that does leak.

1, 2, 4   The accessible source does hold hydraulic oil.

1, 2, 6   The spill is a dangerous oil that does float on the water.

ROSIE relationships can be combined with ROSIE actions to produce rules. A sample ROSIE rule is as follows (parentheses are used to avoid ambiguity):

> If the spill is a dangerous oil
>   from (a source that does appear in the inventory),
>   assert the location of the spill is known
>   and go notify (the field team) about (the location of the spill).

ROSIE rules are organized as rulesets, defined to be either procedures, generators, or predicates. Generators return values of any sort, while predicates determine proposition truth values. The rulesets operate on a global data base but maintain temporary private data bases during execution.

ROSIE supports three types of inference mechanisms: state-driven, where the state of the system directly causes a rule to fire; goal-driven, where backward-chaining is used to find rules that will verify predicates in the rule conditions; and change-driven, where a data-base change causes a rule to fire. ROSIE also supports communication over multiple ports, permitting the user access to the local operating system or communication networks, and incorporates powerful pattern-matching capabilities to facilitate these interactions.

6.2.5.2   The Problem Considered

The ROSIE team concentrated on the problem of locating the spill source but embedded this in the context of an overall system for handling spills. Its members adopted a control strategy that allowed for the inclusion of many more activities than those exclusively concerned with source location. In fact if the spill-monitoring facility were connected via network to remote computers (say, those of other government agencies), ROSIE would be particularly well-suited to coordinating the flow of information in such a system, given its powerful capabilities for communicating with remote systems.

The ROSIE team made the following basic assumptions to constrain the task: a single pollutant source, continuous flow of pollutant, a single observer available for inspection, a possible undocumented pollutant source, and observation time much greater than transit time. The first four assumptions are standard, except for the possible inclusion of undocumented sources. The ROSIE team made an additional assumption that affected the drainage basin search strategy: that the observation time (at a manhole) was much greater than the transit time (between manholes).

6.2.5.3   Design of the Resulting System

The ROSIE model has two primary goals: to locate the spill source and to identify the spill material. The model locates the spill source by eliminating unlikely sources until only one remains. Sources are eliminated either by directing an observer in backtracking through the drainage basin, physically examining manholes and storage containers, or by deduction based on current information regarding the spill material and volume. Likely spill materials are identified on the basis of physical characteristics (smell, color), while volume is estimated from observers' field reports. Sources incompatible with the material or volume estimates are eliminated.

The top-level procedure in the ROSIE model coordinates the investigation (see Appendix 1.6). It reads the report on the spill, plus any replies to its requests for information, and then interprets and assimilates these data. It next attempts to determine the spill material, spill volume, and source location. If the source location is still unknown, the procedure makes further requests for information and repeats the cycle just described.

The model represents domain knowledge as ROSIE assertions and rules, as follows:

> Assert s6-8 is a source in BUILDING 3518.
> Assert s6-8 does hold 32 gallons of sulfuric acid.
> Assert s6-19 is a source in BUILDING 3517.
> Assert s6-19 does hold 10 gallons of sulfuric acid.
>
> If the result of the sulfate ion test is positive,
> deny the material of the spill is undetermined
> and go report 'the material of the spill is sulfuric acid'.

To illustrate how the model might use the preceding assertions and rules, assume a spill situation where the model directs an observer to perform a chemical analysis of the spill and learns that the sulfate ion test is positive. If the observer discovers more than ten gallons of the spill material in the drainage network, the model can use the sulfate ion rule in conjunction with other rules to infer that the spill is sulfuric acid and likely to be from source s6-8 in building 3518. (If the spill source is not found at this location, the model continues the search, looking for an undocumented source.) This, of course, follows only if all other sources containing more than 10 gallons of sulfuric acid have already been eliminated from consideration by direct observation or other analyses.

6.2.5.4   Evaluation of ROSIE

The ROSIE model lacks sophisticated facilities for data-base structure and construction but does contain useful I/O and explanation routines. The model performs the drainage basin search, contains an interrupt mechanism to handle new data on arrival, and processes multiple goals.

The main strength of ROSIE is its English-like syntax. This permits the model-builder to write code that is entirely readable, even to those unfamiliar with programming. The English-like syntax also aids in program development, speeding the tasks of choosing a representation and writing explicit rules within that representation. The development of the ROSIE model was expedited by the ROSIE syntax.

Another strength of ROSIE is its powerful pattern-matching capability, which when used in conjunction with its ability to access the local operating system (and thus other languages or computer installations), provides an extremely useful mechanism for monitoring or controlling off-site computation. In the ROSIE model this ability provided the basis for the interrupt mechanism to accept new data immediately.

A major limitation of ROSIE is its lack of accessibility to its own rules and control mechanisms. There is no easy way to have a ROSIE model add or modify its own rules and no way to change its control structure to fit new problem domains. Another weakness is its lack of predefined AI problem-solving strategies. There is some support for automatic inference, but little support for interpretation, heuristic search, or any other specific AI techniques. Also, as an algorithmic notation, ROSIE is clearly not as succinct as terser programming languages such as LISP.

Another weakness of ROSIE is its inability to handle concurrent, asynchronous operations. Although the ROSIE model simulated asynchronous processing of multiple goals (as did many of the other spill models), it did this without the use of any special ROSIE features. ROSIE programs are relatively inflexible in the ordering of operations.

After the completion of the investigation of expert-system-building tools, the ROSIE model was redesigned and implemented to incorporate many of the ideas mentioned previously (See Fain 1982 for a detailed description of this model.) A trace of the operation of the redesigned ROSIE model is shown in Appendix 1.6. This model contains approximately seventy ROSIE rules. It should be noted that there were no time constraints on the development of this version of the model, as there were on the development of the other models. A diagram of the portion of the ORNL complex used as the data base for this model is given in Appendix 1.5.

6.2.6   RLL

6.2.6.1   Overview of RLL

RLL is a structured collection of tools to help the knowledge engineer construct, use, and modify expert systems (Greiner 1980). In one sense, RLL is itself an expert system—knowledgeable about facts concerning programming in general and its own subroutines in particular. This competency permits RLL to "understand" its internal inference procedures and provides the user with a means for modifying these programs to meet the task specifications. The RLL system contains a collection of useful constructs, including different types of slots, control mechanisms, inheritance schemes, and methods of associating appropriate actions to help access particular facts. RLL organizes these constructs into a library to help the user access them and provides tools to help him or her manipulate, modify, and combine them. For example, the knowledge engineer who needs a new type of slot or inheritance procedure can create one by performing a simple modification on a similar existing slot or procedure. Furthermore, with RLL, the user can create new modes of inference using the same types of steps a program like CASNET would use to incorporate a new fact about a patient or a new type of disease. RLL allows the specifics of the problem to guide the nature and implementation of the final system, rather than forcing the system into some particular formalism. Thus the knowledge engineer has great latitude in determining the type of control as well as the form of the data.

6.2.6.2   The Problem Considered

The RLL team concentrated on the crisis-management problem in general, with special emphasis on determining the source location. The members considered subproblems ranging from identifying the spill material to performing remediation tasks, such as notifying the authorities. The problem of dealing with the timeliness and ordering of subtasks was also considered. (For example: recording the name of a witness to a toxic acid spill should be deferred until after the witness has been warned against inhaling the fumes.) The RLL team made the standard assumptions to constrain the task except that it allowed intermittent pollutant flow.

6.2.6.3   Design of the Resulting System

The RLL model has two primary goals: to locate the spill source and to notify the appropriate agencies of spill violations. The model acts as a spill-crisis-management expert, coordinating many tasks, including directing the activities of the spill observers, sending out new teams, and notifying authorities.

The RLL team attempted to make the model as general and extensible as possible. Domain-specific knowledge in the model is carefully connected to appropriate generalizations. As a result the model could easily be extended beyond the oil spill problem to handle, for example, the problem of locating an escaped convict (by tracing the roads the convict could travel). The team chose to sacrifice "performing a flashy demo" for "representing things the right way" but had to sacrifice both to get even a simple demonstration program running in the short time available. A transcript of the RLL model being applied to the spill problem is given in Appendix 1.7. The model contains approximately 25 rules within 152 knowledge-base units.

The RLL model incorporates facts ranging from very general statements about spills to specific connections between manholes in the drainage basin. Also included are representations of events, such as "Oil spilling into a body of water causes a sheen." Both facts and events are represented as RLL "units" (constructs inherited from KRL and the UNITS package; see Bobrow and Winograd 1977 and Stefik 1978a,b). The following example shows how the model would represent the fact that "The types of oil stored in building 3504 are hydraulic and diesel":

```
B3504
    Isa:            (AnyBuilding)
    Description:    This refers to building 3504.
    HousesOils:     Hydraulic, Diesel

Hydraulic
    Isa:            (AnyOil)
    HousedIn:       B3504

Diesel
    Isa:            (AnyOil)
    HousedIn:       B3504
```

The model would represent the rule "If the spill is gushing, locate the source before trying to contain it," as illustrated below.

Rule#113
    Description: This is used to order spill tasks.
    IfPotentiallyRelevant: (And (Trying to order tasks)
                                (This is a spill problem))
    IfTrulyRelevant: ((Eq 'CurrentState' Gushing))
    ThenOrderTasks: (Put LocateSource before Containment)
    OnTask: OrderTasksForSpillProblem
    Specificity: 368

The specificity number provides one means for the RLL interpreter to choose between rules when more than one rule applies to a given context. Often, the more specific rule (the one with higher valued specificity) is chosen first.

Control of the model is based on an agenda containing an ordered list of tasks to be processed sequentially. Each task performs a particular job, such as determining the spill material, implementing countermeasures, or printing instructions to the user. Tasks may add new tasks to the agenda; for example, the implement-countermeasures task adds tasks for authority notification and for spill containment. Task execution involves collecting relevant rules, ordering them, and firing the list in sequence. The rules may produce new information, add additional rules to the current rule set, add new tasks to the current agenda, or suspend the current task to await necessary new data.

6.2.6.4   Evaluation of RLL

Like the OPS5 and HEARSAY models, the RLL model possesses only rudimentary facilities for input/output, data-base construction, and explanation. It does perform the drainage basin search and does process multiple goals in parallel. However, it does not contain an interrupt mechanism to handle new data as they arrive.

RLL's strengths derive primarily from its competence model of programming and its generality of data structures and algorithms. An RLL model can reason about its own operation and manipulate its own data structures in a general way. The ease with which the RLL team abstracted the model to handle a broader class of problems demonstrates this generality. The team also modified the RLL task interpreter to change the low-level control of the RLL model, demonstrating its modifiability and flexibility. RLL pays for its flexibility in terms of space rather than time (see Lenat 1979a,b; Greiner and Lenat 1980). To offset the additional space requirements, RLL uses a demand-paging algorithm that ignores INTERLISP's 256K storage maximum on the DEC System 20 (Smith 1980).

RLL's weaknesses stem from its immaturity. Its lack of a user-friendly front end proved a serious limitation in developing the RLL model. All code for the model had to be entered in a LISP-like format. A good front end coupled with a high-level representation language would have greatly facilitated the system development.

Another problem with RLL is its lack of constraints. The RLL team found that too much freedom forced them to spend considerable time deciding which was really the best representation and control structure. Some external constraints might have narrowed the search and helped them finish their program in the allotted three days. This, of course, would be much less of a problem with a model developed over a longer period of time.

A third problem is RLL's current "ignorance." By design, it will continuously incorporate new facts about control structures, forms of representation, and modes of inheritance, as it encounters new applications. When the RLL spill model was built, however, RLL had never encountered a search problem like that encountered in spill-crisis management; all its previous work had been directed toward self-directed searches of discovery (Lenat 1977; Davis and Lenat 1980a). RLL knew about tasks like finding interesting generalizations of primes, but not about tasks like finding the source of a spill.

6.2.7   HEARSAY-III

6.2.7.1   Overview of HEARSAY-III

HEARSAY-III is a domain-independent programming facility for developing prototype expert systems in a chosen domain (Balzer, Erman, and London 1980; Erman, London, and Fickas 1981). It was designed to assist the user in developing methods for representing and applying diverse sources of knowledge to a chosen problem area. The HEARSAY-III architecture evolved from earlier work on speech-understanding systems (Lesser and Erman 1977; Erman et al. 1980), particularly the concepts of a blackboard structure for knowledge sources (KSs) and opportunistic scheduling. In HEARSAY-III the blackboard is used by the prototype expert system to store and coordinate information about the domain, partial solutions, and current activities. The blackboard is subdivided into two major components: the domain blackboard for competence reasoning and the scheduling blackboard for performance reasoning. KSs in HEARSAY-III are complex pattern-directed modules, production rules containing most of the domain-specific knowledge for a particular application. A KS becomes eligible for execution when its triggering pattern is matched by information on the blackboard. Execution usually results in the modification of blackboard information. The problem of determining which triggered KS should be executed next is called the scheduling problem. Since scheduling can become quite complicated, special scheduling KSs are used in conjunction with the scheduling blackboard to facilitate the selection of triggered domain KSs.

6.2.7.2   The Problem Considered

The HEARSAY team focused on building a general crisis-management model for the spill domain. The members addressed the problems of spill identification, source location, notification, countermeasures, and minimization of expended resources. The team also addressed the high-level problems of incorporating large amounts of diverse knowledge and managing competing goals whose relative priorities vary as new information is acquired.

   To constrain the task, the basic assumptions standard for most of the teams were made plus the additional assumption that an estimate of pollutant flow rate is available for use by the model.

6.2.7.3   Design of the Resulting System

The HEARSAY model has two major goals: to locate the spill source and to identify the spill material. Factors used to direct the search through the drainage basin included likely sources of the material (constrained by current information, about estimated volume for instance) and the desirability and cost of making the individual observations. The HEARSAY team specified and partially coded knowledge sources for evaluating drainage basin observation points, choosing the next observation point to examine, and reevaluating the worth of the observation points.

   The HEARSAY model is a collection of KSs or complex pattern-directed modules, one of which can execute when its triggering pattern matches the blackboard information. The three major KSs in the model are the observation-request evaluator, the observation-request assigner, and the observation-request reevaluator.

   The observation-request evaluator triggers on the initial detection of a pollutant and associates with each manhole an indication of the desirability of making an observation at that location. It takes into account likely spill sources and information gain. As new information becomes available, the observation-request evaluator can retrigger and recalculate desirabilities.

   The observation-request assigner initially triggers when an observer is chosen to backtrack to the source. It assigns him the task of going to a new location and making an observation there. The choice of next location is based on the amount of information to be gained (as calculated by the observation-request evaluator), transit time, and ease of access. This KS retriggers when the observer finishes his observation. It may also retrigger if its inputs (such as desirability or cost) change; in such cases, it may reassign the observer before the observer's current assignment is finished.

The observation-request reevaluator triggers upon completion of an observation, including an unsolicited one. It uses the results of the observation to reevaluate the desirability of observation for all locations in the basin. This KS needs to execute before the observation-request assigner to minimize its retriggering. Such prioritization of KSs is handled by KSs containing scheduling rules.

6.2.7.4   Evaluation of HEARSAY-III

Like the OPS5 model, the HEARSAY model lacks sophisticated facilities for I/O, data-base construction, and explanation. However, the model does contain facilities for performing the drainage basin search, for interrupting processing to handle new data as they arrive, and for processing multiple goals in parallel.

The major strength of HEARSAY-III is its general-purpose control structure, which supports interaction among numerous, diverse sources of knowledge and competing subproblems. This facilitates both the design of asynchronous processing of information requests and the design of control structures for handling multiple goals in the HEARSAY model. Also, HEARSAY-III provides great flexibility in choosing KS granularity; this allows grouping the knowledge into chunks that seem intuitively natural.

Another strength of HEARSAY-III, not obvious from the HEARSAY model, is the ease with which performance knowledge can be separated from competence knowledge. This permits the independent development of the two types of knowledge and expedites the implementation of differing modes of system interaction (having the system control the crisis management; advising a human manager).

A major weakness of HEARSAY-III is its lack of an external, high-level representation language for describing the domain model. HEARSAY-III currently provides for general (LISP-ish) ways of representing knowledge. A representation language would have assisted the HEARSAY team in expressing taxonomic relations and static domain information, such as the drainage basin map, and generally would have led to a more rapid development of the model.

As a result of designing their model, the HEARSAY team became aware of the potential utility of relaxing the requirement that all KS actions in HEARSAY-III be written in LISP. For example, it would be useful if KS actions could also be written as production systems adapted to allow HEARSAY-III blackboard interaction. This higher level representation would speed development. The team also noted that the granularity usually chosen for HEARSAY-III knowledge sources—larger than rules in most production systems but smaller than, for example, all of MYCIN—seemed well matched to the spill-management task. This granularity is not typical of most expert system applications.

6.2.8   AGE

6.2.8.1   Overview of AGE

The AGE (Attempt to GEneralize) system is a tool for helping knowledge engineers design, build, and test different frameworks for expert systems (Nii and Aiello 1979). It provides an environment in which different representational and control techniques can be explored and developed. For example, with AGE a user can build and test an expert system for some particular application, using a KAS-like framework. The user can then develop the same system within an EMYCIN-like framework to compare the two approaches.

AGE provides the user with two types of entities for constructing expert systems: components and frameworks. A component is a collection of routines that supports basic AI mechanisms; the production-rule component is composed of a rule interpreter and a collection of strategies for rule selection and execution. These components can be modified by the user if the need arises.

A framework is a predefined configuration of components. These can aid users who are not experienced enough to combine the components themselves. Two examples are the back-chaining framework and the blackboard framework. The back-chaining framework uses production rules and goal-directed, backward chaining to complete an inference. It could be used as the basis for constructing a program with an EMYCIN flavor. The blackboard framework uses a blackboard and knowledge sources to create a system that can form hypotheses on the blackboard through mutual cooperation of the knowledge sources. It could be used to develop HEARSAY-like expert systems.

6.2.8.2   The Problem Considered

The AGE team focused on two aspects of the spill problem: information management and on-scene coordination. The former included the collection, organization, and maintenance of information, while the latter included advising the on-scene coordinator of actions to take and hazards to avoid. Because of the limited time available for design and development, the AGE team ignored many aspects of the spill problem, including resource allocation, representation of static knowledge (the drainage basin and inventories), natural language recognition, and many others. The AGE team made the usual basic assumptions to constrain the task.

6.2.8.3   Design of the Resulting System

The AGE model has two primary goals: to recommend spill notification and containment procedures and to locate the spill source. The model uses interacting sources of knowledge to search for the spill source and issue warnings, containment suggestions, and notification directives. It performs backtracking through the drainage basin by directing an observer through it, suggesting the next checkpoints, and analyzing the observer's findings. The model determines missing information by creating expectations and then requesting information that could satisfy those expectations. When new, unexpected information becomes available, the model reassesses its expectations, possibly reordering goal priorities.

The model represents much of the static domain knowledge in LISP property lists. Thus the information "There is a storage tank outside building 3503 with a dike around it" would take the following form:

```
STORAGE-TANK10:   (MEMB/OF PERMANENT-STORAGE-TANK
                   LOCATION (OUTSIDE B3503)
                   TYPE PERMANENT
                   CONTAINMENT DIKED)
```

Procedural domain knowledge is represented in sets of production rules, or knowledge sources (KSs). The knowledge that "Oil spilling into water causes a sheen" would be represented as follows:

```
If      ($VALUE 'DISCOVERER DESCRIPTION LATEST) = 'SHEEN
then    (PROPOSE ch.type MODIFY
                  hypo-element 'DISCOVERER
                  attribute-value (INITIAL-ID 'OIL)
                  support DISCOVERY
                  event.type OA3
                  comment If a sheen is observed,
                            then oil may have been spilled)
```

Control in the AGE model is handled by a blackboard framework with a standard event-driven strategy and first-in, first-out event selection method. Thus the model processes the least recent events first. Once an event (data or hypotheses on the blackboard) is selected for processing, the model executes KSs whose preconditions match the event, causing new events to be placed on the blackboard.

6.2.8.4   Evaluation of AGE

The AGE model lacks useful facilities for I/O, data-base construction, and explanation. It does contain facilities for performing the drainage basin search and for processing multiple goals in parallel. It does not, however, address the problem of providing an interrupt mechanism to handle new data as they arrive.

A major strength of AGE is the ease with which the programmer can apply the general control frameworks supplied by the system. Currently AGE contains two such frameworks, the blackboard framework and the back-chaining framework. If the domain fits one of these, AGE can easily provide the control structure for the user's system. The blackboard framework greatly facilitated the processing of multiple goals in the AGE model.

Another strength of AGE is its flexibility of representation. AGE clearly differentiates between control information, procedural domain information, static domain information, and the evolving solution. Many of the other tools, on the other hand, seem to encourage a blurring of the distinctions between these different types of information.

AGE also contains useful interface, value-marking, and history-recording facilities. The interface facility helps the user design and specify a system. The marking facility permits the user to add time markers or other tags to values added to the hypothesis structure. The marking and recording facilities were particularly useful in the AGE model for generating spill reports and complying with time-dependent government regulations.

A major weakness of AGE is its inability to handle problems requiring a control structure incompatible with its built-in frameworks. Another weakness is its inability to track or explain actions on the right-hand side of rules that do not make changes to the blackboard. These side effects cannot be traced or explained later by AGE because it has no record of them.

6.3   Comparing the Case Studies

The eight knowledge-engineering applications can be compared in many different dimensions. Here we compare them in three basic areas: problem scope, program organization and structure, and representation of knowledge.

6.3.1   Problem Scope

All of the spill models except KAS focused primarily on the problem of locating the spill source. The EMYCIN, EXPERT, RLL, and AGE models were geared toward simple searches of the drainage basin, following paths of contamination back to the source. The OPS5, ROSIE, and HEARSAY-III models performed more sophisticated searches, using inventory information and knowledge about the spill material characteristics to restrict the search dynamically to plausible areas of the drainage system. The HEARSAY-III model also used desirability and cost to help decide where in the basin to search next. By contrast, the KAS model focused on the problem of determining the best strategy to use in searching for the spill source, rather than actually searching for the source. Four strategies were considered, one being the drainage basin backtracking that the other efforts applied.

Some models provided other helpful information for the user; for example, the EMYCIN model provided containment recommendations, and the KAS model provided warnings to the user concerning the handling of the spill material. The EXPERT and RLL models provided containment and notification recommendations. The AGE model provided warnings, containment, and notification recommendations. The OPS5, ROSIE, and HEARSAY-III models focused on spill location and generally ignored other aspects of the problem, such as warnings and recommendations.

6.3.2   Program Organization and Structure

In each of the eight knowledge-engineering applications, the program organization was strongly influenced by the characteristics of the tool used to develop it. Five of the tools (EMYCIN, KAS, EXPERT, OPS5, and ROSIE) are variations of conventional rule-based systems and thus provide the IF—THEN rule as a basic building block. Of these, EMYCIN, KAS, and EXPERT are special-purpose diagnostic systems with relatively rigid control structures (particularly in the case of EMYCIN) but fairly sophisticated interaction and explanation facilities. Thus the models developed using these tools had difficulty performing even a simple tree search of the drainage basin but provided impressive and useful ways to interact with the user, including sophisticated techniques for explaining how conclusions were reached. The EMYCIN model, with its highly constrained backward-chaining control structure, used a call to a LISP function to perform the drainage basin search, while the less restrictive EXPERT used a call to a FORTRAN function to perform this task. KAS avoided the tree search by choosing as its goal the determination of the best strategy to use for locating the spill. These three models also used probabilistic inference, since EMYCIN, KAS, and EXPERT provided facilities for assigning and combining certainty factors.

The representational difficulties encountered by the EMYCIN, KAS, and EXPERT teams stem from the paucity of available control schemes. All three models followed rigid control formats provided by their chosen tool, each being standard production-system control paradigms (forward or backward chaining). This type of control, combined with the rules designed for diagnosis, resulted in too little flexibility to handle the search, asynchronous I/O, and parallel-goal-processing tasks.

The two remaining conventional rule-based tools, OPS5 and ROSIE, are general-purpose programming systems that provide greater flexibility of control and representation than do EMYCIN, KAS, or EXPERT. These two tools are quite different from each other. ROSIE, with its English-like syntax, greatly facilitates the representation problem, compared to OPS5 with its LISP-like syntax. On the other hand OPS5 provides a greater flexibility of control than does ROSIE, and it facilitates the dynamic modification of rules. The models developed in OPS5 and ROSIE concentrated almost exclusively on the problem of locating the spill source, using sophisticated search heuristics to eliminate areas of the drainage basin that were unlikely to contain the source. Both models contained a significant amount of code dealing with I/O, something the EMYCIN, KAS, and EXPERT models did not require. The OPS5 interaction with the user was conventional (the OPS5 team could have incorporated asynchronous I/O into the model in a manner similar to the ROSIE scheme if they had had more time), while the ROSIE model simulated asynchronous processing of requests and reports. It did this by collecting status reports from the observers in the field and requests for information by subroutines in the program. Periodically the requests would be presented to the user and new reports would be processed, without requiring that the requests be answered or the reports made at any specific time. Both models easily handled the parallel (actually breadth-first) processing of goals, the OPS5 model by using a goal-interrupt mechanism, and the ROSIE model by having rulesets communicate via internal status reports sent to a global data base.

The other three tools are general-purpose systems for experimenting with expert system architecture. HEARSAY-III provides a blackboard framework with cooperating knowledge sources as the basic design paradigm, while AGE provides both a blackboard and a backward-chaining paradigm. By contrast, RLL provides a unit representation for both facts and rules. All three of these tools have great flexibility with regard to control of rule processing and can use certain of their rules to control and direct the application of the other rules. RLL carries this idea one step further, containing general knowledge about its own operation. However, all three lack a supportive programming environment. They could make good use of a high-level representation language for describing procedural knowledge and built-in mechanisms for facilitating I/O and explanation.

Both the HEARSAY-III and AGE models were organized as collections of KSs communicating via a blackboard mechanism. These KSs were essentially LISP functions for backtracking through the drainage basin, generating containment recommendations, and notifying appropriate agencies. The RLL model was organized as a collection of units representing both static and procedural knowledge for drainage basin backtracking and agency notification. The units representing procedural knowledge contained slots for the IF and THEN portions of the rules. Pieces of LISP code filled these slots, defining the rule conditions and actions. The RLL model differed from the other models in that its solution to the spill problem was represented in a rather abstract way in order to be applicable to a more general class of problems of this type. The unit formalism and agenda control mechanisms of RLL facilitated the development of this more general knowledge.

The RLL, HEARSAY-III, and AGE models had no trouble providing for drainage basin search and parallel goal processing. Only the HEARSAY-III model provided an asynchronous interrupt facility, although it could just as easily have been incorporated into the RLL and AGE models via rules or KSs that trigger upon receipt of unsolicited messages or reports.

The knowledge representation level or granularity of the rules in the various models was fairly constant in all except OPS5 and RLL. The OPS5 model's rules were somewhat finer grained than those of the other models because of the attention paid to defining and controlling the goal-selection mechanism. The RLL model's rules were also finer grained than those of other models due to the specific control of the agenda mechanism in the rules and the attempt at generality that led to a rather precise taxonomy of objects and events.

6.3.3   Knowledge Representation

The methods for representing knowledge in the eight systems vary greatly. This variation will now be illustrated by representing the same three pieces of knowledge in each system. The first piece is clearly static, descriptive knowledge, while the third is clearly procedural. The second lies somewhere between the others on the spectrum from static to procedural.

6.3.3.1   Statement 1: M6-2 Feeds into M6-1

This first piece of knowledge is static knowledge that represents a portion of the drainage network in the spill problem. It says that pipe M6-2 feeds into pipe M6-1 in the network, a fact that would be used to help define the topology of the drainage network so that it could be searched.

EMYCIN representation. There is no natural way to represent this knowledge directly in the EMYCIN formalism, but it could be represented using LISP property lists, as in

M6-2: ([property] FEEDS.INTO (value) M6-1).

KAS representation. The most natural way to represent this in KAS is in the form of a semantic net, although KAS was not intended for search problems and would have difficulty searching the drainage system represented this way:

        KIND-OF   M6-1   PIPE
        KIND-OF   M6-2   PIPE
        FEEDS-INTO   M6-2   M6-1

EXPERT representation. Like EMYCIN and KAS, EXPERT was not intended for search problems and cannot handle this knowledge in a natural way. In the EXPERT model, this knowledge was represented in a FORTRAN array, with rows representing manholes and columns representing the number and names of manholes feeding into the manhole a row represents.

OPS-5 representation. The drainage network is represented as a collection of data elements, one element for each link in the network. The element for this link is

(FLOW-SEGMENT ^FROM M6-2 ^TO M6-1).

ROSIE representation. The drainage network can be represented quite simply in ROSIE as a series of assertions of the form:

        Assert M6-2 does feed into M6-1.
        Assert each of M6-1 and M6-2 is a pipe.

Then the drainage network can be searched easily by recursive functions. For example, given an expanded version of the above network, the following ROSIE generator returns all pipes in the network that directly or indirectly lead to the given pipe, including the given pipe:

> To generate descendant of given-pipe:
> Produce the given-pipe
> and produce every descendant of
> (every pipe that does feed into the given-pipe).
> End.

One call to this generator might be "Display every descendant of M6-1."

RLL representation. This representation is handled within the units framework, using units that represent M6-1, M6-2, the "feeds into" relation, and the set of all the manholes:

M6-2
    Isa: (AnyManhole)
    FeedsInto: (M6-1)

M6-1
    Isa: (AnyManhole)
    FeedsFrom: (M6-2)

AnyManhole
    Examples: (M6-1, M6-2)
    Description: The class of all manholes.

FeedsInto
    Isa: (AnySlot)
    Description: This slot maps from manholes to manholes.
    Inverse: FeedsFrom
    Definition: [Lisp code that indicates how to deduce the value of the FeedsInto slot of some manhole, i.e., the manhole it maps into.]

HEARSAY-III representation. The drainage system is represented as a network of objects of the types manhole, outfall, and so on, and each of these types is a subtype of the type drainage-node. Each drainage-node has a unique "downhill" drainage-node, represented by the HEARSAY role "pipe." Thus the connection would be represented as

$$(PIPE\ M6\text{-}2\ M6\text{-}1).$$

AGE representation. Since AGE is closely integrated with LISP, the normal way to represent this static information would be as LISP property lists. For example,

M6-2: (NEXTDOWNSTREAM M6-1 NEXTUPSTREAM M6-3).

6.3.3.2 Statement 2: All Permanent Storage Tanks Are Diked

This knowledge, which can be represented either statically or procedurally, means that all the permanent storage tanks have walls or ditches to ensure that spills will be contained.

EMYCIN representation. This knowledge is difficult to represent in EMYCIN. If it means that spills at permanent storage tanks are initially contained, it would be represented implicitly in EMYCIN via rules written for handling on-site detection.

KAS Representation. The most natural way to represent this in KAS is through a taxonomy of containers that includes "diked" and "non-diked." For example,

```
category CONTAINERS
    from        MATERIALS
    subcats     DIKED-CONTAINERS  NON-DIKED-CONTAINERS
category DIKED-CONTAINERS
    from        CONTAINERS
    subcats     PERMANENT-STORAGE-TANKS
category PERMANENT-STORAGE-TANKS
    from        DIKED-CONTAINERS
```

EXPERT representation. The natural way to represent this in EXPERT is through a rule that states: "If it is true that the type of storage tank is permanent, conclude it is diked with certainty 1." This would be represented as:

```
**findings
PERM      The type of storage tank is permanent.

**hypotheses
DIKED      The storage tank is diked.

**rules
f(perm, t) → h(diked, 1.).
```

OPS5 representation. As in EXPERT, the natural way to represent this information in OPS5 is procedurally. If the rule is to be used to infer the type of countermeasure taken at a spill location, it could have the form:

```
(P DEDUCE-COUNTER-MEASURES
    GOAL ^STATUS ACTIVE ^NAME DEDUCE-COUNTER-MEASURES)
(SOURCE ^KIND PERMANENT-STORAGE-TANK ^LOCATION <AT>)
    – (COUNTER-MEASURE ^LOCATION <AT> ^KIND DIKE)
```

$\rightarrow$
(MAKE COUNTER-MEASURE ^LOCATION <AT> ^KIND DIKE))

ROSIE representation. In ROSIE, the "any" construct would be used to assert that all currently defined permanent storage tanks and all permanent storage tanks defined at some later date are diked:

Assert any permanent storage_tank is diked.

RLL representation. One way to represent this in RLL involves two units: AnyStorageTank and a universal variable (called x):

AnyPermanentStorageTank
    Description   The class of all permanent storage tanks.
    UnivElements: (x)
X
    UnivIsa: (AnyPermanentStorageTank)
    MyDefiningSlots: (UnivIsa TimeOfStorage)
    MyAssertionalSlots: (Diked?)
    Description: The facts stored here are true for all
                      permanent storage tanks.
    TimeOfStorage: Permanent
    Diked?:   T

Note that the foregoing unit shows only what the user would have to tell RLL. The system can now compute the value for many additional slots, as needed. The various slots that store executable LISP code (corresponding to these declarations) are computed in this way.

HEARSAY-III representation. As in AGE and OPS5, this knowledge can be represented procedurally in HEARSAY in an inference rule of the form:

(PERMANENT StorageTank) $\rightarrow$ (DIKED StorageTank).

The information could also be represented statically by defining types DikedObject, StorageTank, and PermanentStorageTank and making PermanentStorageTank a subtype of both StorageTank and DikedObject.

AGE representation. In AGE, as in RLL, the most natural way to represent this information is via the unit construct:

PERMANENT-STORAGE-TANK
    TYPE—(role S datatype ATOM value PERMANENT)
    CONTAINMENT—(role S datatype ATOM value DIKED)
    MEMBERS—(STORAGE-TANK10 ...)
    LOCATION—(role U datatype PAIR)

6.3.3.3   Statement 3: If the Chemical Is HF, Tell the Observer Not To Breathe It

This knowledge can be represented procedurally and is an important warning that should be given as soon as the chemical is identified.

EMYCIN representation. This rule could have the form:

If   1) The spilled substance is HF

then   It is definite (1.0) that the following is one of the recommended emergency procedures: Since the spill substance is HF—do NOT breathe it!

The actual representation in EMYCIN is as follows:

```
RULE003
    PREMISE:              (SAME CNTXT SUBSTANCE HF)
    ACTION:               (CONCLUDETEXT CNTXT WARNING (TEXT DANGER))
SUBSTANCE
    ASKFIRST:             T
    EXPECT:               (OIL HF OTHER)
    TRANS:                (the spilled substance)
    PROMPT:               (Is the spilled substance Oil, HF or Other?)
    USED-BY               (Rules 12 3)
WARNING
    MULTIVALUED:          T
    TRANS:                (the recommended emergency procedures)
    LEGALVALS:            TEXT
DANGER
    TRANS:                (Since the spill substance is HF—Do NOT breathe it!)
```

KAS representation. This knowledge would most naturally be represented in KAS as a procedure ("demon") attached to an antecedent or consequent identifying the chemical as HF:

Antecedent: KIND-OF E2 POLLUTANT
                KIND-OF E2 HF

Consequent: DANGEROUS E2
                DEMONS ("This substance is very dangerous, do not breathe it.")

EXPERT representation. A finding can be used to describe the information that the spill is HF, while a hypothesis describes the advice about informing the user of the spill's danger:

```
**findings
*multiple-choice
Type of spill material:
OIL        The material is oil.
HF         The material is HF.

**hypotheses
NBRTH      Inform the observer not to breathe the material.

**rules
f(hf,t) → h(nbrth, 1.)
```

OPS5 Representation. Since it is important that warnings of this kind be generated immediately after the information becomes available, a rule is used that can fire regardless of the current goal of the system:

```
(P ISSUE-WARNING-HF
   (GOAL ^STATUS ACTIVE ^ID <ID>)
   (MATERIAL ^NAME HF)
   -(GOAL ^NAME WARN-OF-HAZARDOUS-SUBSTANCE)
   →
   (MODIFY 1 ^STATUS PENDING)
   (MAKE GOAL ^ID (GINT) ^STATUS ACTIVE ^PARENT-ID <ID>
              ^NAME WARN-OF-HAZARDOUS-SUBSTANCE))

(P WARN-OF-HAZARDOUS-SUBSTANCE
  (GOAL ^STATUS ACTIVE ^NAME WARN-OF-HAZARDOUS-SUBSTANCE)
  (MATERIAL ^NAME <MAT>)
       →
       (WRITE (CRLF) The material has been determined to be <MAT>)
       (WRITE (CRLF) Warn everyone in the area of the spill not
                 to breathe it))
```

ROSIE representation. The information is coded in an event-driven ROSIE ruleset (demon) that is activated when a new assertion indicates that the chemical is HF:

```
Before asserting chemical is HF:
Send {"Warning—do not breathe the spill material!", return}.
End.
```

RLL representation. The information can be represented as an RLL rule, as follows:

```
Rule#332
    Isa:                (AnyRule)
    IfTrulyRelevant:    ((EQ 'Chemical HF))
    ThenTellUser:       "Do not breathe the chemical!!"
    Priority:           High
    OnTask:             ImminentDanger
```

HEARSAY-III representation. This information could be represented by a combination of two knowledge sources that together handle more general cases. OHMTADS-Lookup is a KS that triggers on the pollutant being identified. It looks up the pollutant in OHMTADS and puts its important characteristics on the blackboard.

```
(declare-KS OHMTADS-Lookup (Material Observation)
    Trigger:    (MATERIAL Observation Material)
    Action:     (for each Attribute in (LOOKUP OHMTADS Material)
                    do (AUGMENT Material CHEMICAL-ATTRIBUTE Attribute)))
```

Caustic-Volatile, the other KS, triggers on the discovery of a caustic and volatile pollutant. It runs at very high priority and sends an appropriate warning to the user.

```
(declare-KS Warn-Caustic-Volatile (Material Observation Observer)
    Trigger:        (AND (MATERIAL Observation Material)
                         (CHEMICAL-ATTRIBUTE Material CAUSTIC)
                         (CHEMICAL-ATTRIBUTE Material VOLATILE)
                         (OBSERVER Observation Observer))

    Sched-level:    Emergency-Level
    Action:         (COMMUNICATE Observer
                     "Warning:" Material
                     " is caustic and volatile—DON'T BREATHE IT!"))
```

AGE representation. This rule would be invoked during the initial dialogue with the observer:

```
If      ($VALUE 'MATERIAL-ID CHEMICAL LATEST) = 'HF
        OR
        ($VALUE 'DISCOVERER INITIAL-ID LATEST) = 'HF
then    (PRINT   pr.type PRINTOUT
                 output "*** DO NOT BREATHE SPILL MATERIAL! ***"
                 file TTY:)
```

6.3.3.4   Comparing the Knowledge-Representation
Methods

The representations of these three pieces of knowledge in the eight systems provide certain insights into the structure and usefulness of the languages. The first piece of knowledge, defining a connection in the drainage network, was particularly interesting. The three systems with the specialized representation and control (EMYCIN, KAS, and EXPERT) essentially could not represent the connections in the drainage system in such a way that the network could be searched. Clearly, one must take great care when using these systems to ensure that the problem does indeed match the diagnostic paradigm required by the language. The OPS5, HEARSAY-III, and ROSIE representations of the drainage network were very similar to one another: they were simple and straightforward, and they facilitated network search. The RLL and AGE representations were also straightforward but somewhat more complex, since they both depended on LISP code and representations to define network access.

The second piece of knowledge, stating that permanent storage tanks are diked, was easier than the first piece of knowledge for the more specialized systems to handle. EMYCIN, however, could not represent it in any natural way. In KAS, it had to be represented through a taxonomy of containers, which implied that this was a definition rather than a current state. Such a taxonomy would be awkward to change if it were later discovered that some permanent storage tanks were not diked. In EXPERT, OPS5, ROSIE, and HEARSAY-III, the representation was procedural and seemed fairly natural and useful. RLL and AGE used a static representation via units, which seemed useful although overly complex in RLL.

The third piece of knowledge, involving the warning to the observer, was clearly procedural and was the easiest for all systems to handle. In all the systems it was represented as an IF-THEN rule whose action was the warning concerning the dangerous spill substance. In ROSIE and HEARSAY-III, the representation was particularly simple, since both have trigger mechanisms for responding immediately to newly asserted data.

In all three of the representation examples, the ROSIE language seemed to capture the intended meaning of the given pieces of knowledge most easily. This was due in part to the flexibility of expression inherent in ROSIE due to its natural language syntax. The examples show the ROSIE code to be much easier to read and understand than the code of the other seven systems. ROSIE's flexibility of expression also appears to make it somewhat easier to write and debug its code than code in the other systems.

6.4 Lessons from the Investigation

The question of what has been learned from this investigation of eight tools for building an expert system will be answered with a discussion of the issues involved in choosing or designing such a tool.

6.4.1   Choosing a Tool Appropriate for the Problem

In choosing an appropriate tool, generality, testing, accessibility, development speed, and tool features must be considered. The issue of generality is important. The more general the control and representation, the more time-consuming and difficult is the representation of any particular chunk of knowledge because of excessive degrees of freedom. Thus a tool for knowledge-engineering applications should be as specialized as possible while still being appropriate for the problem area. A tool that provides more generality than is needed will hinder the user by inefficiency and loss of power. By contrast, the more rigid and constrained the control and representation, the easier it is to represent knowledge—if that knowledge can be represented at all within the limited representation paradigm.

The issue of testing the appropriateness of the tool should not be ignored. If possible, the tool should be tested early by building a small prototype system. Although the development of an expert system typically requires many months of effort, it may be possible to test the effectiveness of a proposed tool through an intensive week-long interaction with experts who are well prepared, with well-organized written material describing the problem. This approach worked well for the eight tools discussed in this chapter.

The issue of accessibility must likewise not be overlooked when choosing a tool appropriate for the problem. If possible, the tool should be currently maintained by the developer and already proven robust by other users. An old tool, no longer supported by the developer, may be difficult to get running initially and could have basic system bugs that must be corrected by the user. Even worse, a tool that is still under development may lack documentation and may contain numerous system bugs. When the developer corrects these bugs, the language itself may change radically, hindering development of the expert system.

Development speed often dominates other considerations during building of an expert system. If development speed is critical, the knowledge engineering tool should have built-in explanation and interaction facilities. They will not only speed the expert system development but also result in a more intelligible system.

One of the most difficult aspects of choosing an appropriate tool for a knowledge-engineering application is matching the problem characteristics to the tool features. The features needed in the tool depend strongly upon three things: the characteristics of the problem domain, the characteristics of the likely approach to solving the problem, and the desired characteristics of the expert system to be built. Problem characteristics include the size of the search space; the form of the data (continuous, time-varying, uncertain, inconsistent, containing errors); and the structure of the problem (incomplete knowledge, interacting subproblems, evaluator for partial solutions, fixed partitioning of subproblems). Solution characteristics include the type of search (exhaustive, generate-and-test, dependency-directed backtracking); the representation of knowledge (monotonic data base, abstracted problem space, multiple contexts); and the form of the control (opportunistic scheduling, top-down refinement, parallel processing of subproblems). Characteristics of an expert system include the type of users (trained, inexperienced, skeptical) and the method of extending the system (user modification, system builder modification, self-modification).

To illustrate the process of choosing a tool for a particular application, consider a hypothetical problem whose important characteristics are a large search space, a fallible evaluator for partial solutions, and time-varying data. Assume that the resulting expert system is to be extended by the users. The large search space rules out blind exhaustive search as a solution characteristic; however, the partial-solution evaluator permits pruning via generate-and-test. The fact that the evaluator is fallible suggests the possibility of discarding a good solution from weak early evidence; thus characteristics for reasonable solution might include heterogeneous abstraction spaces, opportunistic scheduling, and multiple models. Time-varying data suggest the need for multiple contexts to handle the problem of referencing the same data at different time intervals.

Now the task is to decide which tool features best support the characteristics of solution and system. In this case the use of a blackboard mechanism with diverse knowledge sources supports generate-and-test, abstraction spaces, opportunistic scheduling, and multiple models. The use of multiple data bases supports the need for multiple contexts, and the use of a readable, manageable, high-level representation language supports the need for extension of the expert system by the user. Thus an appropriate tool for this task would need readability, manageability, multiple data bases, and a blackboard mechanism with diverse knowledge sources.

In summary, the maxims suggested for choosing an appropriate tool are the following:

- Do not pick a tool with more generality than you need.
- Test your tool early by building a small prototype system.
- Choose a tool that is maintained by the developer.
- Choose a tool with explanation/interaction facilities when development speed is critical.
- Use the problem characteristics to determine the tool features needed.

6.4.2   Designing a Tool for Building Expert Systems

The design of a tool for building expert systems involves many considerations, including issues of generality, completeness, language features, data-base structure, and control methods. These issues are discussed briefly below.

One difficult problem is that of deciding on the generality and completeness of the tool. The generality depends on the range of problem domains for which the tool is appropriate. Naturally expert system tool builders want to develop general-purpose tools that will be applicable to a wide range of problems, but the trade-off here is efficiency of design and development versus efficiency and power of application. Resource limitations prohibit fashioning tools tailored to each application, so the approach often followed is to choose the target class of problems and then incorporate only enough generality to cover that class.

The degree of completeness needed depends on the number and importance of the features embodied in the tool (explanation facility, certainty factors). This examination has shown that the most specialized tools (EMYCIN, KAS, and EXPERT) provided the largest number of special support features. This is due in part to the difficulty of implementing many of the desired expert-systems-building features within the context of a generally applicable tool. Specialization also led to more power and efficiency within the restricted application domain.

Certain features all tools must have. One is a high-level representation language for expressing procedural knowledge. The lack of such a language greatly slows down the development process and makes it difficult for the system to be extended by the users. The language should be both readable and manageable; application domain experts should be able to read and understand the rules with little or no previous training, and computer experts should be able to modify or augment the rules with only modest training. And the task of mapping the "raw knowledge" supplied by the expert into the representation language should be simple enough to be performed by a domain expert trained in the use of the language. One way to provide this manageability is to make the syntax of the representation language very close to the syntax of the raw knowledge.

Other very useful, although not indispensable, features to incorporate into tools are facilities for explanation, user-interface interactions, and local operating system accessibility. Built-in explanation and interaction facilities speed prototype system development and facilitate initial testing and evaluation. The design of the tool, however, should not preclude new developments or extension of these facilities. One of the most important (and least publicized) lessons learned from the development of RITA (Anderson and Gillogly 1976a,b) and ROSIE was the usefulness of interaction with the external computer environment. Such interaction extends the power and generality of the expert system, since it enables the system to control other jobs in parallel, accessing them like subroutines. For example, the expert system can perform complex mathematical calculations in FORTRAN or access external data bases via computer nets.

Another issue to consider in the design of a tool for building an expert system is the structure of the data base. The way the tool permits or encourages static knowledge to be represented is extremely important. If it is too restrictive, even simple problems will be unsolvable. If it provides too little guidance (too much freedom), complex problems will seem overly complex. Thus the basic data-representation scheme should be made as general as possible while keeping the representation task reasonably easy (constrained) for the target problems.

A final issue to consider in the design of an expert-system-building tool is the control structure. The power, generality, and accessibility of the control mechanism are important aspects of an expert system language. The form of the control shapes and restricts the representation of procedural knowledge in the system. For example, the use of iteration, recursion, backward-chaining, forward-chaining, and hierarchies (nested subroutine calls) affects decisions regarding the representation of procedural knowledge. Special-purpose systems that have efficient but restrictive inference methods (like EMYCIN, KAS, and EXPERT) have sacrificed generality to gain efficiency. If generality is more important than efficiency, the tool should have an accessible control mechanism that can be augmented by the expert system's builder.

A rigid, constrained control paradigm simplifies and expedites the development of interaction and explanation facilities in an expert system. It also facilitates the incremental extension of the system, providing a higher degree of modularity than would be present with a more general control paradigm. Rigid control simplifies predicting the effect of changes in procedural knowledge and thus makes it easier for the system to decide how to modify itself to achieve some desired goal. Thus if the target problems require learning, self-modification, or sophisticated explanation, a somewhat constrained control paradigm is appropriate.

The maxims suggested for designing tools for building expert systems are as follows:

- Provide a high-level representation language.
- Provide built-in explanation and interaction facilities.
- Provide local operating system accessibility.
- Provide a basic data representation scheme that is as general as possible.
- Provide an accessible control mechanism if generality is more important than efficiency.
- Provide a constrained control mechanism if learning, self-modification, or sophisticated explanation is required.

QUESTIONS

1. Which of the assumptions made by the knowledge-engineering teams seemed most tenuous? What changes in approach would have been necessitated by more appropriate assumptions?
2. Why didn't the tools used help much in representing knowledge or techniques in backtracking the spill to its source? What kind of special tool would help?
3. Identify the important differences among the diagnostic system tools. Why are the tools different?
4. How do tools make knowledge engineering easier? How do they make it harder than it would be without them?
5. What criteria should be used to compare tools? What kind of experiment would be required?

ACKNOWLEDGMENTS

The experiment described in Section 6.1 was part of the Expert Systems Workshop held in San Diego in August 1980, under NSF/DARPA sponsorship. The case studies described in this chapter are based on information provided by the members of the Expert System Workshop teams. The very significant contributions of William van Melle, Carlisle Scott, Richard Duda, Rene Reboh, Sholom Weiss, Peter Politakis, John McDermott, Lanny Forgy, Lee Erman, Philip London, Douglas Lenat, Russell Greiner, Stanley Rosenschein, Daniel Gorlin, Penny Nii, and Nelleke Aiello are gratefully acknowledged.

PART III

Evaluating an Expert System

7

Reasoning about Reasoning

**Douglas Lenat, Randall Davis, Jon Doyle,
Michael Genesereth, Ira Goldstein,
and Howard Schrobe**

*Knowledge has many uses. Most knowledge-based systems
today employ only simple kinds of knowledge in simple ways.
These accomplishments raise our aspirations, and we try to
expand the kinds of knowledge employed and the kinds of
tasks performed by expert systems. Since the tasks of constructing, maintaining, and extending expert systems demand
the power of expert systems themselves, this leads us to investigate metaknowledge and metaexpert systems.*

The performance of expert systems can be improved by supplying
various sorts of knowledge about the knowledge in the system. This
type of metaknowledge comes in many forms:

> Prefer experts' rules to novices' rules.
> This program knows nothing about biology or physics.
> The search for the spill source is exhaustive generate-and-test.
> Exhaustive search is fine, as each type of oil is stored
> in only a few places.

The present chapter examines this phenomenon, by showing how a
rule-based system (for the task of managing a chemical spill crisis)
can utilize various types of metaknowledge.

A knowledge engineer works with a human expert to construct a large knowledge base of facts and rules. Gradually that program approaches competence at its task. Whenever the expert and the program disagree, the expert can usually be coaxed into providing a new rule or changing some old rule. But sometimes the knowledge the human expert provides is not knowledge about the task itself but, rather, knowledge about the knowledge in the program, as in the following metarules:

MR1   Rules that save lives take precedence over rules about notifying agencies.

MR2   Rules about solubility and pH are rarely (if ever) going to be changed.

MR3   Rule #6 works only because lime forms an insoluble compound with sulfuric acid, hence it precipitates out.

The information these rules provide, the content of metarules 1−3, is called *metaknowledge*. The expression "meta-X" means "X about X," so metaknowledge means knowledge about knowledge. The various reasoning activities of expert systems are more or less cognitive; when one reasons about such activities (as is being done in this sentence), one is engaging in metacognition. This chapter illustrates several kinds of metaknowledge and shows how each can be important to building, running, and modifying expert systems.

Metarule 1, for instance, provides strategic guidance in selecting rules. Such metaknowledge can improve the performance of the program by constraining the search for a solution. Some metalevel knowledge, such as MR3, supplies the justification for a rule, its origin, records of how it has performed in actual use, and so on. This makes it easier for a human—or even for the program itself—to make changes in the program. This increased flexibility is often worth the added effort of supplying the descriptive information initially. For instance, if lime runs out, and someone suggests using lye instead, MR3 will help decide whether rule 6 in Section 7.3 ("If sulfuric acid spilled, then dump some lime onto it") can still be relied on. In this case since lye is soluble in sulfuric acid, one should not count on rule 6.

Just as the task-specific knowledge was extracted, codified, and entered into the program's knowledge base, so too is this new meta-level knowledge, knowledge about the program. In the usual mode of building an expert system, a human's expertise is gradually transferred into the knowledge base. This process creates, in the builder's mind, a new body of knowledge: knowledge about the program, about the particular rules in its knowledge base, and about its

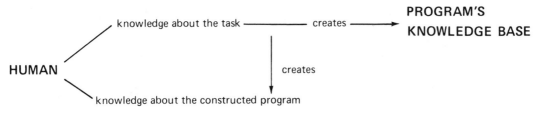

FIGURE 7.1   In the process of building an expert system, the human acquires knowledge about that program.

architecture. (See Figure 7.1.) Just as a human transferred domain knowledge to the program, he or she can now transfer this body of metaknowledge. (See Figure 7.2.) (To the clever reader who now asks "What happens to the new body of knowledge that *that* process spawns?" the reply is that it is largely domain-independent and placed in this chapter.)

As programs grow ever larger and more complex, it becomes increasingly difficult for human beings to stay "on top" of everything that is happening internally. The program itself must assume more and more of the burden of understanding its own behavior, documenting and justifying itself, and even modifying itself. In part this also reflects a broadened perspective on what constitutes competence. Experts are more than people who merely solve problems. They are capable as well of explaining, learning, reorganizing, reformulating, all the while rating the progress they are making.

What is the source of metaknowledge? Paradoxically, much of it derives from an incomplete understanding of the phenomena. Until a task has been completely formalized—and often afterward as well—experts will not discuss it in formal terms. First they provide a base of facts, theorems, equations, categories, lab objects and operations. This constitutes a "zeroth order" theory of their task domain. It contains the factual knowledge present in texts on the subject. Often the

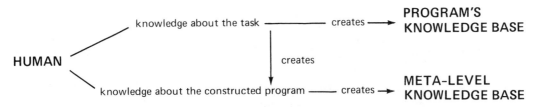

FIGURE 7.2   Just as the task-specific knowledge was extracted, codified, and entered into the program's knowledge base, so too is this new meta-level knowledge, knowledge *about* the program.

experts claim that this knowledge is complete, and only after a pro-gram embodying it fails to perform adequately do they volunteer additional knowledge. This second sort of knowledge is heuristic: rules of thumb, inconsistent advice, inexact judgmental criteria. The heuristic knowledge forms a "first-order correction" to the factual zeroth order theory. But often even this knowledge does not produce results as well as the experts do. Continued pressure on the experts may yield a third type of knowledge, the kind referred to as meta-knowledge: "Well, this last piece of advice really doesn't work for paint spills," or "Those rules about chemical analysis aren't totally reliable." This is a "second-order correction" of the previous system knowledge.

This scenario is not always followed precisely, but it indicates the three levels of information offered by an expert describing a domain and the problem-solving techniques required: factual, heuris-tic, and metalevel. Explicitly or (more often) implicitly, almost all expert systems embody metaknowledge of the sort illustrated.

If metaknowledge is going to be present (and it always seems to be desirable), the knowledge engineer should deal with it explicitly. That is, it should be recognized and represented in a language that is high-level and economical in expression, and that has the appropriate primitives. As a result, the program will function better and will also be easier to build and to modify. Examples given throughout the rest of this chapter illustrate this point.

The spill-crisis-management task domain has already been intro-duced. For the remainder of this chapter, presume that an archetypi-cal expert system is performing that task. Its architecture will start out as simply as possible. Say it is a rule-based program, with rules being cycled through randomly; any time the current rule's "condi-tions" part is satisfied, it will fire (execute) its "actions" part.

Suppose the following are two of the rules in the system:

R1   If the spill is sulfuric acid, then use an anion-exchanger.

R2   If the spill is sulfuric acid, then use acetic acid.

Once a spill has been identified as sulfuric acid, each of these rules will have its if-parts (conditions) satisfied. Which of them will be fol-lowed? Since the control structure is random selection, there is no bias and no way of knowing which rule—and which remedy—will be selected. But in real life there must be some basis for choosing among them, or the expert probably would not have two different methods with which to react to the same situation. That extra information is metaknowledge. The next several sections deal with issues that arise as an attempt is made to add various types of metaknowledge to the spill system.

Most expert systems today contain little or no metaknowledge. In this chapter we are sketching long-term research directions and aspirations, and some of what is anticipated may not turn up as usable "knowledge-engineering products" for several years. However, it is believed that the incorporation of metalevel reasoning into expert systems will probably play an increasingly important role.

7.1 Example: Metaknowledge Selects Rules

Besides R1 and R2, suppose three new rules are added to the system:

R3   Use rules that employ cheap materials before those that employ more expensive materials.

R4   Use less hazardous methods before more hazardous methods.

R5   Use rules entered by an expert before rules entered by a novice.

Note that these new metarules require that the system be able to reason about the cost, danger, and so on, of items mentioned in rules R1 and R2. In particular, there must be in the system the fact that acetic acid is cheap and also that anion-exchanging is generally more expensive; that acetic acid may be more dangerous to work with than anion-exchangers; that R1 was typed in by Carroll Johnson, Oak Ridge's spill expert, and R2 by a college sophomore spending the summer at Oak Ridge.

So both R3 and R5 would cause R2 to be considered before R1, while R4 would recommend that R2 be considered after R1. So which rule—R1 or R2—will be executed first? It comes down to which of R3, R4, R5 will be executed first. If there is a complete separation of rules from metarules, and a separate interpreter for metarules, then the question becomes dependent upon that particular metarule interpreter. If it is pure random selection, then there is a two-thirds chance of R2 being tried before R1 (since two rules favor R2 over R1), and therefore that acetic acid will be the method of choice. If the "majority decides," it is 100 percent certain that R2 would be tried before R1.

But let us take a look at R3–R5 again. All give good advice—and quite general advice. Why not permit them to affect the metarule interpreter as well as the rule interpreter? Consider R5 first. It says to prefer experts' rules over novices' rules. If R4 was typed in by Dr. Johnson, and R3 by the college student, the advice says to prefer R4 to

R3. That would result in anion-exchanging ultimately being chosen. Now consider R4: Prefer less hazardous methods. Suppose R3 is known to cause catastrophes sometimes, R5 is less risky, and R4 is safe but sure. Then even R4 prefers R4 to the other two rules. Finally consider R3: Pinch pennies. Suppose that estimating the cost of various approaches is itself difficult and costly, estimating the risks involved is less costly, but finding out who typed in a rule is impossible since it was never recorded. R3 then prefers R4 to the other two rules. In short, all of R3–R5 (acting in the role of meta-metarules) prefer R4 as the metarule of choice in this problem. But R4 (acting as it was introduced, as a metarule choosing between R1 and R2) prefers R1. Therefore R1 is definitely selected, and it directs the use of an anion-exchanger on the spill.

Of course, in general, the rules for choosing a metarule to follow may not all result in the very same metarule; yet another level of rule interpreter must be specified to resolve such conflicts, and this process threatens to continue ad infinitum. This is not the brink of disaster. One way out is to draw a dark line, at some metalevel, and fix a rule interpreter at that level once and for all, arbitrarily deciding for example that metarules will be present, but no meta-metarules. If there is ever a conflict among the metarules, one is just selected at random and that is that. The system will still reason more deeply than any system without metarules. The previous paragraph hinted at a second way to break the infinite ascent: just refuse to make a distinction between knowledge and metaknowledge; allow the same body of rules to serve as metarules, meta-metarules, and so on. Of more practical importance is the observation that the number of meaningful rules at each metalevel decreases sharply with n. By the time $n = 3$, the only rule one may have left is "Try to maximize utility."

A related point is that one person's metaknowledge is another's knowledge. Consider the following:

K1   The "track the spill back to its source" approach is usually tried first if the source is unknown.

Is it knowledge, or is it metaknowledge? If the task given is to ameliorate the spill, then planning how to do it is at a metalevel to you, and you'd call K1 metaknowledge. Knowledge, to you, comprises pieces of information about how to backtrack, what manhole is connected to what pipe, and so forth. But if your task is planning to clean up the spill, then K1 is just a piece of knowledge to you.

The problem addressed so far in this subsection is often referred to as "conflict resolution"—choosing among the many rules that may be relevant at any given moment. A related problem is the efficient location of potentially relevant rules. As the number of rules in the expert system grows, it becomes less practical to test the conditions of every rule each time the situation changes slightly. There must be some way to find the relevant rules quickly.

The system needs strategies about how to focus quickly upon the relevant categories of rules. An example of this might be a piece of knowledge that said:

> If currently seeking rules about X, look first at rules that mention X somewhere inside them; look next at rules that mention some generalization of X.

Thus when an unknown oil spill is noticed, the first rules the expert system considers are those that explicitly mention oil spills. If none of these is found to be relevant, the system might gather rules about spills in general. Only if none of these rules is found to be relevant would rules about less relevant subjects finally be inspected.

But one does not want to examine every rule in the system, looking for those that mention oil spills! How is this avoided? Presumably there is some indexing scheme whereby "Oil-Spill" is linked associatively to the set of rules that mention oil spills. For example, if knowledge is represented as frames, the Oil-Spill frame may have a slot called RelevantRules, whose value is that list of rules. The same indexing scheme lets one quickly find the generalization of any given concept. So after exhausting the oil spill rules, one quickly finds that the generalization of Oil-Spill is Spill, and then recurs, finding the rules relevant to Spill, etc.

7.2   **Example: Metaknowledge Records Needed Facts about Knowledge**

The strategic metarules described in the last section, such as R3–R5, demand information about the system's domain knowledge and its rules. In order for rule R3 to work, the system must somehow know (or be able to compute) how expensive each chemical is. In order for R4 to work, the system must somehow know which chemicals are more dangerous than others. In order for R5 to work, the system must somehow know which rules were entered by experts and which were entered by novices. The metarules cannot even function unless that type of recordkeeping has been done. But what are those records, after all? They are knowledge about the system's knowledge (both domain knowledge and rules), which means that they, too, are a kind of metaknowledge.

Figure 7.1 illustrated how a human system-builder watches the growing program and builds up knowledge about it. One of the commonest kinds of knowledge acquired is an awareness of resources that the various actions consume: time, space. For example, in the spill task, one crucial bit of descriptive metaknowledge is the fact that it takes several days to get the results of a general chemical analysis back from the lab. Some rule-based systems monitor the methods, rules, and even the metarules in order to accumulate statistics about their average running time, percentage record of success, number of times they stop to ask the human user a question, and so on. These empirically obtained resource data often turn out to be more accurate than an expert's a priori intuitive estimates.

Dealing with resources opens up an important distinction: there are several "modes" that an expert system may be in. Initially, the system is being built up. In this mode resources include real time, experts' time, programmers' time, and so on. The way to conserve these resources is to employ a language that allows the rules to be stated quickly. Later, as the system begins to work on actual problems, it must be monitored and modified to add to and correct its knowledge base. It ought not take too long to find "the right place" to make a needed change. Finally, when the system is being used in production, a different set of economies applies. It is no longer as important how descriptive and malleable the code is; efficiency of running the rules is what is noticed most.

Yet another useful type of metaknowledge is some notion of how accurate is the result obtained from a given method. One may get five digits back, but how many are significant? For example, in the oil spill task, weathering of a sample will reduce the trust that should be put in the results of its chemical analysis.

This new type of metaknowledge—records of origin, empirical behavior, cost, danger—is quite unlike the strategic metaknowledge described in Section 7.1. There, the metaknowledge was effective and executable advice. It constrained and guided a performer searching for the best rules to apply at each moment. Here the metaknowledge is noneffective, descriptive, explanatory. In both cases, though, it has proven useful.

7.3   Example: Metaknowledge Justifies Rules

Suppose the present system contains these three rules:

R6   If spill is sulfuric acid, then use lime.
R7   If spill is acetic acid, then use lime.
R8   If spill is hydrochloric acid, then use lime.

Now suppose lime runs out and lye is suggested as a replacement. Presumably many additional pieces of information about lye are known, for example, that the compound formed by lye and sulfuric acid is soluble. Can one simply go through rules R6−R8 and replace lime by lye? If that is done, some of them still work and some of them become completely useless (or even worse than useless). What is wrong?

A deeper look should be taken into the rationale behind those rules. Suppose some descriptive metaknowledge about each one has been supplied: whenever a rule is typed in, the expert is also asked to specify its justification:

R6   If spill is sulfuric acid, then use lime.
   Justification: Lime neutralizes acid and the compound
       that forms is insoluble and hence will pre-
       cipitate out.
R7   If spill is acetic acid, then use lime.
   Justification: Lime neutralizes the acid.
R8   If spill is hydrochloric acid, then use lime.
   Justification: Lime neutralizes the acid.

The suggestion about using lye instead of lime also had a justification:

S1   If out of lime, then consider using lye instead.
   Justification: Lye can neutralize acids (just as lime does).

What one really wants to do is go through R6−8 and substitute lye for lime only in those rules that use lime solely to neutralize pH, hence not in rule R6. The point is that substitutions work only when one knows why the original compound was being employed in the first place.

To look on the positive side of this issue, suppose a new, cheap base (material with basic pH) is marketed one day. The system will possess the necessary knowledge to go through its rules and make changes where—but only where—the new substance is preferable to the old.

Often there is a need to know just what makes one believe something, what the justification for a rule is. Is it by definition? by appeal to an established authority? by deduction? by induction? by observation? Except for those rare cases of ironclad justifications, most of Polya's rules (1954) for the use of evidence in plausible (inexact) reasoning are quite appropriate here.

Even given the truth of a rule, the rule itself may contain reservations about its conclusion. The expert might qualify the rule's actions-part by saying, "Then it is likely that...," perhaps even assigning a numeric certainty factor or likelihood ratio. In addition to the average or mean truth of a rule, it may be worth recording its variance; this is referred to as the "reliability" of the rule. For instance, in a desperate emergency, one might employ methods with only mediocre average justifications, if their variance were high enough to suggest some chance for success.

A related measure is the risk—just how bad is it if the rule gives incorrect advice? For example, "If we fully automate our retaliatory strike launchings, then global peace is assured" might be right most of the time, but if it is ever wrong . . .

The end users of the expert system may have a healthy disrespect for machines telling them what to do. No doctor wants to rely on a computer program's diagnosis or prescription without first asking for an explanation. The expert system's response to such an inquiry may initially be a listing of the most important (or recent) rule used to reach that conclusion. But what if the expert feels uneasy about that rule? Can he or she ask: Who entered this rule? Why is this rule supposed to work? How well has it performed in practice? By answering such questions, the program convinces the user of its conclusions, and, if there is a bug in the knowledge base, that bug will also surface faster and more clearly.

Often typing out a single rule and answering questions about it is not satisfactory. The user may desire a more complete trace of the program's line of reasoning (the sequence of rule firings). The careful expert may probe deeper, asking about the global diagnosis strategies the system is using.

7.4 Metaknowledge Detects Simple Bugs in Rules

These last few examples of metaknowledge have dealt with the content of the rules and methods in the system. It is possible to deal with the form of the rules (and other knowledge-carrying structures) as well. To illustrate that point, suppose in the middle of a rule-entry session the expert types in the following "rule":

FR1   Use lye.

A rule such as FR1, having no conditions (IF-part) at all, should be noticed and brought to the attention of the person who entered it for confirmation (and correction). Probably, the user meant that the context of this rule (its condition) was assumed to be the same as the one(s) most recently discussed. Actually that is not a bad piece of strategic advice. It is called FR2 and added to the system:

FR2   If a rule is typed in with no conditions,
       then ask the typist if it is supposed
       to have the same conditions as the most
       recently typed rule.

Another bug that occurs frequently is that a rule has conditions that
can never be satisfied:

FR3   If acid must be neutralized, and lye is available,
       and no basic material is available,
       then use lye.

In the case of FR3 the user really meant to type "and no other basic
material is available," but because the word "other" was omitted, the
rule as stated will never fire. This might automatically be detected,
either deductively by proving that FR3's clauses are not simultaneously satisfiable, or empirically by recording the behavior of FR3, and
employing a rule such as FR4:

FR4   If, over the course of many runs, a rule never fires,
       then ask the expert if the condition is for
       some (semantic) reason unsatisfiable,
       and request that it be rephrased.

Both FR1 and FR3 represent rules whose forms have bugs. In the first
case, no condition, the error is syntactic. In the second case, an unsatisfiable condition, the error is semantic. In each case, metaknowledge can be used to detect and correct such bugs. In the first case the
metaknowledge is that all rules should have both conditions and
actions. In the second case the metaknowledge is that all rules should
fire at least sometimes. These pieces of descriptive metaknowledge
are therefore quite useful.

7.5   The Representation Used Is a Form of Metaknowledge

The system-builder selects or, more commonly, modifies a representation system that will hold the domain knowledge, rules, and so on.
Presumably the choice of representation language was made so that it
would be seem natural to the task at hand. Was the system based
around Get/Put or Assert/Match? How big is the average knowledge

structure? How are rules represented? Does the system solve a problem by working forward, or backward, or both at once? The answers to such questions of program design are a subtle yet important form of metaknowledge.

In systems whose knowledge-carriers (rules, frames) have a great deal of structure, knowledge acquisition becomes a process of filling in the schemata. The "dialogue" between system and expert is more like text-editing or prompt-answering than unguided composition. A simple example of this occurs after one has typed in rule R7 and wants to type in R8. The structures and justifications are so similar that it is easiest simply to edit a copy of R7 and replace the word "acetic" by "hydrochloric." Another way to look at this is to say that the vocabulary of legal slots (attributes) embodies metalevel knowledge about the important relationships in this task.

Framelike schemata only help describe the syntax of the knowledge base. Descriptive metaknowledge on interrelations that should exist in the knowledge (either statically, such as inverse links, or dynamically, such as relative running times) can be used to provide checks on the semantics of newly acquired knowledge.

An example of this phenomenon involves the use of information about the representation of knowledge in the system, descriptive metaknowledge about a relation between two of the slots of a frame-structured representation:

FR5   If   a rule has an "If-Potentially-Relevant" slot filled
              with some predicate PR, and an "If-Truly-Relevant"
              slot filled with predicate TR,
          then TR should imply PR, and PR should be much faster to
              execute than TR.

The idea here is that a rule can have two parts to its conditions: a fast but uncertain preconditions check (If-Potentially-Relevant), and a slow, sure, detailed condition (If-Truly-Relevant). For instance, FR3 might have been split into three parts:

FR6   If-Potentially-Relevant: Acid must be neutralized
       If-Truly-Relevant: Acid must be neutralized,
                          lye is available,
                          and no (other) basic material is available,
       Then: Apply lye to the spill to neutralize the acid

FR5 states explicitly how the semantics of the two kinds of If-parts interrelate. It is a piece of descriptive metaknowledge. FR5 declares that the If-Potentially-Relevant slot must be implied by and faster than the If-Truly-Relevant slot, and that is certainly the case in FR6.

Coupled with, say, some statistical data on running times, it might be possible to verify that indeed, for some other rule, its "fast" condition was taking longer to test than its "slow but sure" one. In that case the system might log a message to that effect, interrupt and notify the user to delete the If-Potentially-Relevant slot of the offending rule completely, and so on.

Just as the representation scheme subtly encodes some metalevel knowledge about the task and the rules that exist to solve it, so too does the control scheme chosen. For example, if a backward-chaining search was adopted, one can infer that the rules are not too branchy in that direction. If an exhaustive search was adopted, one can infer that the space of alternatives is not too large.

7.6 Metaknowledge Justifies the Program's Architecture

Sometimes the user's questions will be so deep that they are actually probing the control structure and organization of the expert system itself, its assumptions about the task, and so forth. Answering the following questions typically requires both a domain expert and the system architect: "Why are you doing that by depth-first search? Why was such a slow control structure chosen? Why can't the system 'back up'? Why was each type of oil represented just as a vector of numbers? When there is more than one relevant rule, why is just one chosen at random?"

What is it that a good system designer knows and puts to work in constructing (or even simply selecting from among) such architectures as MACSYMA, HEARSAY-II, MYCIN, HARPY, AM, DENDRAL, or others? Why prefer a blackboard model, or an agenda, or a pure production system? Will resolution work? Does one need metarules? Can one afford to do exhaustive backward-chaining?

Such decisions call for knowledge about the consistency and the completeness and magnitude of the available knowledge, the size and shape of the search space, the required efficiency of the system, and similar parameters of systemic, global scale. For a detailed discussion of these options, see Chapter 4.

Having an expert system handle questions such as these will require adding a great wealth of knowledge about the design of the expert system itself. One such body of knowledge deals with the assumed model of what the task is and how it is to be carried out. Of equal importance is general information about building expert systems: the control structures that are available, the ways of representing knowledge, and the advantages and disadvantages of each choice.

Let us add the following additional metarules to the sample spill system:

R9   If the search space is moderately small,
       then exhaustive search is feasible.

R10   If the ruleset is rarely modified,
       then it is worth compiling it initially into a decision tree.

Thanks to facts such as "There are 33 standard oil types . . . and 1,000 different locations . . . ," the system designer can estimate the size of the search space involved and, employing R9, opt for an exhaustive search.

When might R10 fire? During the development and rule-debugging phases of the project, the ruleset is changing fairly frequently. But once our program has been debugged, tested, and shipped out into the field, the rules will change rarely if at all. R10 might then become relevant and recommend that somebody redesign the basic control structure of the system, so that from then on it follows a decision tree to obtain an answer. Before obeying R10, a new rule could be added easily at any moment. However, once R10's suggestion is acted upon, if one wants to add a new rule, the whole ruleset might have to be recompiled into a new decision tree.

If the program begins to be used on larger and larger problems, R9 may eventually complain that it is being violated and that an exhaustive search may no longer be such a great idea—again, one sees a metarule (R9) suggesting a redesign.

Suppose a user employing the program asks why a particularly unlikely rule was even considered. The system replies that it was executing an exhaustive search, and the user asks "Why?" again. This time, R9 is printed out to answer the query. This is a significant extension to answering "why" questions by typing out the control stack (higher level goals). After it reaches the top of that stack, the system can begin to interpret "Why?" to mean "Why was the system designed like that?"

Consider a program that is in the midst of a square-root calculation. If it is interrupted and asked what it is doing, the answer might be that it was dividing two numbers. If asked why, its answer is "In order to get the square-root of p, via Newton's method." A second "why?" might mean either, "Why are you computing that square-root," or "Why via Newton's method." In the second case one goes outside the goal/supergoal framework of typical explanation systems to explain why one of a number of design choices was made (in this case the choice of Newton's method as the algorithm).

Thus the same metarule, R9, has been used in three distinct roles: to aid in designing a system, to aid in knowing when and how to redesign a system, and to answer "why" questions of a fundamental nature. One desirable feature for a knowledge base is to have its knowledge represented in such a way that it can be used for several distinct purposes; here the same desirability for metalevel knowledge has been apparent. The second of R9's three roles was a kind of dynamic adaptation, and is worth pursuing.

7.7   Metaknowledge Aids a System Adapt to Its Run-time Environment

Can the system reconfigure itself in response to experience, to what it may have learned about the domain? Here are two metarules that support that type of operation:

R11   If a piece of code is called frequently,
then it is worth optimizing.

R12   If (almost) every frame has many entries on its s slot,
then try to replace s by a cluster of more specialized slots.

The original design had rules possessing only an If slot and a Then slot and action slots. If the majority of rules have large conditions (many clauses), then R12 might fire and suggest dividing that slot into a constellation of new, more specialized conditions slots: If-potentially-relevant, If-there-are-enough-resources, If-truly-relevant, If-user-is-a, etc. Instead of each rule having a dozen clauses in its conditions slot, it might then have two or three clauses in each of the new, specialized conditions slots. Note that the "If-truly-relevant" slot need contain only those conditions that are not also present on the other "If-" slots.

The wisdom of such a partitioning rests with the Justification slot of R12, which might cite evidence as solid as "This simplifies the entry of new rules" or as dubious as "This appeals to the aesthetic tastes of the end users."

Changes in the program need not be on so grand a scale; consider these rules:

If one conjunct appears to be false more often than any other conjunct, then reorder the conjuncts so that it comes first in the list.

If each user is using the program only very briefly and never more than once, then throw away the code that spends time building up a model of the user.

If a function is used frequently and changed only occasionally,
then it is worth taking the time to compile it.

If one part of the representation (e.g., one kind of slot)
    is being very heavily used,
then consider replacing it by a cluster of similar, more specialized parts.

While these rules are executable metaknowledge, they can be run only if the system has been keeping track of such things as the frequency of use of each function, the average length of runs. That is, these rules run on data that is itself descriptive metaknowledge.

7.8 Metaknowledge Models the Program's Abilities

If asked "Do you know the phone number at the last place you lived?," you may think hard for a minute or two and then provide an answer. But if you are asked "Do you know the private telephone number of the Premier of the USSR?," your reply will not take very long. Why? Obviously, you are not performing a detailed search over all the phone numbers you know. Rather, you are drawing upon a very useful body of knowledge: your model of what it is you do and do not know, what tasks you can and cannot tackle, how long it would take you to solve some problem.

Suppose rules R13−15 are added to our spill expert system:

R13   If the substance spilled is biologically active,
       then the "Spill knowledge base" is inadequate for the task.

R14   If the substance spilled is not in the OHMTADS data base,
       then the "Spill knowledge base" is inadequate for the task.

R15   If the substance spilled came from an Oak Ridge container,
       then the "Spill knowledge base" is adequate for the task.

The program can now respond quickly to some situations where before its behavior was less than ideal. R14 prevents many long searches that would result in failure anyway. R13 serves the much more useful role of preventing the program from assuming it had handled the situation when in reality it was applying inappropriate and inadequate measures (literally mopping up some viral material, for instance). R15 is a more positive type of metarule, one that can provide immediate assurance that the program expects to succeed on the given task.

One of the most persistent problems with commercially available software, such as statistical subroutine packages, has been the danger of using a program outside the range where its algorithm works and not being able to tell by the output that it is incorrect. As expert systems are developed for high-impact applications, such as air traffic control, or areas already sensitized to malpractice, such as medicine, it becomes increasingly desirable to have a program reason about its own adequacy.

A knowledge base can be used for more than one purpose, as when a collection of medical diagnosis rules is employed to make diagnoses and also to help teach medical students. Similarly a program containing a body of metarules that models its abilities and limitations might be able to use that knowledge to teach would-be users about itself.

7.9   Work to Date

Metalevel knowledge that aided in selecting rules was historically one of the first forms to be recognized, though it was generally encoded implicitly. By "implicitly" is meant that various problem domains forced system builders to contend with it, but they often did so with mechanisms that were added on to their system designs as afterthoughts. The idea has shown up in many places, such as conflict-resolution in production systems (Waterman and F. Hayes-Roth 1978), advice lists in PLANNER (Stallman 1977), metarules in TEIRESIAS (Davis 1982), and choice rules in NASL (McDermott and Doyle 1980).

Certainty factors are added to rules by the physician-experts who build the MYCIN knowledge base (Shortliffe 1976). Similarly the geologist-experts who add rules to PROSPECTOR (Duda 1979) provide two likelihood ratios for each rule. EURISKO (Lenat 1982) keeps track of the average running times, space consumed, success and failure rate, and so on, of its rules, and uses these statistics to affect its choice of which rule to try in new situations. A few expert systems pay attention to the form of the rules. For instance, EURISKO complains if the user tries to type in a rule with no conditions (a piece of syntactic metaknowledge complains). If the user attempts to type in a rule whose pre-preconditions take longer to run than its preconditions, a piece of semantic metaknowledge complains after a great deal of empirical run-time statistics have been accumulated. TEIRESIAS (Davis 1982) may occasionally interject a comment like "Excuse me, doctor, but all rules mentioning x and y have also mentioned patient age as a relevant parameter; are you sure you don't want to add some clause about patient age?"

A number of programs have worked within the model of using descriptive metaknowledge to provide explanations of the program's goals. A digitalis advisor (Swartout 1977) was a slight improvement over MYCIN. Instead of simply replaying the exact rule used, the system determined what generic principle the rule was an instance of and displayed that instead. This produced somewhat more general and often somewhat more comprehensible explanations. While it was still following the "retrace the performance" model of explanation, the restructuring of the program as a collection of domain principles helped to make that performance more understandable.

An early thesis by Low (1976) monitored the manner in which each user accessed a file system, and then dynamically changed the data structures to improve efficiency. More recent work along similar "automatic programming" lines has been done by Barstow (1979) and Kant (1979), the latter performing an analysis of the various options, à la Knuth. At Massachusetts Institute of Technology the MACSYMA advisor project (Martin and Fateman 1971) and the programmer's apprentice project (Rich 1976) pioneered the use of metaknowledge pertaining to the program itself. AM (Lenat 1977) had rules of this form, such as "If a piece of code is executed twice, Then compile it", and EURISKO (Lenat 1982) has employed rules akin to R12. Modern truth maintenance systems gain much power from explicit systemic metaknowledge (Doyle 1980).

This description of work to date seems to be brief, and the reader may get the impression that not much has been done. That is correct. Incorporating metalevel knowledge and reasoning capabilities into expert systems is still in the research stage.

7.10 Conclusions

Many uses have been established for metaknowledge:

- To guide the location and selection of rules.
- To provide information about domain knowledge and rules—how fast a rule runs, who typed a piece of data, and so on. This is the kind of recordkeeping information needed for strategic metarules to make their judgments.
- To justify rules, thereby enhancing the system's explanation abilities.
- To help detect bugs in the form of recently entered rules, thereby aiding knowledge-base expansion.

- To facilitate the entry of new knowledge—terms, facts, heuristic rules—by providing a structured corpus of already existing knowledge of all those types. In such a situation, "entry" can usually be done simply by copying and then editing.

Much of this chapter has dealt with explanation, since it is the simplest sort of metacognition, the best understood, and the only one in routine use in expert systems. Treating explanation separately in several sections of this chapter may seem disconnected, but it reflects the multiple meanings of the English query "Why?" There is an interesting range of precisely what that question can mean:

What is your immediate goal?   (descriptive metaknowledge)
What is an abstraction of your immediate goal?   (descriptive metaknowledge)
What is the justification for that?   (descriptive metaknowledge)
Teleologically, how is it that that action contributes to the goal? (systemic metaknowledge)
Why is that a good choice of methods to accomplish that goal? (strategic metaknowledge)

In this chapter several categories of metaknowledge have been distinguished; this division has been more illustrative than theoretical. In practice, there are no sharp boundaries between the types of metaknowledge one may embed in an expert system. Rule R5, which was presented as a rule to help choose which rule to fire at each moment, is the compiled strategic form of the following two rules, the first of which is descriptive and the second, systemic:

R5a   The experts' spill rules are much much more reliable than the novices'.

R5b   In the long run, it pays for an expert system to use reliable rules.

This illustrates one important kind of process, akin to learning: the compiling of descriptive metaknowledge into strategic form, recasting it into a form in which it can be evaluated efficiently.

Changing a huge program is currently a painful, often impossible task. Static comments and documentation help. Dynamic documentation can be even more useful: the program has available to it, explicitly, a model of its organization, overall design, detailed algorithms and knowledge representations, typical behaviors, and more. Many kinds of metaknowledge combine to provide this type of self-description capability for a program.

Static documentation requires manual updating whenever the program changes, but dynamic self-description ought to be computed by the program itself and should change automatically with the program's executable code. A simple example of this is INTERLISP's MasterScope facility (Teitelman and Masinter 1981): one can ask "Which functions call FIB7?" and the answer will be correct even if one has just defined a new function that calls FIB7. As another example, the expert system grown in this chapter keeps track of the average running times and percentage of success of its rules.

Once self-description is a reality, the next logical step is self-modification. Small, self-modifying, automatic programming systems have existed for a decade; some large programs that modify themselves in very small ways also exist; and the first large fully self-describing and self-modifying programs are being built just now. The capabilities of machines have finally exceeded human cognitive capabilities in this dimension; it is now worth supplying and using meta-knowledge in large expert systems.

NOTE

1. A rule-based system is used as a focus for the discussion, but none of the material here is constrained to a rule representation. All of the discussion is oriented to issues of kinds of knowledge and the appropriate organization for that knowledge; issues that are particular to a specific representation are not dealt with.

QUESTIONS

1. In what sense is one person's metaknowledge another's knowledge?
2. Demonstrate the benefits of distinguishing knowledge from meta-knowledge. What are the costs?
3. Why don't most expert systems use metaknowledge today?
4. Where is metaknowledge in systems like MYCIN, DENDRAL, and HEARSAY-II?
5. What constitutes a sound justification of a heuristic rule? Of an expert decision?

ACKNOWLEDGMENTS

This chapter began as a series of discussions at the 1980 Workshop on Expert Systems, in San Diego, organized by F. Hayes-Roth, D. Waterman, and D. Lenat. Davis was the note-taker at these discussions, and Lenat reorganized the notes, added some additional material, and turned them into prose. Useful comments have been incorporated from Frederick Hayes-Roth, Mark Stefik, and Don Waterman.

8

Evaluation of Expert Systems: Issues and Case Studies

John Gaschnig, Philip Klahr,
Harry Pople, Edward Shortliffe, and
Allan Terry

As evolving software projects of significant size, expert systems require incremental assessments and continued financial support. As finished artificial experts, these systems offer services for a cost. Can the benefits be measured? Can the foibles of imperfect wisdom be tolerated? Can one assess clearly both what has been achieved and what needs to be accomplished? Evaluation can provide an important focus for a project, if made at the right time. But inappropriate evaluation can undermine a healthy and valuable development activity.

8.1 Developing an Expert System: A Long-Term Feedback Process

It is always exciting to develop new ideas, to implement them on a computer, and eventually to relish the satisfaction of achieving a successful result. It may be less exciting to undertake formal evaluations of implemented programs. Why should one take the time to run test cases, gather statistics and observations, and generate graphs and charts?

Some investigators argue that one should not bother to evaluate expert systems because, although the research field is now past its infancy, it is still actively developing. Why spend time and energy evaluating expert systems instead of concentrating on building them? Difficult issues abound, and the continual development of new techniques makes any system a moving target. Some real successes are apparent, yet the systems have many limitations. Thus evaluations only indicate that work should continue, which is what should have been going on anyhow. Besides, the best way to evaluate a system is to get it built, turn it over to friendly users, and solicit and respond to their feedback.

This argument, however, ignores a crucial observation: systems are *always* being evaluated, whether consciously or not. Designing and implementing expert systems involves constant evaluating of the progress by considering questions such as the following:

- Is the knowledge representation scheme adequate or does it need to be extended or modified?
- Is the system coming up with right answers and for the right reasons?
- Is the embedded knowledge consistent with the experts'?
- Is it easy for users to interact with the system?
- What facilities and capabilities do users need?

Expert systems evolve. Rarely do initial designs and implementations last. Feedback from users, expert collaborators, and the system builders themselves suggests improvements that are incorporated into later versions. Evaluations pervade the system-building process and are crucial for improving system design and performance. Every time a rule in the knowledge base is changed, added, or deleted, every time the code of the reasoning program is modified or extended, or every time the knowledge representation scheme is refined, action has been taken in response to an informal evaluation. Another reason for conducting evaluations of expert systems is that controlled experiments, producing hard data, will contribute to AI's scientific respectability.

One reason for the present difficulty in evaluating knowledge-based expert systems is that human experts are seldom evaluated objectively. One therefore cannot simply apply the same standards to machines as those that are applied to people. Human experts must usually pass some tests or standards to become licensed or otherwise certified, but for a problem requiring expertise, one does not select a doctor, geologist, or automobile mechanic according to any numerical rating system. Although there is a vast literature on human testing, few of these results and methods seem to apply directly to the issues faced in evaluating knowledge-based expert systems or their human counterparts. This situation is both a challenge and an opportunity to develop evaluation methods that may shed new light on human as well as machine performance. In other words whatever means are developed for measuring machine performance may also have applicability to human expertise. In the process at least more will be learned about what it takes to become an expert.

Section 8.2 highlights the importance of evaluations for various groups of individuals involved in the expert-system-building process. Different groups benefit from evaluations in different ways. One should keep in mind the needs of those for whom a developing expert system is evaluated. The potential pitfalls of the evaluation process must also be recognized. Evaluations are very easily misinterpreted, and it is therefore extremely important to evaluate at appropriate stages in a system's development, to clarify exactly what is being evaluated, and to interpret the results correctly. These potential pitfalls are also discussed.

Section 8.3 defines the central issues involved in evaluating expert systems: What aspects of an expert system can be evaluated? When during the system-building process should evaluations occur? How should evaluations be performed? Sections 8.4 and 8.5 present case studies of hypothetical evaluations of two expert systems: the R1 system for configuring VAX computers and the ORNL spill problem. The case studies emphasize the important role evaluations play in the evolution of expert systems.

The last section, 8.6, cites lessons learned from these case studies. It is suggested that evaluations be planned as early as possible, when the expert system is first designed, not after it is built, as is usually the case. Planned evaluations help to pinpoint both the specific goals of the system and the objective measures that can be used to determine whether the goals have been achieved. Finally directions for future research and experimentation are suggested.

The principal goal in this chapter is to make future expert systems evaluations easier. An attempt is made to define the key issues, acknowledging that there is no consensus about how to evaluate expert systems (or when or why). By summarizing what has been done and suggesting what types of evaluations can be helpful, one can begin to give some structure to the evaluation process. Most early evaluations of expert systems were unstructured and subjective; even the more formal studies have only begun to define what is possible and appropriate. It is hoped that this chapter will encourage researchers in artificial intelligence and expert systems to direct more of their attention to the issue of evaluation. Research in evaluation methods is scarce, but its impact can be tremendous.

8.2   Why Evaluate Expert Systems?

Expert systems are evaluated primarily to test for program accuracy and utility. Evaluations by domain experts help to determine the accuracy of the embedded knowledge and the accuracy of any advice or conclusions that the system provides. Evaluations by users help to determine the utility of the system—namely, whether it produces useful results, the extent of its capabilities, its ease of interaction, the intelligibility and credibility of its results, its efficiency and speed, and its reliability.

As has been noted, informal evaluations have traditionally been used as routine diagnostic tools during the development and fine-tuning of a system. This chapter argues that the process may also benefit from more formal evaluations at certain key points in system development. However, if done improperly or misinterpreted, such evaluations can result in the demise of an otherwise promising system, in the continuation of a system that holds little potential, or in misdirected effort. In designing an evaluation, one must be aware of its purpose: who it is for, exactly what is being evaluated, and what one hopes to gain from the experiment.

8.2.1   Who Benefits?

Evaluations vary depending on who is making them. Funding agencies may wish to see a system performing in the best possible light. System designers probe for deficiencies and ways to improve a system's operation and performance. End users want to be convinced that the total package represents an improvement over procedures they currently use.

8.2.1.1   System Builders

All evaluations influence the system builders, who are continually evaluating their systems: testing their programs and knowledge bases, identifying problem areas and weak sections needing improvement, making modifications and extensions, and so on. Feedback from users and domain experts provides further evaluation of the knowledge base, the search and reasoning mechanisms used, and the human-engineering aspects of the system.

8.2.1.2   Expert Collaborators and End Users

Domain experts involved in the construction of an expert system are concerned primarily with the embedded domain knowledge and how it is used by the program. Thus the experts repeatedly perform both static and dynamic evaluations. In static evaluation they compare the system's knowledge base with their own, looking for consistency and completeness. In dynamic evaluation they compare the system's line of reasoning and conclusions on a specific case with their own. They make suggestions on improvements in both the knowledge base and the reasoning methods in order to bring the system's expertise closer to their own. Thus the knowledge-acquisition process is intimately linked with ongoing evaluation by the domain experts (see Chapter 5). The ongoing evaluation of a system helps them structure and better understand both their domain and their own expertise.

Evaluations by domain experts also promote communication among members of the development team. The expert typically gains an understanding and appreciation of the system builders' task. At the same time, system builders learn more about the domain being modeled.

Perhaps the ultimate criterion of success is whether an expert system is actually used for expert consultation by individuals other than the system developers. This goal represents a formidable challenge for a young and developing field; only a few expert systems have reached this stage. A key ingredient of success is involving eventual users in evaluations of the system as it is being built. Without a clear understanding of the ultimate users' needs and requirements, system builders may fail to provide crucial capabilities and, consequently, the expert system may have limited utility.

Through evaluations, users can test a system's competence in its domain of expertise and determine whether it produces meaningful results. Users also evaluate their interaction with the system—its facilities for assisting them in using the system, methods for input of knowledge and output of results, and speed of response. All these evaluations help the user decide what capabilities are useful, what others are required and/or desired, and which can be ignored. This feedback in turn allows the system builders to provide capabilities commensurate with the needs of potential users.

Involving end users in the development process can generate user interest in the system as a potential tool for their own use. The psychological benefits of allowing the intended users to feel that their opinions are important in system development cannot be overemphasized. Sometimes users join the system-building team and become advocates for the system in their own work community.

Finally, before an expert system is accepted by a user community, it will necessarily undergo some formal testing and evaluation. The degree of its success will affect the credibility of the system in the users' eyes and the extent to which it will be used. The user's all-important question is whether using the system is worth the trouble.

8.2.1.3 Researchers

Some investigators view structured evaluations of expert systems as "applied AI" (as opposed to research). Such a perspective is questionable on two counts. First, creation of an expert system may require shaping new tools and methods that are not available "off the shelf." Second, the process of identifying the essence of expertise and codifying it is itself a difficult, empirical process in many domains. For both reasons the construction and evaluation of expert systems will generally involve significant components of pure research rather than lying solely at the applied end of the research-and-development spectrum. Researchers in AI and expert systems are always evaluating and comparing alternative systems and techniques, which help them test new ideas, both their own and those of their peers.

Cognitive psychologists evaluate expert systems to explore models of human reasoning. Since an expert system attempts to encode human experts' methods, those used for representing knowledge, for undertaking probabilistic or logical reasoning, and for learning can be compared to the methods of the humans from whom they were derived.

Evaluations often result in the initiation of new research or development efforts. Systems that are particularly slow will inspire efforts to enhance speed. Systems with large knowledge bases will need more efficient memory management. Poor interfaces will result in new user-oriented languages, displays, and explanations.

Some researchers are interested in the evaluation methods themselves, some of which can be applied to many systems. For example, various test cases or particular performance experiments can have wide applicability. Research on evaluation techniques may also lead to a general theory of evaluation or at least to objective criteria for evaluating expert systems over many dimensions.

The development of expert systems is funded primarily by governmental agencies and commercial corporations. Favorable evaluations by these financial sponsors are crucial for continued support. Funding organizations are generally looking to AI research to help them solve problems by providing systems that can eventually be transferred to a routine operational environment. Such systems must provide a variety of capabilities and payoffs, and they must be fairly easy to use. Relevant expenses are also important factors, including the cost of building a system, running it, interpreting the results, and providing for its maintenance.

When expert systems become widely used, they will require intensive evaluations before release to the public. There may be legal considerations as well. Should such systems be certified according to their abilities? Who is ultimately to blame if a system produces negative consequences? On the other hand, will some systems become so expert and accepted that it will be considered inappropriate or illegal to reach decisions without consulting them? Effective evaluation methods will become extremely important in these areas. A demonstration that a system is competent in its limited domain of expertise has to be sufficiently convincing to achieve a consensus of trust from society as a whole. And the legitimate demands of financial sponsors and of society will eventually force expert systems to give a rigorous account of themselves.

8.2.2 Pitfalls in the Design and Conduct of Structured Evaluations

8.2.2.1 Four Evaluation Principles

Evaluations surround us constantly. It is instructive to notice how one goes about performing them and using the results. What does this general experience with evaluations teach about how to evaluate (or not to evaluate) expert systems? One has only to consider the process of evaluating frequently discussed questions, such as automobile performance or the state of the U.S. economy, to realize the need for careful design of an evaluation relative to the predominant questions being asked by those desiring results.

In evaluating an automobile, for example, numerous pertinent criteria come immediately to mind: fuel economy, price, acceleration, handling ability, amount of luggage space, repair record, number of seats, and the like. It is clear that different criteria are emphasized depending on who is doing the assessment. The U.S. government mandated total fleet fuel efficiency standards, so it became interested in the Environmental Protection Agency (EPA) ratings. Manufacturers who must evaluate their cars in the same way are also interested in their appeal to the consumer and in how profitable they are when placed on the market. A salesperson may publicly tout evaluations such as EPA mileage ratings if they make the car look favorable, but may omit the mention of other, less favorable facts. Privately the salesperson evaluates the car by how profitable it is to sell, not by how well it drives. To the potential owner a car is a necessity that must be evaluated in terms of the trade-off between luxury and performance on the one hand and personal finances on the other. Thus the potential customer must evaluate many detailed characteristics of each car under consideration.

Similarly, the U.S. economy can be evaluated (or measured) in terms of the gross national product, the rate of unemployment, the prime interest rate, the size of the federal budget deficit, the number of housing starts, the values of leading indicators, etc. Again, different individuals or organizations emphasize different aspects of the economy's performance.

Such points suggest a series of principles that may be applied to the evaluation of expert systems:

> Principle 1. Complex objects or processes cannot be evaluated by a single criterion or number.

> Principle 2. The larger the number of distinct criteria evaluated or measurements taken, the more information will be available on which to base an overall evaluation.

For example, if no one knew mileage estimates, it would be harder to evaluate a car's relative economy. Given a choice between ordinal categories such as "good," "average," "poor," and the actual measurement (EPA estimate), most people would prefer the number (as long as reason exists to believe that differences between numbers are meaningful), because it contains more information, obviating and subsuming the more aggregate ordinal categories.

> Principle 3. People will disagree about the relative significance of various criteria according to their respective interests.

> Principle 4. Anything can be measured experimentally as long as exactly how to take the measurements is defined.

8.2.2.2   Formal Versus Informal Testing

At some point in the development of an expert system testing for certification or acceptance is required, often at a late stage of development, prior to general release of the system. Many difficulties are encountered in structuring an appropriate certification procedure, the problems resemble those involved in the assessment of the competence of human practitioners (discussed later in this chapter). But what might be more beneficial is conducting formal evaluations during earlier stages of development (before system release is seriously contemplated), when performance statistics might contribute to the ongoing development process. The question of motivation is central; it should be understood clearly by all concerned what purpose is to be served by a formal system evaluation, and who may be expected to benefit from the study. Such considerations can influence the design of the study and, in some cases, bias the results.

Because of the empirical nature of most expert-systems work, it is often the case that a system's failures are more interesting and informative than its successes. Often the richest source of new material is postmortem analysis, conducted impartially as an open inquiry about what happened and why. Such studies can lead to important discoveries concerning the essence of the problem domain and the adequacy of the tools being used. Publication of such results may provide a much more significant contribution to the literature than documentation of a system's success rate. But this may not appear sufficiently rigorous to satisfy those who prefer accountability through controlled, randomized, statistically significant studies of performance.

It can be argued that formal evaluations aim at cutting through rhetoric and obtaining an objective basis for gauging progress. However, serious difficulties in the design of evaluation studies can make the interpretation of results somewhat problematic. In part these difficulties reflect the myriad challenges involved in evaluating human expertise mentioned earlier. The process of certifying the competence of a professional practitioner can often involve a mixture of written and oral examinations and in some cases direct observation of on-the-job performance.

8.2.2.3   The Leeds and Copenhagen Tests: The Impact of Preselected Test Cases

A major source of difficulty in evaluating expert systems stems from the fact that these systems currently tend to be limited to a small portion of the human experts' domain of competence. This might be expected to simplify the evaluation task, as the range of behaviors to be evaluated becomes more constrained. A danger exists, however, that the results of evaluation studies may be unfairly biased by comparing the performance of a limited expert system with that of its more diversified human counterpart. Surprisingly, there is some evidence that this bias tends to work in favor of the restricted computer-based expert.

Because such an expert system cannot deal with the full range of human expert behavior, it is necessary to preselect tasks that fall within its limited purview. Thus many possibilities and complexities that can serve to confound the human expert are simply not at issue in the program. Moreover, the program has a language of discourse pertaining to its restricted subset of possibilities; therefore, if real-world test cases are used, there may be facts reported in the protocol, which—although capable of being interpreted and influencing the behavior of the human expert—cannot even be made known to the program. In effect, the program "knows" only what falls within its limited domain of expertise, and it is capable of "hearing" only pertinent facts related to those possibilities; it thereby perceives what may be a considerable simplification of the issues.

Some evidence in the literature supports this view. De Dombal (1972) has discussed a differential diagnosis program in a very limited domain. His program achieved an accuracy rating significantly better than that of senior clinicians analyzing the same patient data. This diagnostic program employed a Bayesian inference procedure, for which the required probability arrays were determined on the basis of a data base containing records of symptom variables for patients admitted to a department of abdominal surgery with the principal complaint of acute abdominal pain.

In the initial study, conducted at Leeds, England, the range of decision alternatives was restricted to seven diagnostic categories. It was found that in this setting, the program performed at a 91.8 percent level of accuracy, as compared with 79.6 percent for the senior clinicians in the department, 77 percent for registrars (residents) who entered the data, and 65.6 percent for all physicians.

In a subsequent study (Bjerregaard et al. 1976) conducted in Copenhagen, Denmark, the diagnostic domain could not be controlled as narrowly. The authors note that in Leeds, no patients with acute salpingitis or urolithiasis are admitted to the department of abdominal surgery (gastroenterology); instead, they are directed to the appropriate gynecological or urological units. In Copenhagen, however, such patients would first be admitted to the gastroenterology department and transferred to special departments on the next day.

To adapt to this expanded problem domain, forms for collecting input data were changed to contain more symptom variables, and the data base from Leeds was modified to include patients with acute salpingitis and urolithiasis. The list of possible diagnoses increased from seven to nine. The authors observe that "although the list of potential causes of acute abdominal pain is almost endless, in practice about 90% of patients suffer from one of (these) nine disease categories."

In addition to the modified Leeds data base, a local data base was compiled in Copenhagen, prospectively recording the same symptom variables for 623 patients admitted to the gastroenterology depart-

ment. The first 451 of these patient records were analyzed, using probability arrays derived from both the Leeds and the Copenhagen data bases. In neither case was it possible to obtain accuracy ratings for the computer greater than the 65 percent level of the doctors.

The authors explain this rather dramatic drop in system performance in two ways. For the Copenhagen version, the lower performance rating is thought to be due to an inadequate sample of the rarer diseases in that data base. For the Leeds version the lower performance is attributed to regional differences in the prevalence of disease. These are undoubtedly contributing factors, but they fail to take into account the change in definition of the task environment, which increased the number of observational variables that could be reported, as well as the number of decision alternatives to be considered. It is interesting that in this more complex domain, even senior clinicians performed less well than their counterparts in the more constrained environment at Leeds.

While the evidence is not conclusive, it illustrates how a formal evaluation can be seriously misleading—even when methodologically sound in its statistical design. This will result when the study measures performance of an expert system operating in a limited domain, where cases are preselected and presented using a restricted set of descriptors that pertain only to its limited domain.

Since most of the patients in the de Dombal studies underwent surgery, it was possible to use the pathologic diagnosis (the true facts of the case, based on examination of tissue, culture, or other diagnostic procedure) as a basis for judging the accuracy of the diagnostic performance of both the physicians and the computer programs. There is some question whether this might account for what appears to have been a bias in favor of the computer system. More comparable results might have been obtained if an alternative "gold standard" based on some form of peer review process had been employed, for in this case the expert human evaluators would have the same opportunity to be misled as the human decision makers. Thus the process of selecting the standard for an evaluation can itself affect the quality and results of the study. This topic is discussed in greater detail in Section 8.3.

8.2.2.4 Evaluating the Reasoning as Well as the Conclusions

Since the typescript protocol generated by an expert system cannot very well be disguised to resemble a human dialogue, the desire to blind a study necessarily limits the amount of evidence that can be made available to the panel of expert judges concerning the adequacy of the problem-solver's knowledge and methods. In one of the MYCIN studies (Yu et al. 1979a), the evaluators were asked to make their assessment of performance (of both physicians and the MYCIN program) based only on the decision maker's final judgment about therapy. One problem with this emphasis on final performance is that it fails to take into account the microstructure of problem-solving behavior, which can be extremely important in permitting the extrapolation from representative instances of behavior to make judgments concerning overall competence. Evaluators want to be convinced that the system is consistently getting the right answers for the right reasons.

8.2.2.5   Evaluation by Peers

It is important to keep in mind that in evaluating the performance of an expert system, what is being studied is a program, however complex. As with other complex systems that are to be relied on for critical applications (such as operating systems, and programs for air traffic control), the expert system needs to be exercised within a wide-ranging series of test situations aimed at discovering ways to make the system fail. The experts engaged in evaluating system performance must have full access to all aspects of behavior, so that they can push and probe, looking for weaknesses and deficiencies. This would seem to rule out blinded, comparative studies as an appropriate framework for expert-system evaluation, at least at early stages in the development life cycle.

A further benefit of having outside experts interactively probe an expert system is obtaining their judgments as to whether the right problem has been addressed. The bottom line is "Will the system be used?" This is not the same question as "Does it do correctly the subtask selected by its designers?" Indeed the answer to this question may be totally irrelevant. The real question is whether the subset of expertise modeled in the expert system is really of any importance—can it render a service for which a need really exists?

Once a system begins generating performance, it becomes an important part of the laboratory apparatus available to the knowledge engineer and cognitive analyst to gain fresh insights into the domain of expertise for which that system was built. The true goal of evaluation should not be to show how well a system does what it was designed to do but, rather, to gain a greater appreciation of the process, structure, and limits of expertise. This system can later be parlayed into new levels of expert performance in successive system developments.

8.2.2.6   A Checklist of Pitfalls

The following is a list of potential pitfalls that must be avoided in preparing for the evaluation of a developing expert system and in presenting results:

- Evaluators may fail to clarify what is being evaluated.
- Evaluators may fail to clarify for whom the evaluation is intended.
- Preselected cases may bias the results or their interpretation by narrowing the scope of problems with which the system is asked to deal.
- Evaluators may fail to select an appropriate standard against which to compare the performance of the expert system.
- Evaluators tend to overgeneralize from results obtained in a highly constrained environment.
- Confusion may exist about the goals of the study; a designer's attempt to assess new techniques by a modest survey may be seen by others as an evaluation of a proposed performance system.
- The evaluation may be inappropriate for the stage of development (because premature or entwined with conflicting goals of the funding agency and the researcher).
- There are often inherent difficulties in designing elegant tests; these may not have been appreciated and dealt with adequately in the study design.
- A formal evaluation may be a misallocation of scarce resources needed for other project activities (such as funds, computer time, and work time of research staff, evaluators, and those supplying the input data).

Despite these potential pitfalls, the benefits of well-designed evaluation studies justify careful consideration of when to undertake formal studies during the evolution of an expert system. The next section describes these design issues in detail.

8.3   Design Issues for the Evaluation of Expert Systems

Thus far the reasons for doing evaluations of expert systems have been discussed, as well as some pitfalls that must be avoided en route, but the nature of the evaluation process itself has not been addressed in detail. This section defines many of the parameters that determine an appropriate design for an evaluation experiment.

8.3.1   Dependence on Task, System, Goals, and Stage of Development

From the literature on computer performance evaluation (Denning 1981), it is clear that the term *evaluation* is used with a variety of meanings, depending upon the perspective of the authors. Each tends to focus on performance issues specific to the design of the system in question; other aspects warranting formal evaluation are often ignored or deferred. One of the goals of this chapter is to make it clear that there are diverse components of the evaluation process. Validation should occur in stages as an expert system develops over time, from first feasibility demonstration, to formal testing, through field tests with live users solving real-world problems, to annual use statistics and retrospectives.

It is instructive to consider the evaluation of systems that are designed to perform a real-world task, typically to be used by a community of noncomputer scientists. It is assumed that one major goal is the development of a useful system that can have an impact on society by becoming a regularly used tool in the community for which it was designed. Although it is recognized that many basic science problems may arise during the development of such systems, the focus here is the staged assessment of the developing tool rather than techniques for measuring its scientific impact as a stimulus to further research.

8.3.2   What Expert System Characteristics to Evaluate

Some aspects of a computing system's performance are more appropriately evaluated than others at a particular stage in its development. By the time a system has reached completion, however, it is likely that every aspect will have warranted formal assessment, including (1) the quality of the system's decisions and advice, (2) the correctness of the reasoning techniques used, (3) the quality of the human–computer interaction (both its content and the mechanical issues involved), (4) the system's efficiency, and (5) its cost-effectiveness. Each of these points will be discussed in the following sections. The optimal timing for such evaluations is the topic of a subsequent section.

8.3.2.1   Decisions, Advice, and Performance

Expert systems developed to date, including both MYCIN and PROS-PECTOR, have tended to emphasize the program's performance at its decision-making task in their evaluation studies. Since reliably accurate advice is an essential component of an expert consultation system, it is usually the area of both greatest research interest and practical interest and is logically an area to emphasize in evaluation. However, the mechanisms for deciding whether a system's advice is appropriate or adequate may be difficult to define or defend. Expert systems tend to be built precisely for those domains in which the decisions of human experts are highly judgmental and nonstandardized. However, it is clear that no expert system will be accepted by its intended users if they fail to be convinced that the decisions made and the advice given are pertinent and reliable. Typically some approach to performance verification is mandatory.

8.3.2.2   Correct Reasoning

Not all designers of expert systems are concerned about whether their program reaches decisions in a humanlike way, as long as the advice that it offers is appropriate. Both the MYCIN and PROSPECTOR evaluations ignored the question of whether the programs were reaching decisions using reasoning equivalent to that used by comparable human experts. However, as has been made clear earlier in this book, there is an increasing realization that expert-level performance may require heightened attention to the mechanisms by which human experts actually solve the problems for which the expert systems are typically built. It is with regard to this issue that the interface between knowledge engineering and psychology is the greatest; and, depending upon the motivation of the system designers and the eventual users of the expert program, some attention to the mechanisms of reasoning that the program uses may be appropriate during the evaluation process. The issue of deciding whether or not the reasoning used by the program is "correct" will be discussed below.

8.3.2.3   Discourse (I/O Content)

Although the reliability of the reasoning processes of an expert system is crucial to its ultimate success, knowledge engineers now routinely accept the fact that a variety of other parameters influence whether a system is accepted by the intended users. The nature of the discourse between the expert system and the user is particularly important. Relevant are such diverse issues as the following:

- The choice of words used in the questions and responses generated by the program
- The ability of the expert system to explain the basis for its decisions and to tailor those explanations appropriately to the level of expertise of the user
- The ability of the expert system to assist users when they are confused by what is required of them or need assistance for any other reason when using the program
- The ability of the expert system to give advice or to educate the user in a congenial fashion and in the user's own terms, so that the frequently cited psychological barriers to computer use are overcome or avoided

Because issues such as these are every bit as important to the ultimate practical success of an expert system as is the quality of its advice, they also warrant formal evaluation. Many current expert systems have made some effort to develop capabilities along these lines, but the techniques for assessing their utility and for separating one variable from the others in a study design are still rudimentary. Because the issues generally are not amenable to formal study until a system is implemented for use by its intended end users, their evaluation has tended to be ignored in assessments of expert systems to date.

8.3.2.4   Hardware Environment (I/O Medium)

Much effort has gone into the development of congenial terminal interfaces between novice computer users and computer systems. Although some users, particularly when pressed to do so, can become comfortable with a conventional typewriter keyboard as the basis for the interaction with the machine, in many settings this is a skill that has to be learned and the potential users are not motivated. For that reason, light-pen interfaces, touch screens, and specialized keypads have been developed, any of which may be adequate to support a simple interaction between intended users and the expert system. The details of the hardware interface typically influence the design of the system software as well. The intricacies of this interaction cannot be ignored in system evaluation, nor can the mundane details of the users' reaction to the terminal interface. Again, it can be difficult to design evaluations in which dissatisfaction with the terminal interface is isolated as a variable, independent of discourse adequacy or decision-making performance. As will be pointed out subsequently, one purpose of staged evaluations is the resulting ability to allow certain variables to be eliminated during the evolution of the system and the corresponding stages of the evaluation.

8.3.2.5   Efficiency

The impact of an expert system on the process of decision-making in the users' environment must also be analyzed during the system's evaluation. A system that requires an excessive time commitment by users, for example, may fail to be accepted even if it excels at all the other tasks mentioned. Similarly, technical analyses of system behavior are generally warranted. Underutilized CPU power or poorly designed disk-seeking behavior, for example, may introduce resource inefficiencies that severely limit the system's response time or cost-effectiveness.

8.3.2.6   Cost-Effectiveness

Finally, and particularly if it is intended that an expert system become a marketable product, some detailed evaluation of its cost-effectiveness is in order. Only a few AI systems are beginning to reach this stage in system evolution, but there is a wealth of relevant experience in other areas of computer science. Developers of expert systems must be prepared to embark on similar studies. Ultimately, however, the marketplace judges the cost-effectiveness of a product. The first tool for building expert systems to be sold on a commercial basis is AL/X (Reiter 1981). Since it is used to build expert systems and does not itself contain domain expertise, AL/X has not undergone formal evaluations previously, and the marketplace will therefore help define the success of the approach that the program offers.

8.3.3   When to Evaluate Expert Systems

The evaluation process should be continual, beginning with system design, extending in an informal fashion through the early stages of development, and becoming increasingly formal as a developing expert system begins to achieve real-world implementation. Nine stages of system development summarize the evolution of an expert system. These steps, based on a discussion of expert systems by Shortliffe and Davis in SIGART *Newsletter* 55 (December 1975), are discussed in some detail in the paragraphs below (the first three are discussed in greater detail in previous chapters). The stages in the implementation of an expert system are as follows:

1. Top-level design; definition of long-range goals
2. Implementation of prototype Mark-I to show feasibility.
3. Refinement of system, usually by
   a.   Running informal test cases to generate feedback from the expert, resulting in refined prototype Mark-II
   b.   Releasing Mark-II to friendly users and soliciting their feedback
   c.   Revising system on basis of users' feedback
   d.   Releasing revised Mark-II to users and returning to stage 3b
4. Structured evaluation of performance
5. Structured evaluation of acceptability to users
6. Service functioning for extended period in prototype environment
7. Conducting of follow-up studies to demonstrate the system's large-scale usefulness
8. Making program changes to allow wide distribution of the system
9. General release and marketing with firm plans for maintenance and updating

It is important for system designers to be very clear about the nature of their motivations for building an expert system. The long-range goals must also be outlined explicitly. *Thus stage 1 of a system's development, the initial design, should be accompanied by explicit statements of what the measures of the program's success will be and how that failure or success will be evaluated.* It is not uncommon for system designers to ignore this issue at the outset, since the initial challenges appear so great upon consideration of the decision-making task that their expert system will have to undertake. If the evaluation stages and long-range goals are explicitly stated, however, they will necessarily have an impact on the early design of the expert system. If formal explanation capabilities are deemed to be crucial for the user community in question, for example, this will have important implications for the underlying knowledge representation that the expert system must utilize. Thus the evaluation process ideally starts with the conception of an expert system, so that its anticipation may help shape the early design and uncover issues that it would otherwise be tempting to overlook or ignore at that early stage.

Stage 2 in the development of an expert system is a demonstration that the performance task that has been selected is

feasible. No attempt is made to demonstrate expert-level performance; rather, the designers must show that the representation of
knowledge is appropriate for the task domain and that by utilizing
knowledge-engineering techniques, a prototype system can be built
that performs reasonably well on some subtask of the domain. An
evaluation at this stage is typically very informal, simply showing
that a few special cases can be handled by the prototype system. This
result suggests that with increased knowledge and refinement of the
reasoning structures, a high-performance expert system is attainable.

Stage 3 is familiar to all knowledge engineers; in fact, it is as far
as many laboratory systems ever get. This is the period in which
informal test cases are run through the developing system, the
system's performance is observed, and feedback is sought from expert
collaborators and potential end users. This feedback serves to define
the major problem areas in the system's development and guides the
next iteration in the development. This iterative process may go on
for months to years, depending on the complexity of the knowledge
domain, the flexibility of the knowledge representation, and the
availability of techniques adequate to cope with the domain's
specific control or strategic processes. The point can be made, however, that evaluation of an informal nature is part of this iteration.
The question constantly being asked is: How did this system do on
this case? Detailed analyses of strengths and weaknesses lead back to
further research; in this sense evaluation is an intrinsic part of the
system development process.

Once the system is performing well on most cases with which it
is presented, it is appropriate to turn to a more structured evaluation
of its decision-making performance. This evaluation can be performed without assessing the program's actual utility in a potential
user's environment. Thus Stage 4 is undertaken when the test
cases being used in stage 3 are found to be handled with skill and
competence, and a belief accordingly develops that a formal randomized study will show that the system is capable of handling almost
any problem from its domain of expertise. Only a few expert systems
have reached this stage of evaluation. The principal examples are the
PROSPECTOR system developed at SRI International (Gaschnig
1980a, b) and the MYCIN system from Stanford University (Yu et al.
1979a). A formal evaluation with randomized case selection may
show that the expert system is in fact not performing at an expert
level. In this case new research problems or knowledge requirements
are defined and the system development returns to stage 3 for additional refinement. A successful evaluation at stage 4 is required
before a program is introduced into the users' environment.

Stage 5 is system evaluation in the setting where the intended users have access to it. The principal question at this stage

is whether the program is acceptable to the users for whom it is intended. Among current expert systems, only the R1 program for configuring VAX computers (see Section 8.4) has been assessed formally at this stage. The fact that R1 has also melded its stage 4 and 5 evaluations, for reasons discussed below, may lead to confusion in interpreting results. The emphasis in stage 5 is on the discourse abilities of the program, as well as on the hardware environment that is provided. That is the reason that stage 4 ideally should have been successfully completed before stage 5 is attempted. Otherwise failure to accept the program by the end users may result from decision-making errors rather than from problems with the discourse or the hardware environment. If on the other hand expert-level performance has been demonstrated at stage 4, failure of the program to be accepted at stage 5 can be assumed to be due to one of these human factors.

If a system is shown formally to make good decisions and to be acceptable to users, introducing it for extended periods in some prototype environment (stage 6) is appropriate. This stage is intended largely to gain experience with a large number of test cases and with all the intricacies of field functioning that may not have been addressed adequately in system design. Careful attention during this stage must be directed toward problems of scale, the question being what new difficulties will arise when the system is made available to large numbers of users beyond the direct control of the system developers. Evaluation during this stage, which tends to be rather informal, is based upon careful observation of the program's performance and the changing attitudes of those who interact with it.

After service functioning has proceeded in a prototype environment and seems to be running smoothly, it is appropriate to begin some follow-up studies to demonstrate the system's large-scale usefulness (stage 7). These formal evaluations tend to require the measurement of pertinent parameters prior to introducing the system into a large user community that is different from the original prototype environment. Then, after the system is made available in the new setting, careful observation and measurement are required to determine the system's impact. Pertinent issues are the system's efficiency, its cost-effectiveness, its acceptability to users who were not involved in its early experimental development, and its impact on the execution of the task with which it was designed to assist.

During stage 7 it is not uncommon to discover new problems that require attention before the system can be marketed or otherwise distributed freely (stage 8). These may involve programming changes or modifications required to allow the system to run on a smaller or exportable machine.

The last stage in system development is its general release as a marketable product (stage 9). Inherent at this stage are firm plans for maintaining the knowledge base and keeping it current. It might be argued that the ultimate evaluation takes place at this stage when it is determined whether the system can succeed in the open market. However, a system's credibility is likely to be greater if good studies have been done in the first eight stages so solid data support any claims about the quality of the program's performance.

8.3.4   How to Evaluate Expert Systems

It would be folly to claim that detailed study designs for expert systems can be suggested in one section of a book chapter. A wealth of information is to be found in the statistical literature, for example, regarding the design of randomized controlled trials (Armitage 1971), and much of that experience is relevant to the design of expert systems evaluations. The intention here is to provide some general guidelines, concentrating on issues that complicate the evaluation of expert systems and on factors that must be considered during study design.

It is also desirable to distinguish between two senses of the term *evaluation*. In computer science, system evaluation often means optimization in the technical sense—timing studies, for example, that measure the CPU time required or the number of disk accesses. Emphasis here, on the other hand, is on a system's performance at the specific consultation task for which it has been designed.

Unlike many conventional programs, expert systems do not usually deal with problems for which there is clearly a right or wrong answer (sorting a list or inverting a matrix). As a result it is seldom easy to demonstrate in a straightforward fashion that a system's answers are correct and then to concentrate on demonstrating that it reaches the solution to a problem in some optimal way.

The following sections will outline a number of the key issues that affect the decision on how best to evaluate an expert system. There are several items on the list: (1) the need for an objective standard of excellence, (2) concerns regarding biasing and blinding, (3) the elimination of irrelevant variables, (4) the definition of realistic standards of performance, (5) the need for sensitivity analysis, (6) problems with confounding interactions among knowledge sources, and (7) the need for realistic time demands on evaluators.

8.3.4.1   Need for an Objective Standard

Evaluations of new techniques typically require some kind of gold standard, a generally accepted correct answer with which the results of the new methodology can be compared. In the assessment of new diagnostic techniques in medicine, for example, the standard is often the result of an invasive procedure that physicians hope to be able to avoid, even though it may be 100 percent accurate (operative or autopsy results, or the analysis form of angiogram). The sensitivity and specificity of a new diagnostic liver test based on a blood sample can be assessed only by comparing test results with the results of liver biopsies from several patients who also had the blood test. If the blood test is thereby shown to be a good predictor of the results of the liver biopsy, it may be possible to avoid the more invasive procedure with future patients. The parallel to expert system evaluation is obvious: if it can be demonstrated that the expert system's advice is comparable to the standard for the domain in question, it may no longer be necessary to turn to the standard itself if it is less convenient, less available, or more expensive.

In general, there are two views of how to define the standard for an expert system's task domain: (1) what eventually turns out to be the correct answer for a problem (in some objective sense) or (2) what a human expert (or a group of them), presented with the same information available to the program, say is the correct answer. It is unfortunately the case that for many kinds of problems with which expert systems are designed to assist, the first of these questions cannot be answered or is irrelevant.

Consider, for example, the performance of the MYCIN program (Shortliffe 1976). MYCIN's charge is to identify the bacteria causing infection in a patient and, accordingly, to suggest optimal antibiotic therapy. One might therefore suggest that the standard in this domain should be the identity of the bacteria that are ultimately isolated from the patient or the outcome for the patient, if he is treated in accordance with (or in opposition to) the program's recommendation. Suppose, for example, that MYCIN suggests therapy that covers four possibly pathogenic bacteria but that the organism that is eventually isolated is instead a fifth, rare bacterium that was totally unexpected, even by the experts involved in the case. In what sense should MYCIN be considered wrong in such an instance? Since expertise in such a domain is largely based on probabilistic considerations, might it not be reasonable to suggest that MYCIN performed at an expert level and was in fact correct if it agreed with the experts, even if both MYCIN and the experts turned out to be wrong? Similarly, the outcome for patients treated for serious infections is not 100 percent correlated with the correctness of therapy; patients treated in accordance with the best available medical practice may still die from fulminant infection, and occasionally patients will improve on their own, despite inappropriate or unnecessary antibiotic treatment (or lack of treatment). Because of considerations such as these, the stud-

ies of MYCIN's performance used expert opinions rather than outcomes for patients or bacterial identification as the gold standard (Yu
et al. 1979a, b).

A related issue that arises if domain experts are used as the objective standard for performance evaluation is whether the human
experts themselves are subjected to rigorous evaluations of their decisions. If so, such assessments of human expertise may provide a useful set of benchmarks against which to measure the expertise of a developing consultation system (a silver standard, perhaps). An advantage of this approach is that the technique for evaluating human
experts (if any exists) is usually a well-accepted basis for assessing
expertise and thus lends credibility to an evaluation of the
computer-based approach.

Typically, however, human expertise is accepted and acknowledged using less formal criteria (level of training, recommendations
of previous clients, supervisors or teachers, years of experience in a
field, number of publications, salary, and the like). Testimonials
regarding the performance of a computer program have also frequently been used as a catalyst for the system's dissemination, but it
is precisely this kind of anecdotal selling of a system that is being
argued against here. Many fields will not accept technological inno-
vation without rigorous demonstration of the breadth and depth of
the new product's capabilities. This may be particularly true in the
domains in which a computer system is taking on decision-making
tasks previously performed by humans. Both MYCIN and PROSPEC-
TOR encountered this cautious attitude in potential users and
designed their evaluations largely in response to a perceived need for
rigorous demonstrations of performance.

8.3.4.2   Biasing and Blinding

In designing any evaluation study, considerations of sources of bias
are, of course, important. This lesson, learned again by MYCIN's
evaluators, explains many of the differences between the bacteremia
evaluation (Yu et al. 1979a) and the meningitis study (Yu et al.
1979b). During the first of these evaluations, the expert physicians
who were assessing MYCIN's performance knew they were examining
the output of a computer program. Many of their comments and criticisms reflected their own biases regarding the proper role of computers in medical settings ("I don't think the computer has an adequate
sense of how sick this patient is. You'd have to see a patient like this
in order to judge."). As a result, the meningitis study design mixed
MYCIN's recommendations with a set of recommendations from nine
other individuals (ranging from infectious disease faculty members to

medical students) asked to assess the case. When national experts later gave opinions on the appropriateness of therapeutic recommendations, they did not know which proposed therapy was MYCIN's and which recommendations came from the human diagnosticians. This blinded study design removed an important source of potential bias and also provided a sense of where MYCIN's performance lay along a range of expertise from faculty specialists to medical students.

8.3.4.3   Eliminating Variables

As pointed out in the discussion of when to evaluate an expert system, one advantage of a sequential set of studies is that each can assume the results of the experiments that preceded it. Thus for example, if a system has been shown to reach satisfactory decisions in its domain of expertise, the system's failure to be accepted by its intended users in an experimental setting can be assumed to reflect inadequacies in an aspect of the system other than its decision-making performance. One key variable that could account for system failure has been removed in this way. For example, MYCIN's designers explained in evaluating the program's decision-making performance (Yu et al. 1979b) that they did not intend to implement it to assess its clinical utility until they had demonstrated that it reached decisions at the level of an expert in the field. In this way they wanted to assure that any subsequent failure of acceptance by physicians was due to human-engineering problems rather than decision-making errors.

8.3.4.4   Realistic Standards of Performance

Before assessing the capabilities of an expert system, it is necessary to define the minimal acceptable standards that will permit the system to be called a success. Ironically, in many domains it is difficult to decide what level of performance qualifies as expert. Thus it is important to measure the performance of human experts in a field if they are assessed by the same standards to be used in the evaluation of the expert system. This point was demonstrated in the MYCIN evaluations. In the bacteremia studies (Yu et al. 1979a), MYCIN's performance was approved by experts in approximately 75 percent of cases, a figure that seemed disappointingly low to the system developers. They felt that the system should be approved in at least 90 percent of cases before it was made available for actual clinical use. The blinded study design for the subsequent meningitis evaluation (Yu et al. 1979b), however, showed that even infectious disease faculty members received at best a 70–80 percent rating from other experts in the field. Thus the 90 percent figure originally sought may have been unrealistic, inadequately reflecting the level of disagreement that can exist even among experts in a field such as clinical medicine.

8.3.4.5   Sensitivity Analysis

A special kind of evaluation procedure pertinent for expert systems is the analysis of a program's sensitivity to slight changes in the knowledge represented, inference weighting values, input data supplied by the user, and so on. Similarly it may be pertinent to ask which interactive capabilities were necessary for user acceptance of an expert consultant. Experiments that compare two versions of the system, one with and one without (or with a different version) of the feature under consideration provide one approach to assessing these issues. Identical results from two parallel studies tend to suggest that the feature may not be crucial to system performance after all.

Examples of studies of this kind are the experiments that MYCIN's developers have done in assessing their certainty factor (CF) model of inexact reasoning (Shortliffe and Buchanan 1975). Clancey and Cooper showed, in experiments, (Buchanan and Shortliffe, 1983) that the decisions of MYCIN changed minimally from those of the meningitis evaluation (Yu et al. 1979b) over a wide range of possible CF intervals for the inferences in the system. This *sensitivity analysis* helped MYCIN researchers decide that the details of the CFs associated with their rules mattered less than the semantic and structural content of the rules themselves.

8.3.4.6   Interaction of Knowledge

Preserving good performance when correcting the bad is important. A problem can be encountered when an evaluation has revealed system deficiencies and new knowledge has been added to the system in an effort to correct them. In complex expert systems, the interactions of new knowledge with old can be unanticipated and lead to detrimental effects on problems that were once handled very well by the system. An awareness of this potential problem is crucial as system-builders iterate from stage 3 to stage 4 and back to stage 3. One method for protecting against the problem is to keep a library of old cases available on-line for batch testing of the system's decisions. Then, as changes are made in the system in response to stage 4 evaluations of the program's performance, the old cases can be run through the revised version to verify that no unanticipated knowledge interactions have been introduced (to show that the program's performance on the old cases does not deteriorate). Automated tools can facilitate such *quality-control* efforts by making such tests routine and not time-consuming.

8.3.4.7   Realistic Time Demands on Evaluators

A mundane issue that must still be considered because it can lead to failure of a study design or, at the very least, to unacceptable delays in completing the program's assessment is the time required for evaluators to judge the system's performance and for others to supply input data for the test. If expert judgments are used as the gold standard for adequate program performance, the opinions of the experts must be gathered for the cases used in the evaluation study. A design that picks the most pertinent two or three issues to be assessed and concentrates on obtaining the expert opinions in as easy a manner as possible will therefore have a much better chance of success. MYCIN's staff experienced over a year's delay in obtaining the evaluation booklets back from the experts who had agreed to participate in the bacteremia evaluation (Yu et al. 1979a); focusing on fewer variables and designing a checklist that allowed the experts to assess program performance much more rapidly allowed the meningitis evaluation to be completed in less than half that time (Yu et al. 1979b). Even a half-year will seem discouragingly long to some readers.

8.4   A Case Study: R1

Perhaps the most mature knowledge-based expert system, in terms of the developmental stages discussed previously, is the R1 system developed by John McDermott and his colleagues at Carnegie-Mellon University. This program, which helps in configuring VAX computer systems, was developed under contract with the Digital Equipment Corporation. As this contract specified a form of acceptance testing for the system, the experience of this project provides a unique case study in formal systems evaluation. In this section, the purpose and task domain of the R1 system are reviewed briefly, then the evaluation process examined. In part, the background material derives from technical reports (McDermott 1980a, b) describing the R1 system and a retrospective article about the stages of R1's development (McDermott 1981); additional insights, particularly with respect to the acceptance testing procedure, were obtained through personal interviews and discussions with John McDermott in 1980.

8.4.1   The Computer Configuration Task

The following description of the VAX-11/780 configuration task is taken from McDermott (1980b):

> The VAX-11/780 is the first implementation of Digital Equipment Corporation's VAX-11 architecture. It is similar in many respects to the PDP-11, though its virtual address space is 2^{32} rather than 2^{16}. The VAX-11/780 uses a high speed synchronous bus, called the sbi (synchronous backplane interconnect), as its primary interconnect. The central processor, one or two memory control units, one to four massbus interfaces, and one to four unibus interfaces can be connected to the sbi. The massbuses and particularly the unibuses can support a wide variety of peripheral devices. Because the number of system variations is so large, the VAX configuration task is non-trivial.
>
> A VAX configurer must have two sorts of knowledge. . . . First, he must have information about each of the components that a customer might order. For each component, the configurer must know the properties that are relevant to system configuration—e.g., its voltage, its frequency, how many devices it can support (if it is a controller), how many ports it has . . . "component information." Second, he must have rules that enable him to associate components to form partial configurations and to associate partial configurations to form a functionally acceptable system configuration. These rules must indicate what components can (or must) be associated and what constraints must be satisfied in order for these associations to be acceptable: "constraint knowledge."
>
> . . . On the average, a configurer must know eight properties of a component in order to be able to configure it appropriately. Currently about 420 components are supported for the VAX. Thus there are over 3300 pieces of component information that a VAX configurer must have access to.
>
> Before R1 was developed, it would have been difficult to estimate accurately the amount of constraint knowledge required for the configuration task. Much of the required knowledge was not written down anywhere and thus the only source of estimates would have been individual human experts. But the experts find the task of quantifying their constraint knowledge foreign. As I extracted this knowledge from them, it became clear that their knowledge takes two forms: (1) The experts have a sparse but highly reliable picture of their task domain. When asked to describe the configuration task, they do so in terms of the subtasks involved and the various temporal relationships among these subtasks. (2) They also have a considerable amount of very detailed knowledge that indicates the features that particular partial configurations and unconfigured components must have in order for the partial configurations to be extended in particular ways. I extracted 480 rules. Of these, 96 define situations in which some subtask should be ini-

tiated. The other 384 rules define situations in which some partial configuration should be extended in some way.

8.4.2   The History of R1 to Date

The development of R1 followed a rapid progression through the nine stages of development. The concept was first proposed to Digital Equipment management in December 1978. Somewhat dubious, they agreed to proceed informally with a preliminary study. After approximately two weeks of intensive briefing by experts in the configuring task, McDermott undertook the implementation of a prototype system, which was completed and demonstrated in May 1979. This pilot version, implemented in OPS4 (Forgy 1979a), contained about 300 rules. Although not perfect, this prototype system served to convince management of the potential of this approach, so a formal agreement was drawn up providing for delivery of a finished system in October of that year, with acceptance testing to begin October 1.

8.4.2.1   The Initial Acceptance Tests for Demonstrating Feasibility

The initial plan called for use of the R1 system to configure fifty orders on October 1; these would be evaluated by a panel of experts, who would go over each order carefully, noting any errors or inadequacies in R1's handling of the configuration. Then, at three-week intervals, the process would be repeated: an additional batch of fifty orders would be selected and run through R1 (along with any not correctly configured during the preceding cycle), with the results fed back to the implementors for correction of the system, if necessary. The process would continue until an acceptable level of accuracy and reliability had been demonstrated.

The criteria for evaluation were not clearly defined in the contract, which specified only that the results should prove acceptable to the selected panel of experts. It was recognized that, in most cases, there would be no one right answer as to how to configure a system and that at a low level of detail, it was likely that no two experts would configure a given order in the same way. Agreement about the difference between acceptable and unacceptable configurations appeared to be pretty good. Knowledge about constraints was gained during system refinement between May and October of 1979, when an improved version of R1 was developed and the number of rules increased from 300 to over 800. McDermott reports that the expansion went smoothly, with no need for significant changes in the overall system design. Among considerations that needed to be taken into account in designing the knowledge base were four major categories of constraints identified by McDermott:

1. Violating engineering restrictions may mean that the system will not work correctly or not perform as well as possible. For example, if UNIBUS modules are ordered suboptimally, there might be data-late errors. One of the reasons for doing configuration is to determine the optimal order for putting devices on the bus. Other considerations include determining when it is necessary to put in a repeater and what is the alternating-current load on the backplane. There are many such engineering constraints, which are relatively clear cut.

2. A second set of constraints derives from the way in which the configuration process was previously carried out. Formerly two groups of people were involved: the paper configurers and the technicians. The paper configurers had the job of preparing a high-level description of the system layout, a task that did not require significant technical expertise, as the assignment was mainly to determine whether the various parts of an order would work together. The paper configurer merely produced a single sheet of paper displaying the cabinet layout of items ordered: the contents of the CPU cabinet and CPU expansion cabinets if any, the UNIBUS cabinet and expansion boxes if any, and so on.

3. This layout was then used by the technicians who actually physically assembled the system; what they did was follow the high-level description but make decisions on their own at a lower level. McDermott discovered a great deal of lore among technicians in the manufacturing organization about how these systems should be configured, some of which does tend to make the assembly process easier. However, much of the lore is completely ad hoc (there may be ten ways to do something, but a particular technician may habitually do it only one way), and some of it even conflicts with engineering standards. Nonetheless, such lore constitutes an important factor in the subjective determination of whether a configuration seems—to the technicians at least—acceptable or unacceptable.

4. A third set of constraints arises from decisions taken at the manufacturing plants, which send sets of components to the assembly factory, some of which may be partially configured; a backplane might arrive with a module in it, or a cabinet with a massbus adapter in it. The placement of these prepackaged components is not done with any particular configuration in mind and must therefore be changed in some cases in order to satisfy engineering (or other) constraints in the final assembly. However, the technician should not be directed to move such preinstalled modules unless there is

a good reason to do so; thus practices of the manufacturing plants in partially configuring components must be factored into the decisions made by the system configurer.

5. Market considerations constitute a final source of constraints because, as a matter of policy, the company has chosen to limit the range of combinations of components that will be considered complete systems. These marketing constraints do not affect the configuration task directly, but they do enter into the assessment of whether a system configuration is considered acceptable.

8.4.2.2   Formal Performance Tests

The enrichment of R1's knowledge base was completed on schedule, and the acceptance testing procedure was initiated on October 1, with some modifications in the initial plan. Instead of selecting a set of fifty orders to analyze, modification reduced the number to ten per cycle. The selection criterion was naive: the orders to be processed were the last ten to come through; thus no attempt was made to look for difficult configuration tasks (many orders that come through are actually trivial) on which the system might fail.

The evaluation team consisted of twelve people, drawn from the ranks of paper configurers, technicians, and engineering staff; of these, six or seven participated in the evaluation of any particular order. In an evaluation session the participants worked together, as opposed to working independently and then comparing conclusions. The process of evaluation required eight hours for the first order, four hours for the second, and one to two hours for the rest of the orders. McDermott reported that one of the things that the evaluators learned in processing the first few orders was that there was significant disagreement among themselves as to the right way to do the configurations. Here was a clear example of the lack of an objective, accepted gold standard.

The evaluation continued for two months, during which R1 was given fifty orders to configure. In the examination of the configurations produced, twelve orders were found to contain errors, which were of seven types. After the rules responsible for the errors were corrected, the orders were resubmitted to R1 and configured correctly. By December 1979, just one year after the first discussions of the project, R1 was judged to be expert enough to be used routinely in the configuration task.

8.4.2.3   Release to Users: Reactions and Limitations

At the time of the interview with McDermott, approximately one year after the evaluation and acceptance testing, it was not clear what impact the R1 implementation was having on VAX assembly operations. The role of paper configurer had continued but with altered responsibilities. Now, instead of preparing a one-page layout, this person was assigned the job of reviewing the first page of R1's output to see if any obvious problems had occurred; if problems are detected, they are sent to the ongoing review committee. Similarly, if the technicians get directions they do not trust, they are supposed to report this to the committee.

According to McDermott, one of the things that emerged from this postevaluation review of the actual implementation of R1 was that the program was adding things to orders (in order to satisfy the various sorts of constraints mentioned above) that reviewers considered too costly. In situations where formerly the technicians would leave a system unconfigured until advised by the customer about how to proceed, R1 would go ahead and add the necessary components and complete the configuration. Such problems are now caught by the paper configurer during the review process, which reduces by 40 to 50 percent the number of R1 configurations that actually reach the technicians.

On the final stage of the configuration process, when technicians actually assemble the system, McDermott had no direct evidence whether the detailed low-level layout specified by R1 was actually being adhered to. However, under pressure to determine the answer to this question, management had recently brought the technicians together for a type of postmortem review, which elicited what McDermott described as extremely important feedback, albeit a bit overdue, as to what is important and what is not in carrying out the configuration task.

In a retrospective article concerning the formative years of R1, McDermott (1981) makes the following observation concerning the relationship between expectations and the reality of R1 performance during the shakedown period after its formal acceptance:

> Many people were disturbed by the poor performance of R1 over this eight month period; the expectation after the validation stage was that R1 would soon be configuring at least 90% of the orders correctly. But in retrospect, it is clear that at the end of the validation stage R1 was still a very inexperienced configurer. It had encountered only a tiny fraction of the set of possible orders, and consequently its knowledge was still very incomplete.

8.4.3   Lessons

The main lesson from this experience is that the process of acceptance testing of an expert system cannot be considered complete until it can be demonstrated that the system is actually employed routinely in the capacity for which it was designed. In this case the evaluation procedure employed in the acceptance testing of R1 failed to reveal a number of important barriers to the eventual acceptance and implementation of that system. What seems to have been missing in the acceptance testing process was any real involvement by the user in the exercise of the system. There can be no better way to expose the weaknesses of a purported expert system than to invite those whose task domain it is to have a go at breaking the system. Real acceptance will come only when such a system can gain the respect of the most skeptical of its potential users by surviving the worst trials that they can devise.

8.5   A Case Study: The ORNL Spill Problem

8.5.1   The Spill Crisis Management Problem

Since the Oak Ridge National Laboratory (ORNL) spill-management problem (Chapter 10) is used as an example throughout this volume, it seemed useful as a hypothetical case study in expert system evaluation. As a *Gedanken* experiment, a procedure was designed for evaluating the performance of this unbuilt system—not only the pieces built at the 1980 Expert Systems Workshop but the entire hypothetical system. Data came from Chapter 10 and from discussions with Carroll Johnson and Sara Jordan, authors of that chapter.

Briefly, a toxic substance incident begins when any employee notices something unusual on the grounds or witnesses an actual spill and reports it to the Environmental Management Office. This office then becomes the focal point for an effort, first to identify and trace the substance back to its source through a complex system of drains, then to contain the leak, and finally to neutralize the substance. Depending upon the nature and severity of the spill, the manager must notify various governmental agencies during the incident and follow up with specific required reports. Although well-defined roles do exist, this task is complicated because the expertise of the individuals that fill them varies considerably, the night shift being on the whole less expert than the day shift, for example.

8.5.2   Selecting Performance Criteria

It was surprisingly difficult to select performance criteria for this problem. Two complications in particular were encountered. First, the background report about the spill problem sets out the task domain but does not specify exactly what the expert system program should do. Second, the experts in this case are not really experts at spills management; they are scientists involved in the early stages of formulating a program to aid in spills management. Many specific questions about performance and function had not yet been considered by them. In fact these questions forced the experts to think more closely about how to design their system: what kind of performance would be required, how the system would interact with its users, and so on.

This experience reinforced emphasis on the importance of formulating evaluations in the early stages of system design. The formulation process serves as a useful device for focusing attention on the details and requirements of the final system.

8.5.3   A Hypothetical VM-Style Crisis Monitoring System

The program definition decided on is similar to the Ventilator Manager (VM) program (Fagan et al. 1979) in its functional specification. The spills-management program will essentially act as a crisis monitor. In the event of an oil or chemical spill, it will aid the people working in the emergency center and in the field. It will function as a repository for all incoming reports about the spill and will thus have the most comprehensive and current view of the situation possible. This data-collection facility allows it to act as a coordination point for the various people working during the crisis and enables it to generate the required federally mandated reports.

The system also plays a more active role. Given a set of crisis scenarios, it will provide advice when asked and issue warnings when appropriate. For example, if it deduces from physical descriptions that the spilled chemical is toxic, it will warn field personnel to wear protective clothing. Finally the program will act as an intelligent access to the oil and chemical inventories and to the On-Line Hazardous Material Technical Assistance Data System (OHMTADS) data base on toxic chemicals. The spills program is intended to augment experts, not to replace them. Spills management is marked by necessary haste and uncertainty (or confusion); this system would act as a second opinion and back-up, ensuring that no vital step is omitted as well as monitoring for mistakes.

8.5.4   The Design for an Evaluation

Once the form and function of the proposed expert system were defined, it was time to suggest ways in which the system could be evaluated. Even assuming the system's functions are well-defined and that measurable performance criteria do exist, evaluation is still not a straightforward task. Three separate groups are interested in this system, each having different goals, motivations, and expectations.

The most remotely involved group includes various state and federal regulatory agencies such as the EPA, whose primary goal is to ensure that regulations are satisfied and that ORNL is dealing with spills in a competent manner. This group will want a thorough evaluation of the system's competence, if ORNL relies on the program to any large extent. These agencies would not be interested in other aspects of the system, except perhaps as a possible model for other installations. One approach to satisfying these regulatory agencies might be for the system to produce reports on its various recommendations and have the agencies measure the extent to which the reports and conclusions are considered adequate.

The eventual users (ORNL environmental management and field personnel) form the second group. They want to develop an efficient spills countermeasures operation but do not require an extensive computerized solution. Indeed they are under regulatory pressure to come up with a spills-management plan in the near future, so they would probably have to proceed along more conventional paths even if convinced of the feasibility and desirability of the proposed system. The user group wants evaluations at stages 4 and 5 as soon as possible. It might be difficult for them to separate performance from acceptance, because they are the ones who would most use and rely on the program. For them form is as important as content. If the system cannot perform in an acceptable manner, its degree of competence is irrelevant because nobody will use it. One final note about this group: these are busy people. However useful to the system builders or their own eventual welfare such steps might be, they probably do not have much time to participate in feasibility studies, system refinement, and performance evaluations before participating in a full-scale evaluation.

The final group is composed of the developers of the system, whose primary, stated goal is a demonstration of a feasible prototype. They think in terms of a stage 2 evaluation aimed at securing further support from ORNL management and gaining continued cooperation from collaborators and potential users of the system. Although some sort of feasibility study is necessary, it will consume a large portion of already-scarce research time.

Another issue is that solid, significant evaluations will be hard to obtain and easy to misinterpret. For example, it would be very difficult to evaluate a partially expert system. Because of the nature of the domain, the functioning of the system will be difficult to segment into independent subparts. The system will coordinate many different information sources and people; the nature of the system is substantially changed when only a small part of the total system is considered.

The other problem with a feasibility demonstration is that it is difficult to differentiate between the system's performance as an expert and its acceptability to users. A partial system will perform less competently and much less acceptably than a completed system. The evaluators will need to be very clear about what they are testing and what they expect to see. Although significant results might be obtained from testing a prototype system, they are not likely to predict much about the finished system.

There is a conflict in the motivations of the users and the builders of this system. The AI group at Oak Ridge is trying to bootstrap its exploratory efforts into a funded program, and their orientation is toward the examination of the applicability of current AI technology to ORNL problems. In this context, they look for tasks where AI tools can be applied profitably. They cannot be concerned primarily with developing new methodology or long-term problem involvement until they and their management are satisfied that such efforts are worthwhile. Consequently, the principal goal of this group is to provide either positive or negative evidence that knowledge engineering is a productive approach to this problem domain.

This is a different motivation from that of the spills-management people, who have a very specific problem that requires an immediate solution, in whatever form. The environmental management at Oak Ridge is open to an expert systems solution. Still, their goal is the completion and certification of a practical fielded system.

Without explicitly stating what is being tested, why it is being tested, and for whom, the evaluation could easily waste time and resources. It would be unfortunate if the EPA saw results of a stage 2 test.

8.5.5   A *Gedanken* Experiment at Stage 4

To continue the thought experiment, assume the project has reached stage 4. The knowledge engineers believe the system is ready for use and wish to test its competence before subjecting it to a more general user-acceptance test. This domain permits limited objective testing criteria so the program's performance must be compared against expert performance. There are two primary methods of doing this. The easier, and less formal, is the testimonial method, in which the evaluators put together a comprehensive set of test cases and perhaps a checklist of important features. The system is run on all the cases and if it is correct (or at least correctable) on all or most of them, the system passes. This testimonial method is widely used but is of limited utility because such results are difficult to interpret and generalize.

A better test design is the formal, blinded, statistical study. In this case the comparison would have to proceed event by event since a total process is being evaluated. The comparison would be between the program and its potential users: the three people at ORNL who can do the same job as the program, somebody from the night shift, and somebody from the field personnel. Protocols could be created by giving each tested agent step-by-step information about an incident and asking what response, if any, is best. Each protocol then could be rated by expert judges in a blind fashion. It is unrealistic to aim for results like "The program is 89 percent as good as our top expert," but this study could support a conclusion like "The program can perform with more expertise than both an average night-shift person and an average field worker but not as well as a typical expert."

There are still many questions to consider before a good evaluation can be accomplished. First, to what exactly is the program being compared? There are three people who could do the same job the program is designed to do, but they do not currently do it. The program represents a change in the way spills are handled. Since the program mimics a simulated expert, it is not clear what constitutes reasonable performance. The only evaluation of human performance at similar tasks is when a violation occurs. In such cases a formal report is made to the EPA for them (or sometimes the courts) to evaluate. Nobody tests the experts' routine competence. Besides not knowing what standards to apply, there is the problem of time and effort. The experts estimate it would take twenty to twenty-five cases to provide a fair sample that covered all significant variables and expertise. Doing step-by-step protocols of twenty cases would consume an enormous amount of time. Even if one is convinced of the test's value, perhaps other factors, such as fatigue, could cause poor performance. If all these variables are not considered, one might end up with a very expensive but inappropriate testimonial.

8.5.6   Lessons

The conclusions drawn from the thought experiment can be summed up in two words: caution and explicitness. Caution is necessary when conducting an evaluation experiment because many factors can invalidate the results. Explicitness in stating the goals of the experiment design is a good way to prevent these difficulties from occurring. If knowledge engineers state the methods and intent of their evaluation, they are forced to consider all the details and their results are more likely to resist misinterpretation.

8.6   Conclusions and Recommendations

The technology of expert systems is still in its infancy. Existing techniques for evaluating these systems are few and primitive. Certainly many criteria, like correctness, efficiency, or friendliness, used to evaluate other computerized or human systems also apply to expert systems. But expert systems are unique in that they contain human expertise and are thus most often compared and evaluated with respect to human performance. In this context it is not always clear whether a correct solution (for an expert system) is one that a human expert would give, one that a group of experts would agree upon, or one that represents the ideal solution (after subsequent testing and analysis). No one knows how to evaluate human expertise adequately, let alone how to evaluate the expert systems that attempt to recreate that expertise.

This chapter has summarized what is currently known about evaluating expert systems. At this stage of expert systems' evolution, the evaluation process is more of an art, however primitive, than a science. Although precise procedures and requirements for performing evaluations cannot be provided, some advice can be given as in the following recommendations and checklist.

Attention here has been focused on characteristics common to all expert systems, independent of the domain being modeled. Each particular domain will most likely have unique characteristics that will affect evaluation procedures and measurements. Nonetheless evaluations play a crucial role in the development and acceptance of all expert systems. Hence,

Recommendation 1. Plan evaluation checkpoints as part of system design.

We cannot stress strongly enough the need to design performance evaluations of an expert system *before* it is built, not after. Designing evaluations helps pinpoint both the specific goals of the system and the objective measures that can be used to determine whether the goals have been achieved. It is important for knowledge engineers to be very clear about the nature of their motivations for building an expert system. The system's goals should be accompanied by explicit statements of what the measures of the program's success will be and how that failure or success will be evaluated. Evaluation checkpoints should be set up corresponding to various stages of expert system implementation, and evaluations should be integral to the system's development. They should be formulated at the time of system design, extend in an informal fashion through the early stages of development, and become increasingly formal as the expert system moves toward field testing.

Recommendation 2. Involve eventual users in the design of a system.

The key question "Will the system be used?" should motivate the system-building process. This question should not be withheld until the evaluation stage; it should dominate every stage of system specification, design, and implementation. The expert system must render a service for which a need really exists. It will not be sufficient for the system to produce good answers; the system must also be usable and useful. To create a system that will be acceptable to users, knowledge engineers must acquaint themselves with the users' needs and desires and become familiar with the users' terminology, daily routines, and main headaches or worries. To introduce a system successfully into routine production use, they must strive to make it match closely the users' current needs and habits. The new tool must be as nondisruptive as possible, imposing few (if any) new requirements and demanding little training in its use and interpretation.

Recommendation 3. Be cautious when interpreting evaluation results.

Pitfalls to avoid in preparing and interpreting evaluations were listed earlier. Evaluation procedures often fail to capture the scope and depth of expert systems. It is often easy to criticize expert systems because they fail to perform up to (or even beyond) expectations. On the other hand successful test performances may result in unfounded generalizations. The few who are performing more structured evaluations are like a scouting party, exploring new and challenging areas of research. Many report the wondrous things discovered. Others speak of the frustrations and faults that lie in premature and inappropriate evaluations. More people are needed to map and cultivate these areas more comprehensively.

Many potential difficulties can be avoided by explicitly stating the methods and intent of an evaluation experiment. The following checklist is intended to force evaluation designers to consider all the details and thereby leave the results less open to misinterpretation.

1. Specify for whom the evaluation is intended. This greatly influences the design of the evaluation. Clearly, the informal evaluations

usually performed for system builders and expert collaborators would not be sufficient for financial supporters or for society.

2. Define precisely what is being evaluated. Isolate those aspects of the system that are being tested. Is it the quality of the system's decisions and advice, the correctness of the reasoning mechanism, the quality of the human–computer interaction, the system's efficiency, its cost-effectiveness, or some other aspect?

3. Select an appropriate gold standard against which to compare the expert system's performance.

4. Define realistic standards of performance; it may be unreasonable, for example, to expect better performance from the expert system than from a human expert.

5. Specify who will be evaluating the results. It could be human experts or end users, it could be individuals or a group evaluating by consensus, and so on. (Note that persons evaluating the results need not be the same as those for whom the evaluation is intended.)

6. Eliminate potential bias, for example by avoiding presenting the results in the form of computer output, which may bias judges who feel negative toward computer technology.

7. Specify the type of test cases presented—random cases or cases preselected to range over a broad spectrum of difficulty.

For a variety of reasons much more effort has been devoted to designing and constructing knowledge-based expert systems than to measuring their resulting performance. Some productive performance evaluations have been done, but opportunities abound for extending such efforts. One should not be content with building expert systems and turning them over to users. It is highly unlikely, for example, that physicists who have just completed the construction of a new, more powerful particle accelerator would unplug it, to turn to other matters, as soon as it passed the acceptance tests. It is clear, then, that AI researchers can profit by the physicists' example, by considering expert systems as scientific instruments, sources of observable behavior and hard data by which to define and investigate problem-solving behavior in detail, as well as ends in themselves.

QUESTIONS

1. How does developing an expert system differ from other software development tasks? In what ways are the two similar?

2. What advantages accrue to setting performance criteria before building a system? What disadvantages?

3. What knowledge is required to determine the way an expert system will be used? Where does this knowledge now reside?

4. Identify three types of contemporary knowledge purchasers. What else do they obtain with the knowledge that expert systems cannot provide? What added benefits can an automated system provide?

5. How can you measure the level of performance of an expert system? How can you bound its error rate? Which important qualities can you not assess?

PART IV

Expert System Tools

9

Languages and Tools for Knowledge Engineering

David R. Barstow, Nelleke Aiello,
Richard O. Duda, Lee D. Erman,
Charles L. Forgy, Daniel Gorlin
Russell D. Greiner, Douglas B. Lenat,
Philip E. London, John McDermott,
H. Penny Nii, Peter Politakis,
Rene Reboh, Stanley Rosenschein,
A. Carlisle Scott, William van Melle, and
Sholom M. Weiss

A comprehensive survey of tools widely used in knowledge engineering is provided in this chapter. Each tool reflects a special emphasis on kinds of problems, kinds of overall designs, or kinds of implementations deemed desirable. Although none of the tools meets industrial standards for wide-scale utilization, an order-of-magnitude reduction in development time can be realized by applying an appropriate tool. Today's tools foreshadow a vast array of future industrial implements. Knowledge engineering means forming and assembling knowledge, and the tools make this possible.

Whereas previous chapters described different ways of representing and using knowledge in expert systems, this one presents detailed descriptions of eight important expert-systems-building tools, using one of them to illustrate current knowledge-engineering techniques. Focus is on eight rule-based systems because of their conceptual simplicity: EMYCIN, KAS/PROSPECTOR, EXPERT, ROSIE, OPS5, RLL, HEARSAY-III, and AGE.

Experienced builders of expert systems develop a general paradigm or computational framework for building an expert system quite early to help them choose a programming language or system with which to work. A variety of options exist, ranging from general-purpose programming languages such as LISP, PASCAL, and FORTRAN to general-purpose representation systems developed specifically for knowledge engineering.

9.1   General-Purpose Programming Languages

One obvious strategy is to implement from scratch in one of the standard programming languages. LISP is chosen for most work in AI for several reasons. First, LISP is oriented toward symbolic computation; the programmer can code such terms as "chemical" and "spill." Although such terms have no direct meaning in LISP, the LISP program can conveniently manipulate such symbols and their relations. The interactiveness of most LISP systems greatly facilitates the evolutionary development so essential to knowledge engineering. Finally, the programmer is freed from certain burdens (including excessive worry about memory management) that could slow down the experimental process.

The several LISP dialects differ primarily in the features of their programming environments, the two most common being INTERLISP and MACLISP. The choice of one of them (or of any other LISP system) is probably more a matter of personal preference and availability than of clear technical superiority, although discussions among advocates of INTERLISP and MACLISP often take the tone of theological disputes.

Whatever programming language or dialect is chosen, an expert system requires two major components: an inference engine and a body of rules. The best strategy is probably to consider the rules first, developing a language or set of concepts in which they can be expressed. Depending on the general framework, each rule will have to satisfy a set of conditions to be relevant and perform a set of actions when invoked. In identifying the nature of a chemical spill, for example, the informal rule,

Oil spilling into water causes a sheen,

might be represented as follows:

> (IF   (DISTURBANCE WATER SHEEN)
> THEN   (SUBSTANCE SPILL OIL))

Note that the rule is represented as a statement of the corresponding inference, rather than as a direct statement about oil causing a sheen.

The rule language in this case might be as shown in the following Backus–Naur form (BNF) as follows:

```
<rule>          ::= (IF {<antecedent>}+ THEN {<consequent>}+)
<antecedent>    ::= <associative-triple>
<consequent>    ::= <associative-triple>
<associative-triple> ::= (<attribute> <object> <value>)
```

where <attribute>, <object>, and <value> would be domain-specific terms. This example is too simple for any realistic expert task, of course, but it illustrates the general idea.

Once the rule language has been defined, the inference engine can be built in terms of the general framework or architecture selected. In the ideal expert system, the inference engine never needs modification; all changes in system behavior result from changing the rule set. For example, the following is a simple backward-chaining inference engine for the rule language just given:

> To test whether hypothesis X is true:
>   if X is stored in the global data base
>   then X is true
>   else if there are any rules whose consequents include X
>   then for each such rule:
>   if all antecedents are true
>   then add all consequents to the global data base
>   and X is true
>   else if the user says that X is true
>   then X is true
>   else X is false

Note that checking the antecedents of a rule causes the inference engine to be invoked recursively; this recursion implements backward-chaining.

Any expert system is far more complicated than this illustration indicates, and a set of LISP programming techniques has been developed for implementing various pieces of expert systems (as well as other artificial intelligence programs), to which the textbook by Charniak, Riesbeck, and McDermott (1980) is an excellent guide.

9.2   Skeletal Systems

Rather than building an expert system by starting from scratch, it is sometimes possible to borrow a great deal from a previously built expert system. This strategy has resulted in several new software tools for knowledge engineering that may be described as skeletal systems: EMYCIN (derived from MYCIN), KAS (derived from PROSPEC- TOR), and EXPERT (derived from (CASNET). In a skeletal system all domain-specific knowledge is represented explicitly as rules, rather than as code in the inference engine. Permitting the replacement of those rules by rules for a different task greatly simplifies the process of building an expert system for the second task, although in practice this process is rarely quite this simple. The following are among the problems that may occur:

- The old framework may be inappropriate to the new task. This is both the most likely and the most serious problem.
- The control structure embodied in the inference engine may not sufficiently match the new expert's way of solving problems.
- The old rule language may be inappropriate to the new task.
- There may be task-specific knowledge hidden in the old system in unrecognized ways.

If these difficulties can be overcome, however, using a skeletal system makes it possible to build a system for a new task relatively quickly. For example, PUFF (Fagan et al. 1979) was built by replac- ing MYCIN's infectious disease rules by rules for pulmonary function diagnosis. Perhaps the greatest benefit of this strategy is that any extra facilities in the first system (for example, explaining how a con- clusion was reached) are also available in the next.

9.3   General-purpose Representation Languages

Another category of software tools for building expert systems consists of general-purpose programming languages developed specifically for knowledge engineering. ROSIE, OPS5, RLL, and HEARSAY-III fall into this category. Generally less constrained than skeletal systems, since they are not as closely tied to particular frameworks or paradigms, they allow for a wider variety of control structures. They can thus be applied to a broader range of tasks, although the process of applying them may be more difficult than with skeletal systems.

AGE, another tool, is not a general-purpose representation language, but it can help the user construct such a tool. It is better classified as a computer-aided design tool for expert systems. Such a system can aid the builder in selecting a framework, designing a rule language, and assembling the pieces into a complete system.

The remainder of this chapter presents detailed descriptions of the eight knowledge-engineering tools mentioned above, concluding with a detailed description of implementing an example expert system in KAS.

9.4   EMYCIN

9.4.1   Overview of EMYCIN

EMYCIN, basically a domain-independent version of MYCIN, is an appropriate skeletal system for developing a consultation program that can request data about a case and provide an interpretation or analysis. It is particularly well-suited to deductive problems such as fault diagnosis, in which a large body of possibly unreliable input measurements (symptoms, laboratory tests) is available and the solution space of possible diagnoses can be enumerated.

EMYCIN allows the MYCIN inference engine to be applied to a new problem domain whose problem-specific knowledge can be represented in the MYCIN rule language, providing all of MYCIN's features (such as its versatile explanation facility) as well as a human-engineered system-building environment, which greatly facilitates entering and debugging the knowledge base. This section describes the main characteristics of EMYCIN's representation language and inference engine (for a more detailed and complete description see van Melle 1980a, b).

9.4.2   Knowledge Representation in EMYCIN

Most of the domain-specific knowledge in EMYCIN is represented in terms of production rules. To a first-order approximation, EMYCIN employs the following rule language:

$$
\begin{aligned}
\text{<rule>} &::= \text{(IF <antecedent> THEN <action> (ELSE <action>))}\\
\text{<antecedent>} &::= \text{(AND \{<condition>\}}^{+}\text{)}\\
\text{<condition>} &::= \text{(OR \{<condition>\}}^{+}\text{) |}\\
&\qquad \text{(<predicate> <associative-triple>)}\\
\text{<associative-triple>} &::= \text{(<attribute> <object> <value>)}\\
\text{<action>} &::= \text{\{<consequent>\}}^{+} \text{ | \{<procedure>\}}^{+}\\
\text{<consequent>} &::= \text{(<associative-triple> <certainty-factor>)}
\end{aligned}
$$

A rule links an antecedent to one action if the antecedent is true, and (optionally) to another action if the antecedent is false. The antecedent is always the conjunction of one or more conditions, a condition being either (1) the disjunction of one or more conditions or (2) a predicate applied to an attribute-object-value triple. Since the predicate can include negation, an antecedent can be thought of as an arbitrary Boolean combination of predicates of associative triples, which happens to be expressed in conjunctive normal form.

For example, the antecedent of one of MYCIN's bacterial infection rules is:

```
(AND
    (SUSPECTED (IDENTITY ORGANISM CORYNEBACTERIUM-NON-DIPHTHERIAE))
    (OR
        (NOT-SUSPECTED (CONTAMINENT ORGANISM TRUE))
        (SUSPECTED (SIGNIFICANT ORGANISM TRUE))        ))
```

In English, this antecedent is true if and only if the organism under consideration is suspected to be of a particular type (corynebacterium-nondiphtheriae) and is either not considered a contaminent or believed to be associated with a significant disease.

The objects in the associative triples (called "contexts" in the EMYCIN terminology) are variables corresponding to domain entities. They are organized into a simple hierarchy called the context tree. For example, in the MYCIN domain the objects might be PATIENT-1, CULTURE-1, ORGANISM-1, and ORGANISM-2, and the context tree would indicate that ORGANISMs belong to CULTUREs and CULTUREs belong to PATIENTs. The context tree provides some of the inheritance mechanisms of a frame representation. For example, since cultures also have sites, the system can discover the site of ORGANISM-2 by knowing that ORGANISM-2 came from CULTURE-1 and looking up the site of CULTURE-1.

To accommodate uncertainty, EMYCIN associates a certainty factor with every attribute-object-value triple (Shortliffe and Buchanan 1975). This number, a normalized probability, ranges from −1 (when the triple represents a false assertion) through zero (no opinion) to +1 (unquestionably true). Predicates such as SUSPECTED can either evaluate to T (true) for some certainty interval (such as 0.2 to 1) or can be fuzzy-set functions that indicate a degree of truth. As in fuzzy-set theory, AND returns the minimum and OR returns the maximum of the certainty values of its arguments (Zadeh 1965). As a condition of applying a rule, however, an antecedent is considered to be true if its final certainty is greater than some threshold (typically 0.2) and "false" if its final certainty is less than another threshold (typically -0.2).

The action part of a rule consists either of updating the certainties of the specified consequents or of evaluating a set of attached procedures. More specifically, updating the certainty of a consequent means modifying the certainty that the attribute of the object has a particular value in light of evidence from the antecedent. In doing this, the system combines (1) the certainty of the antecedent, (2) the present certainty of the consequent, and (3) the certainty factor associated with the rule according to the certainty-theory formulas of Shortliffe and Buchanan (1975). The alternative action of evaluating the attached procedures is an escape mechanism that allows the execution of arbitrary LISP code.

9.4.3 The EMYCIN Inference Engine

The basic control strategy employed by EMYCIN is backward-chaining, its initial goal being to determine the value of a (typically artificial) top-level goal attribute. At any subsequent time, EMYCIN is working on the goal of establishing the value of the attribute of some object. To do this, it retrieves a precomputed list of rules whose consequents are known to bear on that goal, and it systematically attempts to apply the rules until it either establishes the value with complete certainty or exhausts the rule list. If no value can be deduced—whether because there are no rules or because the rules were unsuccessful—it resorts to asking the user for the value.

In attempting to apply a rule, EMYCIN must first establish the truth of its antecedent, which requires determining the certainty of each of its conditions. To do this, the system typically has to establish the values of other attributes of objects. This sets up subgoals that are addressed by using the same mechanism recursively. Thus to a first degree of approximation EMYCIN uses the following control strategy:

To determine the value V of property P of object O:
    retrieve the rules bearing on V(P,O);
    while there is an untried rule R and the certainty of V(P,O) < 1 do

      begin
      for every condition C in the antecedent of R do
          for every property-object pair (P',O') accessed in
          evaluating C do
              if the value V(P',O') has not been determined
              then apply this procedure to (P',O');
        if every condition is "true" then execute the THEN action;
        if at least one condition is "false" then execute the ELSE action
      end
    if V(P,O) is not known then ask the user.

Thus applying one rule sets up subgoals, which in turn invoke other rules, and the attempt to achieve goals drives the consultation. Ultimately the user must supply information, that determines the truth or falsity of the antecedents. While they may also determine the antecedents of rules not currently under consideration, no attempt is made to recognize this possibility. Since EMYCIN tries all applicable rules, these other rules will be encountered eventually, and the information acquired earlier will be used at that time.

9.4.4 EMYCIN Facilities

One of the reasons for using a skeletal system is to exploit an existing rule language and inference engine. Another equally important reason is to take advantage of the numerous facilities that have been developed to support a large system.

EMYCIN's explanation program, already mentioned, allows a user to examine both the reasons for the conclusions reached in a particular session and the information in the static knowledge base. This can be done either through the use of simple "WHY" and "HOW" commands when the system requests the value for an attribute, or through a keyword parser that can interpret simple requests given in English (Scott et al. 1977).

In addition EMYCIN provides a well-engineered environment for developing the knowledge base. Rules can be entered in Abbreviated Rule Language, a convenient formal representation that is more English-like than LISP, and modified with a high-level knowledge-base editor that checks them for syntactic validity and sees that they do not contradict or subsume existing rules. (A contradiction occurs when two rules with the same antecedents have conflicting consequents; subsumption occurs when the antecedent of one rule is a subset of that of another and their consequents are the same.) Once the legal values for properties are specified, the system uses them to prompt for needed values and to check for errors.

Finally EMYCIN provides valuable tracing and debugging facilities. Libraries of test cases are maintained, and a debugger based on the one in the TEIRESIAS program is available to guide the designer through the program's reasoning process (Davis 1976). Such features greatly facilitate the development of a new system.

9.5 KAS

9.5.1 Overview of KAS

PROSPECTOR is a consultation program developed for diagnosis problems that arise in mineral exploration (Duda, Gaschnig, and Hart 1979). KAS (Knowledge Acquisition System) is the PROSPECTOR consultation program without its domain-specific knowledge. Related to PROSPECTOR in basically the same way as EMYCIN is to MYCIN, KAS allows the PROSPECTOR inference and control mechanisms to be used on new problems when the domain-specific knowledge can be represented in KAS rule language.

Viewed abstractly the problems for PROSPECTOR/KAS are very similar to those that are suitable for EMYCIN, the primary difference being that PROSPECTOR relies more directly on information volunteered by the user to steer the consultation. Thus the KAS/PROSPECTOR inference engine is distinguished from EMYCIN mainly by performing both forward- and backward-chaining. This allows significant changes in the choice of high-level goals to occur in response to information acquired. Furthermore, instead of doing backward-chaining depth-first, KAS tries to avoid low-payoff questions by using a heuristic evaluation function to choose the most promising rules.

The price that KAS's designers have chosen to pay in order to obtain this versatility is to restrict the use of variables severely . Thus where EMYCIN allows repeated use of the rules by creating different instantiations of the objects in its attribute-value-object triples, KAS allows only one, namely the one for which the situation described by the triple is thought to be most certain. (KAS does allow multiple instantiations through permitting itself to be called recursively; however, the paths for communication between calls are very limited.) This restriction allows KAS to interconnect its rules into a static network before run time, thereby eliminating the need for searching through the rules to propagate inferences.

This section presents the main characteristics of KAS's rule language and inference engine. Many details that have been suppressed for the sake of brevity can be found in Duda et al. (1978a) and Duda, Gaschnig, and Hart (1979).

9.5.2   Knowledge Representation in KAS

Viewed abstractly, the rule languages employed by EMYCIN and KAS are very similar. To a first degree of approximation, KAS's rule language can be described as follows:

```
          <rule> ::= (IF <antecedent>
                     THEN <rule-strength> <rule-strength> <consequent>)
     <antecedent> ::= <statement>
     <consequent> ::= <descriptive-statement>
      <statement> ::= <logical-statement> | <descriptive-statement>
<logical-statement> ::= (AND {<statement>}⁺) |
                     (OR {<statement>}⁺) |
                     (NOT <statement>)
```

Temporarily ignoring the optional context, one sees that a rule links an antecedent to a consequent. Both the antecedent and the consequent are propositional statements—assertions about the world that may or may not be true. Statements can be either logical or descriptive, logical statements being arbitrary Boolean combinations of other statements. In particular, the antecedent of a rule can be the conjunction of disjunctions of other statements.

Both consequent statements and the ultimate components of logical statements are always descriptive statements, which are basically a generalization of attribute-object-value triples to more general semantic networks (Hendrix 1975; Duda et al. 1978b). This allows a descriptive statement to represent a situation involving n-ary relations among any number of objects.

For example, to represent a situation in which a polluting oil is coming from a storage tank, one might use the description:

```
          ((COMPOSITION-OF O1 OIL)
           (TYPE-OF O1 POLLUTANT)
           (TYPE-OF O2 STORAGE-TANK)
           (SOURCE-OF O1 O2)).
```

Here COMPOSITION-OF, TYPE-OF, and SOURCE-OF are binary relations, and the system would know about their legal arguments. O1 and O2 are symbolic objects; while they are never formally instantiated and thus are not true variables, the inference engine knows that if such objects exist they are distinct. OIL, POLLUTANT, and

STORAGE-TANK are domain terms that occur in a taxonomy such as:

```
(UNIVERSAL
    (PHYSICAL-OBJECTS
        (BUILDINGS ...)
        (CONTAINERS
            (STORAGE-TANKS HOLDING-PONDS ...)) ...)
    (MATERIALS
        (SOLIDS ...)
        (LIQUIDS
            (ACIDS ...)
            (OILS
                (HEATING-OIL GASOLINE ...)) ...) ...)
    (ABSTRACT-OBJECTS
        (POLLUTANTS ...) ...) ...).
```

KAS's inference engine uses the taxonomy to make useful deductive inferences about logical relations among the descriptive statements.

The semantic network description is a rather direct generalization of the attribute-object-value triples of EMYCIN; KAS employs it a bit differently. Whereas EMYCIN is constantly attempting to establish the values of attributes of objects whose existence has been established, KAS is constantly trying to establish the possible existence of situations. For example, where EMYCIN might ask "What is the composition of Object O1," KAS would ask about the entire situation: "Is polluting oil coming from a storage tank?" A "yes" answer would then be taken to establish the existence of both an O1 and an O2 satisfying the description.

To accommodate uncertainty, KAS associates a probability value with every statement. This number measures the degree to which the statement is currently believed to be true. The probability of a logical statement is computed from the probability of its components, using Zadeh's rules for fuzzy sets (Zadeh 1965). The probability of a descriptive statement is determined either from a user's answer to a direct question or—in the case of a consequent—through the use of Bayes' Rule (Duda, Hart, and Nilsson 1976).

Each rule includes two numerical rule strengths that are used to update the probability of its consequent. The first one is used if the antecedent is determined to be true, while the second is used if the antecedent is determined to be false. When the probability of the antecedent is somewhere between zero and one, an appropriate intermediate rule strength is used. Thus, there is no threshold probability for deciding whether or not to apply a rule; whenever the probability of an antecedent changes, the Bayesian procedure is invoked to update the probability of the consequent, which in turn can chain forward to update the probabilities of other statements.

Finally it must be mentioned that any KAS statement can be linked to one or more other statements called "contexts." Recall that EMYCIN applied two different kinds of predicates to associative triples—one that returned a certainty value and one that evaluated to true if the certainty of the triple fell in a prespecified interval. In KAS these different functions are formally distinguished. Antecedents always have an associated probability value, and that value always affects the probability of the consequent. However, the probability of an antecedent is considered to be undefined until all of its context is established. A statement is said to be established if all possible actions have been taken to determine its truth, and its final certainty (in exactly the EMYCIN sense) falls in some specified certainty interval. A rule that has a context cannot be applied until its context has been established. Thus even though contexts do not directly affect probability calculations, they have a major effect through enabling rules and by influencing the sequence in which questions get asked.

9.5.3   The KAS Inference Engine

In KAS there is no formal top-level goal, but certain consequents are distinguished as top-level hypotheses. A consultation narrows down this list of goal hypotheses continually, working to establish the truth or falsity of the most promising ones. Even when no clear conclusions can be reached, the identification of the missing information that would be most effective in resolving the situation is a valuable output of the program.

At any given time KAS is either trying to identify the best top-level hypothesis to pursue or trying to identify the best question to ask the user to establish that hypothesis. The first mode will be called the goal-selection mode and the second, the question-asking mode.

Goal selection is guided by information the user supplies during the session. Initially the user is allowed to volunteer (in simple English statements) any information that seems relevant. Such statements are parsed and represented as semantic networks, each assertion being matched against the descriptive statements in the knowledge base. When either exact or partial matches are detected, the system updates a heuristic score for each of the top-level hypotheses that statement supports. This scoring function (described in detail in Duda, Gaschnig, and Hart 1979) takes into account the certainty of the evidence, the nature of the match, and—by tracing through the rules—whether the evidence is favorable or unfavorable for the hypothesis. While the best-scoring hypothesis is typically selected as the one to pursue, the user always has the ability to overrule the system in selecting the current goal hypothesis, H. Thus, mixed-initiative control is supported.

Once the goal-hypothesis H has been chosen, the program enters the question-asking mode. The statements one level below H are inspected in order to find the one that is expected to have the greatest effect on the probability of H. Let S denote that statement. If S is marked as askable and if the user was not asked about S previously, the system asks whether S is true, forward-chains to propagate the consequences of the answer, and returns to the goal-selection mode. If S is not askable, S becomes a new goal, and the same procedure is reapplied, resulting in "best-first" backward-chaining.

Before a formal description of this procedure is presented, a bit more precision is needed about how the statement having the greatest effect on H is determined. To begin with, if any required contexts for H have not been established, their determination immediately becomes a new goal; this mechanism (which is subject to abuse) is often employed by the knowledge engineer to shape a desired questioning sequence.

Once the needed contexts are established, the next step depends upon whether H is a logical statement or a descriptive statement. For logical statements, a special procedure (called Select-Argument in the following description) chooses the least likely unexhausted argument for conjunctions and the most likely unexhausted argument for disjunctions. This procedure can fail if all the arguments are exhausted or (more interestingly) if the certainty of the logical expression can be appropriately bounded. For descriptive statements, a special procedure (called Select-Rule in the following description) uses heuristic criteria to score the rules having H as a consequent. The scoring function (described in detail in Duda 1979b) takes into account the current certainty of both the antecedent and the consequent, as well as the strengths of the rules. As with Select-Argument, Select-Rule can fail if a worst-case computation shows that all the remaining rules cannot have a significant effect on the consequent's certainty. Thus lines of reasoning are not pursued more deeply if their effects on conclusions can be shown to be small.

Summarizing, to a first-order of approximation, KAS's control strategy can be described in terms of the following two procedures:

Procedure Select-Goal:
    begin
    TOP ← list of top-level hypotheses;
    match volunteered information against statements in the knowledge base;
    while TOP is not empty do

```
begin
score the hypotheses in TOP;
interactively select a goal hypothesis H;
repeat
    begin
    call Ask-Question(H);
    update the scores for the top-level hypotheses;
    if H is exhausted
    then remove it from TOP and reset its score
    end
until the score for H drops and
        H is not the highest-scoring hypothesis
end

Procedure Ask-Question(H)
    begin
    S ← H;
    while S is not exhausted do
        begin
        while S is blocked by unsatisfied contexts do
                if any unsatisfied contexts of S are exhausted
                then mark S "exhausted" and return
                else S ← an unsatisfied context of S;
        if S is a logical statement
         then begin
                S' ← Select-Argument(S);
                if Select-Argument failed
                then mark S "exhausted" and return
                else S ← S'
                end
        else if S is unaskable or has been asked
                then begin
                        R ← Select-Rule(S);
                        if Select-Rule failed
                        then mark S "exhausted" and return
                        else S ← the antecedent of R
                        end
                else  begin
                        ask the user about S;
                        if the user responds with enough certainty
                           or there are no rules for deducing S
                        then mark S "exhausted" and return;
                        propagate the consequences
                        end
        end
    end
```

9.5.4   KAS Facilities

KAS provides a well-engineered environment for developing and debugging rules, semantic networks, and taxonomic structures. Its knowledge-based editor has three particularly valuable features: (1) it operates directly on network structures, (2) it uses knowledge about representational formalisms to assist the knowledge-base designer, and (3) it facilitates development by allowing the designer to get immediate feedback on the consequences of changes to the knowledge base. Each of these features will be considered in turn.

The advantages of structure editing are well known to programmers who have used both text and structure editors for programming languages. KAS brings these advantages to editing network structures, so that the designer works directly in terms of the different kinds of nodes and arcs, without having to know the details of their internal representations.

KAS is acquainted with many of the special properties of networks. It protects against various kinds of common errors (such as providing illegal parameter values) or potential errors (such as accidentally disconnecting sections of the network). It also keeps records of unfinished work, automatically providing reasonable default values wherever possible. As a simple example, KAS knows that terminal statements always represent askable assertions but that nonterminal statements may or may not be askable. Thus it will automatically assign a terminal node an askable status but will put the status of a nonterminal statement on the list of information needed for that statement. If subsequent editing causes a terminal node to become nonterminal (or vice versa), this is dealt with correctly. At any time the designer can inquire about unfinished business and have the system prompt to supply the missing information.

Finally, KAS's knowledge-based editor can be used at virtually any time in the development cycle. In particular, it can be invoked in the middle of a run to modify the current knowledge base. After changes are made, controlled experiments can be performed to observe their consequences; when satisfactory performance is achieved, the results of the editing can be saved and the run resumed. Such features in the programming environment can be of great value in developing a knowledge-based system.

9.6   EXPERT

9.6.1   Overview of EXPERT

EXPERT (Weiss 1979, 1981) is a general system for developing consultation models. Although designed independently of any specific application, it has been strongly influenced by the system designers' experience developing medical consultation models. Experimental models have also been developed in other areas, such as chemistry, oil well log analysis, and automobile repair. The types of consultation problems best suited for EXPERT are classification problems, which have a predetermined list of potential conclusions from which the program may choose. PROSPECTOR and EMYCIN are also knowledge-based systems that specialize in forms of classification problems.

The design of EXPERT has been deliberately streamlined to emphasize certain themes, including:

- Ease of model design. Prototype models should be capable of running in relatively brief periods of time.
- Efficient system performance.
- Predictable performance. Interaction among decision rules should be relatively easy to understand.
- Empirical testing. A model's performance should be matched to a data base of stored cases, providing a degree of verification and consistency checking.

9.6.2   Knowledge Representation in EXPERT

In EXPERT three representational components are used to design a consultation model: hypotheses, findings, and decision rules. Unlike EMYCIN or PROSPECTOR, EXPERT makes a major distinction between findings and hypotheses. Findings, observations, or measurements, such as a patient's height or blood pressure, are reported in the form of true, false, numerical, or unavailable responses to questions from EXPERT. Hypotheses are conclusions that may be inferred by the system, for example, a diagnosis. A measure of uncertainty is usually associated with a hypothesis. Three types of production rules are employed to describe logical relationships between findings and hypotheses: finding-to-finding rules (FF); finding-to-hypothesis rules (FH); and hypothesis-to-hypothesis rules (HH).

The FF rules, which specify truth values of findings that can be directly deduced from an already established finding, are used to establish local control over the sequence of questions. A simple example of such a rule is "If A is true then B is false." FH rules are logical combinations of findings that indicate confidence in the confirmation or denial of hypotheses. The next few examples are taken from the prototype model for giving advice on handling oil or chemical spills. (See Chapter 6, Section 6.2.3.) Mnemonics are used to abbreviate English text in the EXPERT language. For example, the following is an FH rule from this model:

$$f(oil,t) \,\& \, f(DOE,f) \rightarrow h(viol,.9)$$

Read this rule as: If the finding has been made that an oil spill has occurred, and the Department of Energy has not been notified, then conclude that (the hypothesis of) a noncompliance violation exists with a confidence of 0.9.

The HH rules allow the model-builder to specify inferences between hypotheses. In contrast to EMYCIN and PROSPECTOR, in EXPERT a hypothesis specified in an HH production rule is stated for a fixed interval of confidence. This effectively limits the propagation of scoring weights for the left-hand side of the production rule. For example,

$$h(matrl,.2:1) \,\& \, h(helth,.1:1) \rightarrow h(haz,1)$$

Read this rule as: If the material has been identified (with a confidence of 0.2 to 1), and it is felt that there is a potential health hazard (confidence 0.1 to 1), then conclude that a complete hazard analysis is required.

The following example is a highly abstracted session from the prototype spill-management model. The system asks questions; user responses are entered following the asterisk. These responses are the findings. The interpretive analysis is the set of hypotheses selected by the program as appropriate, based on the set of production rules invoked for this case.

1. Type of spill:
   1) source
   2) containment
   3) stream
   Choose one:
   *3
2. Agencies notified:
   1) DEM
   2) ORO-DOE
   Checklist:
   *no
3. Initial spill location drain code m6:
   *dx

INTERPRETIVE ANALYSIS

Notify DEM of spill Discovery.
Source and location must be determined to halt spill.

The chemical has not yet been identified.
Path flow and volume should be determined to evaluate
success of cleanup and potential propagation pattern.
Containment is usually the first priority of the OSC.
For oil floating on water, booms and absorbent
material are indicated. Cleanup and mitigation depend
on the specific causes of the spill.

3. Initial spill location drain code m6:
   *5

4. Material type:
   1) oil - film or sheen
   2) chemical
   Choose one:
   *1

9.6.3   The EXPERT Inference Engine

The major issues of control in EXPERT are directed to the related
goals of reaching accurate conclusions and asking reasonable questions that aid in interpretation. Although EXPERT is a system applied
to problems that require approximate reasoning, every effort has been
made to simplify the control strategies. This may require that additional knowledge be specified by the knowledge engineer. In particular, implied orderings of evaluation are involved in a given representation of an EXPERT model. For example, in many applications the
order of a set of questions can be stated in advance. By declaring a
group of questions to be part of a questionnaire, the model designer
can eliminate much of the need for a complicated control mechanism.
Within the questionnaire, control is handled by very simple mechanisms such as FF rules. Another important ordering is that of
production-rule evaluation. Instead of using a backward-chaining
mechanism for production-rule evaluation as in EMYCIN, EXPERT
evaluates rules in an ordered fashion that has been prespecified by
the model designer. Because of the ordering of the production rules
and the relatively efficient implementation of EXPERT, reevaluation
of all rules can take place after each new response is received, just as
in PROSPECTOR/KAS. In a case when different rules are satisfied
and applicable to the same hypothesis, EXPERT selects the rule with
the maximum absolute value of confidence in that hypothesis (where
confidence measures are assigned from -1 to 1). A bonus scheme is
available that mimics scoring functions such as those found in EMY-
CIN and PROSPECTOR. A bonus may be added to the score of a

hypothesis that is supported by a relatively large number of findings. In most applications, however, scoring by maximum value has proven satisfactory, yielding highly predictable results.

The questioning strategy selects questions of the following types:

- The least costly question (where cost is an ordering as opposed to real cost)
- The questions appearing in those production rules that imply hypotheses related to responses already received
- The questions that appear in production rules for the hypothesis currently weighted highest
- The questions that can potentially increase the maximum absolute value of the score of a hypothesis

9.6.4 EXPERT Facilities

Creating and running an EXPERT model is similar to writing and running a computer program. A standard text editor is used to create a file that contains statements in a special-purpose programming language used to describe a model. The model is checked for syntactic errors and translated into an efficient internal representation by the compiler. The model may then be executed, and cases may be entered for consultation. Because the system has been programmed in FORTRAN, it is relatively efficient and transferable between machines, and versions exist for both DEC and IBM equipment. EXPERT has many facilities proven useful for designing consultation models, such as explaining the program's interpretations and accepting information volunteered by the user. All consultation facilities of EXPERT are fully sequential. For example, one may ask for the system's interpretation at any point in a consultation session. Extensive work has been done on interfacing EXPERT models to data bases of stored cases, and many utilities are available for the empirical analysis of cases, including a complete data-base system for searching through cases for patterns of both user-entered data and model-interpretations.

9.7 OPS5

9.7.1 Overview of OPS5

OPS5 and the earlier languages in the OPS family have been used for a variety of applications in the areas of AI and cognitive psychology.

The first application of OPS in the area of knowledge engineering was the R1 system for configuring VAX computers (McDermott 1980c).

OPS5 incorporates general control and representation mechanisms. Although it provides the basic mechanisms needed for knowledge engineering, it is not biased toward particular problem-solving strategies or representational schemes. OPS5 allows the programmer to use symbols and represent relations between symbols, but no symbols or relations have predefined meanings. The meanings are determined entirely by the production rules written by the programmer. The control mechanism of the OPS5 interpreter is a simple loop called the recognize-act cycle, which the user elaborates as desired. Rather than changing the interpreter, the programmer writes rules to effect the control strategies chosen. In short, control is brought into the purview of the system itself and treated as a kind of knowledge to be represented and reasoned about, just as other kinds are.

9.7.2   Knowledge Representation in OPS5

OPS5 provides a single global data base called *working memory*, which consists of a set of constant symbol structures. Two kinds of symbol structures can occur in working memory: (1) vectors of symbols and (2) objects with associated attribute-value pairs. The elements are represented as follows:

$$<element> ::= <vector-element> \mid <av-element>$$
$$<vector-element> ::= (\{<value>\}^+)$$
$$<av-element> ::= (<object>\{\hat{}<attribute><value>\}^+)$$

The following is a typical vector element:

(TASK-ORDER SOURCE-LOCATION CONTAINMENT)

This element, which was taken from the spills-management system, (See Chapter 6, Section 6.2.4) is an assertion that the system should do the task of locating the source of the spill before the task of containing the spilled material. The following is a typical attribute-value element (the carat is the OPS5 operator that distinguishes attribute names from values):

(MATERIAL ^NAME H2SO4 ^COLOR COLORLESS ^CLASS ACID)

This is a statement that a material named H2SO4 is colorless and belongs to the class of acids.

The elements in working memory can vary dynamically in size at run time. Vectors can gain or lose values, and attribute-value elements can gain or lose attribute-value pairs.

The rules in OPS5 are, of course, able to process both vector and attribute-value elements. However, to keep the description of the rules reasonably short, vector elements and other features, such as AND's and OR's in the antecedent, will not be considered here. The simplified OPS5 language can be described as follows. (The antecedents and consequents for vector data elements are similar to the ones shown here. The principal difference is that sequences of values replace the attribute-value pairs.)

```
        <rule> ::= ( P <rule-name> <antecedent> → <consequent> )
  <antecedent> ::= {<condition>}+
   <condition> ::= <pattern> | - <pattern>
     <pattern> ::= (<object>{^<attribute><value>}+)
  <consequent> ::= {<action>}+
      <action> ::= (MAKE <object>{^<attribute><value>}+) |
                   (MODIFY <pattern-number>{^<attribute><value>}+) |
                   (REMOVE <pattern-number>) |
                   (WRITE {<value>}+)
```

The values in antecedents and consequents may be numbers, symbols, or variables. In OPS5 a variable is a symbol that begins and ends with an angle bracket, for example <X> or <FIRST>.

The patterns in antecedents are partial descriptions of data elements. The interpreter determines whether a pattern matches a data element by comparing the subelements of the pattern to the corresponding subelements of the data element. Every subelement of the condition element must match the corresponding data subelement, according to the following rules: (1) A constant symbol or number matches only an equal constant. (2) A variable matches any symbol or number, but if a variable occurs multiple times within an antecedent, all occurrences of the variable must match the same value.

A variable is said to be bound to the element it matches. Thus for example, the pattern

(MATERIAL ^CLASS ACID ^NAME <MAT>)

would match the data element

(MATERIAL ^NAME H2SO4 ^COLOR COLORLESS ^CLASS ACID)

binding <MAT> to (H2SO4). (Note that it is not necessary for the pattern to describe every attribute of the data element.) As another example, the pattern

(TASK-ORDER <FIRST>)

would match the data element

(TASK-ORDER SOURCE-LOCATION CONTAINMENT)

binding <FIRST> to (SOURCE-LOCATION).

OPS5 provides a number of operators for modifying the meaning of a condition subelement. Three of the operators are particularly important: the prefix operator, ≠, and the two kinds of brackets, { } and << >>. The first operator is the not-equal operator. The pair ≠ *value* will match anything except what is matched by *value*. The brackets, { }, indicate that the enclosed values are all to match the same working memory subelement. Thus the following:

^VALUE { <X> ≠ NIL }

would match any VALUE that was not equal to NIL and bind the variable <X> to it. The other kind of bracket, << >>, indicates that the working memory subelement can match any one of the subelements within the brackets.

As the description of <condition> shows, the patterns in an antecedent may be preceded by the operator, −. An antecedent is satisfied if all of the patterns not preceded by minus match data elements and none of the patterns preceded by minus match data elements. Thus the following antecedent:

(GOAL ^STATUS ACTIVE ^NAME DEDUCE-COUNTER-MEASURES)
(SOURCE ^KIND PERMANENT-STORAGE-TANK ^LOCATION <AT>)
− (COUNTER-MEASURE ^LOCATION <AT> ^KIND DIKE)

could be expressed in English as follows:

IF there is an active goal to deduce the countermeasures that already exist, and there is a source that is a permanent storage tank, and there is not a countermeasure of kind dike at the same location, . . .

The most important action types are [MAKE], [REMOVE], [MODIFY], and [WRITE]. [MAKE] creates and adds one new element to working memory. For example,

(MAKE MATERIAL ^NAME H2SO4 ^COLOR COLORLESS ^CLASS ACID)

would add the element

(MATERIAL ^NAME H2SO4 ^COLOR COLORLESS ^CLASS ACID)

(REMOVE) deletes one or more elements from working memory.
The action

(REMOVE 1)

would delete the element matched by the first pattern of the
antecedent. MODIFY changes one or more subelements of an existing
element. The action

(MODIFY 1 ^STATUS PENDING)

would change

(GOAL ^STATUS ACTIVE ^WANT PROCESS-HAZARDOUS-SUBSTANCE)

to

(GOAL ^STATUS PENDING ^WANT PROCESS-HAZARDOUS-SUBSTANCE)

WRITE types information on the user's terminal. The action

(WRITE (CRLF) ENTER THE NAME OF THE MATERIAL SPILLED:)

would start a new line (CRLF is a function that returns the end of line
symbol) and then type

ENTER THE NAME OF THE MATERIAL SPILLED:

The following is typical of the rules in the OPS5 production system for the chemical spill problem. (The rules in the chemical spill
system are actually somewhat more complex than the one shown
here. To make the example easier to understand, some of the information in the goal elements has been omitted.) This rule is one of those
used to coordinate the activity of the system as a whole. This rule
essentially says that if the system is trying to coordinate its activities
and it has not yet decided the best order for its subtasks, then it
should determine the order. The text after the semicolons is a more
detailed explanation of what the rule means.

```
(P COORDINATE-A                        ; If there is a goal
   (GOAL
      ^NAME COORDINATE                 ; to coordinate the system's tasks
      ^STATUS ACTIVE                   ; which is active
 − (TASK-ORDER)                        ; And there is not a preferred order

→

   (MAKE GOAL                          ; Then make a subgoal
      ^NAME ORDER-TASKS                ; to determine the preferred order,
      ^STATUS ACTIVE                   ; making its status active
   (MODIFY 1                           ; And modify the coordinate goal,
      ^STATUS PENDING))                ; changing its status to pending
```

9.7.3   The OPS5 Inference Engine

The OPS5 interpreter executes a production system by performing the following operations:

1. Determine which rules have satisfied antecedents.
   (This step is called *match*.)
2. Select one rule with a satisfied antecedent.
   If no rules have satisfied antecedents, halt execution.
   (This step is called *conflict resolution*.)
3. Perform the actions of the selected rule.
   (This step is called *act*.)
4. Go to 1.   (Go back to the first step.)

This sequence of actions may be thought of as the outline of a control structure that the user fills in as desired, for in OPS5 the production system itself determines what control and problem-solving strategies will be used.

Control in a production system can be implemented using explicit goals, that is, elements in working memory that designate desired states. Every rule in the system contains a pattern to match a particular kind of goal, and hence each rule fires only when goals of that type are in working memory. For example, the first pattern in the COORDINATE-A rule shown above matches goals of type COORDINATE, and the rule thus executes only when an active goal of this type is in working memory. A production system is able to direct its own processing by putting goals into working memory and removing them as appropriate for the strategy to be used. For example, the COORDINATE-A rule causes the system to attend to a new task—

generating a preferred sequence for later processing—by putting the ORDER-TASKS goal into working memory and making it active.

Although rules can be written to do all the processing of goals necessary to implement any control strategy, it has been found convenient to allow the interpreter to do some of the processing automatically. This is one of the purposes of *conflict resolution*. Among the control functions of conflict resolution are ensuring that subgoals are processed before supergoals, permitting the system to know when it has finished processing a particular goal, and preventing certain kinds of loops. (For more information on conflict resolution, see McDermott 1978.)

9.7.4   OPS5 Facilities

The OPS5 interpreter provides the programmer with a conventional interactive programming environment much like that of a typical LISP interpreter; OPS5 allows the programmer to trace and break runs, to examine the state of the system, to change the system in the middle of a run, and so on.

Three facilities seem to be particularly important in working with large production systems. One is a function that determines how close a given rule is to being satisfied. The programmer calls the function, passing it the name of a rule, and the function returns (1) a list of the elements in working memory that satisfy each pattern and (2) certain information about the partial matches for the complete antecedent. This function is used primarily to determine why a rule did not fire when the programmer thought it should. The second facility, PPWM, is a function to print selected parts of working memory. The programmer supplies the function with a description of a data element, and it prints every element that matches the description. If the programmer types, for example,

(PPWM GOAL ^STATUS ACTIVE)

the function will print every active goal in working memory. This function is used when the programmer needs to find a few elements in a working memory of several hundred elements. The third facility is a function to single-step the system backward, undoing changes to working memory. When the system gets into an incorrect state, the programmer can call this function to back it up to an earlier state. The system can be traced as it backs up to see where it went wrong; when the incorrect rule is found, it can be changed and the run continued from that point.

9.8   HEARSAY-III

9.8.1   Overview of HEARSAY-III

HEARSAY-III is a domain-independent framework for knowledge-based expert systems.[1] Although HEARSAY-III is specifically not a speech-understanding system (and we know of no one who expects to use it for building a speech-understanding system), it draws very strongly on the architectures of the HEARSAY-I (Reddy et al. 1973) and HEARSAY-II (Erman et al. 1980) speech-understanding systems. HEARSAY-II's concepts of large-grained, modular knowledge sources and systemwide communication via a structured global blackboard remain central to HEARSAY-III. (Erman, London, and Fickas 1981 describes HEARSAY-III more fully and includes a more extensive example of its use.)

The overall design goal for HEARSAY-III was the development of representation and control facilities with which a user could construct an expert system for a chosen domain. Deemed particularly important were facilities to do the following:

1. Support codification of diverse sources of knowledge. The desire is to avoid commitment to any particular class of application domains and, instead, to provide as much generality as possible in the types of knowledge that might be brought to bear on a problem from the chosen application domain.

2. Support application of these diverse sources of knowledge. Beyond mere application of the knowledge sources, an important design goal is to allow flexible coordination of the knowledge sources in their pursuit of an acceptable solution.

3. Represent and manipulate competing solutions that are constructed incrementally. This aspect of the HEARSAY-III architecture distinguishes it from the "diagnosis-system-building systems," such as KAS, EMYCIN, and EXPERT.

4. Reason about partial solutions. That is, not only does HEARSAY-III allow for incremental construction of competing solutions but it also supports in a straightforward way the ability to reason about and manipulate those solutions during the various stages of their construction.

5. Describe and apply domain-dependent consistency constraints to the competing partial solutions. Thus the system supports application of knowledge globally so as to aid in reducing the search for a solution.

6. Support long-term, large-system development and, in particular, experimentation with varying knowledge for the application domain and varying schemes for applying that knowledge.

In summary, the goal for HEARSAY-III is to develop, debug, and experiment with theories of domain expertise. One important area not emphasized is performance of the application system. It is intended that one use HEARSAY-III to gain an understanding of the problem-solving principles of a chosen domain—to study the domain. Later, it is appropriate to use a more efficient formalism to construct a performance system for the domain.

9.8.2   Knowledge Representation in HEARSAY-III

9.8.2.1   The Underlying Relational Data Base

HEARSAY-III is built on a foundation that consists of a relational database system and its corresponding control facilities. The data-base language is called AP3 (Goldman 1978) and is embedded in INTER-LISP (Teitelman 1978). As will be seen in subsequent sections, HEARSAY-III relies critically on the facilities provided within AP3. The AP3 data base is similar in structure to those available in the PLANNER-like languages (Hewitt 1972), but it also includes strong typing on assertion, retrieval, and parameter passing in function calls. This type of facility is available to a HEARSAY-III user for application domain modeling, in addition to being used to advantage within the HEARSAY-III system itself. The HEARSAY-III blackboard (Section 9.8.2.2) and all publicly accessible HEARSAY-III data structures are represented in the AP3 database. Additional annotations required by the application knowledge sources may also be placed in the AP3 data base. Because knowledge-source triggers are implemented uniformly as AP3 demons, modification to the data base gives rise to knowledge-source activity (as described in Section 9.8.3).

AP3 also makes available to HEARSAY-III applications a context mechanism similar to those found in AI programming languages such as QA4 (Rulifson 1972) and CONNIVER (McDermott 1974). HEARSAY-III supports contexts in such a way as to make them an integral part of the reasoning mechanisms made available to an application. This is a unique feature in systems for expert-system writing. The context mechanism supported in HEARSAY-III allows reasoning along independent paths, which may arise both from a choice among several competing knowledge sources and from a choice among several competing partial solutions.

The AP3 data-base system also provides facilities for inference rules and constraints. In addition to being used in the implementation of HEARSAY-III itself, these facilities are also available to the user for encoding global domain-dependent relationships. For example, the inference rule

$$\text{Inference: (AND (CONTAINS Vessel 'WATER)}$$
$$\text{(CONTAINS Vessel 'OIL))}$$
$$\rightarrow \quad \text{(SHEEN-ON-CONTENTS Vessel)}$$

represents that the presence of both oil and water in a vessel results in a sheen visible in the vessel. Constraints and contexts are supported by HEARSAY-III so that reasoning that produces a constraint violation results in marking as poisoned the context in which the reasoning was performed.

9.8.2.2   The Blackboard Structure

The blackboard, the central communication medium provided by HEARSAY-III, is used by an application program as a repository for a domain model, for representation of partial solutions, and for representation of pending activities. HEARSAY-III supports the representation on the blackboard of graph structures consisting of structured nodes called *units* and labeled arcs called *roles*. The blackboard is segmented into two parts: the domain blackboard and the scheduling blackboard. The domain blackboard is intended as the site for competence reasoning (that is, for reasoning within the task domain), while the scheduling blackboard is intended as the site for performance reasoning (that is, for reasoning about scheduling). The application writer can further subdivide each of these blackboards.

Blackboard units are the fundamental components of the representations built by application programs in HEARSAY-III. Units are typed AP3 objects; their types are called *unit-classes*. In fact, the segmentation of the reasoning space into distinct blackboards is accomplished simply as the decomposition of the unit-class *Unit* into several distinct subclasses. Thus, the domain blackboard consists solely of units of class *Domain-Unit* (and its subclasses); the scheduling blackboard consists solely of units of class *Scheduling-Unit*. When desired, access can be restricted to a given blackboard simply by using type-restricted AP3 data-base retrievals.

Units have structure in addition to their types. One of their interesting features is that they can be augmented to represent unresolved decisions explicitly. Such units are called *choice sets*. Associated with a choice-set unit is a set of alternatives or a generator of alternatives (or both). A choice set can be viewed as a partial elaboration of a decision point; the alternatives represent still further elaborations (and they themselves might be choice sets). For example, a choice-set unit representing "containment" might have as alternatives units that represent "absorbent-boom" and "dam." These competing problem solutions may be represented with the single locus "containment." Furthermore, structure common to all alternatives may be factored out and associated with the choice-set unit itself. Choice sets allow for pending decisions to be data about which the system can reason.

HEARSAY-III provides two mechanisms for resolving the ambiguity represented by a choice set. These mechanisms interact in an integrated fashion with the context mechanism of AP3. The first mechanism is called a *deduce-mode Choose* of the choice set. An application program may perform a deduce-mode Choose when it has conclusive evidence that one alternative is the correct solution for the problem represented by the choice set and that there will be no desire to retract that choice based on further evidence. In this case the choice set is replaced by the alternative (their properties are merged) in the context in which the choice is made. In this context all evidence that the choice set ever existed is eliminated and the blackboard structure appears as if this choice set had never been there.

The other mechanism for choice is called an *assume-mode Choose*. An assume-mode Choose also replaces the choice set with a unit that represents a merge of the properties of the choice set and the chosen alternative. However, an assume-mode Choose makes these changes in a newly created context derived from the one in which the choice was made. The blackboard structure in the new context is identical to that resulting from a deduce-mode Choose. The choice-set unit still exists in the earlier context with its structure modified only to eliminate the alternative just chosen. In this way, if subsequent reasoning indicates that this alternative may not be best, it is possible to return to the original context and select a different alternative.

As mentioned earlier, HEARSAY-III supports the construction of labeled graphs on the blackboard. Units are the nodes in those graphs. The labeled arcs are called *component roles* (or simply *roles*) and are represented as typed relations connecting two units. The typing of roles is of significant convenience because it allows the use of type-restricted AP3 retrievals to simplify searching the structure. Roles, in addition to being typed, are also placed in classes called *role sets*. One use for role sets is to define distinct component hierarchies in which units are related by the transitive closure of the roles in a given role set. This allows the suppression of detail along chosen dimensions when examining the blackboard structure.

Blackboard structures are used to represent both static and dynamic aspects of the application problem. For example, a statically represented structure would be the topology of the drainage network in the chemical spills problem. Roles would represent connections between the pipes and manholes, and the pipes and manholes would be represented by units. Dynamic problem-specific information can also be represented on the blackboard. For example, the relationships between units representing "mitigation" and units representing "containment" would be expressed using blackboard roles.

9.8.3   The HEARSAY-III Inference Engine

9.8.3.1   Knowledge Sources

Much of the domain-specific knowledge for an application built in HEARSAY-III is embodied in knowledge sources (KSs). Each KS can be thought of as a large-grained production rule; it reacts to blackboard changes produced by other KS executions and in turn produces new changes.

To define a KS, the user provides a *triggering pattern*, *immediate code*, and a *body*. Whenever the pattern is matchable on the blackboard, HEARSAY-III creates an *activation record unit* for the KS and runs the immediate code. At some later time the activation record may be selected and executed; that is, the body, which is arbitrary LISP code, is run. In more detail:

1. The triggering pattern is expressed as an AP3 pattern. As such, it is a predicate whose primitives can be AP3 fact templates and arbitrary LISP predicates, composed with AND and OR operators. Whenever the AP3 data base (which includes the HEARSAY-III blackboard—the units and roles) is modified so that any of the AP3 templates in the pattern is matched, the entire pattern is evaluated. If the entire pattern is matchable, an activation record is created that stores the KS's name, the AP3 context in which the pattern matched (called the *triggering context*) and the values of the variables instantiated by the match.

2. At the point the activation record is created, the immediate code of the KS is executed. This code, which is also arbitrary LISP code, may associate information with the activation record that might be valuable later in deciding when to select this activation for execution. The immediate code is executed in the triggering context and has available to it the instantiated pattern variables. The immediate code must return as its value the name of some unit class

of the scheduling blackboard. The activation record is then placed on the blackboard as a unit of that class.

3. At some subsequent time, the system's base scheduler (see below) may call the HEARSAY-III *Execute* action on the activation record. The usual result of this is that the body of the KS is run in the triggering context and with the pattern variables instantiated. If at the point of execution, the triggering context of the activation is poisoned and the KS has not been marked as a *poison handler*, the body is not run; rather, the activation record is marked as *awaiting unpoisoning*, and will have its status changed to *ready* if the poison status of the context is ever removed.

Each KS execution is indivisible; it runs to completion and is not interrupted for the execution of any other KS activation. This insulates the KS execution and simplifies the coding of the body; there need be no concern that during a KS execution anything on the blackboard will be modified except as effected by the KS itself.

9.8.3.2 Scheduling

Frequently, many knowledge-source activation records vie for execution. For instance, knowledge sources that deal with spill source location might be competing for computational and physical resources with knowledge sources that deal with containment. HEARSAY-III is intended for use in domains in which knowledge-source scheduling schemes are likely to be complex and in which one might need to experiment freely with various schemes. Since the scheduling problem itself has characteristics similar to domain problems, the blackboard-oriented knowledge-based approach is appropriate for its solution as well, and HEARSAY-III supplies the same mechanisms for its solution.

Because of the indivisibility of KS execution, the scheduling problem in HEARSAY-III can be stated as follows: At the end of each KS execution, determine, from the state of the system, the KS activation to execute next. To help solve this problem, the following concepts, features, and mechanisms are useful.

As described before, the time of execution of a KS body is delayed arbitrarily long from its triggering, with the activation record unit on the scheduling blackboard used as the mechanism for representing the activation. Also, the immediate code of the KS is run on creation of the activation record, allowing KS-specific scheduling information to be added to the activation record.

Some knowledge sources, termed *scheduling KSs*, may make

additional changes on the scheduling blackboard to facilitate the selection of activation records. Scheduling KSs may respond to changes both on the domain blackboard and on the scheduling blackboard, including the creation of activation records. The actions they may take include associating information with activation records (e.g., assigning and modifying priorities) and creating new units to represent metainformation about the domain blackboard (for example, pointers to the current highest-rated units on the domain blackboard). The scheduling blackboard is the data base for solving the scheduling problem.

The application writer provides a *base scheduler* procedure that is called by HEARSAY-III after startup and actually calls the primitive Execute operation for executing each selected KS activation. The base scheduler is intended to be simple; most of the knowledge about scheduling should be embodied in the scheduling KSs. For example, the base scheduler might consist simply of a loop that removes the first element from a queue, maintained by scheduling KSs, and calls for its execution; if the queue is ever empty, the base scheduler simply terminates, marking the end of system execution.

9.9   RLL

The task of building an expert system demands a large amount of expertise; it entails many subtasks (choosing the computer's role, choosing an expert, finding or building the right inference engine, designing an appropriate representation scheme for the knowledge), and those subtasks interact heavily. But the two criteria—much expertise, many interacting subtasks—are precisely those that make a task suitable to an expert systems approach. One ought to be able to build an expert system whose "task domain" is itself the building of expert systems. RLL (Greiner and Lenat 1980), which is such a system, helps a KE design, construct, use, and modify a (new) expert system. The knowledge base in RLL contains information about AI programming in general and its own subroutines in particular.

9.9.1   Overview of RLL

Like other programs that help KEs build expert systems, the RLL system begins with a store of primitives and a collection of tools for combining them: a large collection of types of slots, control mechanisms, and inheritance schemes. The user picks and chooses from among these options, and RLL knows enough to combine them into what the user then perceives as a representation language—a particular set of representations, a control scheme, an inheritance, and so on, in which the user can now begin building up a knowledge base. Hence the name RLL, for *representation-language language.*

Surely not every conceivable expert system primitive is present initially in RLL. For instance, a geneticist may want to have a primitive inheritance mode of "skipping a generation." So RLL provides tools that aid knowledge engineers in constructing new primitives, rather than compelling their coding from scratch in LISP. The geneticist, for example, might browse through the known types of inheritance, select one that is vaguely similar to the kind needed, have it copied, and spend a few minutes editing that description. RLL then converts the modified description into executable LISP code. RLL creates new modes of inference with the same types of steps that MYCIN takes to incorporate a new fact about a patient or a new type of disease.

9.9.2   Knowledge Representation in RLL

The philosophy in designing RLL's representation was to opt for uniformity. Thus for any structure more complex than a list of values, a framelike data structure or a unit is provided. Thus there is a unit for oil, for each type of oil, for pipes' connectivity, and so forth. More than that, there is a unit in RLL for each type of slot, for each type of inheritance mechanism, for each type of control structure, for the abstract user (and for specific individuals), and even for RLL itself (and separate units for each running of RLL). See Figure 9.1.

The first unit in the figure, M6-3, represents the third manhole in drainage basin six. The third unit, Manhole, represents a more abstract concept: the set of all manholes. The final pair of units represent still more abstract notions. The FeedsInto unit provides the following information: FeedsInto is a relation that can hold between two manholes. FeedsInto is the name of a slot. Any manhole *m* may have a FeedsInto slot. If it does, it must be filled by the name of another manhole *m2*. In that case, the *m2* unit can and should list *m1* as one of the entries on its FeedsFrom slot. To compute which manholes *m* feeds into, first locate all the downstream pipes, find their ends, and return one of those values (other than "*m*" itself, of course). At a higher level, this slot can be thought of as being defined as the composition OtherEnd 0 DownstreamPipes, that is, as being built by composing two other slots.

But those facts are not merely a description of the FeedsInto type of slot; rather, the unit actually defines the FeedsInto slot. If any of

```
M6-3
    Isa:              Manhole
    FeedsInto:        M6-2
    LocatedUnder:     (MainStreet and OakDrive)
```

```
M6-2
    Isa:              Manhole
    FeedsFrom:        (M6-3)
    LocatedUnder:     (MainStreet and RidgeRoad)
```

```
Manhole
    Isa:              Set
    Generalizations:  (PhysObject, CircularObject, Artifact)
    Examples:         (M6-2, M6-3, . . .)
    Description:      This represents the collection of all manholes.
    Prototype:        TypicalManhole
    NewSlots:         (FeedsInto, FeedsFrom, LocatedUnder)
```

```
LocatedUnder
    Isa:              Slot
    Description:      The street(s) above the manhole.
    Format:           List
    Datatype:         Streetname
    MakesSenseFor:    (Manhole)
    Inverse:          LocatedAbove
```

```
FeedsInto
    Isa:              Slot
    Description:      Whatever is directly downstream.
    Inverse:          FeedsFrom
    MakesSenseFor:    (Manhole)
    HighLevelDefn:    (Compose: OtherEnd DownstreamPipes)
    Format:           Singleton
    Datatype:         Manhole
    ToCompute:        (lambda (m)
                      (OneOf (Remove m (Ends (DownstreamPipes m)))))
```

FIGURE 9.1   Examples of RLL units.

those slots were ever changed, the way FeedsInto behaves would be affected. For example, declaring the Format of FeedsInto to be a List (instead of a Singleton) would cause RLL to do two things: it would make into lists all the existing FeedsInto entries on all the manholes (enclose the value in parentheses) and it would redefine the ToCompute slot of FeedsInto by eliminating the call on "OneOf."

Similarly each rule in RLL is stored as a unit. What attributes (slots) does a rule have? Throughout this book, rules have been spoken of as antecedent-consequent pairings, as having IF and THEN parts. So a first pass is to to give each rule an IF and a THEN slot. But one wants the user to be spared the task of entering the actual LISP code to be run. So in RLL the user provides a higher level specification of what the rule is to do, and RLL "expands" the definition into that code. As Figure 9.2 indicates, this is done by providing many special kinds of IF and THEN slots, each having its own concise format. RLL eventually combines these into a big, coded IF and THEN slot and ultimately into a single lump of compiled LISP code.

Rule#332	
Isa:	Rule
Description:	Tell the user to hold his breath if the chemical is toxic.
IfWorkingOnTask:	AscertainImminentDanger
IfPotentially Relevant:	(chemical Toxicity is High ?)
IfTrulyRelevant:	(chemical Location is (Nearby user) ?)
ThenTellUser:	"Do not breath this chemical!!"
ThenAddToAgenda:	(SummonAmbulance WarnOthers)
Priority:	High
Worth:	900
AvgRunningTime:	.1 seconds
FrequencyOfUse:	considered 985 times, used 4 times
Generalizations:	(Rule#899, Rule#45)
Specializations:	(Rule#336)
Justification:	Breathe&DieScenario
Author:	Johnson
CreationDate:	17:30 on 9-July-81

FIGURE 9.2   Example of RLL rule.

Notice that the code for this rule is scattered about, stored in several distinct slots. This enables more than one kind of rule interpreter to be employed. For instance, one interpreter might collect a set of rules, run all their IfPotentiallyRelevant tests (which are quick and cheap), see how many rules still remained in the set, and then decide on a course of action based on that result. A second, perhaps more traditional, interpreter would run all the If parts of the rules, and employ some conflict resolution scheme if more than one were truly relevant. A third interpreter might first see how much time was available, eliminate any rule whose AverageRunningTime was too high, run the IfPotentiallyRelevant slots, and (if many still remain) eliminate those that would define new units or add tasks to the agenda (those with any entries on their ThenDefineNewUnits or ThenAddTo-Agenda slots), and finally run the IfPotentiallyRelevant slots of the few rules that survived all the preceding screening tests.

The user can select which interpreters to use in various circumstances, modify the interpreters, define new ones, etc. It is relatively easy to change the rule interpreter(s) because each such block of code is itself an RLL unit. Like the rules, each interpreter is decomposable into nice-sized chunks that can be independently inspected and modified.

Besides the effective (executable) slots—IFs and THENs—there are many nonexecutable, "declarative" attributes stored for each rule. It has already been shown how the AverageRunningTime can be used to decide whether a rule should even be considered if time is tight; another such slot is Author. It may be used by other rules such as:

IF   two rules disagree,
THEN follow the one typed in by the expert

IF   many of the rules typed in by x have declined in value,
THEN lower all of x's rules even more.

Similar mechanisms exist for processing agenda, or tasks, or other control regimes (for example, a blackboard architecture).

In RLL all of the executable code is made explicit, and the user is permitted to modify it to suit the design. To change a piece of the control structure (such as the order in which pieces of rules get evaluated) or representation (such as the format of some slot), the user need only browse through the unit representing that knowledge and edit it. There is thus no distinction between this type of modification and the editing of the domain-specific knowledge base.

Suppose the user realizes one day that Pipe#406 really joined Pipe#317, rather than Pipe#316, as had been thought. The user begins to edit the unit for Pipe#406, sees the slot called "JoinedTo," and replaces the value there, Pipe#316, with the value Pipe#317. As the unit editor is exited, RLL automatically looks up JoinedTo to find its inverse, and goes to the two other units involved, Pipe#316 and Pipe#317) to update the information stored there. This kind of correction can be performed easily in most languages used for building expert systems.

But now suppose the user realized that a pipe could really join many pipes, rather than just one. This change would be difficult to make in many languages—indeed it might require defining a totally new JoinedTO link. After that, all of the existing data would have to be transferred, regrettably by hand. Not so in RLL. The user edits the unit called JoinedTo, notices it has a slot called Format, currently filled with "Singleton," and changes that entry to read "List." As the user exits the editor, RLL percolates the change throughout the system: in this case, all existing JoinedTo entries get enclosed in parentheses; all future entries on JoinedTo will be checked to ensure they are lists, and so on.

9.9.3 The RLL Inference Engine

Each knowledge-engineering task has its own particular priorities, options, trade-offs—and there should not be a single control structure to which the knowledge engineer is forced to adhere. For example, in the spill task, there are some very crucial actions ("Tell the person not to breathe fumes from the spill!") and some less so ("Notify the department within 30 days"). Moreover, many small details must be attended to eventually. A natural kind of control scheme for this task is an agenda mechanism, a queue of little jobs executed in a best-first order (according to a dynamic scheduler). When the oil spill task was first encountered, this mechanism was not among those possessed by RLL, but it took only a matter of a few hours to assemble an adequate initial agenda scheme.

One goal of the work on RLL is to produce a library of various successful AI control structures and, even better, a small collection of tools from which those (and new ones) can be built quickly. At present, however, the RLL system developers are still example-driven and have built control structures only for the few tasks that have been coded in RLL so far.

The oil-spill agenda works as follows. (See Chapter 6, Section 6.2.6.) A task is selected from the agenda. It is declared the "current task," and all the rules look it over to see if (and how) they apply. Metarules break any ties among the relevant rules, and the rules are then executed, one after another. The spirit is that while some rules are better than others, many rules are better than one. Only after some time limit has expired does RLL pause and see if (how well) the task has been satisfied. Often, while trying to satisfy a task, a rule will add one or more new tasks to the agenda. Each task has a list of symbolic reasons justifying it, and from these a numeric priority value is derived. Thus some new tasks may be placed high on the agenda and others placed very low.

The processor for the agenda (get task, execute it, perform a post-mortem) is almost the same as the one for an individual task, once it is chosen (get rule, execute it, perform a postmortem), and even for executing a rule once it is chosen (get slot, execute it, perform a post-mortem). Although agenda processing had to be defined from scratch, the rule-processor could be copied and edited (trivially) to produce the task-processor, and a copy of that edited again to produce the agenda-processor.

One final point is worth making about control in RLL. The language pays for its flexibility in space, not in time (efficiency). It might seem that looking things up constantly uses vast amounts of processing time. Rather, each time an answer is found (What is the inverse of JoinedTo? What are all the examples of X?), that value is *cached* (redundantly stored) so that the next time the query is made the answer can be retrieved quickly. As the knowledge base changes, RLL must explicitly erase in various units cached information that is no longer current. What this means in terms of efficiency is that in the first few minutes RLL runs very slowly, but the system gradually speeds up to the point where one does not notice its intrusion. The slowness temporarily returns after any major editing or changing of the system; the more fundamental the change, the more appreciable the slowdown.

9.9.4   Conclusion

RLL began as a two-week project to build a representation language on which the EURISKO system (Lenat 1982) would be built. The developers soon realized many nontrivial research issues had to be addressed before such a general, self-encoding language could be constructed and eventually abandoned the quest for this ultimate language.

The current system plays a necessary bootstrapping role: certain parts of the system must be present, as these are used to fill in other parts. (For example, the code used to expand high-level definitions must be present, or at least enough of it to generate the rest of it.) The initial control mechanism was the one needed for the EURISKO work, which was an Agenda structure.

Other languages for building expert systems have proven expedient for tackling particular problems in particular domains. Such systems will always be limited in the scope of problems they can solve, however. Even when adequacy is not at issue, small personal preferences of the system-builders slowly magnify until they decide to write their own language; a dozen cases of this phenomenon have appeared. This problem seems to be intrinsic to such programs, at least until they, like the human programmers they are trying to emulate, are capable of crudely understanding the code they are composing at something more than the superficial level now attained. At that stage they can then assume much of the responsibility for modifying themselves to suit new system-builders, or at least of providing them with a concise language in which to state changes in representation and control mechanisms. This sounds like automatic programming, and indeed this research grew out of that field and still draws upon it for its major source of power. RLL was written with the goal of attaining the necessary understanding to make possible this massive automatic programming task.

9.10   ROSIE

9.10.1   Overview of ROSIE

Many expert systems can be built simply by instantiating a prepackaged skeletal system. For systems of this type, special-purpose tools like KAS and EMYCIN are appropriate. Some expert systems do not fit such a schema, however, and might best be programmed in a general-purpose AI language. ROSIE (Fain et al. 1981, 1982) was designed for such applications, but it can be used to build skeletal systems as well. In addition to providing the capabilities characteristic of any general-purpose programming language, ROSIE makes it easy for assertional descriptions to be created, manipulated, and accessed, using a form of stylized English. ROSIE's English-oriented assertional data base, easily adapted to a wide variety of domains, aids the expert-system builder in rapidly defining specialized world models.

ROSIE is not a natural-language understanding system, since it makes no attempt to grasp unrestricted English input and has no built-in knowledge of the English lexicon beyond a few function words. A formal language that resembles a useful fragment of English in its syntax, ROSIE mirrors in its semantics much of the logical structure of English. Thus the system-builder can describe a domain using ROSIE syntax along with ordinary English vocabulary, especially domain-dependent content words (nouns, verbs, adjectives). The semantic content of these descriptions, as revealed by the system's behavior, will conform to most expectations of an English speaker. ROSIE achieves this result without preprogrammed knowledge of the meaning of content words by paying close attention to the grammatical and logical role of such words in a few very common sentence types. Experience with the system shows that even this limited form of "understanding" greatly facilitates the passage from unformalized knowledge to a formal model.

9.10.2   Knowledge Representation in ROSIE

ROSIE's view of knowledge representation is much like that to be found in the PLANNER family of languages. In these languages, atomic facts are held in a "declarative" data base, which may also hold some deductive rules. The inference engine does pattern matching for retrieval and rule application and controls the process of deduction and transformation of the data base. Facts in the data base are ordinarily used representationally in much the same way as the formulas of a logic.

In ROSIE, too, there is a data base of facts. Most of the deductive rules are stored separately, however, in modules called *rulesets*. The data base is used to hold simple relational facts, as well as some simple deductive facts like "Any P is a Q."

The ROSIE user thinks of the data-base entries as elementary assertions in English. For example, the following assertions could be stored in ROSIE's data base to indicate three-place relations.

> JOHN will be flying to HAWAII in 1982.
> JOHN does live in HAWAII during MAY.
> SAM did not see MARY on TUESDAY.

In general, the elementary assertions express relations among objects using the following common English forms (square brackets indicate optional items, and braces indicate zero or more repetitions):

element is	[not] a noun	{preposition element}
element was	[not] a noun	{preposition element}
element will	[not] be a noun	{preposition element}
element is	[not] adjective	{preposition element}
element was	[not] adjective	{preposition element}
element will	[not] be adjective	{preposition element}
element does	[not] verb [element]	{preposition element}
element did	[not] verb [element]	{preposition element}
element will	[not] verb [element]	{preposition element}

Clearly, these forms provide the user with options as to how a particular relation will be expressed. For instance, some ternary relation like FOO(x,y,z) could be expressed in the data base in any of the following ways (among others):

> x does FOO y at z.
> x will FOO to y during z.
> x is a FOO of y in z.
> x was FOO at y over z.

The choice among these forms will depend critically on the English word expressing the relation FOO, and on what types of objects x, y, and z are. Consider:

> John does THROW water at Bill.
> John will DEFER to Bill during MEETING #33
> John is an OPPONENT of HOUSE-BILL #335 in Congress.
> John was ANGRY at Bill over salaries.

ROSIE intentionally provides the user with a range of options for expressing arbitrary n-ary relations; the goal is to make it easy to define new data bases quickly, since the "naive" English relational expression used by the expert-system builder is likely to already be in one of the allowable forms (or can be easily brought into that form).

The "elements" that fill the slots in the relation can be instances of any built-in ROSIE data type. These include symbols (JOHN), numbers (4.2), tuples (<1, 2 <JOHN, BILL>>), and strings ("This is a string"). In addition, ROSIE has "proposition" as a built-in data type and allows nesting. Thus it would be a valid operation to assert that JOHN does believe "Mary is living in Bermuda." These propositional data types are useful for representing "metafacts" about what other people know or about the state of a hypothetical data base.

Rulesets are the ROSIE equivalent of procedural knowledge. One way rulesets may be used is as conventional procedures to be invoked in an English-like fashion. For example, the expression "Go alert John of the danger" will cause the procedure "alert" to be called with two arguments: "John" and the object currently asserted to be a danger. Upon entry, a local data base is available, with inheritance from the global data base.

Another way to use rulesets is to implement forward-chaining or backward-chaining inference rules. The exact manner in which this is done will be described in the next section.

Syntactically, a ruleset consists of a sequence of rules. A rule is either an action (which may be simple, compound, or iterative) or a conditional (IF−THEN) form. Primitive actions include those that manipulate the data base (ASSERT, DENY, and CREATE), those that do input/output (DISPLAY, SEND, READ), and those that manipulate the file system (DIR, COPY, APPEND), among others. The compound actions include forms of sequenced actions, WHILE, and IF−THEN−ELSE.

9.10.3   The ROSIE Inference Engine

ROSIE's inference engine is responsible for interpreting the rules entered at the terminal or taken from rulesets and for providing deductive access to the data base. These two functions will now be discussed.

The rulesets are interpreted very much like conventional program modules, with some special features. One such feature is the ability of users to specify an execution order (such as cyclic), should they wish to view their rules as production rules triggered by conditions in the data base rather than as conventional program statements. This feature can be used for a variety of applications, such as rule-based simulation. Using standard sequential execution, rulesets are executed as ordinary procedures, each rule being fired in turn.

The interpreter recognizes two special types of rulesets— *generators* and *predicates*—and uses them to define sets and relations via rules in a manner that resembles limited deduction. The generator ruleset acts as a function or generator of elements of a computed set, and the predicate ruleset acts as a recognizer of tuples satisfying some computed relation.

For example, one could define a generator ruleset for "Officer in Unit" to generate all persons either asserted to be officers of that unit or found to be officers in any subunit of the unit. The interpreter filters out duplicates, so the programmer can iterate over "officers" as if it were a primitive relation in the data base.

The ROSIE data base may be accessed and manipulated using English-like constructions of far greater expressiveness than those that record the primitive assertions in the data base itself. A "description" is an expression in the language that serves to pick out individual elements from the data base. For instance,

> boy from Wisconsin who did not read every assigned book

is a description that when evaluated against the data base, will find one or more such boys (if they exist), say, JOHN, BILL, and HARRY. The number of elements to be found depends on the description's context of use.

An oversimplified syntax for descriptions is

[adjective] noun {preposition term} [relclause].

Relclause, in turn, looks like

who/which/that <sentence fragment>,

or

such that <sentence>.

An example of <sentence fragment> is "does live in NEW YORK."

Descriptions are interpreted by breaking them into elementary assertions and finding objects that satisfy all the component assertions. For example,

"big mean kid from Brooklyn who does terrorize the neighborhood"

would be broken down into the components:

> x is a kid
> x is big
> x is mean
> x does terrorize the neighborhood.

The embedded term "the neighborhood," of course, contains a description consisting of the bare noun "neighborhood" and would be evaluated against the data base as well.

ROSIE provides both implicit and explicit ways to iterate through a set of elements. For implicit iteration, iterative determiners (every, some) are provided. When such a determiner occurs in a description within an imperative command, it is interpreted to mean: iterate over elements satisfying the description, executing the command for each one, for the first one, etc. If the iterative determiner occurs in a description with "assertional" force, it is treated as an ordinary quantifier of the appropriate type (as an extended AND or OR).

Explicit iteration is achieved by using the construct

FOR EACH description, <statement>.

There are also conventional *while* and *until* statements. Less conventionally, looping is supported by the cyclic execution option for rulesets.

9.10.4   ROSIE Facilities

The ROSIE programming environment attempts to incorporate as much from the INTERLISP concept as can be accommodated to the quite different nature of the language. ROSIE makes it easy to edit and maintain rulesets, automatically remember what has been parsed and compiled whenever changes are made, keep a history (a list that can be used to redo certain actions), do operations on files and directories from the ROSIE environment, and communicate easily with the operating system.

Of course, some differences are inevitable, primarily because ROSIE's syntax is not as structurally uniform as undifferentiated LISP structures. Thus for example, no system-resident structural editor is provided. However, the system does make it easy to move back and forth between a screen-oriented text editor and the ROSIE environment—a solution some users may even prefer.

While ROSIE's development is still under way, the current prototype system provides a useful level of support by way of helpful error messages, graceful error recovery, interrupts, and so on. In all, ROSIE provides a congenial programming environment for building expert systems.

9.11   AGE

AGE (Nii and Aiello 1979) is a software tool that aids in the design, construction, and testing of a variety of frameworks for knowledge-based programs. AGE differs from other skeletal systems in one major dimension. Its objective is to provide an environment in which the user can choose or specify a variety of knowledge representation and processing methods. For example, an AGE user is able to build and run a program that behaves in ways similar to a program built using EMYCIN or one built using HEARSAY-III. AGE is a tool with which a problem-solving framework can be constructed and a knowledge base built in ways most suited to the application problem at hand.

9.11.1   Overview of AGE

The AGE system provides the user with a set of predefined modules called *components* or *building blocks*. A component is a collection of LISP functions and variables that support conceptual, as well as concrete, entities. For example, the *production-rule component* consists of: (1) a rule interpreter that supports the syntactic and semantic description of production-rule representation, as defined in AGE, and (2) strategies for rule selection and execution. The components have been preprogrammed for convenience, but they can be modified or replaced by the user as long as the changes conform to the definitional constraints.

The components in AGE have been carefully selected, defined, and modularly programmed to be usable in various combinations. Using different combinations makes it possible to construct programs that display different problem-solving behaviors. For those users not familiar enough to experiment with combining components, AGE provides predefined configurations of components. Each configuration is called a *framework*. A framework is conceptually similar to a prefabricated house—the basic design decisions have been made, but many of the final decisions have been left to suit individual tastes and needs. Similarly the components of the framework can be rearranged or modified to suit the problem at hand.

One such framework, the *backchain framework*, is used for building a program that uses production rules as its primary knowledge representation, and goal-directed, backward-chaining of rules as its inference method. With this framework the user can build a program whose behavior is similar to a program written in EMYCIN. In contrast to EMYCIN, the AGE backchain framework requires that the user provide the rule predicates, specify the structure of the objects to be chained, define the computation to be applied to the certainty factors, and so on. The backchain framework in AGE is therefore at once more flexible and more difficult for a novice knowledge engineer to use. Another element of flexibility in AGE is the fact that, if at some point it becomes desirable to use forward execution of the rules, this can be done simply by respecifying the control component.

Another framework, the *blackboard framework*, is useful primarily for building a program whose design is rooted in the blackboard model developed for the HEARSAY-II speech-understanding system (Erman et al. 1980). The blackboard model uses the concepts of a globally accessible data structure called a blackboard and independent sources of knowledge that cooperate to form hypotheses incrementally on the blackboard. In AGE the original blackboard model has been augmented with a variety of control and representation concepts. Some of these augmentations include production rules and object-centered representations of knowledge, an extended blackboard, and a scheme for generating and processing expectations and goals. The blackboard framework in AGE has been designed to give the user flexibility in the representation, selection, and utilization of the domain knowledge.

Because the blackboard framework is intended to be a general as well as a practical problem-solving method, it will be described in some detail in the following sections. One should remember, however, that if a simpler method or framework will solve the problem at hand, that is what should be used.

9.11.2   The Blackboard Framework

A blackboard-based program written in AGE consists of three major components: the blackboard, the knowledge base, and the control. The blackboard is designed to hold input data, intermediate results, and solutions. It is a hierarchical data structure organized to represent the problem domain as a hierarchy of analysis levels. In addition the blackboard holds some dynamic control information accessible to the user program.

The knowledge of the problem domain can be represented in two different ways. The description of the objects, both conceptual and actual, and the relationships among them can be represented in an object-centered representation as implemented in the UNITS package (Stefik 1978b). Production rules represent the knowledge that uses these facts and information on the blackboard in order to perform a specific task. A set of related rules is called a *knowledge source* (KS).

The methods of selection and activation of the knowledge sources and the selection of items on the blackboard for focus of attention are designed to be independent of the knowledge representation. By specifying different control mechanisms, programs can be made to display different behaviors even with the same knowledge base.

The combined process of KS selection and incremental changes to the blackboard is viewed as a general process of hypothesis formation. Consequently the data structure that holds the input data and the intermediate, as well as the final, results is referred to as the *hypothesis structure*. In addition to this structure, the blackboard holds information related to the various control mechanisms. Control information on the blackboard can also be accessed by the KSs, and KSs can be built that act as control or metaknowledge sources.

The *hypothesis structure* is organized hierarchically. Depending on the problem, there may be more than one hierarchy needed to define the hypothesis structure. Each hierarchy consists of hypothesis elements integrated by links that represent support from above and support from below; these links are called *expectation-links* (or model-derived links) and *reduction-links*, respectively.

A hypothesis element is a named node (object) in the hypothesis structure that represents an abstraction (summary, interpretation, integration, aggregation) of lower level hypothesis elements. Each element contains a description in the form of attribute–value–weight triples that are meaningful at the particular level of the hypothesis.

A link in the hypothesis structure represents a relationship between elements in the hypothesis. Since the links are created by the actions of the rules, they indirectly represent the rule(s) that created them. A link can point to a hypothesis element from any other element, including one from its own level. Thus the user can structure the hypothesis as a general directed graph, as a simple linear sequence, or more usually, as a strict hierarchy. A hypothesis structure appropriate for the problem at hand is specified by the user during the design phase.

The actual solution hypothesis is built incrementally by rules that add or modify the hypothesis elements or relationships between the elements. Hypothesis formation can be thought of as a process whereby the rules do the following:

1. Interpret data (support from below);
2. Specialize or instantiate a more inclusive hypothesis element (support from above); or
3. Generate expectations that must be verified by data. These expectations can be generated based on:
   a. A model (theoretical support), or
   b. A higher level hypothesis element.

The knowledge necessary to accomplish the goals of the program is represented in production rules. These rules are organized into one or more sets of rules, the knowledge sources. The user program may consist of one KS that contains a set of homogeneous rules—these may be chained to represent a line of reasoning in the style of EMYCIN programs or left loosely organized. Alternatively the user program may contain many KSs that are invoked in an appropriate manner and are used as hypothesis generators and validators (Nii and Aiello 1979).

A KS is a labeled set of production rules that are a priori deemed to belong together. For example, a model KS may contain rules organized around some objects or concepts; a data-oriented KS may contain rules that generate hypotheses from data elements.

A KS can be thought of as a large chunk of knowledge or, because of its organization, as a large-grained rule. With each are associated preconditions for its invocation. Such preconditions indicate the specific situations under which the rules in the KS are applicable. A KS is invoked when one of its preconditions matches the currently focused event, which represents the situation. An event is a token, generated by rules, that summarizes the actions taken by the rules. For example, a rule may modify an attribute (x) in some hypothesis element. It will generate a token, (x-modified), which is also the event name. A KS that knows what to do with (x) will have in its preconditions (x-modified)—the KS will be invoked after (x) is changed. KSs can thus be chained dynamically in different orders, depending on the events generated by the firing of different rules.

The local context applicable to the rules within the KS can be established before the rules are actually executed. A context includes a strategy for rule evaluation for the KS (single hit, multiple hit, once-only), links that are allowed to be generated by the rules in the KS, and binding of local variables.

The rules in a KS can access control information on the blackboard. Such a KS can manipulate other KSs, and it can be thought of as a part of the control structure. These KSs can contain rules that know about problem-solving strategies for the specific application at hand, manipulation of other knowledge sources, and other control heuristics.

Each production rule consists of a left-hand-side (LHS) and a right-hand-side (RHS). The LHS specifies a set of conditions or patterns for the applicability of the rule. The term *applicability* can mean that all of the specified conditions must be true or only that some need be true. Because of the wide range of possibilities for defining applicability, AGE asks the user to define it in the form of a function to serve as the LHS Evaluator. Some simple LHS-evaluators, such as all-conditions-must-be-true, are provided; the user can use one of them rather than programming a new one. The RHS represents the implication to be drawn, under the situation specified in the LHS. These implications are represented in the form of changes to be made to the hypothesis structure or to the UNITS knowledge base. Currently the changes the RHS can make are limited to the following three:

1. Actual changes to the hypothesis element, link, or UNITS. These changes are called *events* and are posted on the *event-list* on the blackboard after the changes have been made. As mentioned earlier, the event-list is a part of the control information on the blackboard that is available to the KSs.

2. Expected changes, either to the hypothesis structure or UNITS. These are to be posted on the *expectation-list*. No actual changes are made until the expected changes occur. The expectation-list is also available to the KSs as a part of the control information.

3. Desired changes to the hypothesis structure or UNITS. These are

posted on the *goal-list*. No actual changes are made until the goals have been achieved. The goal-list is also available to the KSs.

A change inferred by the RHS of a rule can have associated with it a probability, or some informal weight, that reflects the confidence in the implication to be drawn under the particular conditions specified in the LHS. This informal probability will need to be reflected in the attribute-value-weight triples of the affected hypothesis element when the rule is executed. The a priori specified weights in the rules and the probability already assigned to the attribute of the hypothesis element in question need to be integrated. This can be accomplished in many ways. One possible method is used in EMYCIN and another in KAS. To allow maximum flexibility, AGE asks the user to provide the necessary computation in the form of a function to serve as a weight adjuster. There are some predefined weight-adjuster functions available in AGE.

Several functional components are grouped under the heading of Control. They are as follows:

1. The *input* component, for inputting the data. The format and the names of the input data, as well as the manner in which the data are to be acquired, need to be specified by the user. For example, the input may come from a terminal or a file; the input may be acquired at the beginning of the program or only when a rule first needs the information.

2. The *initialization* component, for preprocessing of data, if necessary, and returning the name of the first KS to be invoked.

3. The *kernel control* component, for specifying the inference mechanisms to be used. This component will be discussed in some detail below.

4. The *termination* component, for specifying the condition under which the program is to terminate, for example, the occurrence of some specific event.

5. The *postprocessing* component, for processing after the termination of rule executions; for example, printing the hypothesis or printing an explanation.

The primary function of the kernel control is to select an item on the blackboard to process next and to invoke KSs appropriate to that item and consistent with the goal of the program. Thus the kernel control component consists of two conceptually distinct sub-components whose separate functions are *inference generation* and *focus of attention*.

For inference generation, within the invoked KS the rules either (1) *propose* changes in the hypothesis elements or UNITS, (2) indicate that some changes are *expected* to occur, or (3) indicate that the KS desires a particular value or state to be *achieved* within the hypothesis structure. Each of these actions taken by the RHS is called a *step*.

For focus of attention, first select a step-type (an event, an expectation, or a goal) to process next. From the appropriate control information associated with the step-type (event-list, expectation-list, or goal-list), choose a specific step; this has the effect of selecting a hypothesis element or a unit for focus of attention. Then choose a relevant KS—a KS whose precondition matches the focused event. Finally, invoke that KS. KS selection may require complex processing associated with each step-type; for example, for a goal step-type, backward-chaining of rules might be an appropriate method for achieving the goal.

To allow flexibility, both in the selection of focus-of-attention items and in the invocation of KSs, these control subcomponents are further divided into smaller subcomponents. Because the control mechanisms have many details that are confusing to novice users, AGE provides two rather simple, prepackaged control structures called *control macros*. They are useful for event-driven and expectation-driven control.

Event-driven hypothesis formation is characterized by incremental formation of hypothesis elements from evidence found in data or in lower level hypothesis elements. The modified elements can be focused for further processing, on the basis of first-in, first-out, or first-in, last-out, or best-first. These generally correspond to breadth-first, depth-first, and best-first processing of the hypothesis space. (When an element is chosen to be processed, it is termed *focused*.) The event name (assigned by the user) associated with the focused element determines which KS is to be invoked next.

Event-driven processing can be summarized as a two-step process: (1) A rule modifies the hypothesis elements or UNITS and causes an event, with associated event token. (2) If the focused event name matches a precondition of a KS, then invoke that KS. Loop back to 1.

Within an *expectation-driven* system, states expected to occur within the hypothesis structure are generated by the rules. The expectation can be data consistent with some current hypothesis or some intermediate results. The expectation generated can be based on some previously generated hypothesis elements or on models or schemata represented in the UNITS knowledge base or as rules.

If a set of rules is used as a model to generate the expectations, the rules are generally grouped around objects, much like the way frames are organized. These groups form models of objects from which properties of the objects can be inferred or expected to occur.

For example, consider a rule of the form:

> if   (isa disease oad) and
>   (isa severity severe)
> then   (expect RV > 20) and/or
>   (expect RV/TLC>RATIO > 20)

This rule has a schemalike flavor. Of course, the model—in this case a model of an obstructive airway disease—can be represented as a group of UNITS. If a UNITS reprsentation is used, there are both access and storage interfaces between the information represented in the UNITS knowledge base and the production rules.

In order to determine if a specified expectation has been met or can be met, the user must provide an expectation evaluation function. Independent of the user-provided expectation evaluation function, AGE will always monitor the incoming data and events to see if the expected situation has occurred.

Expectation-driven processing involves three simple steps: (1) A rule generates expectation(s). (2) If an expectation is met, the hypothesis elements or UNITS are modified as specified. This action generates an event with an associated event token. (3) If the *focused event name* matches a precondition of a KS, that KS is invoked. Loop back to 1.

The AGE control macros are simply collections of preset control variables and preprogrammed control functions. For example, both macros use for the LHS-evaluator $AND, one of the AGE functions available to the user. It takes as its argument LISP expressions and returns T if none of the expressions evaluate to NIL. Both macros also use a common initialization function, $INITIALIZE, which is a null function that returns as its value the name of the first KS to be invoked (specified during the design phase). If the macros do not perform exactly as the user wishes, unsatisfactory parts can be modified; for example the user can replace the $INITIALIZE function with one specialized to the problem at hand. In this manner the user can evolve an arbitrarily complex control structure from a rather simple initial macro.

9.11.3   AGE Facilities

AGE provides a user environment that facilitates the construction and detailed specification of each of the components. Currently designed to be usable by persons knowledgeable in the appropriate uses of various AI problem-solving methods, AGE is unable to help a novice knowledge engineer translate a problem into an appropriate framework. However, once a framework has been chosen, AGE does provide some help in designing its components.

The AGE system consists of four major subsystems: the *design* subsystem guides the user in the design and construction of an application program that fits a predefined framework; the various *editors* help the user enter detailed domain-specific information as well as control information for each of the components; the *interpreter* executes the user program and provides a variety of debugging aids; and the *explainer* provides a complete trace of the execution of the user program.

9.12 Using the Tools to Build an Expert System

9.12.1 The Example Problem

A variety of languages and tools being used to build expert systems have been examined. The process of putting these tools to use, which remains to be discussed, will be explained by selecting a particular problem, sketching the steps involved in designing a system to solve that problem, and giving concrete illustrations of interesting parts of the solution. Although only one of many possible approaches to the problem can be illustrated, it will give a more concrete view of the process of knowledge engineering.

This is a portion of the problem of containing chemical spills described in Chapter 10. The overall problem is one of crisis management and resource allocation and has many facets. Here only one subproblem will be considered—the determination of the best strategy for locating the source of a spill detected in a river. (See Chapter 6, Section 6.2.2.) It is assumed the goal is to provide assistance to a possibly inexperienced, off-hours security officer, although the program can also be viewed as one module in a more comprehensive expert system for the entire crisis-management problem.

From discussions with experts, it is known that once a spill has been detected there are only a few standard procedures for locating its source. If the spill is flowing continuously, one can go upstream to the offending drain pipe and work backward through the storm drain system to its source. If the basin from which the spill is coming is known, and if the identity of the pollutant is known, one can check an inventory list for buildings in that basin; if only a few buildings contain that material (in sufficient quantity), one can telephone the building supervisors and enlist their help. For the more unusual substances, one can check a separate, facilitywide source inventory, and—if there are not too many potential sources—send people out to check each potential source. Finally, for certain kinds of pollutants (such as oil associated with construction projects) that show up in certain circumstances (such as following a heavy rain), one can initiate a search for nondocumented sources.

This description of the problem suggests the construction of a simple decision tree:

```
if spill-is-flowing-continuously
then use find-outlet-and-search-storm-drains-strategy
elseif basin-is-known and identity-is-known
      then use building-inventory-list-strategy
elseif identity-is-unusual
      then use facility-wide-inventory-strategy
else try special-strategies-for-special-situations.
```

However, even if some obvious defects with this primitive program are ignored, a little more probing discloses that actual situations are never as simple as first described. It may be observed that a spill is occurring intermittently. It may not be entering the river through the storm drain system. The identity of the pollutant may be totally unknown, or several different possibilities may be suspected. Estimates of the quantity of the spill may be crude and subject to large error. Many other factors may also have to be considered, such as the fact that a guard does not want to telephone a building supervisor during off-hours unless there is a serious emergency. The uncertainties and probable need for periodic future revision and refinement preclude a simple decision-tree solution.

If the problem is characterized as a diagnosis task involving uncertain and incomplete information, it appears to fit the general EMYCIN/KAS/EXPERT paradigm, and one may be able to take the skeletal-system approach. Although any of these systems could be used equally well, KAS is chosen, perhaps because one anticipates the eventual need for forward-chaining to respond to critical volunteered information.

9.12.2   Designing the Knowledge Base

The basic problem is to express the knowledge about choosing a source-location strategy in the KAS rule language. This is generally best done in a top-down fashion, the first step being to identify the top-level hypotheses. In the example, this is done as follows:

H1   Backtrack through the storm drain system.
H2   Call the building supervisor.
H3   Check the known sources.
H4   Seek an undocumented source.

Evidence exists that might support or rule out each of these top-level hypotheses. Instead of going immediately to the relevant evidence (which might be quite extensive), one usually tries to identify a small number of general factors that bear on each hypothesis. For example, the following factors clearly have a first-order effect on deciding whether to try the backtracking strategy:

F1   The pollutant is flowing continuously.
F2   It is entering the river from a known drain pipe.
F3   A map of the storm-drain system for the corresponding basin is available.

Each of these factors is in turn a subhypothesis that might be supported by other factors. Thus the same process of identifying the directly relevant factors is repeated until factors are obtained that correspond to basic observational evidence. This example considers F2 and F3 to be primitive but elaborates F1 in terms of the following three subfactors:

F1a   There is a liquid pollutant in the river.
F1b   It is visually observable.
F1c   It is flowing more or less steadily.

At this point it has been decided that H1 depends on F1, F2, and F3, and that F1 depends on F1a, F1b, and F1c. Instead of moving on to develop a similar substructure for the other top-level hypotheses, the nature of these dependencies will be clarified.

Since one does not want to recommend a backtracking strategy (H1) if any of the major factors F1, F2, or F3 is definitely false, one might consider expressing H1 as the conjunction (AND F1 F2 F3). This will have the right behavior in the extreme cases where the truth or falsity of the supporting factors is known with complete certainty. However, it will probably not behave appropriately in less clear-cut situations. In particular, suppose that nothing is currently known about F2 or F3, but that one learns that the spill is flowing continuously: that F1 is true. This should at least arouse some interest in hypothesis H1. However, since the probability of a conjunction is computed as the minimum of the probabilities of its components, a change in the probability of F1 from its initial or prior value all the way to unity may not cause any increase at all in the probability of H1. (Exactly what would happen depends on the prior probabilities of F2 and F3. For simplicity it is assumed that all prior probabilities are equal, so that the probability of (AND F1 F2 F3) increases only if the probabilities of all the components increase.)

An alternative is to use three rules of the form:

R1   (IF F1 THEN t1 f1 H1)
R2   (IF F2 THEN t2 f2 H1)
R3   (IF F3 THEN t3 f3 H1).

Here each factor contributes "votes" (which can be effectively positive or negative) toward H1. For example, F1 casts t1 votes if it is true, f1 votes if it is false, no votes if it is at its prior probability, and some interpolated intermediate number of votes in intermediate situations. This provides considerable flexibility. The different factors can be weighted differently to reflect their differing degrees of importance. Thus knowing that a map is available (F3) would probably have less of a positive effect on selecting H1 than knowing that the pollutant is flowing steadily from a particular drain pipe. Making the negative votes sufficiently strong guarantees that if any one of the factors is definitely false H1 will get a very low score, essentially achieving the effect of conjunction in such cases. To avoid excessive detail, the question of exactly how numerical values for these votes are determined is ignored and the interested reader referred to Duda, Hart, and Nilsson (1976).

Note that factors F1, F2, and F3 are not independent. Until F1 is established one cannot consider F2, and until F2 is established it makes no sense to consider F3. These strong dependencies do not invalidate the voting scheme, provided the designer recognizes, for example, that F2's positive votes t2 should be considered as an increment to t1. The major effect of these dependencies lies in their implications for control. Even if the factor F2 is more important than F1, the system should not pursue F2 before F1 has been reasonably established. Thus F2 should have F1 as a context (in KAS's terminology) and F3 should have F2 as a context.

After one has decided how the various factors interact, the question of producing semantic network representations for them can be addressed. At first this seems like an enormous task. If a complete representation is sought, even the simple-sounding assertion F6, that there is a liquid pollutant in the river, can lead to thorny representation problems. How, then, is one to represent assertion F1, that the pollutant is flowing more or less continuously, or hypothesis H1, that a backtracking strategy should be used?

The answer to these questions becomes clearer when one asks how these representations are used. One major use is to allow automatic recognition of certain logical relations among factors. For example, even the rudimentary representation of F1 and F2 as

> F1   ((TYPE-OF O1 POLLUTANT)
>   (PROPERTY-OF O1 CONTINUOUSLY-FLOWING))

and

> F2   ((TYPE-OF O2 DRAIN-PIPE)
>   (DISCHARGING O2 O1))

would allow the system to recognize that if F1 is false (there is no object O1 possessing the specified properties), then F2 is undefined, thereby eliminating the need for the designer to identify explicitly F1 as a context for F2.

The other major reason to create representations is to allow the system to connect volunteered information to the rules. This is obviously important if the user begins by mentioning a potentially dangerous pollutant that demands special treatment. In this example, if Fa were represented as

> Fa   ((TYPE-OF O3 POLLUTANT)
>   (STATE-OF O3 LIQUID)
>   (LOCATION-OF O3 RIVER)),

and the system possessed a taxonomy of pollutants, then if an observer mentioned the presence of gasoline in the river, the system could automatically deduce the truth of F1 and propagate the results. By contrast, if it is assumed that the user will never say anything immediately relevant to H1 (such as "I cannot send out anyone to search the storm drains"), no articulated representation of H1 would be needed. Thus one crafts the semantic network representations to support anticipated use.

9.12.3   Using KAS to Implement the System

Having represented at least a portion of the system in KAS's rule language, one may see how KAS can be used to create and debug the actual code. Since the purpose here is merely to convey the flavor of what it is like to use any skeletal system, a systematic explanation of the actual KAS rule language, commands, and features will not be attempted. Instead a glance will be taken at snapshots of a slightly edited KAS session.

After invoking KAS, one begins by defining the major assertions and the connections among them. Every statement (or "space" in the KAS terminology) has a name and the KAS commands operate on those names. To use something a bit more suggestive than H1 or F1b, the following names will be employed:

H1	BACKTRACK
F1	FLOWING
F2	KNOWN-ENTRY
F3	HAVE-MAP
F1a	LIQUID-SPILL
F1b	VISIBLE-SPILL
F1c	STEADY-FLOW

The spaces H1, F1, F2, and F3 and the rules R1, R2, and R3 are created through the following commands (the user's input is enclosed in angle brackets):

** <CONNECT RULES FROM FLOWING KNOWN−ENTRY HAVE−MAP TO BACKTRACK>

Although it has not yet been decided just how F1a, F1b, and F1c are to determine F1 (whether through logical connectives or through rules), it is possible to record the fact that connections are desired as follows:

** <CONNECT FROM LIQUID−SPILL VISIBLE−SPILL STEADY−FLOW TO FLOWING>

This defines the topology of the rule network shown in Figure 9.3 but leaves a lot of unfinished business. To see the minimum that must be specified to allow execution, one uses the NEEDS command:

** <NEEDS ALL>

Spaces

BACKTRACK	(PRIOR DESCRIPTION)
FLOWING	(PRIOR ASKABLE DESCRIPTION)
KNOWN-ENTRY	(PRIOR ASKABLE DESCRIPTION)
HAVE-MAP	(PRIOR ASKABLE DESCRIPTION)
LIQUID-SPILL	(PRIOR UPCONNECTION ASKABLE DESCRIPTION)
VISIBLE-SPILL	(PRIOR UPCONNECTION ASKABLE DESCRIPTION)
STEADY-FLOW	(PRIOR UPCONNECTION ASKABLE DESCRIPTION)

Rules

FLOWING:BACKTRACK	(LAMBDA LAMBDABAR)
KNOWN-ENTRY:BACKTRACK	(LAMBDA LAMBDABAR)
HAVE-MAP:BACKTRACK	(LAMBDA LAMBDABAR)

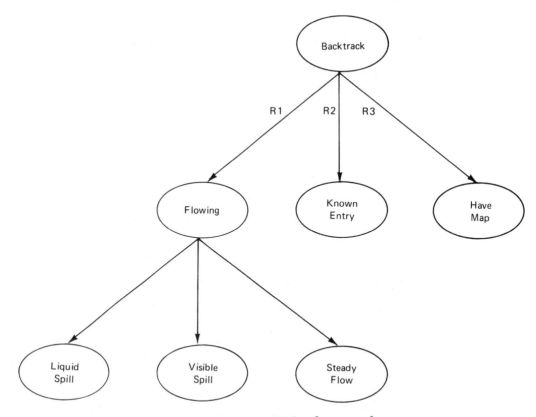

FIGURE 9.3   A KAS rule network.

Each space needs an initial or prior probability and an English description that can be used in asking questions (such as "To what degree do you believe" <STEADY-FLOW-description>). In addition, except for the top-level and logical spaces, the system needs to know which spaces are askable, how LIQUID-SPILL, VISIBLE-SPILL, and STEADY-FLOW are to be connected to FLOWING, and the strengths (LAMBDA) and (LAMBDABAR) of the three rules.

It is arbitrarily decided to define F1 (FLOWING) as the conjunction (AND) of F1a, F1b, and F1c, and complete all the needs for that space. The connection type is defined first.

** <CTYPE AND FLOWING>

Next a prompting mode is entered:

** <FILLNEEDS FLOWING>

In English, this is "a visible liquid pollutant is flowing steadily in the river." Note that the system did not ask for the prior probability or for the askability status. That is because after the space had been defined as a conjunction, the system knew that its prior probability will be computed from its components and that logical spaces are never askable.

The FILLNEEDS ALL command is used to have the system prompt the user for the remaining information needed to obtain a running system, choosing numerical parameters (prior probabilities and rule strengths) somewhat arbitrarily. After this has been done, the final results can be viewed by commanding KAS to print the knowledge base in its external format, as shown in Figure 9.4.

At this point the knowledge engineer can cause the knowledge base to be interpreted by KAS's inference engine by supplying the top-level hypothesis, BACKTRACK. Since no semantic networks were defined, KAS goes directly to the backward-chaining mode, examines the three spaces supporting BACKTRACK, and decides from the rule weights that KNOWN-ENTRY should be explored first:

** <RUN BACKTRACK>

1—To what degree do you believe that the flowing pollutant is
   entering the river from a known drain pipe ? <QUIT>

Unfortunately, it is obvious at once that the contexts were forgotten and that the model will have to be edited. Typing "QUIT" causes one to exit the run and return to KAS. The contexts are easily specified:

**<CONTEXT FLOWING FOR KNOWN-ENTRY>

**<CONTEXT HAVE-MAP OF KNOWN-ENTRY>

Now the run proceeds as desired. Answers to the questions are certainties expressed on a −5 to 5 scale. A trace (which is normally suppressed) shows how the answers propagate. In particular, note that since FLOWING is a conjunction, no propagation occurs until the certainty of the third conjunct is specified.

** <RUN BACKTRACK>

1—To what degree do you believe that the pollutant in the river is a liquid ? <5>

2—To what degree do you believe that the pollutant in the river is clearly visible ? <3>

3—To what degree do you believe that the pollutant is flowing steadily (as opposed to stopped for long periods of time) ? <4>

** <PM>

---

space	BACKTRACK

text   description /* The best strategy is to backtrack through
                        the drain system to the source*/

inference prior .2

	rules	antecedents	FLOWING	t1 3.0 f1 0.001
			KNOWN-ENTRY	t2 9.0 f2 0.001
			HAVE-MAP	t3 4.0 f3 0.001

control   unaskable

---

space	FLOWING

text   description /* a visible liquid pollutant is flowing
                        steadily in the river*/

inference prior .2

logical definition AND LIQUID-SPILL VISIBLE-SPILL STEADY-FLOW

control   unaskable

---

space	HAVE-MAP

text   description YN /* Do you have (or can you get) a map of
                        the storm drain system from which the pollutant
                        is entering the river */

inference prior .2

control   askable

---

space	KNOWN-ENTRY

text   description /* the flowing pollutant is entering the river
                        from a known drain pipe*/

inference prior .2

control   askable

---

space	LIQUID-SPILL

text   description /* the pollutant in the river is a liquid*/

inference prior .2

control   askable

---

space	STEADY-FLOW

text   description /* the pollutant is flowing steadily (as opposed
                        to stopped for long periods of time) */

inference prior .2

control   askable

---

space	VISIBLE-SPILL

text   description /* the pollutant in the river is clearly visible*/

inference prior .2

control   askable

**FIGURE 9.4   External representation of the KAS inference
network.**

Only one goal has been considered so far: my certainty in
1. The best strategy is to backtrack through the drain system to the
    source is now 3.88
Do you wish to see additional information? ⟨YES⟩

I suspect that
1 — (* The best strategy is to backtrack through the drain system to
    the source) (3.88)

There are two favorable factors:
  1. A visible liquid pollutant is flowing steadily in the river 3.0
  2. You were sure that the flowing pollutant is entering the river from
     a known drain pipe 5.0   ** dominating factor **

There is one factor that has not yet been considered:
  3. Do you have (or can you get) a map of the storm drain system
     from which the pollutant is entering the river 0.0

For which of the above do you wish to see additional information? ⟨1⟩

On a scale from −5 to .5, my certainty that
1.1 — (* a visible liquid pollutant is flowing steadily in the river)
    is now 3.0

There are several favorable factors:
  1. You were sure that the pollutant in the river is a liquid 5.0
  2. You were sure that the pollutant is flowing steadily (as
     opposed to stopped for long periods of time) 4.0
  3. You suspected that the pollutant in the river is clearly
     visible 3.0   ** limiting factor **

For which of the above do you wish to see additional information?
⟨NONE⟩

---

5 — Do you have (or can you get) a map of the storm drain system from
    which the pollutant is entering the river ? ⟨YES⟩

Changing the certainty of (* The best strategy is to backtrack through
the drain system to the source) from 3.83 to 4.68

I suspect that
H — (* The best strategy is to backtrack through the drain system to
the source) (4.68)

Do you wish to see additional information ? ⟨NO⟩

FIGURE 9.5 **KAS's summary of the current situation.**

343

Changing the certainty of (* a visible liquid pollutant is flowing steadily in the river) from 0.0 to 3.0

Changing the certainty of (* The best strategy is to backtrack through the drain system to the source) from 0.0 to 0.86

4—To what degree do you believe that the flowing pollutant is entering the river from a known drain pipe ? <5>

Changing the certainty of (* The best strategy is to backtrack through the drain system to the source) from 0.86 to 3.88

5— Do you have (or can you get) a map of the storm drain system from which the pollutant is entering the river ? <SUMMARIZE>

Instead of giving a certainty answer, the user has exploited an advantageous feature of a skeletal system by executing a built-in command: SUMMARIZE. This command allows the user to explore the rule network top-down to examine the state of the consultation. (See Figure 9.5.)

9.12.4   Observations

The process of building an expert system has begun. With relatively little effort a program has been created that seems to be behaving appropriately. Much remains to be done, however. Since no semantic networks were defined, this program works only in the backward-chaining mode. Moreover, since it has only one top-level hypothesis, how effective it is in homing-in on the right diagnosis cannot be judged. As the knowledge base grows and the program's potential for interesting behavior increases, the problem of verifying the correctness of the knowledge base will be encountered. These are typical of the problems faced in building a full-scale system and are solved primarily by expending more effort.

The skeletal-system approach has allowed relatively rapid progress to be made, but at a price: only that portion of the problem covered by the system's capabilities can be addressed. Even then, some characteristics of a desirable solution had to be sacrificed. For example, it is presumed that a system that recommends actions would have some explicit notion of the costs of the various alternatives and the resources available. However, diagnosis systems try to determine the most certain (as opposed to the least costly) solution, and thus the present approach addresses just one component of what a full crisis-management system would need.

QUESTIONS

1. How do knowledge-engineering tools differ from conventional software tools?
2. Why is nearly all knowledge engineering grounded in LISP?
3. Identify subcomponents of these tools that would provide a tool-building tool-kit.
4. What is the highest-level tool you can imagine?
5. How do tools differ from programming languages or systems? What common problems do tool builders and programming language designers face?

NOTES

1. This research was supported by Defense Advanced Research Projects Agency Contract DAHC15 72 C 0308. Views and conclusions contained in this section are those of the authors and should not be interpreted as representing the official opinion or policy of DARPA, the U.S. government, or any other person or agency connected with them.

PART V

A Typical Problem for Expert Systems

10

Emergency Management of Inland Oil and Hazardous Chemical Spills: A Case Study in Knowledge Engineering

Carroll K. Johnson and Sara R. Jordan

This chapter describes in some detail a typical problem in knowledge engineering: an expert system is needed to help consult with regular workers or to augment the limited experience of off-shift workers facing a difficult task. Like several other applications, this belongs to the class of crisis-management problems. The oil and hazardous chemical spill-management task demands a system that can integrate diverse sources of knowledge, reason heuristically with incomplete and errorful data, accept data and advice continuously as they become available, and allocate limited resources to various tasks in a reasonable order. The clarity with which the problem is presented reflects great effort on the part of the authors. Ordinarily knowledge engineers encounter less lucid statements of need. Nevertheless, readers should find this sample problem ideal for testing their own skills at building expert systems.

An accidental spill of an oil or chemical at Oak Ridge National Laboratory (ORNL) may be an emergency, depending on the properties and quantity of the substance released, the location, and whether or not the material enters a body of water. Emergency countermeasures must be applied immediately, particularly if the situation presents a health, safety, or environmental hazard. Appropriate countermeasures for various types of spill situations are governed by extensive reasoning. The U.S. National Oil and Hazardous Substances Pollution Contingency plan dictates the handling of many situations. Regional, federal, state, city, and installation contingency plans also exist. In addition, at the individual installation level, a spill prevention, control, and countermeasures plan (SPCC plan) is required by federal law for nontransportation facilities that may release oil spills to navigable waters. Even one quart of oil can pollute a city's water supply, and many installations such as Oak Ridge have inventories containing 100,000 gallons of oil or more. With this volume, accidental spills constitute serious potential threats, requiring expeditious and expert response.

One of several regulations on the discharge of oil is Environmental Protection Agency regulation 40 CFR 110, which states, "No person shall discharge or cause or permit to be discharged quantities of oil into or upon waters of the United States which violate applicable quality standards or cause a film or sheen upon or discoloration of the surface of the water or a sludge or emulsion deposited beneath the water surface or on the shoreline." A simple calculation based on the fact that a layer of oil 0.001 millimeters thick is visible as a silvery sheen on a water surface shows that 1 liter of oil could cause a visible sheen covering a 100-meter by 100-meter body of water. This is an idealized calculation, and there are always natural mitigating factors. Nevertheless a small quantity of oil can cause a visible oil sheen. Although oil is never discharged intentionally, accidental spills can and do occur and the ORNL spill problem prevention, control, and countermeasure plan (Kelly and Oakes 1980) is the basis for this knowledge-engineering study.

10.1   Overview of the Problem

10.1.1   The Operational Environment

Although the complete spill scenario outlined in Figure 10.1 will not be covered in detail, evaluation is discussed in some depth through the portion on global hazards. That portion of the spill scenario is often carried out under hectic conditions before the scope of the spill emergency is understood. Mistakes in early containment, notifications, and hazard appraisal can be costly, and the more organized those early steps can be made, the better. Knowledge engineering may be viewed simply as a technique for formalizing commonsense heuristic solutions into an understandable and computationally practicable form.

A consulting system covering all the initial phases could be quite useful, particularly during off-shift hours, when decisions must sometimes be made by personnel less familiar with the overall problem. A system is envisioned that will act in consulting mode while gathering information concerning a spill. Meanwhile, in the background, the system will use its various knowledge sources plus the accumulating facts to model and simulate the spill, to monitor for actions that should be taken or additional information that should be gathered, and to issue any appropriate messages and warnings.

The users of the computer system will be the ORNL's Department of Environmental Management (DEM) personnel during regular workdays and the staff of ORNL's shift supervisor's office at night and on weekends. It is assumed that a computer such as a small DEC-20 or DEC-VAX is dedicated to emergency response problems, with backup computing capability available from the Laboratory's timeshared computer systems. The person at the terminal acts as an intermediary between the computer system and field personnel who communicate by telephone or two-way radio. Further into the future, one foresees wireless, hand-held terminals (with a small display screen, keyboard, and function keys) used by all DEM staff, making the intermediary operator unnecessary, but for now only the more conventional computer environment is assumed. Since the consulting system will be interacting with people inexperienced with computers, substantial effort should be devoted to developing a friendly interface.

10.1.2 The Physical Setting

The setting for a case study concerning inland oil spill countermeasures knowledge engineering is the Oak Ridge National Laboratory. Located 10 miles from the city of Oak Ridge, Tennessee, on a 200-square-mile government reservation, ORNL has approximately 200 buildings and 5,800 employees. ORNL is one of three U.S. Department of Energy (DOE) installations within the Oak Ridge reservation. White Oak Creek runs along one side of the main ORNL complex and, 3 miles farther on, enters White Oak Lake. Water released from White Oak Lake Dam flows into the Clinch River just below Melton Hill Dam, which forms one of the Tennessee Valley Authority (TVA) lakes. The Clinch River, a navigable waterway for barge traffic, serves as a water supply for several communities, the closest of which are the Oak Ridge Gaseous Diffusion Plant and Kingston. The Clinch River is also used for commercial and sport fishing and for recreational purposes. White Oak Lake is on the Oak Ridge reservation and is not used for recreation or fishing.

For regulation purposes White Oak Creek is also defined as a navigable waterway. It is a small stream of width varying from 0.6 to 1.2 meters and depth ranging from 10 to 25 centimeters before coming into contact with the Laboratory discharge. The average White Oak Creek flow leaving ORNL is 0.34 cubic meters (90 gallons) per second, including the ORNL contribution of approximately 0.04 cubic meters per second.

There are 93 discharges entering White Oak Creek from ORNL. Most of the discharges are storm drains from various parts of the ORNL grounds, but a number of other discharges, including sanitary sewer facilities and process waste drains, are also present. Two additional small creeks join White Oak Creek within ORNL.

White Oak Creek is well-equipped with instruments for monitoring radioactivity because of the extensive atomic energy research programs that have been carried out at Oak Ridge over nearly four decades. The chemical instrumentation on White Oak Creek is less extensive, consisting of pH monitors, flow meters, and sampling stations for 24-hour composite water samples.

10.1.3 Definitions

Definitions of some of the terms used in the regulations and in the following discussions are given in this section, and a flowchart with some of the operational relationships between problem factors is shown in Figure 10.1. Computational solutions to all the subproblems listed in Figure 10.1 seem feasible, but some are less straightforward than others. Drainage systems topography, for example, is a tedious but straightforward computational problem. Hazard assessment and propagation forecasting are two of the more difficult subproblems.

Many specific concepts are involved in this task domain. They should be incorporated in the expert system and should underlie any cooperative problem-solving communication between humans and computers. Some of these concepts are illustrated here.

- Oil. Oil of any kind or in any form, including but not limited to petroleum fuel oil, sludge, oil refuse, and oil mixed with dredged spoil.
- Reportable quantities. Oil discharges defined in 40 CFR 110.3 as

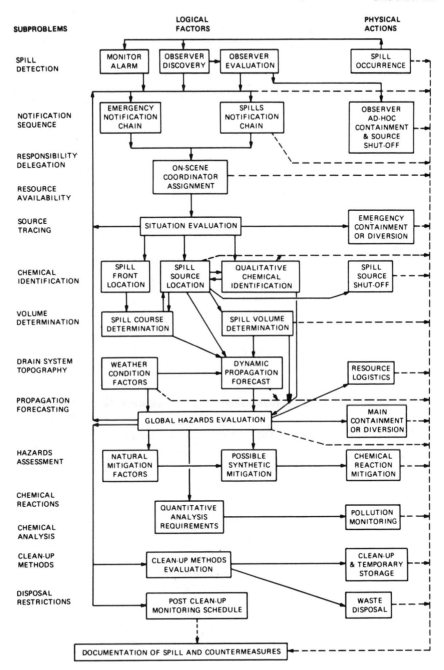

FIGURE 10.1   Elements of an expert system for spill crisis management.

353

discharges that: "(a) violate applicable water quality standards or (b) cause a film or sheen upon or discoloration of the surface of the water or adjoining shorelines or cause a sludge or emulsion to be deposited beneath the surface of the water or upon adjoining shorelines."

- Hazardous substance. Any substance designated as hazardous under subsection (b) (2) of Section 311 of the Clean Water Act.

- Harmful quantities. The EPA regulations on the determination of harmful quantities for hazardous substances (40 CFR 110, 117) list 299 controlled substances categorized by the code letters X, A, B, C, and D, denoting reportable quantities of 1, 10, 100, 1,000, and 5,000 pounds, respectively. The 23 X-rated chemicals are mainly organic pesticides such as DDT, but also included are the inorganic chemicals mercury cyanide, phosphorus, potassium cyanide, and silver nitrate. The polychlorinated biphenyls mixture, which is sometimes found in transformer oil, is an A-rated chemical. Dichlorobenzene rates a B, benzene a C, and naphthalene a D.

- Minor discharge. A discharge of 1,000 to 10,000 gallons of oil to the inland waters, or a discharge of a hazardous substance greater than or equal to a harmful quantity.

- Major discharge. A discharge of more than 10,000 gallons of oil to the inland waters or a discharge of a hazardous substance that poses a substantial threat to public health or welfare or results in critical public concern.

- Phases. Response actions fall into five classes or phases in federal regulations. Phase I is discovery and notification; phase II, evaluation and initiation of action; phase III, containment and countermeasures; phase IV, removal, mitigation, and disposal; and phase V, documentation and cost recovery. Elements of any phase may coincide with other phases.

- Hazard. Safety, health, and environmental dangers.

- Propagation. Predicted or observed position of the spilled substance as a function of time.

- Containment. Enclosure or entrapment that prevents further propagation of the spilled material.

- Mitigation. Factors decreasing the hazardous effect of the discharge.

- Cleanup. The removal of oil or hazardous substances from the water or shorelines or taking necessary actions to minimize or mitigate damage.

- Disposal. Transportation of spilled and cleanup material from the spill site to disposal facilities approved for that material.

10.1.4   Spill Sources

A spill of an oil or hazardous substance can occur from either a stationary source or a mobile source. The most likely stationary sources are storage facilities, construction sites, laboratories, and shops. Spills from mobile sources, such as vehicles, are most likely to occur in parking areas, on roads and railroads, and at construction sites.

An inventory of potential oil spill substances at stationary sites in ORNL is maintained with periodic updates (see Oakes et al. 1980). This inventory provides the location, quantity, and identification of roughly 1,000 oil sources of 1 gallon or more. For example, the inventory states that there are 10 gallons of transformer oil contained in an X-ray generator in Room C-8 of Building 4500-N. There is a total of 247,000 gallons of oil at ORNL, and 50,000 gallons of waste oil are generated annually.

10.2   Discovery and Notification

10.2.1   Discovery of Spills

Many spills are discovered by those working in the vicinity of the spill source, and this situation can be called a "source discovery." The source container is easily found, and the spill material and its volume can often be determined by reading labels and checking records, if they exist.

In "containment discovery," the spilled material is found trapped in a dike or some other form of containment before it has reached a stream. It would be convenient if all potential spill sources were situated so that a spill of maximum volume will be enclosed in some type of secondary containment, such as a diked area. Most spill-prevention programs emphasize secondary containment facilities. If the secondary-containment is close to the source, containment discovery is equivalent to source discovery; in other cases, however, the containment may be some distance away so that the source of the spill is not immediately apparent.

Alarm must be raised in the event of "stream discovery," in which the spilled substance is found in a stream, river, or lake. The alarm for this case might be given by monitoring equipment, or by an observer noting pollution indicators such as an oil slick, discoloration, dead fish, or unusual odor. When the spill is discovered in the stream or in a sump, some detective work is required to identify the material and trace its origin, a process described in a later section.

However the spill is discovered, the observer must evaluate the problem and decide what to do about it besides notifying the Department of Environmental Management. If the observer can safely and competently do so, he or she should also take several other steps. These include characterizing the spill and its probable hazards when reporting it to the DEM and warning others in the area about the probable hazards. In addition, it is important to prevent the spilled material from reaching a stream, to contain the spilled material, and to stop any further release. If the observer cannot carry out these steps, however, the minimum acceptable reaction to a spill discovery is prompt notification of the DEM.

10.2.2   The Notification Sequence

The spill discoverer notifies the DEM, but if there is no answer during off-hours or weekends, the discoverer calls the shift supervisor's office. The shift supervisor, the emergency director of the laboratory during off-hours, may contact someone from DEM at home if necessary. Either the shift supervisor or the DEM representative will act as the initial on-scene coordinator for the current spill emergency.

If the spill is reportable or is in imminent danger of becoming so, the DEM office alerts the DOE Environmental Protection Branch, Oak Ridge Operations (ORO). Off-shift and weekend reporting is made to the DOE security patrol of ORO. Any spill that may reach the stream must be reported to ORO, regardless of the quantity involved.

Oak Ridge Operations then reports the spill to the Emergency Operations Center of the Washington, D.C., headquarters of the Department of Energy. The Federal Clean Water Act requires notification of *any* discharge of oil or hazardous substances into navigable waters of the United States; consequently, if a reportable quantity spill reaches the stream, ORO also reports the spill to the National Spill Response Center (U.S. Coast Guard) in Washington and to the Regional Response Center of the Environmental Protection Agency in Atlanta, Georgia. If the situation is significant enough, the Water Quality Control Office of the State of Tennessee Public Health Department will also be alerted.

Since ORNL-ORO-DOE is the organization responsible for the spill, it bears the primary burden for taking care of it. The Water Quality Control Board, responsible for the state's interests, will keep track of progress made. Finally the regional and national branches of EPA are responsible for the federal interests and stand ready to help or step in if no one else can handle the problem to their satisfaction. State and federal agencies would also be involved in preparing legal action against the ORNL-ORO-DOE organization for violations of regulations associated with any aspect of the spill including occurrence, cleanup, notification, or documentation. Criminal penalties of not more than $10,000 fine or one year's imprisonment or both are authorized for failure to institute appropriate measures or for failure to notify specified bodies of a reportable incident within the time permitted.

All reports of spills should contain as many of the following facts as possible: (1) name, address, and telephone number of the person reporting the spill; (2) exact location of the spill; (3) company name and location; (4) name of material spilled; (5) estimated quantity; (6) source of spill; (7) cause of spill; (8) name of water body involved or body of water nearest to the spill area; and (9) action taken for containment and cleanup.

In addition to the regulatory notification chain another notification chain is needed to alert downstream water users if health hazards accompany the spill. The two closest users to ORNL are the Oak Ridge Gaseous Diffusion Plant, known locally as the K-25 Plant, and the Kingston community, both of which use Clinch River water. Oak Ridge Operations would make the notifications and probably would also alert the Tennessee Valley Authority. TVA can increase the dilution of spills with its flood control system of dams. The State of Tennessee's Water Quality Control Group in Knoxville would extend the alert to other communities along the Clinch River. A pollutant could reach the K-25 water intake in about fifteen hours after release at ORNL.

A third notification chain is concerned with marshaling support personnel and equipment to carry out the containment, cleanup, and disposal stages of the spill countermeasures. The Executive Director of Support and Services at ORNL would be alerted by the ORNL Department of Environmental Management if the spill reached reportable-spill status. The executive director has authority to place the appropriate service groups on alert. During off-shift schedules, the shift supervisor would carry out this function, using the skeleton maintenance crew. The support divisions at ORNL that might be required are (1) operations division for facility-related work to contain a spill; (2) plant and equipment division to supply equipment and manpower; (3) construction engineering to provide liaison with construction contractors; (4) analytical chemistry division to provide chemical identification and analysis.

10.3   Characterization of Spills

10.3.1   Evaluation and Containment

The on-scene coordinator (OSC) assigned by the DEM supervises and coordinates the entire spill treatment process from initial assessment through report documentation. The initial task the OSC must undertake is to perform a situation evaluation, first verifying and supplementing the information given by the discoverer. For effective spill treatment, the initial information must be broadened to include at least the following: (1) the spill source location, (2) the spill front location, (3) the spill path, (4) the spill chemical or oil identification, (5) the spill volume, and (6) the hazards associated with this particular oil or chemical. The OSC must establish priorities for determining the unknown factors and simultaneously start countermeasures for containment and cleanup of the spill.

Containment is usually the first priority of the OSC. For example, suppose an oil slick was sighted on White Oak Creek. The OSC's first action might be to locate the spill front and set up an absorbent boom to stop the oil from spreading any further. On the other hand, if an oil spill were seen to enter a storm drain but had not yet appeared at the outfall into the creek, the OSC might try pulling a manhole cover at some intermediate location in the drain path and inserting absorbent material to stop the oil spill front before it reached the creek. The OSC usually postpones identifying the source and the chemical content of the oil until the emergency containment steps are well underway.

Containment of oil floating on water is relatively straightforward because of the use of booms and absorbent material. Pollutants that are insoluble and heavier than water sink to the bottom and are comparatively easy to contain by damming. Soluble pollutants can be contained only by diversion away from the water flow. Slowly soluble materials require a greatly accelerated cleanup phase, bypassing other phases in the operation, to separate the materials from the water before they dissolve. In the case of valuable materials, salvage or reclaiming operations may be given very high priority.

ORNL has three different underground drain systems: storm, process, and sanitary. The process waste system services all the chemical laboratories. The process system, originally designed for minor radioactive spill control, is also suited ideally for chemical and oil spills because of the extensive facilities for separation operations. Process settling basins provide for automatic containment of spills, holding a spill for a week or longer, and providing ample time for cleanup operations. Spills contained and treated in the process system do not reach the status of reportable spills.

10.3.2   Location of Spill Source

If the source location is unknown to the spill discoverer, that information must be obtained. If the spill is flowing continuously, direct methods based on backtracking are possible. If the flow has stopped, indirect methods, usually involving chemical analysis and inventory comparisons, are required.

Backtracking is often used to find the source of a spill sighted at the stream. A general technique is to send one person in a truck containing absorbent booms down the road along the creek to find the front of the oil slick. A boom is positioned across the stream at that point to stop the oil flow and form a containment. A second person performs the actual backtracking by walking upstream along the ninety-three numbered discharge points looking for the one discharging the pollutant. The number on the relevant one is looked up in a table to identify the drainage basin containing the spill source. Absorbent material may be positioned at the outflow to prevent additional pollution from entering the creek. If the discharge contains a hazardous chemical in dangerous quantity but is not too large in volume, a large balloon-type plug may be used to cut off the flow completely.

An atlas of engineering drawings showing the complete drain system is kept in the Office of the Department of Environmental Management, so that the appropriate drainage basin can be selected and examined. This tree structure contains drain inlets at the tips, the drain discharge at the root, and manhole access points at some of the node points. The tree is pruned in a search for the spill path by selecting certain manholes for examination and seeing if the spill flow exists there. Finally the drain inlets of the surviving branch are examined to locate the spill entry point, and the spill path is then backtracked above ground to the spill source. An example diagram of one basin of the storm drain system is shown in Figure 10.2.

Typically that spill source might be a pool of oil—such as that left by a leaky piece of construction equipment—being washed into a storm drain by a rain shower. Even a rain shower during a street paving operation might cause a reportable spill if proper precautions are not observed.

If backtracking is not feasible, indirect methods based on chemical identification must be used. Chemical analysis requires one to several days unless priorities for the analytical chemistry workload are shifted. In addition, the spill sample may have weathered extensively so that comparison of the chemical results with standard samples may not produce a conclusive result. There are thirty-three standard oil types in the ORNL inventory and roughly 1,000 different locations with a gallon or more of oily material. Thus, on the average, there will be thirty possible locations for the spill source. There are also many special-purpose oils in the inventory besides the thirty-three standard types, which may make the identification a quite different chemical analysis problem. General strategies for locating spill sources are shown in Figure 10.3. An estimate of the quantity of oil spilled

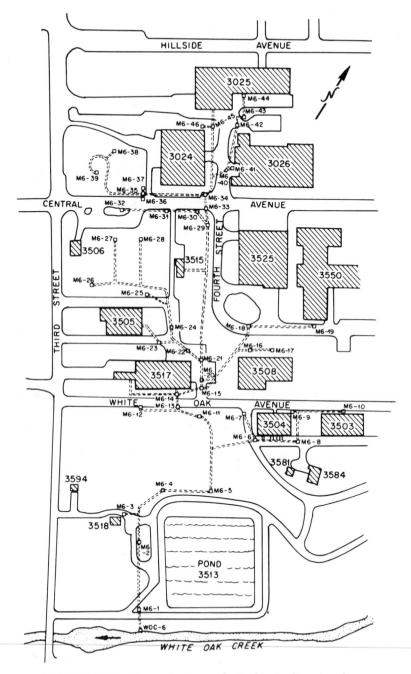

FIGURE 10.2   Example storm drain basin drawing for one outfall into White Oak Creek.

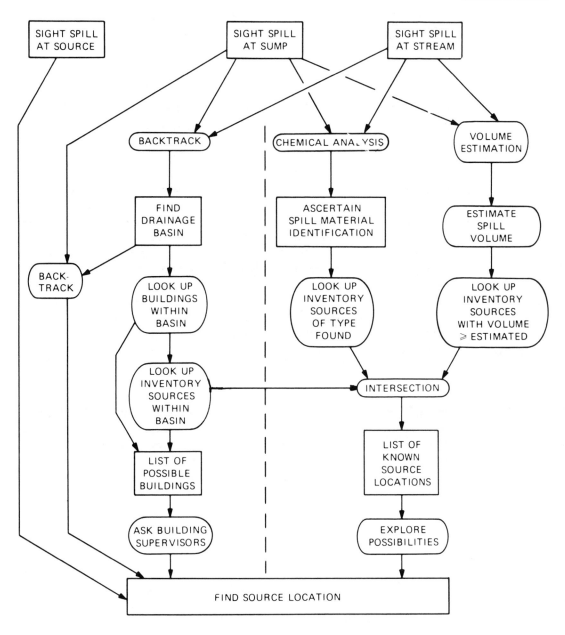

FIGURE 10.3 Diverse methods available to assist in locating a spill source.

can be valuable, since it would eliminate all source possibilities containing quantities less than the spill volume.

10.3.3 Spill Volume Estimation

An estimate of spill volume for an oil can be derived from the area covered by the oil slick times the concentration per unit area. Concentration can be roughly estimated on the basis of a field judgment of the slick's color level and brightness. However, a more accurate estimate involves a Polaroid color camera and a comparison chart produced by the American Petroleum Institute. For best quantitative results the picture should be taken with the camera axis nearly vertical. Color photographs also provide valuable documentation for the final report on the spill, and the spill kit carried by the on-scene coordinator contains a Polaroid camera used for that purpose.

Not all oil types form an oil sheen. Some oils form a cloudy, colloidal suspension layer that floats at the surface. In this case it is necessary to collect a sample from a known surface area using a sorbent filter inside a cylinder. A standard oil-and-grease analysis can be run by the Environmental Management group in roughly one to four hours.

In general, the easiest way to estimate spill volume is to find the source container and check the records concerning supply and usage, if such records exist. Often both types of volume estimates are needed because part of the material may be trapped somewhere along the spill path with the potential to get free and cause another incident. A material balance of volume spilled versus amount recovered in the cleanup operation may be required for the final report on the spill. General strategies for chemical identification and volume determination are shown in Figure 10.4.

10.3.4 Spill Course Determination

From the location of the spill source, the spill path can be determined by referring to the atlas of engineering drawings mentioned previously. The spill path must be known in order to set up a dynamic propagation model to predict the movement of the spill and its dispersion by the water flow. This propagation forecast is useful in planning countermeasures, such as when to curtail the water intake for a community downstream from a spill or how and where to contain a spill for further cleanup.

The most uncertain phase of the propagation requires estimating the transit time from the source to the creek. Numerous factors influ-

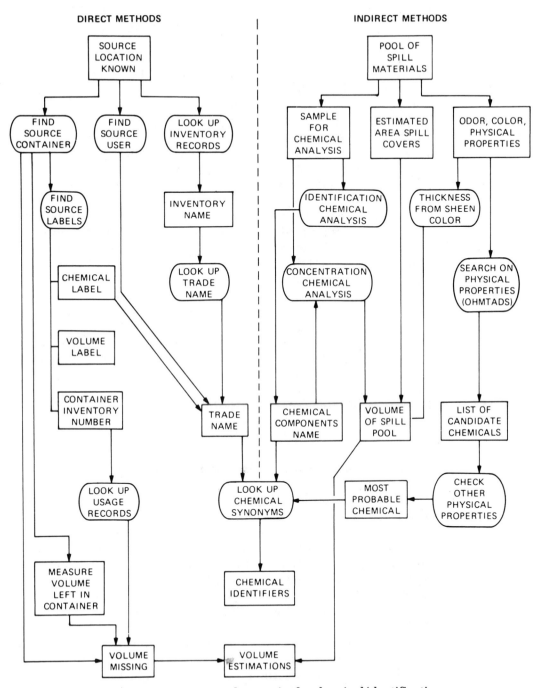

FIGURE 10.4   General strategies for chemical identification and spill volume determination.

ence that transit time because there are so many different path possibilities, depending upon the spill source location. Delay times in elements such as sumps are almost unpredictable. Sumps, low accumulation points usually designed to handle waste water in basements that are lower than the drain system, are usually emptied automatically when full, but the filling time may vary from a few minutes for some sumps to four months in others.

Estimating propagation time on White Oak Creek is less uncertain, because the results of some dye studies made in 1962 are available. A spill from Building 4500 would take about 7.3 hours to reach White Oak Dam, the entry point into the Clinch River, with an average velocity of about 0.5 feet/second. Very little dispersion occurs along White Oak Creek; consequently, the head and tail of the spill body do not separate appreciably in that creek. That fact can be extremely important if the spill must be separated from the stream by isolating the polluted portion. Considerable dispersion occurs in White Oak Lake, and the flow in White Oak Creek moves twice as fast when the flow volume is increased sevenfold by moderately heavy rains.

Water flow rates through the drain systems also provide additional important variables, but those rates change drastically during a rain. Between rains most of the storm drains are dry. An extensive tabulation of plant effluent flow (gallons/day) and type of substance involved is available for each building and each of the three drain systems. From this tabulation can be obtained a rough estimate of the flow rate at any given point in a drain network and an indication as to whether it will be continuous or intermittent.

10.3.5   Information Sources for Hazard Evaluation

Chemical hazards are of three types: flammability, reactivity (instability), and toxicity. The National Fire Protection Association (NFPA) has a scheme called the 704 system for identifying the hazards of a chemical in terms of health, flammability, and reactivity (stability) with a diamond-shaped identification label. The severity of the hazard is indicated by a number—placed in the appropriate block of the diamond—ranging from 4 (most severe) to 0 (no danger). The NFPA label eventually will appear on all chemical containers at ORNL.

The valuable information on the various labels implies that the first task, once on the scene, is to find the source container and read the labels. The observer should note the chemical name, the hazard codes, the manufacturer, and any special directions. The manufacturer's name is important because extensive information on the product, often unique and more reliable than general compilations, can be obtained by a single phone call to the manufacturer.

Several information services are available to help in the hazards evaluation. For a transportation accident, the Chemical Transportation Emergency Center (CHEMTREC) provides information twenty-four hours per day, seven days per week, also serving as a clearing-house for referral to several manufacturers' emergency information systems.

The EPA maintains the Oil and Hazardous Materials Technical Assistance Data System (OHMTADS), which has information on about 1,000 different items. That interactive information retrieval system is part of the NIH-EPA Chemical Information System currently maintained by the Information Sciences Corporation (ISC). This data base is also available on microfiche, which provides a good back-up reference in case of computer system failure.

The Coast Guard has a Chemical Hazards Response Information System (CHRIS) which will eventually become an interactive system. The information in that system is also available in a series of four manuals entitled: *Condensed Guide to Chemical Hazards, Hazardous Chemical Data Manual, Hazard Assessment Handbook*, and *Response Methods Handbook*, which can be obtained from the U.S. Government Printing Office. Particularly useful for predicting air pollution and explosion problems, hazard assessment is based on a model derived by Arthur D. Little, Inc., which evaluates some equations with certain coefficients from chemical property files and others from variables at the accident scene. The NFPA code, CHEMTREC, OHMTADS, and CHRIS are information sources that may be available to the On-Scene Coordinator.

10.3.6   Organization of Goals and Parameters

Given the general description of the spills problem, it is now possible to begin to organize the necessary procedures and facts into goals, plans, and variables that may be useful for an expert system. Table 10.1 lists some abstract and operational goals which may be used to guide the system. Table 10.2 gives a list of spill problem parameters that may be used to describe the problem and its solution.

The following spill scenario, which is slightly fictional, may be used to demonstrate the organization in the early phases of a spill problem's solution. The example begins with a report summarizing a spill incident, required for the files maintained at the ORNL DEM office as documentation of the incident.

TABLE 10.1   Goals List for Spills Problem.

Abstract goals (used in setting priority of other goals)

1. Prevent spills (minimize spill flow)		MIN:FLOW
2. Protect people from spill emergency		MIN:EMER
3. Protect environment and property from spills hazards		MIN:HARM
4. Prevent violation of regulations		MIN:VIOL
5. Prevent delays (minimize time)		MIN:TIME
6. Prevent overhead (minimize costs)		MIN:COST

Operational Goals

1. Spill discovery	GOAL:DISCOV
2. Spill characterization	
2.1 Emergency, hazards	GOAL:EMER
2.2 Source	GOAL:SRCE
2.3 Material	GOAL:MAT
2.4 Flow	GOAL:FLOW
3. Regulation violation analysis	GOAL:VIOL
4. Notification	GOAL:NOTIF
5. Countermeasures on spill flow	GOAL:CMEAS
5.1 Containment trapping	GOAL:CMEAS/TRAP
5.2 Cleanup	GOAL:CMEAS/CLEAN
5.3 Mitigation	GOAL:CMEAS/MITIG

10.4   Spill Incident Report

An oil slick was observed on White Oak Creek near outfall WOC-3 about 2:00 P.M., March 16, 1979, by two painters, Carlson and Thomas. They reported the slick to their supervisor, Scott, in the Operations Division, who called the DEM at 2:20 P.M. Further reporting to ORNL management and DOE followed.

Mr. Scott immediately traced the discharge up the creek to outfall WOC-6 and from there up to the first manhole north of settlement pond 3513 (M6-4), where he placed a boom in the manhole. Since a permanent boom system was already in place downstream at the Lagoon Road weir (WEIR1), these containment actions had the spill under control. By 4 P.M., samples showed 87 milligrams of oil per liter of water at the WOC-6 discharge point and 8 milligrams of oil per liter of water farther along White Oak Creek.

The next day, March 17, the oil slick was traced to the manhole south of Building 3025 (M6-45). Further investigation showed that oil leaking from the hydraulic elevator in 3025 was accumulating in the

TABLE 10.2.   Specification of Spill Problem Parameters.

Description	Mnemonic
Material spilled	MAT
Name	MAT/NAME
Chemical	MAT/NAME/CHEM*
Trade	MAT/NAME/TRADE
Inventory	MAT/NAME/INV
Physical properties	MAT/PHYS
State of ambient temperature	MAT/PHYS/STATE
Color	MAT/PHYS/COLOR
Odor	MAT/PHYS/ODOR
Water soluble	MAT/PHYS/SOLUB
Specific gravity	MAT/PHYS/SP-GR
Melting point	MAT/PHYS/MELT
Boiling point	MAT/PHYS/BOIL
Flash point	MAT/PHYS/FLASH
Hazards	MAT/HAZ
National Fire Protection Association	MAT/HAZ/NFPA
Health	MAT/HAZ/NFPA/HEALTH*
Fire	MAT/HAZ/NFPA/FIRE*
React	MAT/HAZ/NFPA/REACT*
Other	MAT/HAZ/NFPA/OTHER*
EPA index	MAT/HAZ/EPA-INDEX
Oil-PCB content	MAT/HAZ/PCB
Source of spill	SRCE
Location	SRCE/LOC
Building	SRCE/LOC/BLDG*
Room of building	SRCE/LOC/BLDG/ROOM*
Grounds of building	SRCE/LOC/BLDG/GRDS*
Area	SRCE/LOC/AREA
Construction site	SRCE/LOC/CONST
Container	SRCE/CONT
Type	SRCE/CONT/TYPE
Label	SRCE/CONT/LABEL
Material name	SRCE/CONT/LABEL/NAME*
Inventory number	SRCE/CONT/LABEL/INV-NO
Capacity of container	SRCE/CONT/LABEL/CAPAC
Hazards code	SRCE/CONT/LABEL/HAZ-NPFA
Volume of material	SRCE/CONT/VOL*
Before spill	SRCE/CONT/VOL/BEFORE
After spill	SRCE/CONT/VOL/AFTER
Leak flow rate	SRCE/CONT/FLOW-RATE*
Personnel	SRCE/PEOPLE*
Supervisor	SRCE/PEOPLE/SUPER
User's name	SRCE/PEOPLE/USER
Records	SRCE/REC
Flow of spill (with locations, times)	FLOW

TABLE 10.2. (*Continued*)

Description	Mnemonic
Edge	FLOW/EDGE
Front location	FLOW/EDGE/FRONT-LOC@T
Rear location	FLOW/EDGE/REAR-LOC@T
Concentration	FLOW/CONC
Sample for analysis	FLOW/CONC/SMPL @ LOC,T
Analysis results	FLOW/CONC/SMPL-RESULT,T
Volume	FLOW/VOL
Secondary containment	FLOW/VOL/SEC-CONT @ LOC,T
Ground pool	FLOW/VOL/GRND-POOL @ LOC,T
Ground absorption	FLOW/VOL/GRND-ABSOR @ LOC,T
Sump	FLOW/VOL/SUMP @ LOC,T
Pipe absorption	FLOW/VOL/PIPE-ABSOR @ LOC,T
Stream	FLOW/VOL/STREAM @ LOC,T
Streambed absorption	FLOW/VOL/STREAM-ABSOR @ LOC,T
Lake	FLOW/VOL/LAKE @ LOC,T
Total	FLOW/VOL/TOTAL @ T
Observed visually	FLOW/OBS @ LOC,T
Detected nonvisually	FLOW/DET @ LOC,T
Countermeasures (with locations, times)	CMEAS
Containment method (e.g., boom)	CMEAS/TRAP @ LOC,T
Cleanup method	CMEAS/CLEAN @ LOC,T
Disposal	CMEAS/DISP @ LOC,T
Mitigation method	CMEAS/MITIG @ LOC,T
Route	RT
Surface	RT/SUR
Source	RT/SUR/SRCE
Secondary containment	RT/SUR/SECNT
Underground network	RT/UND
Inlet	RT/UND/IN
Access points	RT/UND/ACCESS
Sump	RT/UND/SUMP
Outfall	RT/UND/OUT
Waterway	RT/WAT
White Oak Creek	RT/WAT/WOC
Discharge outfall	RT/WAT/WOC/FALL
Weir 1	RT/WAT/WOC/WEIR1
Weir 2	RT/WAT/WOC/WEIR2
White Oak Lake	RT/WAT/WOL
White Oak Dam	RT/WAT/WOL/WOD
Clinch River	RT/WAT/CLNCH
Gaseous Diffusion Plant	RT/WAT/CLNCH/GAS-DIF
Kingston	RT/WAT/CLNCH/KING
Emergency	EMER
Fire or explosion	EMER/FIRE
Air pollution	EMER/AIR

TABLE 10.2. (*Continued*)

Description	Mnemonic
Water pollution	EMER/WATER
Chronic toxicity	EMER/CHRONIC
Violation of Regulations	VIOL
Federal Water Pollution Act	VIOL/FWPCA
Effluent discharge	VIOL/FWPCA/NPDES
Average (10 milligrams/liter)	VIOL/FWPCA/NPDES/AVG
Maximum (15 milligrams/liter)	VIOL/FWPCA/NPDES/MAX
pH limits (6−9)	VIOL/FWPCA/NPDES/PH
Oil discharge, EPA	VIOL/FWPCA/OIL-DIS
Film	VIOL/FWPCA/OIL-DIS/FILM
Discolor	VIOL/FWPCA/OIL-DIS/DISCOL
Sludge	VIOL/FWPCA/OIL-DIS/SLUDGE
Tennessee Water Quality Control	VIOL/TN-WQC
Impaired use	VIOL/TN-WQC/IMP-USE
Tennessee effluence limit	VIOL/TN-EFF-LM
Maximum (30 milligram/liter)	VIOL/TN-EFF-LM/MAX
Visible sheen	VIOL/TN-EFF-LM/VISIB
Notification	NOTIF
Regulatory channels	NOTIF/REG-CHN
Supervisor	NOTIF/REG-CHN/SUPER
DEM	NOTIF/REG-CHN/DEM
Shift supervisor	NOTIF/REG-CHN/SHIFT-SUP
Oak Ridge Operations	NOTIF/REG-CHN/ORO
DOE	NOTIF/REG-CHN/DOE
National Spill Response Center	NOTIF/REG-CHN/NSRC
Regional Spill Response Center	NOTIF/REG-CHN/RSRC
Tennessee Water Quality Commission	NOTIF/REG-CHN/TNQC
Water users	NOTIF/W-USER
Gaseous diffusion plant	NOTIF/W-USER/GAS-DIF
Kingston water works	NOTIF/W-USER/KINGSTON
Tennessee Valley Authority	NOTIF/W-USER/TVA
Logistics	NOTIF/LOGIS
Operations Division	NOTIF/LOGIS/OP-DIV
Plant and Equipment Division	NOTIF/LOGIS/P-AND-E
Construction Engineering	NOTIF/LOGIS/ENG
Analytical Chemistry	NOTIF/LOGIS/AN-CHEM
Background for spill	BKGRND
Cause	BKGRND/CAUSE*
Weather	BKGRND/WEATHER*
Liable department	BKGRND/LIABLE-DEPT
Time of spill	BKGRND/T-SPILL*
Time of report to DEM	BKGRND/T-CALL-DEM
On-scene coordinator	BKGRND/OSC
Name	BKGRND/OSC/NAME
Department	BKGRND/OSC/DEPT
Arrival time	BKGRND/OSC/START

TABLE 10.2. (Continued)

Description	Mnemonic
Discovery of spill	DISCOV
By	DISCOV/BY
Name	DISCOV/BY/NAME
Department	DISCOV/BY/DEPT
Type of spill	DISCOV/TYPE*
Location description	DISCOV/LOC*
Time	DISCOV/TIME

*ASK DISCOVERER: these items should be ascertained at the time of initial spill report, if possible.

building sump and was being pumped along with surface water to the storm sewer. In wet weather surface water enters the building basement and the bottom of the elevator shaft. These areas are lower than the building's footer drains. The total spill volume was estimated at less than 5 gallons.

The oil was cleaned up and removed from the sump and from the floor of the elevator shaft. A temporary solution for the elevator piston leak consisted of placing a bucket under the piston mechanism's drain spout. Somewhat less than 1 quart of oil per week is being collected there.

No further oil sheen is detectable in White Oak Creek, or at the outfall WOC-6, or at any point in the WOC-6 drain network that allows visual inspection.

10.5 Spill Incident Analysis

This analysis of the spill example maps the verbal description onto the parameters defined previously. The intelligent consulting system is acting like the prompter in a theatrical rehearsal, using the transcription as the script for the play in the language of the consulting system.

The action starts with the discovery of the spill on White Oak Creek by Carlson and Thomas.

```
GOAL: DISCOV
      DISCOV/BY/NAME        — Carlson, Thomas
      DISCOV/BY/DEPT        — Operations
      DISCOV/TYPE           — Stream
      DISCOV/LOC            — Near WOC-3
      DISCOV/TIME             3/16/79, 14:00
```

The discovery observations provide a preliminary characterization of the spill.

GOAL: MAT

MAT/PHYS/STATE	— Liquid (oil)
MAT/PHYS/SP-GR	— <1.0 (floats)
MAT/PHYS/SOLUB	— Not soluble (slick)
FLOW/VOL/STREAM	— Visible sheen @ WOC near WOC-3, 3/16/79, 14:00

The workmen are required to notify their supervisor.

GOAL: NOTIF/REG-CHN

NOTIF/REG-CHN/SUPER	— Scott, 3/16/79, 14:00 +

Carlson and Thomas have now passed on their observations to supervisor Scott, who notifies DEM.

GOAL: NOTIF

NOTIF/REG-CHN/DEM	— Oakes, 3/16/79, 14:20

The next requirement is to determine the source location. Since the spill was discovered on the stream, the source location was unknown at that time. Backtracking, the preferred method of source location for a stream discovery, requires a continuous visible flow, which exists here.

GOAL: SRCE

FLOW/OBS	— NEAR WOC-3 @ 3/16/79, 14:00

The initially known portion of the spill route is the visible sheen near WOC-3, which is between WEIR-1, where the existing boom is located, and the unknown discharge point. Through backtracking, Scott found the discharge point of the spill route to be WOC-6.

RT/WAT/WOC/FALL	— WOC-6

The outfall number provides an identification of the specific underground network involved.

RT/UND/OUT	— WOC-6

Reference to the engineering drawings for WOC-6 provides access points for checking flow of oil in the underground network. A convenient manhole is chosen where further countermeasures can be applied. M6-1 was not used because of potential large-volume discharges from Pond 3513. M6-2 could have been used, but M6-4 is farther off the road and a safer place to work.

RT/UND/ACCESS	— M6-4
FLOW/OBS	— M6-4 @ 3/16/79, 14:20+
CMEAS/TRAP	— Boom @ M6-4, 3/16/79, 14:20

Since the flow rate of the discharge is small enough to produce only an oil sheen, the countermeasures now in place provide effective temporary containment; however, it is necessary to provide quantitative data showing that the spill is under control. The source location goal is suspended for the remainder of the workday to collect samples and have them analyzed.

GOAL: VIOL	SMPL-1, WOC-6, 3/16/79,
FLOW/CONC/SMPL	— 16:00
	SMPL-2, downstream from
	WOC-6, 3/16/79,
	16:00
FLOW/CONC/SMPL-RESULT	— SMPL-1, 87 Mg/1,
	3/16/79, 16:00
	SMPL-2, 8 Mg/1,
	3/16/79, 16:00
VIOL/FWPCA/NPDES/AVG	— <10 (In Compliance)
VIOL/FWPCA/NPDES/MAX	— UNK

Tom Oakes of DEM can now notify the regulatory chain that the spill is under control.

GOAL: NOTIF/REG-CHN	
NOTIF/REG-CHN/ORO	— 3/16/79 16:00
NOTIF/REG-CHN/DOE	— 3/16/79 16:00

Rather than continue the backtracking into the evening with overtime rates, it is decided to invoke GOAL: MIN:COST and delay that task until the following day.

GOAL: SRCE/LOC	
RT/UND/ACCESS	— M6-11
FLOW/OBS	— M6-11 @ 3/17/79, 08:30
—	—
—	—
—	—
RT/UND/ACCESS	— M6-45
FLOW/OBS	— M6-45 @ 3/17/79, 09:30

The last access point available is M6-45. From Figure 10.2, it is clear that the source must be within Building 3015. The field engineer for 3025, G.E. Pierce, who is contacted, notes that one connection to the storm drain system is the building sump, which provides drainage for the elevator shaft located below the drain line. Upon examination of the sump, a layer of oil is found.

FLOW/OBS   — 3025 @ 3/17/79, 10:00
RT/UND/SUMP   — 3025 Sump
SRCE/LOC/BLDG   — 3025 Elevator

The "programmed maintenance reference data sheet" for the elevator gives the inventory code for the hydraulic oil as "BE" and lists six suppliers of compatible products of the type (for example, Gulf Harmony 32).

GOAL: MAT
    MAT/NAME/TRADE   — Hydraulic Oil
    MAT/NAME/INV   — BE
    SRCE/REC   — Prog. Maint. Ref. Data Sheets

The only hazardous oils that must be watched for are those containing polychlorinated biphenyls (PCBs). These oils are usually transformer and capacitor oils, and type BE oils are not in that classification. However, to be sure, a chemical analysis will be requested.

GOAL: EMER
    FLOW/CONC/SMPL   — SMPL-3, 3025 Elevator Sump, 3/17/79, 10:30
    FLOW/CONC/SMPL-RESULT   — SMPL-3, neg. PCB, 3/18/79
    MAT/HAZ/PCB   — Negative
    EMER/WATER   — Negative

The spill may now be considered a non-PCB oil spill with negligible emergency status. The volume estimation subproblem is complicated by the fact that it is not known how long the slow leak has been in progress or when the automatic sump last emptied. The problem appeared because of an unusually heavy rainfall, which caused minor flooding into the elevator sump. The volume of oil needed to refill the hydraulic cylinder tank provides an upper limit estimate for the spill volume.

```
GOAL: FLOW
      FLOW/VOL/TOTAL          — 1–5 gal, 3/17/79
      SRCE/CONT/VOL/BEFORE    — 5 gal
      SRCE/CONT/FLOW-RATE     — 1 qt/week
```

The spill has now been characterized and contained. The remaining tasks (not covered here) involve cleanup, mitigation, and final notifications, including a spill incident report.

```
GOAL: CMEAS/CLEAN
GOAL: CMEAS/MITIG
GOAL: NOTIF
```

The idealized expert system discussed in this chapter has been partially implemented at Oak Ridge National Laboratories. Based on experience to date, there is reason to believe that the techniques of knowledge engineering hold great promise for increasing human ability to manage and overcome crises of the sort that motivated this chapter.

QUESTIONS

1. Identify ten kinds of heuristic knowledge that spill management requires.
2. Identify five resources limited during a crisis. How should these be allocated?
3. What changes to the crisis management system would be required to handle gas leakages? What common capabilities could be shared?
4. What difficulties would arise if the crisis management system were implemented in FORTRAN?
5. Identify three other tasks that are very similar to the spills task. What parts of the expert systems could they all share? How could you minimize the work required to develop the set of four expert systems?

ACKNOWLEDGMENTS

The authors gratefully acknowledge the wholehearted participation of the ORNL Department of Environmental Management personnel in this study. The collaboration of Tom Oakes, Brian Kelly, and Chris Bird was particularly valuable. Discussions with the other members of the Oak Ridge Programmed Reasoning Methodology Panel, particularly John Allen, Robert Meacham, Karl Haeuslein, and Jonas Holdeman, were also extremely valuable and stimulating.

Transcripts Illustrating the Operation of Prototype Expert Systems for the Spill Crisis-Management Application

1.1 Trace of EMYCIN Spill Program

The following trace was generated by the EMYCIN spill model. User input is shown in boldface type, while annotations explaining the trace are shown in square brackets.

27-Aug-80 16:35:13 [consultation of 25-Aug-80 11:57AM]
        --------SPILL-100--------
    1) Is the spilled substance Oil, Acid, or Other?
    **   ?
    What is the spilled substance?
    Expected responses are: OIL, ACID, or OTHER
    Enter HELP for list of user options.
    **   **OIL**
    2) Where was the spill first spotted?
    **   **ALONG-CREEK**
    3) Is the liquid flowing?
    **   **YES**

4) Please walk upstream along the creek looking for the outfall from which the liquid is draining. If you find one, please enter the outfall number.

**   **WHY**   [i.e., WHY is it important to determine the outfall from which the liquid is draining?]

[1.01]   This will aid in determining the spill basin.
It has already been established that
   [1.1] the location where the spill was first reported is along-creek
Therefore, if
   [1.2] the outfall from which the liquid is draining is known
then
   it is definite (1.0) that the outfall from which the liquid is draining is the spill basin
[RULE001]

**   **WOC-6**   [The answer to question 4]
5) Please inspect M6-1. Is the liquid flowing in this manhole?
**   **YES**
6) Is there flow in M6-1 from direction of P3513A?
**   **NO**
7) Please inspect M6-2. Is the liquid flowing in this manhole?
**   **YES**
8) Please inspect M6-4. Is the liquid flowing in this manhole?
**   **YES**
9) Please inspect M6-5. Is the liquid flowing in this manhole?
**   **YES**
10) Please inspect M6-11. Is the liquid flowing in this manhole?
**   **NO**
11) Please inspect B3504A. Is the liquid flowing in this manhole?
**   **NO**
12) Please inspect M6-6. Is the liquid flowing in this manhole?
**   **YES**
13) Please inspect M6-7. Is the liquid flowing in this manhole?
**   **NO**

14) Are there stationary sites listed in the inventory from which the observed volume of oil might have originated?

** **NO**

The recommended emergency containment procedures are as follows:
  Locate the spill front and set up an absorbent boom to stop further flow.
  Suggestions for discovering the source of the spill are as follows:
  Check possible sources near, or that drain into, M6-6.
  Consider possible mobile sources.
  Request chemical analysis to assist in identification.

1.2 Trace of KAS Spill Program

The following trace was produced by the KAS PROSPECTOR spill model. User input is shown in boldface type.

RUN A: Flowing acid

———————————————————

    PROSPECTOR — — — MARK IV — — — Version iv
    SRI International
    27-Aug-80 21:57:29

SPILL — version 1

Do you want instructions ? **NO**

———————————————————

I understand that there is the possibility of a spill in White Oak Creek.
Do you want to volunteer any information? **YES**

Do you know what substance (or type of substance) might have spilled? **YES**

———————————————————

Please name the suspected substance(s).

(If you need instructions, type HELP; terminate by typing DONE.)

――――――――――――――――――

1:OIL OF VITRIOL
OIL-OF-VITRIOL = SULFURIC-ACID? **YES**

WARNING!! Potentially highly corrosive, and yields toxic combustion products.

Wear protective clothing.
(SULFURIC-ACID) (5.0)

――――――――――――――――――

2:DONE

――――――――――――――――――

1 — Are there any other signs of pollution in White Oak Creek? **NO**

2 — Can you estimate the volume of the spill? **YES**

3 — What is the amount (minimum-gallons maximum-gallons)?
   .5   1.5
What is your confidence in this estimate? **4**

4 — To what degree do you believe that the source of the spill is known? **−4**

――――――――――――――――――

We should work on determining the source of the spill.

――――――――――――――――――

5 — To what degree do you believe that the spill is flowing continuously? **4**

6 — Is the basin that is the source of the spill known? **YES**

Find the buildings containing at least the amount (if known) of the pollutant (if identified) in the basin (if known).

Find the location of the sources containing at least the amount (if known) of the pollutant (if identified) in the basin (if known).

[Note: these are substitutes for calls to retrieval functions.]

7 — To what degree do you believe that a map of the storm drains for the basin is available? **5**

I recommend that you trace the spill back through the storm drains for this basin to the source.

I have nothing more to ask about this hypothesis.

— — — — — — — — — — — — — — — — —

On a scale from − 5 to 5, my certainty that H − (* A spill source strategy is clear) is now 4.718

There are several favorable factors; in order of importance:
1. The best method is to backtrack through the drain system to the source 4.718   ** establishes H **
2. the best method is to call the building supervisor 1.875
3. the best method is to track down recorded sources 1.875

There is one factor that has not yet been considered:
4. the best method is to seek a nondocumented source 0.0

For which of the above do you wish to see additional information? (Type ? for available options) **1   2**

— — — — — — — — — — — — — — — — —

I suspect that
1 − (* The best method is to backtrack through the drain system to the source) (4.718)

There are several favorable factors; in order of importance:
1: 1. You were sure that the spill is flowing continuously 4.0
1: 2. You were sure that a map of the storm drains for the basin is available 5.0
1: 3. You were sure that the basin that is the source of the spill is known 5.0

For which of the above do you wish to see additional information?
     NONE

— — — — — — — — — — — — — — — — —

I suspect that
2 − (* the best method is to call the building supervisor) (1.875)

There is one favorable factor:
2: 1. You were sure that the basin that is the source of the spill is known 5.0

There are two negative factors with neutral effect that, if positive, could have been significant; in order of importance:

2:   2.   Off hours and urgent −1.895

** Would have helped if positive **

2:   3.   the spill is not flowing continuously −4.0

** would have helped if positive **

There are two factors that have not yet been considered; in order of importance:

2:   4.   There is at least one but not many buildings to check 0.0
2:   5.   Are we in off hours 0.0

For which of the above do you wish to see additional information?
   2

_ _ _ _ _ _ _ _ _ _ _ _ _ _ _ _ _ _ _

On a scale from −5 to 5, my certainty that 2.2 − (* Off hours and urgent) is now −1.895

There is one unfavorable factor:

2.2:   1.   this spill could be serious −1.895   ** limiting factor **

There is one factor that has not yet been considered:

2.2:   2.   Are we in off hours 0.0

For which of the above do you wish to see additional information?
   NONE

Do you wish to see additional information about
2 − (* the best method is to call the building supervisor)? **NO**

Do you wish to see additional information about
H − (* A spill source strategy is clear)? **NO**

This terminates this run of PROSPECTOR.

1.3 Trace of EXPERT Spill Program

The following trace was generated by the EXPERT spill model. User input is shown in boldface type while annotations explaining the trace are shown in square brackets.

Enter File Name: **spill**

Type ? for a summary of valid responses to any question asked by
the program.

Enter Name or ID Number: **C. Johnson**
Case Type: (1)Real (2)Hypothetical *2
Enter Date of Visit: **8/26/80**
Enter Initial Findings (Press RETURN to begin questioning):
*

1. type of spill:
    1)   source
    2)   containment
    3)   stream
    Choose one:
    *3

2. Agencies notified:
    1)   DEM
    2)   ORO-DOE
    Checklist:
    *n   [Telling the program that no agencies have been notified]

3. initial spill location drain code M6:
    *dx   [Show the current analysis]

INTERPRETIVE ANALYSIS

Notify DEM of spill discovery.
Source and location must be determined to halt spill.
The chemical has not yet been identified.
Path flow and volume should be determined to evaluate
success of cleanup and potential propagation pattern.
"Containment is usually the first priority of the OSC."
    For oil floating on water, booms and absorbent material are
    indicated. Cleanup and mitigation depend on the specific
    causes of the spill.

3. initial spill location drain code M6:
    *fix 2

FIX: Agencies notified:
    1)   DEM
    2)   ORO-DOE
    Checklist:
    *1   [Telling the program that DEM has been notified]

3. initial spill location drain code M6:
    *5

4. material type:
    1) oil – film or sheen
    2) chemical
    Choose one:
    *1

5. initial known spill characteristics:
    1) source, location
    2) identity of spill material
    3) flow or volume
    4) emergency, hazards
    Checklist:
    *n

6. spill flow:
    1) continuous
    2) intermittent/stopped
    Choose one:
    *1

7. source drain code:
    *dx   [Show the current analysis]

INTERPRETIVE ANALYSIS

- - - - - - - - - - - - - - - - - - -

Notify ORO-DOE of possible violation.
Backtracking is indicated to determine next drain basin to examine. Type RUN(map).
Source and location must be determined to halt spill.
The chemical has not yet been identified.
Path flow and volume should be determined to evaluate success of cleanup and potential propagation pattern.
"Containment is usually the first priority of the OSC." For oil floating on water, booms and absorbent material are indicated.
Cleanup and mitigation depend on the specific causes of the spill.

7. source drain code:
    *fix 2

FIX: Agencies notified:
1) DEM
2) ORO-DOE
Checklist:
*1,2 [Telling the program that both agencies have been notified]

7. source drain code:
*run(map)

[Running Program.

Is spill observed at Drain M6- 11 (Y/N): n

Is spill observed at Drain M6- 6 (Y/N): n

Is spill observed at Drain M6- 8 (Y/N): n

BACKTRACKING RESULTS

_ _ _ _ _ _ _ _ _ _ _ _ _ _ _ _ _ _

Source spill is near DRAIN M6-5
Potential buildings/grounds source is 3595. . . [Done]

8. material code:
*568

9. spill volume:
*50

10. effluent discharge sample average mg/1:
*7

11. hazards:
1) health
2) fire
3) reaction
4) epa index
5) oil pcb content
Checklist:
*n

. . . .

SUMMARY

_ _ _ _ _ _ _ _ _ _ _ _ _ _ _ _ _

Name: C. Johnson   [HYP]
Case   1: Visit   1   Date: 8/26/80

type of spill:
  stream

Agencies notified:
  DEM
  ORO-DOE

initial spill location drain code M6: 5

material type:
  oil – film or sheen

spill flow:
  continuous

source drain code: 5

source building/grounds code: 3595

material code: 568

spill volume: 50

effluent discharge sample average mg/1: 7

INTERPRETIVE ANALYSIS

_ _ _ _ _ _ _ _ _ _ _ _ _ _ _ _ _ _

source is known.
substance is identified.
spill volume is known.
hazard analysis has been performed.
"Containment is usually the first priority of the OSC." For oil
floating on water, booms and absorbent material are indicated.
Cleanup and mitigation depend on the specific causes of the
spill.
Currently in compliance with fresh water pollution act.
(Spill may be contained.)

1.4   Trace of OPS5 Spill Program

In the OPS5 trace the model interviews the user, finds that three agents
can work on the task, assigns one of them to find a spot where the
spill can be contained (the head of the spill), another to determine

which outflow is the source of the contaminant, and the third to collect a sample of the contaminant and have it analyzed. When the second agent reports that outfall WOC-6 is the source of the contaminant, the model directs him through the drainage basin until the spill source is found. Boldface type in the trace indicates the user input.

A sample OPS5 interaction with SPILL:

IF THE ANSWER TO A QUESTION IS UNKNOWN ENTER NIL

ENTER THE NAME OF THE PERSON WHO REPORTED THE SPILL AND THE DATE:
* **cooper**
* **18-sept-80**

ENTER THE TIME AT WHICH THE SPILL WAS REPORTED BY COOPER
* **20:30**

IS THE PERSON WHO REPORTED THE SPILL A SPILL EXPERT:
* **yes**

ENTER THE LOCATION AND LOCATION-TYPE — CREEK LAKE STORM-DRAIN GROUND — WHERE THE SPILL WAS SIGHTED
* **weir-1**
* **creek**

ENTER THE CLASS OF THE MATERIAL SPILLED:
* **oil**

ENTER THE ESTIMATED VOLUME OF MATERIAL SPILLED:
* **30**

ENTER THE NAME OF THE MATERIAL SPILLED:
* **nil**

ENTER THE HAZARD LEVEL OF THE MATERIAL SPILLED:
* **nil**

ENTER THE COLOR OF THE MATERIAL SPILLED:
* **black**

ENTER THE NUMBER OF PERSONNEL AVAILABLE TO DEAL WITH THE SPILL:
* **3**

WHAT IS THE NAME OF PERSON 1:
* **smith**

WHAT IS THE NAME OF PERSON 2:
* **jones**

WHAT IS THE NAME OF PERSON 3:
* **larson**

[6] LARSON   :   FIND THE HEAD OF THE SPILL

[10] JONES   :   DETERMINE WHICH OUTFLOW UPSTREAM OF
WEIR-1 IS THE SOURCE OF THE CONTAMINANT

[12] SMITH   :   COLLECT A SAMPLE OF THE CONTAMINANT
AND TAKE IT FOR ANALYSIS
Nil
(response 10 woc-6)

[15] JONES   :   DETERMINE WHETHER MANHOLE M6-1 IS
CONTAMINATED
Nil
(response 15 yes)

[16] JONES   :   DETERMINE WHETHER MANHOLE M6-2 IS
CONTAMINATED
Nil
(response 16 yes)

[17] JONES   :   DETERMINE WHETHER MANHOLE M6-4 IS
CONTAMINATED
Nil
(response 17 no)

[18] JONES   :   DETERMINE WHETHER MANHOLE M6-3 IS
CONTAMINATED
Nil
(response 18 yes)

STATUS REPORT: BLDG-3518 MAY CONTAIN THE SOURCE

[20] JONES   :   SEARCH BUILDING BLDG-3518 FOR DAMAGED
CONTAINERS OF OIL WITH CAPACITY
GREATER THAN 30 GALLONS

1.5   **Drainage Map: Oak Ridge National Laboratory**

Figure A.1 shows the portion of the Oak Ridge National Laboratory
that comprises the data base for the ROSIE model of environmental

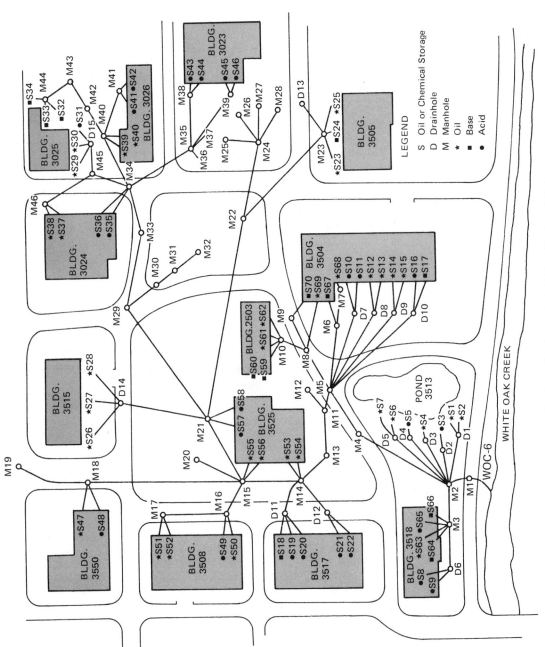

Figure A.1   One drainage basin at Oak Ridge National Laboratory

crisis management. See Appendix 1.6 for a trace of this model in operation.

1.6 Trace of the ROSIE Spill Model

The top-level procedure in the ROSIE model is shown, followed by a trace of the model's operation. This procedure, called "investigate," receives a report from the user and attempts to determine the spill material, volume, and source. If the source is not determined at this point, the procedure requests more information and the cycle continues.

To investigate:

Execute cyclically.

[1] Go get-a-report.

[2] If the material of the spill is undetermined go try-to-determine-the-material.

[3] If the volume of the spill is undetermined go try-to-determine-the-volume.

[4] If the source of the spill is undetermined go try-to-determine-the-source.

[5] If the source of the spill is still undetermined go echo-the-requests-for-information
otherwise,
      go clean-up
      and return.

End.

The two primary procedures are "try-to-determine-the-material" and "try-to-determine-the-source." The former procedure uses inventory information and the results of field and laboratory tests to narrow the list of possible pollutant materials. The latter controls the search for the source location, narrowing the list of possible inventory locations by (1) eliminating those containing materials already ruled out and (2) searching the drainage basin using an investigator to decide whether or not the pollutant exists at any particular point in the network.

The determine-source procedure uses a search algorithm designed to minimize the number of manhole examinations by the investigator. During each cycle of the "investigate" procedure, the program calculates which manhole investigation will eliminate the most potential sources and then asks the investigator to examine that manhole. The search algorithm is quite straightforward. The program uses the list of remaining potential sources and the drainage map to find the node (manhole or source) that represents the "midpoint" of the drainage basin, the node that has approximately as many other sources "above" it (draining into it) as "below" it (into which it drains). Then if pollutant is found at the node, all sources below it are eliminated. If no pollutant is found, all sources above the node are eliminated. See Fain (1982) for a more complete description of the ROSIE model.

The output of the ROSIE model, SPILLS, is shown below. User input is shown in boldface. See Appendix 1.5 for a map of that portion of ORNL used as the SPILLS data base. Note that M6-1 refers to M1 on the map, the "6-" indicating that the outfall of this section of drainage basin is WOC-6.

[ROSIE™   Version 1.1   6-Apr-82   10:09:27]

⟨1⟩ **Go investigate.**

Ready for report: **The spill is detected at WOC-6.**
The solubility of the spill does appear low.
The pH of the spill does approximate 8.
End of report.
Report received.

'SPILL #1 is detected at WOC-6' has been recorded.
'SOLUBILITY #1 does appear LOW' has been recorded.
'PH #1 does approximate 8' has been recorded.

Now attempting to determine the material type.
'TYPE-OF-MATERIAL #1 is an oil'.

Now attempting to determine the spill-material.
'SODIUM HYDROXIDE is not a possible-material of SPILL #1'.
'POTASSIUM HYDROXIDE is not a possible-material of SPILL #1'.
'SULPHURIC ACID is not a possible-material of SPILL # 1'.
'HYDROCHLORIC ACID is not a possible-material of SPILL # 1'.
'ACETIC ACID is not a possible-material of SPILL # 1'.

Now attempting to determine the spill volume.

Now trying to determine the source of the spill.
Locations eliminated (wrong material):

S6-64	S6-65	S6-66	S6-8	S6-9
S6-3	S6-5	S6-10	S6-11	S6-16
S6-17	S6-67	S6-70	S6-59	S6-60
S6-18	S6-19	S6-20	S6-21	S6-22
S6-49	S6-48	S6-57	S6-58	S6-24
S6-35	S6-36	S6-43	S6-44	S6-45
S6-46	S6-41	S6-42	S6-32	S6-33
S6-34	S6-31			

What does the spill smell like?
Please characterize the spill's appearance: a colorless film, a silvery
    film, a lightly colored film, a brightly colored film, a film
    with colors turning dull, or a film with very dark colors.
What is the area of the spill (in square meters)?
Please check M6-15 for signs of the spill.

Ready for report: **The spill is detected at m6-15.**
    The spill does have no odor.
    End of report.
Report received.

'SPILL #1 is detected at M6-15' has been recorded.
'SPILL #1 does have NO ODOR' has been recorded.

Now attempting to determine the spill-material.
    'GASOLINE is not a possible-material of SPILL #1'.
    'DIESEL OIL is not a possible-material of SPILL #1'.

Now attempting to determine the spill volume.

Now trying to determine the source of the spill.
Locations eliminated (below a dirty inspection site):

S6-63	D6-6	M6-3	S6-1	S6-2
D6-1	D6-2	S6-4	D6-3	D6-4
S6-6	S6-7	D6-5	D6-7	S6-12
S6-13	D6-8	S6-14	S6-15	D6-9
D6-10	S6-68	M6-7	M6-6	S6-69
M6-9	S6-61	S6-62	M6-10	M6-8
M6-12	S6-53	S6-54	D6-11	D6-12
M6-14	M6-13	M6-11	M6-5	M6-4
M6-2	M6-1			

Locations eliminated (wrong material):

S6-1	S6-2	S6-4	S6-6	S6-7
S6-61	S6-62	S6-47	S6-23	S6-25
S6-39	S6-40	S6-29	S6-30	

Please characterize the spill's appearance: a colorless film, a silvery
            film, a lightly colored film, a brightly colored film, a film
            with colors turning dull, or a film with very dark colors.
What is the area of the spill (in square meters)?
Please check M6-29 for signs of the spill.

Ready for report: **The spill is detected at m6-29.**
                     The spill does form (a film with colors turning
   .   **dull).**
                     The spill does cover 78000 m**2.
                     End of report.

Report received.

   'SPILL #1 is detected at M6-29' has been recorded.
   'SPILL #1 does form FILM #1' has been recorded.
   'SPILL #1 does cover 78000 M**2' has been recorded.

Now attempting to determine the spill-material.

Now attempting to determine the spill volume.
   'SPILL #1 does involve 20.592 GALLONS of MATERIAL'.

Now trying to determine the source of the spill.
Locations eliminated (below a dirty inspection site):

S6-55	S6-56	S6-50	S6-51	S6-52
M6-17	M6-16	M6-19	M6-18	M6-20
S6-26	S6-27	S6-28	D6-14	D6-13
M6-23	M6-25	M6-26	M6-27	M6-28
M6-24	M6-22	M6-21	M6-15	

Locations eliminated (too little volume):

S6-63	S6-12	S6-13	S6-14	S6-15
S6-68	S6-69	S6-53	S6-54	S6-55
S6-56	S6-51	S6-26	S6-27	S6-28
S6-38				

Please check M6-34 for signs of the spill.

Ready for report: **The spill is detected at m6-34.**
                     End of report.

Report received.

'SPILL #1 is detected at M6-34' has been recorded.

Now attempting to determine the spill-material.

Now trying to determine the source of the spill.
Locations eliminated (below a dirty inspection site):

M6-32   M6-31   M6-30   M6-33   M6-29

Please check M6-40 for signs of the spill.

Ready for report: **The spill is not detected at m6-40.
End of report.**
Report received.

'SPILL #1 is not detected at M6-40' has been recorded.

Now attempting to determine the spill-material.

Now trying to determine the source of the spill.
Locations eliminated (above a clean inspection site):

M6-40   M6-41   M6-42   M6-43   M6-44

Please check M6-35 for signs of the spill.

Ready for report: **The spill is not at m6-35.**
Improper report form.
Please try again.
                     **The spill is not detected at m6-35.
                     End of report.**
Report received.

'SPILL #1 is not detected at M6-35' has been recorded.

Now attempting to determine the spill-material.

Now trying to determine the source of the spill.
Locations eliminated (above a clean inspection site):

M6-35   M6-36   M6-37   M6-38   M6-39

Please check M6-46 for signs of the spill.

Ready for report: **The spill is detected at m6-46.
                     End of report.**
Report received.

'SPILL #1 is detected at M6-46' has been recorded.

Now attempting to determine the spill-material.

Now trying to determine the source of the spill.
Locations eliminated (below a dirty inspection site):

D6-15   M6-45   M6-34

Please check S6-37 for signs of the spill.

Ready for report: **The spill is detected at s6-37.**
                     End of report.
Report received.

　'SPILL #1 is detected at S6-37' has been recorded.

Now attempting to determine the spill-material.

Now trying to determine the source of the spill.
Locations eliminated (below a dirty inspection site):

M6-46

The spill does originate at S6-37.
The material of the spill is HYDRAULIC OIL.
The source is located in BUILDING 3024.

1.7   Trace of RLL Spill Program

The following trace was produced by the RLL spill model. User input
is shown in boldface type, and the model's description of task processing is indented.

34__Process (HandleSpills]
Starting the 'How to handle a spill' program.

Do you have a spill problem for me to work on? **Yes**

　　Processing the Topic, Spill Problem7
　　Processing the Task, Spill Discovery7

In what type of place was the spill discovered? **Stream**

　　***Suspending the Task SpillChar1.
　　Halting work on the Task, SpillChar1.
　　***Adding tasks to agenda: (SpillFlow MaterialName Source-
　　Location)

Processing the Task, Countermeasures1.
Halting work on the Task, Countermeasures1.
***Adding tasks to agenda: (Containment Cleanup Mitigation)
Processing the Task, MaterialName1.

What did you notice? **Sheen**

***Suspending the Task MaterialName1.
Processing the Task, SpillFlow1.
Halting work on the Task, SpillFlow1.
Processing the Task, EmergencyHazard1.
Halting work on the Task, EmergencyHazard1.
Processing the Task, RegulationViol1.
Halting work on the Task, RegulationViol1.
Processing the Task, SpillDiscovery1.

Can you pinpoint the location as precisely as possible? **WOC-6**
Is the material flowing steadily, intermittently, or not at all? **Steady**
Your name: **John Smith**

***Suspending the task SpillDiscovery1.
Processing the Task, MaterialName1.

Due to sheen, I will assume that the spill material was Oil

Halting work on the Task, MaterialName1.
Processing the Task, Notification1.
Halting work on the Task, Notification1.
[User interrupt: report state of agenda
SpillProblem7 replies: fullist = TEL-Notif1 TWQC-Notif1
    OD-Notif1 FWPCA-Notif1 SourceLocation1]
Processing the Task, TEL-Notif1.

Has this situation violated the Tennessee Effluence Limitation Act? **y**
They've been notified.

Halting work on the Task, TEL-Notif1.
Processing the Task, TWQC-Notif1.

Has this situation violated the Tennessee Water Quality Control
  Act? **y**
They've been notified.

Halting work on the Task, TWQC-Notif1.
Processing the Task, FWPCA-Notif1

Has this situation violated the Fresh Water Pollution Act? **n**

Halting work on the Task, FWPCA-Notif1.
Processing the Task, SourceLocation1.
*** Suspending the task SourceLocation1.
Processing the Task, CleanUp1.
Halting work on the Task, CleanUp1.
Processing the Task, Mitigation1.
Halting work on the Task, Mitigation1.
Processing the Task, SpillDiscovery1.

What department do you work for? **Computer Science**
At what time of day did you observe the spill? **3:45**
I am logging this entry as officially reported at this time.

Halting work on the Task, SpillDiscovery1.
Processing the Task, SourceLocation1.

Since the flow is not stopped, you may be able to backtrack it to its
  source.
Are you willing to try this? **y**

Halting work on the Task, SourceLocation1.
***Adding task to agenda: (BackTrack)
Processing the Task, BackTrack1.
Halting work on the Task, BackTrack1.
Processing the Task, BackTrack1.
Processing the Task, BackTrack1.

I'm now considering the pipes (Pipe2 Pipe3)
Seems the Pipe2 has no manhole to check.
Which of these has spill material in it? (SW3513 M6-2) **M6-2**
I'm now considering the pipes (Pipe4 Pipe5).
Which of these has spill material in it? (M6-3 M6-5) **M6-3**
Found the Source: SW3518

Halting work on the Task, BackTrack1.
Halting work on the Topic, SpillProblem7.

Do you have a spill problem for me to work on? **no**
I worked on 1 problem
Process evaluated

Glossary

agenda. A prioritized list of pending activities, usually the applications of various pieces of knowledge.

architecture. (1) The organizing framework imposed upon knowledge applications and problem-solving activities. (2) The knowledge-engineering principles that govern selection of appropriate frameworks for specific expert systems.

attribute. See **property**.

back-chaining. A control procedure that attempts to achieve goals recursively, first by enumerating antecedents that would be sufficient for goal attainment and second by attempting to achieve or establish the antecedents themselves as goals. (Also **backward-chaining**.)

backtracking. A search procedure that makes guesses at various points during problem-solving and returning to a previous point to make another choice when a guess leads to an unacceptable result.

belief. (1) A hypothesis about some unobservable situation. (2) A measure of the believer's confidence in an uncertain proposition.

blackboard. A globally accessible data base used in HEARSAY-II and other systems for recording intermediate, partial results of problem-solving. Typically, the blackboard is partitioned for representing hypotheses at different levels of abstraction and mediates the cooperative activities of multiple "subexperts" or specialists.

certainty. A measure of the confidence placed by a user or expert system in the validity of a proposition, hypothesis, or inferential rule.

chaining, backward. See **back-chaining**.

chaining, forward. See **forward-chaining**.

concept. A descriptive schema for a class of things or a particular instance of the schema with some of its general properties specialized to characterize the specific subclass or element that instantiates the class description.

control (of expert systems). Any procedure, explicit or implicit, that determines the overall order of problem-solving activities; the temporal organization of subprocesses.

data-directed inference. See **forward-chaining**.

dependency. A relation between the antecedents and corresponding consequents produced as a result of applying an inferential rule. Dependencies provide a record of the manner in which decisions are derived from prior data and decisions.

evolutionary development (of software). The practice of iteratively designing, implementing, evaluating, and refining computer applications, especially characteristic of the process of building expert systems.

expectation-driven reasoning. A control procedure that employs current data and decisions to formulate hypotheses about yet unobserved events and to allocate resources to activities that confirm, disconfirm, or monitor the expected events.

expert system. A computer system that achieves high levels of performance in task areas that, for human beings, require years of special education and training.

expertise. The set of capabilities that underlies the high performance of human experts, including extensive domain knowledge, heuristic rules that simplify and improve approaches to problem-solving, metaknowledge and metacognition, and compiled forms of behavior that afford great economy in skilled performance.

explanation. Motivating, justifying, or rationalizing an action by presenting antecedent considerations such as goals, laws, or heuristic rules that affected or determined the desirability of the action.

facet. See **slot**.

fact. A proposition or datum whose validity is accepted.

forward-chaining. A control procedure that produces new decisions recursively by affirming the consequent propositions associated within an inferential rule with antecedent conditions that are currently believed. As new affirmed propositions change the current set of beliefs, additional rules are applied recursively.

frame. A knowledge representation scheme that associates one or more features with an object in terms of various *slots* and particular *slot-values*. Similar to *property-list*, *schema*, *unit*, and *record* in various writings.

goal-directed reasoning. See **back-chaining**.

HEARSAY-II architecture. The organization of a problem-solving system in terms of several cooperating, independent specialists representing diverse areas of knowledge, which exchange partial results via a blackboard and collectively assemble an overall solution incrementally and opportunistically.

Heuristic Programming Project. The research group at Stanford University that principally pioneered the field of knowledge engineering and produced the largest collection of expert systems.

heuristic rule. A procedural tip or incomplete method for performing some task. (Also **heuristic**.)

human engineering. (A misnomer.) The task of designing human—machine interfaces to achieve effective human utilization of machine capacities.

inference, data-directed. See **forward-chaining**.

inference, model-directed. See **expectation-driven reasoning**.

inferential rule. An association between antecedent conditions and consequent beliefs that enables the consequent beliefs to be inferred (deduced) from valid antecedent conditions.

instantiation. An object that fits the general description of some class or, specifically, a pending process that associates specific data objects with the parameters of a general procedure.

INTERLISP. An elaborate programming system providing extensive programming support for constructing and maintaining large LISP programs.

knowledge. Facts, beliefs, and heuristic rules.

knowledge acquisition. The extraction and formulation of knowledge derived from extant sources, especially from experts.

knowledge base. The repository of knowledge in a computer system.

knowledge engineering. The discipline that addresses the task of building expert systems; the tools and methods that support the development of an expert system.

knowledge source. Generally, a body of domain knowledge relevant to a specific problem. In particular, a codification made applicable for an expert system. See **specialist**.

learning. The process of improving performance by changing knowledge or control.

LISP. The principal programming language of AI, which provides an elegant, recursive, untyped, and applicative framework for symbolic computing; actually a family of variants.

MACLISP. The variant of LISP developed and promulgated by workers at MIT.

meta-. Prefix designating reflexive applications of the associated concept.

metacognition. The capability to think about one's own thought processes.

metaknowledge. Knowledge about knowledge.

metarule. A rule that prescribes the manner in which rules should be employed.

natural language. The conventional method for exchanging information between people, such as English as a means of communication for human speakers and various formal written systems as a means of representing intentions in technical disciplines (chemical graphs, DNA sequences, engineering diagrams, and so on).

problem-solving methods, weak and strong. Heuristic for control. Weak methods are domain independent, while strong methods exploit domain knowledge to achieve greater performance.

property. See **slot.**

property list. A construct in LISP that associates with an object called an atom a set of one or more pairs, each composed of a "property" and the "value" of that property for that object.

rule. A pair, composed of an antecedent condition and a consequent proposition, which can support deductive processes such as backchaining and forward-chaining. (See also **heuristic rule.**)

rule-based program. A computer program that explicitly incorporates rules or ruleset components.

ruleset. A collection of rules that constitutes a module of heuristic knowledge.

satisfice. Achieve a solution that satisfies all imposing constraints. (Opposed to "optimize".)

scheduling. Determining the order of activities for execution, usually based on control heuristics. (See also **agenda.**)

schema. See **frame.**

semantic. Pertaining to the meaning, intention, or significance of a symbolic expression, as opposed to its form. (Contrast **syntactic.**)

slot. A feature or component description of an object in a frame. Slots may correspond to intrinsic features such as name, definition, or creator; or may represent derived attributes such as value, significance, or analogous objects.

specialist. An expert in a narrow problem domain, especially one of the several expert subsystems that cooperate in a HEARSAY-II architecture.

syntactic. Pertaining to the form or structure of a symbolic expression, as opposed to its meaning or significance. (Contrast **semantic.**)

tools for knowledge engineering. Programming systems that simplify the work of building expert systems, especially generic task packages such as EMYCIN and very high-level languages for heuristic programming such as ROSIE.

truth maintenance. (A misnomer.) The task of preserving consistent beliefs in a reasoning system whose beliefs change over time.

VLSI. Very large system integration; the construction of extremely complex and powerful circuits on small chips.

References

Abbreviations for journals, technical reports, and conference proceedings:

AAAI	National Conference of the American Association for Artificial Intelligence, Proceedings of the
AFIPS	American Federation of Information Processing Societies
CACM	*Communications of the Association for Computing Machinery*
IEEE	Institute for Electrical and Electronic Engineers
IFIPS	International Federation of Information Processing Societies, Proceedings of the
IJCAI	International Joint Conference on Artificial Intelligence, Proceedings of the
SIGART	*Newsletter* of the ACM Special Interest Group on Artificial Intelligence

Aikins, J.S. 1980. Prototypes and production rules: A knowledge representation for computer consultations. Ph.D. Diss., Rept. STAN-CS-80-814, Computer Science Department, Stanford University, Stanford, Calif.

Amarel, S. 1982. Expert behavior and problem representations. Rept. CBM-TR-126, Laboratory for Computer Science Research, Rutgers University, New Brunswick, N.J.

Anderson, J. 1976. *Language, memory, and thought.* Hillsdale, N.J.: Lawrence Erlbaum Associates.

———. 1983. A general learning theory and its application to the acquisition of proof skills in geometry. In R.S. Michalski, J. Carbonell, and T.M. Mitchell, eds., *Machine learning: An artificial intelligence approach.* Palo Alto, Calif.: Tioga Press.

Anderson, R.H., and J.J. Gillogly. 1976a. Rand intelligent terminal agent (RITA): Design philosophy. Rand paper R-1809-ARPA, Rand Corp., Santa Monica, Calif.

———. 1976b. The Rand intelligent terminal agent (RITA) as a network design access aid. In *Proceedings of the AFIPS National Computer Conference,* pp. 501–509.

Armitage, P. 1971. *Statistical methods in medical research.* New York: John Wiley and Sons.

Badre, N.A. 1973. CLET: A computer program that learns arithmetic from an elementary textbook. IBM Research Rept. RC 4235.

Balzer, R., L.D. Erman, P. London, and C. Williams. 1980. HEARSAY-III: A domain-independent framework for expert systems. In *AAAI1,* pp. 108–110.

Barnett, J.A., and M.I. Bernstein. 1977. Knowledge-based systems: A tutorial. Rept. TM-(L)-5903/000/00 (NTIS: AD/A-044 833), System Development Corp., Santa Monica, Calif.

Barr, A., and E.A. Feigenbaum, eds. 1981. *The handbook of artificial intelligence,* vol. 1 (see also vol. 2, 1982). Los Altos, Calif.: William Kaufman.

Barstow, D.R. 1977. A knowledge-based system for automatic program construction. In *IJCAI* 5, pp. 382–388.

———. 1979. An experiment in knowledge-based automatic programming. *Artificial Intelligence* 12:7–119.

Bennett, J.S., and R.S. Engelmore. 1979. SACON: A knowledge-based consultant for structural analysis. In *IJCAI* 6, pp. 47–49.

Bjerregaard, B., S. Brynitz, J. Holst-Christensen, E. Kalaja, J. Lund-Kristensen, J. Hilden, F.T. deDombal, and J.C. Hurrocks. 1976. Computer aided diagnosis of the acute abdomen: A system from Leeds used on Copenhagen patients. In F. Gremy and F.T. de Dombal, eds., *Decision making and medical care.* Amsterdam: North-Holland, pp. 165–171.

Bobrow, D.G. 1975. Dimensions of representation. In D.G. Bobrow and A. Collins, eds., *Representation and understanding: Studies in cognitive science.* New York: Academic Press, pp. 1–34.

Bobrow, D.G., and A. Collins, eds. 1975. *Representation and understanding: Studies in cognitive science.* New York: Academic Press.

Bobrow, D.G., and T. Winograd. 1977. An overview of KRL, a knowledge representation language. *Cognitive Science* 1:3–46.

Borning, A.H. 1979. THINGLAB: A constraint-oriented simulation laboratory. Ph.D. Diss., Rept. STAN-CS-79-746, Computer Science Department, Stanford University, Stanford, Calif.

Brachman, R.J. 1977. What's in a concept: Structural foundations for semantic networks. *International Journal of Man-Machine Studies* 9:127–152.

———. 1979. On the epistemological status of semantic networks. In N.V. Findler, ed., *Associative networks: The representation and use of knowledge by computers.* New York: Academic Press.

Brachman, R.J., and B.C. Smith. 1980. *SIGART* 70 (special issue on knowledge representation).

Brown, J.S., and R.R. Burton. 1975. Multiple representations of knowledge for tutorial reasoning. In D.G. Bobrow and A. Collins, eds., *Representation and understanding: Studies in cognitive science.* New York: Academic Press, pp. 311–349.

Brown, J.S., R.R. Burton, and A.G. Bell. 1974. SOPHIE: A sophisticated instructional environment for teaching electronic troubleshooting [an example of AI in CAI]. BBN Rept. 2790, Bolt Beranek and Newman, Cambridge, Mass.

Bruner, J.S., J.J. Goodnow, and G.A. Austin. 1956. *A study of thinking.* New York: John Wiley and Sons.

Buchanan, B.G. 1982. New research on expert systems. In J.E. Hayes, D. Michie, and Y.H. Pao, eds., *Machine intelligence,* vol. 10. Edinburgh: Edinburgh University Press, pp. 269–299.

Buchanan, B.G., and E.A. Feigenbaum. 1978. DENDRAL and Meta-DENDRAL: Their applications dimension. *Artificial Intelligence* 11:5–24.

Buchanan, B.G., and T.M. Mitchell. 1977. Model directed learning of production rules. Rept. STAN-CS-77-597, Computer Science Department, Stanford University, Stanford, Calif.

Buchanan, B.G., and Shortliffe, E.H. 1983. (in press). Rule-based expert systems: The MYCIN experiments of the Heuristic Programming Project, Reading, Massachusetts: Addison-Wesley.

———. 1978. Model-directed learning of production rules. In D.A. Waterman and F. Hayes-Roth, eds., *Pattern-directed inference systems.* New York: Academic Press, pp. 297–312.

Buchanan, B.G., D.H. Smith, W.C. White, R.J. Gritter, E.A. Feigenbaum, J. Lederberg, and C. Djerassi. 1976. Applications of artificial intelligence for chemical inference XXII: Automatic rule formation in mass spectrometry by means of the meta-DENDRAL program. *Journal of the American Chemical Society* 98:6168–6178.

Buchanan, B.G., G.L. Sutherland, and E.A. Feigenbaum. 1969. Heuristic DENDRAL: A program for generating explanatory hypotheses in organic chemistry. In B. Meltzer and D. Michie, eds., *Machine intelligence,* vol. 4. Edinburgh: Edinburgh University Press, pp. 209–254.

———. 1970. Rediscovering some problems of artificial intelligence in the context of organic chemistry. In B. Meltzer and D. Michie, eds., *Machine intelligence,* vol. 5. Edinburgh: Edinburgh University Press, pp. 253–280.

Bundy, A., L. Byrd, G. Lager, C. Mellish, and M. Palmer. 1979. Solving mechanics problems using meta-level inference. In *IJCAI* 6, pp. 1071–1027.

Burton, R.R. 1976. Semantic grammar: An engineering technique for constructing natural language understanding systems. BBN Rept. 3453, Bolt Beranek and Newman, Cambridge, Mass.

Carbonell, J.R. 1970. AI in CAI: An artificial intelligence approach to computer assisted instruction. *IEEE Transactions on Man-Machine Systems*, MMS-11:190–202.

Charniak, E., C.K. Riesbeck, and D.V. McDermott. 1979. *Artificial intelligence programming.* Hillsdale, N.J.: Lawrence Erlbaum Associates.

Clancey, W.J. 1979. Tutoring rules for guiding a case method dialogue. *International Journal of Man-Machine Studies* 11:25–49.

Clancey, W.J., E.H. Shortliffe, and B.G. Buchanan. 1979. Intelligent computer-aided instruction for medical diagnosis. In *Proceedings of the Third Annual Symposium on Computer Applications in Medical Care*, pp. 175–183.

Davis, R. 1976. Applications of meta-level knowledge to the construction, maintenance and use of large knowledge bases. Ph.D. Diss. Rept. STAN-CS-76-564, Computer Science Department, Stanford University, Stanford, Calif. Reprinted in R. Davis and D.B. Lenat, eds., *Knowledge-based systems in artificial intelligence.* New York: McGraw-Hill, 1980.

――――. 1977. Interactive transfer of expertise: Acquisition of new inference rules. In *IJCAI* 5:321–328.

――――. 1978. Knowledge acquisition in rule-based systems: Knowledge about representation as a basis for system construction and maintenance. In D.A. Waterman and F. Hayes-Roth, eds., *Pattern-directed inference systems.* New York: Academic Press, pp. 99–134.

――――. 1980. Meta-rules: Reasoning about control. *Artificial Intelligence* 15:179–222.

――――. 1982. Expert systems: Where are we? And where do we go from here? *AI Magazine* 3, no. 2:3–22.

Davis, R., and B.G. Buchanan. 1977. Meta-level knowledge: Overview and applications. *IJCAI* 5:920–928.

Davis, R., B. G. Buchanan, and E. Shortliffe. 1977. Production rules as a representation for a knowledge-based consultation program. *Artificial Intelligence* 8:15–45.

Davis, R., and J. King. 1976. An overview of production systems. In E.W. Elcock and D. Michie, eds., *Machine intelligence*, vol. 8. New York: John Wiley and Sons, pp. 300–332.

Davis, R., and D. Lenat. 1980. *Knowledge-based systems in artificial intelligence.* New York: McGraw-Hill.

de Kleer, J. 1979. Causal and teleological reasoning in circuit recognition. Ph.D. Diss. Massachusetts Institute of Technology, Cambridge, Mass.

de Kleer, J., J. Doyle, G.L. Steele, and G.J. Sussman. 1979. Explicit control of reasoning. In P.H. Winston and R.H. Brown, eds., *Artificial intelligence: An MIT perspective*, vol 1. Cambridge, Mass.: MIT Press, pp. 93–116.

de Kleer, J., and G.J. Sussman. 1980. Propagation of constraints applied to circuit synthesis. *Circuit Theory and Applications* 8:127–144.

Denning, P.J. 1981. Performance analysis: Experimental computer science at its best. *Communications of the ACM*, 24:725–727.

Director, S.W., A.C. Parker, D.P. Siewiorek, and D.E. Thomas. 1981. A design methodology and computer aids for digital VLSI systems. *IEEE Transactions on Circuits and Systems*.

Doyle, J. 1979. A truth maintenance system. *Artificial Intelligence* 12:231–272.

———. 1980. A model for deliberation, action, and introspection. Ph.D. Diss. Tech. Rept. AI-TR-581. Artificial Intelligence Laboratory, Massachusetts Institute of Technology, Cambridge, Mass.

Doyle, J., and P. London. 1980. A selected descriptor-indexed bibliography to the literature on belief revision. *SIGART Newsletter* 71:7–23.

Duda R.O., and J.G. Gaschnig. 1981. Knowledge-based expert systems coming of age. *BYTE* 6, no. 9:238–281.

Duda, R.O., J.G. Gaschnig, and P.E. Hart. 1979. Model design in the PROSPECTOR consultant system for mineral exploration. In D. Michie, ed., *Expert systems in the micro-electronic age*. Edinburgh: Edinburgh University Press, pp. 153–167.

Duda, R.O., P.E. Hart, P. Barrett, J. Gaschnig, K. Konolige, R. Reboh, and J. Slocum. 1978. Development of the PROSPECTOR consultation system for mineral exploration. Final Rept. SRI Projects 5821 and 6415, Artificial Intelligence Center, SRI International, Menlo Park, Calif.

Duda, R.O., P.E. Hart, and N.J. Nilsson. 1976. Subjective Bayesian methods for rule-based inference systems. In Proceedings of the AFIPS 1976 National Computer Conference, vol. 45, pp. 1075–1082.

Duda, R.O., P.E. Hart, N.J. Nilsson, and G. Sutherland. 1978. Semantic network representations in rule-based inference systems. In D.A. Waterman and F. Hayes-Roth, eds., *Pattern-directed inference systems*. New York: Academic Press, pp. 203-221.

Eastman, C. 1981. Recent developments in representation in the science of design. In *Proceedings of the 18th Design Automation Conference*, IEEE Computer Society and ACM.

Edelson, E. 1982. Expert systems—computers that think like people. *Popular Science* Sept.:48–52.

Engelman, C. 1971. The legacy of MATHLAB 68. In *Proceedings of the*

Second Symposium on Symbolic and Algebraic Manipulation, Los Angeles.

Ennis, S.P. 1982. Expert systems: A user's perspective on some current tools. In *AAAI* 2, 1982, pp. 319–321.

Erman, L.D., F. Hayes-Roth, V. Lesser, and D. Reddy. 1980. The HEAR-SAY-II speech-understanding system: Integrating knowledge to resolve uncertainty. *Computing Surveys* 12, no. 2:213–253.

Erman, L.D., P.E. London, and S.F. Fickas. 1981. The design and an example use of HEARSAY-III. In *IJCAI* 7, pp. 409–415.

Fagan, L.M. 1980. VM: Representing time-dependent relations in a medical setting. Ph.D. Diss. Computer Science Department, Stanford University, Stanford, Calif.

Fagan, L.M., J.C. Kunz, E.A. Feigenbaum, and J. Osborn. 1979. Representation of dynamic clinical knowledge: Measurement interpretation in the intensive care unit. In *IJCAI* 6:260–262.

Fain, J., D. Gorlin, F. Hayes-Roth, S.J. Rosenschein, H. Sowizral, and D. Waterman. 1981. The ROSIE language reference manual. Tech. Rept. N-1647-ARPA, Rand Corp., Santa Monica, Calif.

Fain, J., F. Hayes-Roth, H. Sowizral, and D. Waterman. 1982. Programming in ROSIE: An introduction by means of examples. Tech. Rept. N-1646-ARPA, Rand Corp., Santa Monica, Calif.

Faught, W.S., P. Klahr, and G.R. Martins. 1980. An artificial intelligence approach to large-scale simulation. In *Proceedings of the 1980 Summer Simulation Conference,* Seattle, Wash. pp. 231–236.

Feigenbaum, E.A. 1977. The art of artificial intelligence: Themes and case studies of knowledge engineering. In *IJCAI* 5, pp. 1014–1029.

Feigenbaum, E.A., B.G. Buchanan, and J. Lederberg. 1971. On generality and problem solving: A case study using the DENDRAL program. In B. Meltzer and D. Michie, eds., *Machine intelligence,* vol. 6. Edinburgh: Edinburgh University Press, pp. 165–190.

Fenves, S.J. and T. Norabhoompipat. 1978. Potentials for artificial intelligence applications in structural engineering design and detailing. In J.C. Latombe, ed., *Artificial intelligence and pattern recognition in computer aided design. Proceedings, IFIP Working Conference, Grenoble, France,* pp. 105–119.

Fikes, R.E. 1975. REF-ARF: A system for solving problems stated as procedures. *Artificial Intelligence* 1:27–120.

Forgy, C.L. 1979a. The OPS4 user's manual. Technical Rept. CMU-CS-79-132, Department of Computer Science, Carnegie-Mellon University, Pittsburgh, Pa.

_____. 1979b. On the efficient implementation of production systems. Ph.D. Diss. Computer Science Department, Carnegie-Mellon University, Pittsburgh, Pa.

_____. 1981. The OPS5 user's manual. Technical Rept. CMU-CS-81-135, Computer Science Department, Carnegie-Mellon University, Pittsburgh, Pa.

————. 1982. RETE: A fast algorithm for the many pattern/many object pattern match problem. *Artificial Intelligence* 19:17–38.

Forgy, C., and J. McDermott. 1977. OPS: A domain-independent production system language. In *IJCAI* 5, pp. 933–939.

Freeman, P., and A. Newell. 1971. A model for functional reasoning in design. In *IJCAI* 2, pp. 621–640.

Freiherr, G. 1980. The seeds of artificial intelligence. NIH no. 80-2071. SUMEX-AIM, Washington, D.C.

Gardner, A. 1981. Search. In A. Barr and E.A. Feigenbaum, eds., *Handbook of artificial intelligence*, vol. 1. Los Altos, Calif.: William Kaufman, pp. 19–139.

Gaschnig, J. 1980a. Development of uranium exploration models for the PROSPECTOR consultant system. Final rept. SRI Project 7856, Artificial Intelligence Center, SRI International, Menlo Park, Calif.

————. 1980b. An application of the PROSPECTOR system to the DOE's national uranium resource evaluation. In *AAAI* 1, pp. 295–297.

Gelvernter, H.L., A.F. Sanders, D.L. Larsen, K.K. Agarwal, R.H. Boivie, G.A. Spritzer, J.E. Searleman. 1977. Empirical explorations of SYNCHEM, *Science* 197:1041–1049.

Goldman, N. 1978. AP3 user's guide. Unpublished memorandum, Information Sciences Institute, University of Southern California, Los Angeles.

Greiner, R., and D. Lenat. 1980. A representation language language. In *AAAI* 1, pp. 165–169.

Grinberg, M.R. 1980. A knowledge-based design system for digital electronics. In *AAAI* 1, pp. 283–285.

Haas, N., and G. Hendrix. 1980. An approach to acquiring and applying knowledge. In *AAAI* 1, pp. 235–239.

Hanson, A.R., and E.M. Riseman, eds. 1978. *Computer vision systems*. New York: Academic Press.

Hart, P.E. 1980. What's preventing the widespread use of expert systems? Position paper, Expert Systems Workshop, San Deigo, Calif., pp. 11–14.

Hart, T. 1961. Simplify. Memo 27, Artificial Intelligence Group, Project MAC, Massachusetts Institute of Technology, Cambridge, Mass.

Hayes-Roth, B., and F. Hayes-Roth. 1978. Cognitive processes in planning. Rand Paper R-2366-ONR, Rand Corp., Santa Monica, Calif.

Hayes-Roth, F. 1974. Schematic classification problems and their solution. *Pattern Recognition* 6:105–113.

————. 1981. Building expert systems: Putting knowledge to work. Invited tutorial presented at IJCAI 7.

————. 1983. Using proofs and refutations to learn from experience. In R.S. Michalski, J. Carbonell, and T.M. Mitchell, eds., *Machine learning: An artificial intelligence approach*. Palo Alto, Calif: Tioga Press.

Hayes-Roth, F., D. Gorlin, S. Rosenchein, H. Sowizral, and D. Water-man. 1981. Rationale and motivation for ROSIE. Tech. Note N-1648-ARPA, Rand Corp., Santa Monica, Calif.

Hayes-Roth, F., P. Klahr, J. Burge, and D.J. Mostow. 1978. Machine methods for acquiring, learning, and applying knowledge. Rept. P-6241, Rand Corp., Santa Monica, Calif.

Hayes-Roth, F., P. Klahr, and D.J. Mostow. 1980a. Advice-taking and knowledge refinement: An iterative view of skill acquisition. In J. Anderson, ed., *Learning and cognition.* Hillsdale, N.J.: Lawrence Erlbaum Associates.

———. 1980b. Knowledge acquisition, knowledge programming, and knowledge refinement. Rand Paper R-2540-NSF. Rand Corp., Santa Monica, Calif.

Hayes-Roth, F., D.J. Mostow, and M.S. Fox. 1978. Understanding speech in the HEARSAY-II system. In L. Bolc, ed., *Speech communication with computers.* Munich: Carl Hansen Verlag.

Hayes-Roth, F., D.A. Waterman, and D.B. Lenat. 1978. Principles of pattern-directed inference systems. In D.A. Waterman and F. Hayes-Roth, eds., *Pattern-directed inference systems.* New York: Academic Press, pp. 577–601.

Hendrix, G.G. 1975. Expanding the utility of semantic networks through partitioning. In *IJCAI* 4, pp. 115–121.

———. 1979. Encoding knowledge in partitioned networks. In N.V. Findler, ed., *Associative networks: The representation and use of knowledge in computers.* New York: Academic Press, pp. 51–92.

Hewitt, C.E. 1972. Description and theoretical analysis (using schemata) of PLANNER: A language for proving theorems and manipulating models in a robot. Tech. Rept. TR-258. Artificial Intelligence Laboratory, Massachusetts Institute of Technology, Cambridge, Mass.

Kant, E. 1979. A knowledge-based approach to using efficiency estimation in program synthesis. In *IJCAI* 6, pp. 457–462.

Kelly, B.A., and T.W. Oakes. 1980. The spill prevention control and countermeasures plan for Oak Ridge National Laboratory. ORNL/TM-7677.

Kleene, S.C. 1967. *Mathematical logic.* New York: John Wiley and Sons.

Knuth, D.E. 1973. *The art of computer programming, Vol. 1. Fundamental algorithms.* Reading, Mass.: Addison-Wesley.

Korsvold, K. 1965. An on-line algebraic simplification program. Artificial Intelligence Project, Memo 37, Stanford University, Stanford, Calif.

Kulikowski, C.A. 1980. Artificial intelligence methods and systems for medical consultation. In *IEEE Transactions on Pattern Analysis and Machine Intelligence,* pp. 464–476.

Kunz, J.C., R.J. Fallat, D.H. McClung, J.J. Osborn, R.A. Votteri, H.P. Nii, J.S. Aikins, L.M. Fagan, and E.A. Feigenbaum. 1978. A physiological rule-based system for interpreting pulmonary function test results. Rept. HPP-78-19, Heuristic Programming Project, Computer Science Department, Stanford University, Stanford, Calif.

Lenat, D.B. 1976. AM: An artificial intelligence approach to discovery in mathematics as heuristic search. Ph.D. Diss. Memo AIM-286, Artificial Intelligence Laboratory, Stanford University, Stanford, Calif.

————. 1977. Automated theory formation in mathematics. In *IJCAI* 5, pp. 833–842.

————. 1980a. On automated scientific theory formation: A case study using the AM program. In R. Davis and D.B. Lenat, *Knowledge-based systems in artificial intelligence.* New York: McGraw-Hill.

————. 1980b. The nature of heuristics. Rept. HPP-80-26, Heuristic Programming Project, Computer Science Department, Stanford University, Stanford, Calif.

————. 1982. The nature of heuristics. *Artificial Intelligence* 19:189–249.

Lenat, D.B., F. Hayes-Roth, and P. Klahr. 1979a. Cognitive economy. Rept. HPP-79-15, Heuristic Programming Project, Computer Science Department, Stanford University, Stanford, Calif.

————. 1979b. Cognitive economy in artificial intelligence systems. In *IJCAI* 6, pp. 531–536.

Lenat, D.B., W.R. Sutherland, and J. Gibbons. 1982. Heuristic search for new microcircuit structures: An application of artificial intelligence. *AI Magazine* 3:17–33.

Lesser, V.R., and L.D. Erman. 1977. A retrospective view of the HEARSAY-II architecture. In *IJCAI* 5, pp. 790–800.

Lindsay, R.K., B.G. Buchanan, E.A. Feigenbaum, and J. Lederberg. 1980. *Applications of artificial intelligence for organic chemistry: The DENDRAL project.* New York: McGraw-Hill.

Low, J.R. 1976. Automatic coding: Choice of data structures. In *Interdisciplinary Systems Research,* vol. 16. Basel: Birkhaeuser.

Lowerre, B.T. 1976. The HARPY speech recognition system. Ph.D Diss. Computer Science Department, Carnegie-Mellon University, Pittsburgh, Pa.

McAllester, D.A. 1980. An outlook on truth maintenance. Memo no. 551, Artificial Intelligence Laboratory, Massachusetts Institute of Technology, Cambridge, Mass.

McCarthy, J. 1968. Programs with common sense. In M. Minsky, ed., *Semantic information processing.* Cambridge, Mass.: MIT Press, pp. 403–409.

McCarthy, J., and Hayes, P.J. 1969. Some philosophical problems from the standpoint of artificial intelligence. In B. Meltzer and D. Michie, eds., *Machine intelligence*, vol. 4. Edinburgh: Edinburgh University Press, pp. 463–502.

McDermott, D., and J. Doyle. 1980. Non-monotonic logic, I. *Artificial Intelligence*. 13:41–72.

McDermott, D., and G.J. Sussman. 1974. The CONNIVER reference manual. Memo 259a, Artificial Intelligence Laboratory, Massachusetts Institute of Technology, Cambridge, Mass.

McDermott, J. 1980a. R1: A rule-based configurer of computer systems. Technical Rept. CMU-CS-80-119. Department of Computer Science. Carnegie-Mellon University, Pittsburgh, Pa.

_____. 1980b. R1: An expert in the computer systems domain. In *AAAI* 1, pp. 269–271.

_____. 1980c. R1: An expert configurer. Rept. no. CMU-CS-80-119, Computer Science Department. Carnegie-Mellon University, Pittsburgh, Pa.

_____. 1981. R1: The formative years. *AI Magazine* 2, no. 2:21–29.

McDermott, J., and C. Forgy. 1978. Production system conflict resolution strategies. In D.A. Waterman and F. Hayes-Roth, eds., *Pattern-directed inference systems*. New York: Academic Press, pp. 177–199.

Manove, M., S. Bloom, and C. Engelman. 1968. Rational functions in MATHLAB. In D.G. Bobrow, ed., *Symbol manipulation languages and techniques*. Amsterdam: North-Holland, pp. 86–102.

Mark, W.S. 1976. The reformulation model of expertise. Ph.D. Diss. Rept. MIT-LCS-TR-172, Laboratory for Computer Science, Massachusetts Institute of Technology, Cambridge, Mass.

Martin, W.A., and R.J. Fateman. 1971. The MACSYMA system. In *Proceedings of the Second Symposium on Symbolic and Algebraic Manipulation*, Los Angeles, pp. 59–75.

Michalski, R.S. 1977. A system of programs for computer-aided induction: A summary. In *IJCAI* 5, pp. 319–320.

_____. 1980. Pattern recognition as rule-guided inductive inference. *IEEE Transactions on Pattern Analysis and Machine Intelligence* 2, no. 4:349–361.

Michie, D., ed. 1979. *Expert systems in the micro-electronic age*. Edinburgh: Edinburgh University Press.

Miller, R.A., H.E. Pople, and J.D. Myers. 1982. INTERNIST-I, an experimental computer-based diagnostic consultant for general internal medicine. *New England Journal of Medicine* (August 19):468–476.

Minsky, M. 1963. Steps toward artificial intelligence. In E.A. Feigenbaum and J. Feldman, eds., *Computers and thought*. New York: McGraw-Hill, pp. 406–450.

_____. 1975. A framework for representing knowledge. In P. Winston, ed., *The psychology of computer vision*. New York: McGraw-Hill.

Mitchell, T.M. 1978. Version spaces: An approach to concept learning. Ph.D. Diss. Rept. STAN-CS-78-711, Computer Science Department, Stanford University, Stanford, Calif.

———. 1982. Generalization as search. *Artificial Intelligence* 18:203–226.

Mitchell, T.M., P.E. Utgoff, and R.B. Banerji. 1983. Learning problem-solving heuristics by experimentation. In R.S. Michalski, J. Carbonell, and T.M. Mitchell, eds., *Machine learning: An artificial intelligence approach*. Palo Alto, Calif.: Tioga Press.

Moses, J. 1967. Symbolic integration. Ph.D. Diss. Rept. MAC-TR-47, Department of Computer Science, Massachusetts Institute of Technology, Cambridge, Mass.

Mostow, D.J. 1981. Mechanical transformation of task heuristics into operational procedures. Ph.D. diss. Computer Science Department, Carnegie-Mellon University.

———. 1983. Machine transformation of advice into a heuristic search procedure. In R.S. Michalski, J.Carbonell, and T.M. Mitchell, eds., *Machine learning: An artificial intelligence approach*. Palo Alto, Calif.: Tioga Press.

Newell, A. 1962. Some problems of basic organization in problem-solving programs. In M.C. Yovits, G.T. Jacobi, and G.D. Goldstein, eds., *Proceedings of the Second Conference on Self-Organizing Systems*. Washington D.C.: Spartan Books, pp. 393–423.

———. 1969. Heuristic programming: Ill-structured problems. In A. Aronofsky, ed., *Progress in operations research*, vol. 3. New York: John Wiley and Sons, pp. 360–414.

———. 1973. Production systems: Models of control structures. In W.G. Chase, ed., *Visual information processing*. New York: Academic Press, pp. 463–526.

———. 1975. A tutorial on speech understanding systems. In D.R. Reddy, ed., *Speech recognition: Invited Papers of the IEEE Symposium*. New York: Academic Press, pp. 3–54.

———. 1980. Physical symbol systems. *Cognitive Science* 4:135–183.

Newell, A., and J. McDermott. 1976. PSG manual. Department of Computer Science, Carnegie-Mellon University, Pittsburgh, Pa.

Newell, A., and H.A. Simon. 1963. GPS: A program that simulates human thought. In E.A. Feigenbaum and J.A. Feldman, eds., *Computers and thought*. New York: McGraw-Hill.

———. 1976. Computer science as empirical enquiry: Symbols and search. [The 1975 ACM Turing Lecture.] *Communications of the ACM* 19, no. 3:113–126.

Nii, H.P., and N. Aiello. 1979. AGE (Attempt to Generalize): A knowledge-based program for building knowledge-based programs. In *IJCAI* 6, pp. 645–655.

Nii, H.P., and E.A. Feigenbaum. 1978. Rule-based understanding of signals. In D.A. Waterman and F. Hayes-Roth, eds., *Pattern-directed inference systems*. New York: Academic Press, pp. 483–501.

Nilsson, N.J. 1980. *Principles of artificial intelligence*. Palo Alto, Calif.: Tioga Press.

Oakes, T.W., J.C. Bird, K.E. Shank, B.A. Kelly, B.R. Clark, and F. Rodgers. 1980. Waste oil management at Oak Ridge National Laboratory. ORNL/TM-7712.

Pauker, S.G., G.A. Gorry, J.P. Kassirer, and W.B. Schwartz. 1976. Towards the simulation of clinical cognition—taking a present illness by computer. *American Journal of Medicine* 60:981–996.

Pednault, E.P.D., S.W. Zucker, and L.V. Muresan. 1981. On the independence assumption underlying subjective Bayesian updating. *Artificial Intelligence* 16:213–222.

Plotkin, G.D. 1971. A further note on inductive generalization. In B. Meltzer and D. Michie, eds., *Machine intelligence*, vol. 6. Edinburgh: Edinburgh University Press, pp. 101–124.

Politakis, P., and S.M. Weiss. 1981. A system for empirical experimentation with expert knowledge. Technical Rept. CBM-TM-091, Computer Science Department, Rutgers University, New Brunswick, N.J.

Polya, G. 1954. *Mathematics and plausible reasoning*, vol. 2. New York: John Wiley and Sons.

Pople, H.E., Jr. 1977. The formation of composite hypotheses in diagnostic problem solving: An exercise in synthetic reasoning. In *IJCAI* 5, pp. 1030–1037.

———. 1981. Heuristic methods for imposing structure on ill-structured problems: The structuring of medical diagnostics. In P. Szolovitz, ed., *Artificial intelligence in medicine*. American Association for the Advancement of Science. Boulder Colo.: Westview Press, pp. 119–185.

Pople. H.E., Jr., J.D. Myers, and R.A. Miller. 1975. *DIALOG: A model of diagnostic logic for internal medicine. In IJCAI* 4, pp. 848–855.

Quinlan, J.R. 1982. INFERNO: A cautious approach to uncertain inference. Rand Note N-1898-RC, Rand Corp. Santa Monica, Calif., September.

Reboh, R. 1979. The knowledge acquisition system. In R.O. Duda, P.E. Hart, K. Konolige, and R. Reboh, *A computer-based consultant for mineral exploration*. Final Rept. SRI Project 6415, Artificial Intelligence Center, SRI International, Menlo Park, Calif.

Reddy, D.R., L.D. Erman, R.D. Fennell, and R.B. Neely. 1973. The HEARSAY speech understanding system: An example of the recognition process. In *IJCAI* 3, pp. 185–193.

Reiter, J.E. 1981. AL/X: An inference system for probabilistic reasoning. M.S. Thesis. Computer Science Department, University of Illinois, Urbana.

Rich, C., and H.E. Schrobe. 1976. Initial report on a LISP programmer's apprentice. Rept. TR-354, Artificial Intelligence Laboratory, Massachusetts Institute of Technology, Cambridge, Mass.

Rieger, C., and M. Grinberg. 1977. The declarative representation and procedural simulation of causality in physical mechanisms. In *IJCAI* 5, pp. 250–256.

Rulifson, J.F., R.J. Waldinger, and J.A. Derksen. 1972. A language for writing problem-solving programs. In IFIPS 71. Amsterdam: North-Holland, pp. 201–205.

Sacerdoti, E.D. 1973. Planning in a hierarchy of abstraction spaces. In *IJCAI* 3, pp. 412–422.

———. 1974. Planning in a hierarchy of abstraction spaces. *Artificial Intelligence* 5, no. 2:115–135.

———. 1975. The nonlinear nature of plans. In *IJCAI* 4, pp. 206–214.

———. 1977. *A structure for plans and behavior.* New York: American Elsevier.

Scott, A.C., W.J. Clancey, R. Davis, and E.H. Shortliffe. 1977. Explanation capabilities of knowledge-based production systems. *American Journal of Computational Linguistics*, Microfiche 62.

Shortliffe, E.H. 1976. *Computer-based medical consultation: MYCIN.* New York: American Elsevier.

Shortliffe, E.H., and B.G. Buchanan. 1975. A model of inexact reasoning in medicine. *Mathematical Biosciences* 23:351–379.

Simon, H.A. 1983. Why should machines learn? In R.S. Michalski, J. Carbonell, and T.M. Mitchell, eds., *Machine learning: An artificial intelligence approach.* Palo Alto, Calif.: Tioga Press.

Slagle, J.R. 1961. A heuristic program that solves symbolic integration problems in freshman calculus. Symbolic Automatic Integrator (SAINT). Ph.D. Diss. Rept. 5G-0001, Lincoln Laboratory, Massachusetts Institute of Technology.

Sleeman, D., and J.S. Brown. 1982. *Intelligent tutoring systems.* New York: Academic Press.

Smith, D.E. 1980. CORLL. A demand paging system for units. Rept. HPP-80-8 (Working Paper), Heuristic Programming Project, Computer Science Department, Stanford University, Stanford, Calif.

Smith, D.H., B.G. Buchanan, R.S. Engelmore, J. Adlercreutz, and C. Djerassi. 1973. Applications of artificial intelligence for chemical inference IX. Analysis of mixtures without prior separation as illustrated for estrogens. *Journal of American Chemical Society* 95:6078.

Sridharan, N.S. 1980. Representational facilities of AIMDS: A sampling. Rept. CBM-TM-86, Computer Science Department, Rutgers University, New Brunswick, N.J.

Stallman, R., and G.J. Sussman. 1977. Forward reasoning and dependency-directed backtracking in a system for computer-aided circuit analysis. *Artificial Intelligence* 9:135–196.

Stefik, M. 1978a. Inferring DNA structures from segmentation data. *Artificial Intelligence* 11:85–114.

———. 1978b. An examination of a frame-structured representation system. Rept. HPP-78-13, Heuristic Programming Project, Computer Science Department, Stanford University, Stanford, Calif.

———. 1981a. Planning with constraints (MOLGEN: Part 1). *Artificial Intelligence* 16:111–139.

———. 1981b. Planning and meta-planning (MOLGEN: Part 2). *Artificial Intelligence* 16:141–169.

Stefik, M., J. Aikins, R. Balzer, J. Benoit, L. Birnbaum, F. Hayes-Roth, and E. Sacerdoti. 1982. The organization of expert systems: A tutorial. *Artificial Intelligence* 18:135–173.

Suppes, P. 1957. *Introduction to logic.* Princeton, N.J.: D. Van Nostrand Reinhold.

Sussman, G.J. 1977. Electrical design: A problem for artificial intelligence research. In *IJCAI* 5, pp. 894–900.

Sussman, G.J., and G.L. Steele, Jr. 1980. CONSTRAINTS: A language for expressing almost hierarchical descriptions. *Artificial Intelligence* 14:1–39.

Swartout, W.R. 1977. A digitalis therapy adviser with explanations. In *IJCAI* 5, pp. 819–825.

Szolovits, P., L.B. Hawkinson, and W.A. Martin. 1977. An overview of OWL, a language for knowledge representation. Rept. LCS-TM-86, Artificial Intelligence Laboratory, Massachusetts Institute of Technology, Cambridge, Mass.

Teitelman, W. 1978. *INTERLISP reference manual.* Zerox Palo Alto Research Center, Palo Alto, Calif.

Teitelman, W., and Masinter, L. 1981. The INTERLISP programming environment. *Computer* 14, no. 4:25–33.

van Melle, W. 1979. A domain-independent production-rule system for consultation programs. In *IJCAI* 6, pp. 923–925.

———. 1980. A domain-independent system that aids in constructing knowledge-based consultation programs. Ph.D. Diss. Rept. STAN-CS-80-820, Computer Science Department, Stanford University, Stanford, Calif.

———. 1981. *System aids in constructing consultation programs.* Ann Arbor, Michigan: UMI Research Press.

van Melle, W., E.H. Shortliffe, and B.G. Buchanan. 1981. EMYCIN: A domain-independent system that aids in constructing knowledge-based consultation programs. *Machine Intelligence, Infotech State of the Art Report* 9, no. 3.

Vere, S.A. 1975. Induction of concepts in the predicate calculus. In *IJCAI* 4, pp. 281–287.

Waterman, D.A. 1970. Generalization learning techniques for automating the learning of heuristics. *Artificial Intelligence* 1:121–170.

_____. 1979. User-oriented systems for capturing expertise: A rule-based approach. In D. Michie, ed., *Expert systems in the micro-electronic age.* Edinburgh: Edinburgh University Press, pp. 26–34.

_____. 1981. Rule-based expert systems. *Machine Intelligence, Infotech State of the Art Report* 9, no. 3.

Waterman, D.A., and F. Hayes-Roth, eds. 1978. *Pattern-directed inference systems.* New York: Academic Press.

Waterman, D.A., and B. Jenkins. 1979. Heuristic modeling using rule-based computer systems. In R. Kupperman and D. Trent, eds., *Terrorism, threat, reality, response.* Stanford University: Hoover Institution Press.

Waterman, D.A., and A. Newell. 1971. Protocol analysis as a task for artificial intelligence. *Artificial Intelligence* 2:285–318.

_____. 1980. Rule-based models of legal expertise. In *AAAI* 1, pp. 272–275.

Waterman, D.A., and M. Peterson, 1981. Models of legal decision-making. Rand Report R-2717-ICJ. Rand Corp., Santa Monica, Calif.

Webster, R. and L. Miner. Expert systems: Programming problem solving. *Technology* 2:62–73.

Weiss, S.M., and C.A. Kulikowski. 1979. EXPERT: A system for developing consultation models. In *IJCAI* 6, pp. 942–947.

_____. 1981. Expert consultation systems: The EXPERT and CASNET projects. *Machine Intelligence, Infotech State of the Art Report* 9, no. 3.

Weiss, S.M., C.A. Kulikowski, and A. Safir. 1977. A model-based consultation system for the long-term management of glaucoma. In *IJCAI* 5, pp. 826–832.

_____. 1978a. A model-based method for computer-aided medical decision-making. *Artificial Intelligence* 11:145–172.

_____. 1978b. Glaucoma consultation by computer. *Computers in Biology and Medicine* 8:25–40.

Weyhrauch, R.W. 1980. Prolegomena to a theory of mechanized formal reasoning. *Artificial Intelligence* 13:1–2.

Wilensky, R. 1981. Meta-planning: Representing and using knowledge about planning in problem solving and natural language understanding. *Cognitive Science* 5:197–233.

Wilkins, D.E. 1979. Using plans in chess. In *IJCAI* 6, pp. 960–967.

_____. 1980. Using patterns and plans in chess. *Artificial Intelligence* 14:165–203.

Winograd, T. 1980. Extended inference modes in reasoning by computer systems. *Artificial Intelligence* 13:5–26.

Winston, P.H. 1970. Learning structural descriptions from examples. Ph.D. Diss. Rept. TR-76, Artificial Intelligence Center, Massachusetts Institute of Technology, Cambridge, Mass.

Winston, P.H., and B.K.P. Horn. 1981. *LISP*. Reading, Mass.: Addison-Wesley.

Wipke, W.T. 1976. Computer planning of research in organic chemistry. In E.V. Ludena, N.H. Sabelli, and A.C. Wahl, eds., *Computers in chemical education and research*. New York: Plenum Press, pp. 381–391.

Wooldridge, D. 1963. An algebraic Simplify program in LISP. Memo AIM-11, Artificial Intelligence Laboratory, Stanford University, Stanford, Calif.

Yasaki, E.K. 1981. AI: More than science. *Datamation* September 27:63–64.

Yu, V.L., B.G. Buchanan, E.H. Shortliffe, S.M. Wraith, R. Davis, A.C. Scott, and S.N. Cohen. 1979a. Evaluating the performance of a computer-based consultant. *Computer Programs in Biomedicine* 9:95–102.

Yu, V.L., L.M. Fagan, S.M. Wraith, W.J. Clancey, A.C. Scott, J.F. Hanigan, R.L. Blum, B.G. Buchanan, and S.N. Cohen. 1979b. Antimicrobial selection by a computer: A blinded evaluation by infectious disease experts. *Journal of the American Medical Association* 242:1279–1282.

Zadeh, L.A. 1965. Fuzzy sets. *Information and Control* 8:338–353.

———. 1979a. A theory of approximate reasoning. In J.E. Hayes, D. Michie, and L.I. Mikulich, eds., *Machine intelligence*, vol. 9. New York: John Wiley and Sons.

———. 1979b. Possibility theory and soft data analysis. Rept. UCB/ERL M79/66, Electronics Research Laboratory, University of California at Berkeley.

Suggested Reading

Aho, A.V., J.E. Hopcroft, and J.D. Ullman. 1974. *The design and analysis of computer algorithms*. Reading, Mass.: Addison-Wesley.

Alan, B.G., A. Bundy, L. Byrd, G. Luger, C. Mellish, and M. Palmer. 1979. Solving mechanics problems using meta-level inference. In D. Michie, ed., *Expert systems in the micro-electronic age*. Edinburgh: Edinburgh University Press, pp. 50–64.

Amarel, S. 1978. Basic themes and problems in current AI research. In *Proceedings of the* 4th *AIM Workshop*, Rutgers University, New Brunswick, N.J. Also available as Rept. CBM-TR-91, Department of Computer Science, Rutgers University.

Anderson, J.R., and G.H. Bower. 1973. *Human associative memory*. Washington D.C.: Winston-Wiley.

Anderson, J.R., and P.J. Kline. 1977. Design of a production system for cognitive modeling. Proceedings of the Workshop on Pattern-Directed Inference Systems. *SIGART Newsletter* 63:60–65.

Barbacci, M., and D. Siewiorek. 1974. The CMU RT-CAD system: An innovative approach to computer aided design. *CMU Computer Science Research Review 1974–1975*. pp. 39–53.

Bennett, J.S., L.A. Creary, R.S. Engelmore, and R.E. Melosh. 1978. A knowledge-based consultant for structural analysis. Rept. HPP-78-23, Heuristic Programming Project, Computer Science Department, Stanford University, Stanford, Calif.

Biermann, A.W. 1976. Regular LISP programs and their automatic synthesis from examples. Rept. CS-1976-12, Computer Science Department, Duke University, Durham, N.C.

Bobrow, D.G., and B. Raphael. 1974. New programming languages for AI research. *ACM Computing Surveys* 6:153–174.

Boden, M.A. 1977. *Artificial intelligence and natural man*. New York: Basic Books.

Brooks, R.A., R. Greiner, and T.O. Binford. 1979. The ACRONYM model-based vision system. In *IJCAI* 6, pp. 105–113.

Buchanan, B.G. 1979. Issues of representation in conveying the scope and limitations of intelligent assistant programs. In J.E. Hayes, D. Michie, and L.I. Mikulich, *Machine intelligence*, vol. 9. New York: Wiley, pp. 407–425.

Burstall, R., and J. Darlington. 1977. A transformation system for developing recursive programs. *Journal of the ACM* 24:44–67.

Callero, M., D. Gorlin, F. Hayes-Roth, and L. Jamison. 1981. Toward an expert aid for tactical air targeting. Rept. N-1645, Rand Corp., Santa Monica, Calif.

Coles, L.S. 1975. Methodologies for heuristic modeling. Rept. 3372, Artificial Intelligence Center, SRI International, Menlo Park, Calif.

Cooke, S., C. Hafner, T. McCarty, M. Meldman, M. Peterson, J. Sprowl, N. Sridharan, and D.A. Waterman. 1981. The applications of artificial intelligence to law: A survey of six current projects. *AFIPS Conference Proceedings* 50:689–696.

de Dombal, F.T., D.J. Leaper, J.R. Staniland, et al. 1972. Computer-aided diagnosis of acute abdominal pain. *British Medical Journal*, pp. 9–13.

Dietterich, T.G., and R.S. Michalski. 1979. Learning and generalization of characteristic descriptions: Evaluation criteria and comparative review of selected methods. In *Proceedings of the Sixth Internatonal Joint Conference on AI*, pp. 223–231.

Duda, R.O. 1980. The PROSPECTOR system for mineral exploration. Final Rept., SRI Project 8172, Artificial Intelligence Center, SRI International, Menlo Park, Calif.

Duda, R.O., and P.E. Hart. 1980. Rule-based modeling of ore deposits for mineral exploration. Presented at AAAS Symposium, Machine Intelligence and Perception: The Past, Present, and Future.

Duda, R.O., P.E. Hart, K. Konolige, and R. Reboh. 1979. A computer-based consultant for mineral exploration. Final Rept., SRI Project 6415, Artificial Intelligence Center, SRI International, Menlo Park, Calif.

Eastman, C. 1978. The representation of design problems and maintenance of their structure. In J.C. Latombe, ed., *Artificial intelligence and pattern recognition in computer aided design*. New York: North-Holland, pp. 335–373.

Engelmore, R., and A. Terry. 1979. Structure and function of the CRYSALIS system. In *IJCAI* 6, pp. 250–256.

Erman, L.D., and V.R. Lesser. 1978. System engineering techniques for artificial intelligence systems. In A. Hanson and E. Riseman, eds., *Computer vision systems*. New York: Academic Press, pp. 37–45.

Faught, W., D.A. Waterman, S. Rosenschein, D. Gorlin, and T. Tepper. 1980. EP-2: An exemplary programming system. Rand Report R-2411-ARPA, Rand Corp., Santa Monica, Calif.

Freeman, P., and A. Newell. 1971. A model for functional reasoning in design. In *IJCAI 2*, pp. 621–640.

Garvey, T.D., and M.A. Fischler. 1979. Machine-intelligence-based multisensor ESM system. Technical Rept. AFAL-TR-79-1162, Artificial Intelligence Center, SRI International, Menlo Park, Calif.

Gaschnig, J. 1979. Preliminary performance analysis of the PROSPECTOR consultant system for mineral exploration. In *IJCAI 6*, pp. 308–310.

_____. 1981. PROSPECTOR: An expert system for mineral exploration. *Machine Intelligence, Infotech State of the Art Report* 9, no. 3.

Genesereth, M.R. 1977. An automated consultant for MACSYMA. In *IJCAI 5*, p. 789.

_____. 1979. The role of plans in automated consultation. In *IJCAI 6*, pp. 311–319.

_____. 1980. Metaphors and models. In *Proceedings of the AAAI Conference 1980*, pp. 208–211.

Goldberg, R., and S.M. Weiss. 1980. An experimental transformation of a large expert system knowledge-base. Working Paper, Computer Science Department, Rutgers University, New Brunswick, N.J.

Gorry, G.A. 1974. Research on expert systems. MAC Technical Memorandum 56, Project MAC, Massachusetts Institute of Technology, Cambridge, Mass.

Gorry, G.A., J.P. Kassirer, A. Essig, and W.B. Schwartz. 1973. Decision analysis as the basis for computer-aided management of acute renal failure. *American Journal of Medicine* 55:473–484.

Green, C. 1976. The design of the PSI program synthesis system. In *Proceedings of the Second International Conference on Software Engineering*, pp. 4–18.

Green, C., R. Waldinger, D. Barstow, R. Elschlager, D. Lenat, B. McCune, D. Shaw, and L. Steinberg. 1974. Progress report on program-understanding systems. Memo AIM 240, Artificial Intelligence Laboratory, Stanford University, Stanford, Calif. Also in Rept. STAN-CS-74-444, Computer Science Department, Stanford University.

Hart, P.E. 1975. Progress on a computer-based consultant. In *IJCAI 4*, pp. 831–841.

Hart, P.E., R.O. Duda, and M.T. Einaudi. 1979. Computer-based consultation system for mineral exploration. In A. Weiss, ed., *Computer methods for the 80's*. New York: American Institute of Mining, Metallurgical, and Petroleum Engineers, pp. 127–140.

Hayes-Roth, B., and F. Hayes-Roth. 1979. A cognitive model of planning. *Cognitive Science* 3:275–310.

Hayes-Roth, F., P. Klahr, and D. Mostow. 1980. Advice-taking and knowledge refinement: An iterative view of skill acquisition. Rept. P-6518, Rand Corp., Santa Monica, Calif.

Hempel, C.G. 1952. *Fundamentals of concept formation in empirical science.* Chicago: University of Chicago Press.

Hewitt, C. 1975. How to use what you know. In *IJCAI* 4, pp. 189–198.

Klahr, P. 1978. Planning techniques for rule selection in deductive question-answering. In D.A. Waterman and F. Hayes-Roth, eds., *Pattern-directed inference systems.* New York: Academic Press, pp. 223–239.

———. 1979. Conditional answers in question-answering systems. In *IJCAI* 6, pp. 481–483.

Klahr, P., and W.S. Faught. 1980. Knowledge-based simulation. In *AAAI* 1, pp. 181–183.

Langley, P. 1977. Rediscovering physics with BACON 3. In *IJCAI* 6, pp. 505–507.

Larkin, J., J. McDermott, D.P. Simon, and H.A. Simon. 1980. Expert and novice performance in solving physics problems. *Science* 20:208.

Lenat, D.B. 1975. Beings: Knowledge as interacting experts. In *IJCAI* 4, pp. 126–133.

———. 1977. Automated theory formation in mathematics. In *IJCAI* 5, pp. 833–842.

———. 1977. On automated scientific theory formation: A case study using the AM program. Ph.D. Diss. Rept. STAN-CS-76-570, Computer Science Department, Stanford University, Stanford, Calif. Reprinted in R. Davis and D.B. Lenat, *Knowledge-based systems in artificial intelligence.* New York: McGraw-Hill, 1980.

London, P.E. 1978. Dependency networks as a representation for modelling in general problem solvers. Rept. TR-698 NSG-7253, Computer Science Department, University of Maryland, University Park.

Mark, W.S. 1977. The reformulation approach to building expert systems. In *IJCAI* 5, pp. 329–335.

Martin, N., P. Friedland, J. King, and M. Stefik. 1977. Knowledge-base management for experiment planning in molecular genetics. In *IJCAI* 5, pp. 882–887.

McCorduck, P. 1979. *Machines who think: A personal inquiry into the history and prospects of artificial intelligence.* San Francisco: W.H. Freeman.

Millen, J.K. 1968. CHARYBDIS, a LISP program to display mathematical expressions on typewriter-like devices. In M. Klerer and J. Reinfelds, eds., *Interactive systems for experimental and applied mathematics.* New York: Academic Press, pp. 79–90.

Minsky, M.L. 1967. *Computation: Finite and infinite machines.* Englewood Cliffs, N.J.: Prentice-Hall.

Model, M.L. 1979. Monitoring system behavior in a complex computational environment. Ph.D. Diss. Rept. STAN-CS-79-701, Computer Science Department, Stanford University, Stanford, Calif.

Newell, A. 1973. Artificial intelligence and the concept of mind. In R.C. Schank and K.M. Colby, eds., *Computer models of thought and language.* San Francisco: W.H. Freeman.

Newell, A., and H.A. Simon. 1972. *Human problem solving.* Englewood Cliffs, N.J.: Prentice-Hall.

Nilsson, N.J. 1971. *Problem-solving methods in artificial intelligence.* New York: McGraw-Hill.

Reboh, R. 1980. Using a matcher to make an expert consultation system behave intelligently. In AAAI 1, pp. 231–234.

Rosenberg, S. 1980. An intelligent support system for energy resources in the United States. In *Proceedings of the Third Biennial Conference of the Canadian Society for Computational Studies of Intelligence,* pp. 34–40.

Rubin, A. 1975. The role of hypotheses in medical diagnosis. In *IJCAI* 4, pp. 856–862.

Rychener, M.D. 1979. A semantic network of production rules in a system for describing computer structures. In *IJCAI* 6, pp. 738–743.

Shortliffe, E.H. 1978. Medical consultation systems: Designing for doctors. Rept. HPP-78–29, Heuristic Programming Project, Computer Science Department, Stanford University, Stanford, Calif.

Shortliffe, E.H., B.G. Buchanan, and E.A. Feigenbaum. 1979. Knowledge engineering for medical decision making: A review of computer-based clinical decision aids. *Proceedings of the IEEE* 67:1207–1224.

Simon, H.A. 1969. *The sciences of the artificial.* Cambridge, Mass.: MIT Press.

————. 1983. Why should machines learn? In R.S. Michalski, J. Carbonell, and T.M. Mitchell, eds., *Machine learning: An artificial intelligence approach.* Palo Alto, Calif.: Tioga Press.

Stansfield, J.L. 1977. COMEX: A support system for a commodities expert. Rept. 423, Artificial Intelligence Laboratory, Massachusetts Institute of Technology, Cambridge, Mass.

————. 1980. Qualitative reasoning about time series. In *Proceedings of the Third Biennial Conference of the Canadian Society for Computational Studies of Intelligence,* pp. 41–48.

Stefik, M. 1980. Planning with constraints. Ph.D. Diss. Rept. HPP-80-2, Heuristic Programming Project, Computer Science Department, Stanford University, Stanford, Calif. Also Rept. STAN-CS-80-784, Computer Science Department, Stanford University.

Stolfo, S. 1980. Automatic discovery of heuristics for nondeterministic programs from sample execution traces. Ph.D. Diss. Institute of

426 Suggested Reading

Vere, S.A. 1979. Induction of reliable productions in the presence of background information. In *IJCAI* 5, pp. 349–355.

Waterman, D.A. 1976. An introduction to production systems. Rept. P-5751, Rand Corp., Santa Monica, Calif. Also in *AISB Newsletter* 25.

———. 1978. A rule-based approach to knowledge acquisition for man-machine interface programs. *International Journal of Man-Machine Studies* 10:693–711.

Waterman, D.A., W.S. Faught, P. Klahr, S.J. Rosenschein, and R. Wesson. 1980. Design issues for exemplary programming. Rept. Note N-1484-RC, Rand Corp., Santa Monica, Calif. Also in A. Biermann, G. Guiho, and Y. Kordratoff, eds., *Automatic program construction techniques*. New York: Macmillan, 1983.

Wesson, R.B. 1977. Planning in the world of the air traffic controller. In *IJCAI* 5, pp. 473–479.

Winston, P.H. 1977. *Artificial intelligence*. Reading, Mass.: Addison-Wesley.

Author Index

Subject Index

design issues in, 253–266

discourse in, 255–256

efficiency in, 257

end users and, 245–246, 278

expert system characteristics in, 254–257

explicitness in, 276–277

feasibility demonstration in, 268–271, 274–275

formal, blinded, statistical study in, 276

formal versus informal testing in, 248–249

hardware environment in, 256–257

of hazard in spill problem, 264–265

of human experts, 242–243

interaction of knowledge in, 265–266

issues and case studies in, 241–280

key issues in best use of, 261–266

long-term feedback process in, 241–244

Oak Ridge National Laboratory (ORNL) case study in, 272–277

objective standard in, 261–263

by peers, 252

performance standards in, 264–265

pitfalls in design and conduct of, 247–253

preselected test cases in, 249–251

principles of, 247–248

questions used in, 242

reasoning in, 219–239, 251–252, 255

reasons for, 244–253

recommendations in, 277–279

researchers and, 246–247

R1 case study in, 266–272

sensitivity analysis in, 265

stages of, 258–261

systems builders and, 244–245

testimonial method in, 275–276

time demands on evaluators in, 266

timing of, 257–261

use of term, 254

variable elimination in, 264

EXPERT, 9, 38, 135, 180–183, 213, 297–301

evaluation of, 182–183

explanation system in, 151

facilities of, 301

inference engine in, 180, 300–301

knowledge-base revision in, 152–153

knowledge representation in, 202, 204, 206–207, 209, 298–300

Oak Ridge National Laboratory (ORNL) problem with, 170, 173, 180–183

overview of, 180–181, 297–298

problem scope in, 181, 199

program construction and structure in, 181–182, 199, 200, 388–392

as skeletal system, 286

support features of, 212

Expertise

expert system with, 43–45

features of, 41–43

finding solutions efficiently and, 44–45

high performance and, 44

Experts

evaluation of, 242–243

see also Domain experts

Expert systems

artificial intelligence research with, 60

case history of use of, 32–35

characteristics of, 50–55, 170

codification of knowledge and, 28

commercial exploitation of, 28

components of, 16–19

construction of, 23–27

data processing systems different from, 5

definition of, 32, 43, 169

developmental lines within, 7–11

emphasis on knowledge in, 4–5

fundamental qualities of, 41–50

history of development of, 35–41

knowledge-based, 59–60

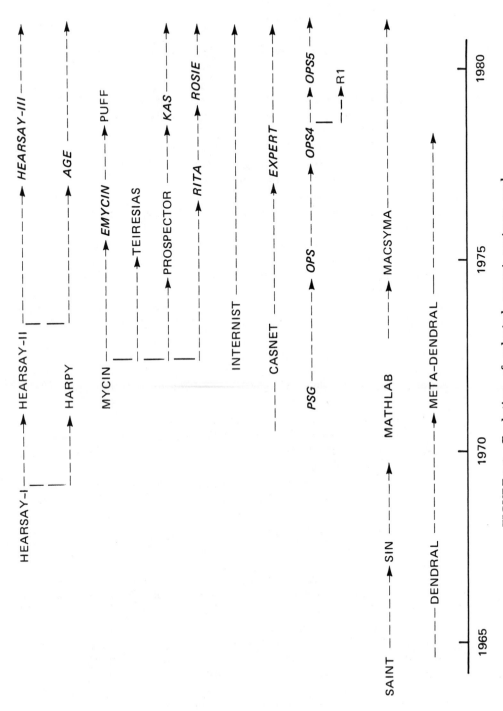

FIGURE 1.1 Evolution of selected expert systems and expert system building languages. (Italics indicate system building languages).

was dominated by a naive belief that a few laws of reasoning coupled with powerful computers would produce expert and superhuman performance. As experience accrued, the severely limited power of general-purpose problem-solving strategies ultimately led to the view that they were too weak to solve most complex problems (Newell 1969; Newell and Simon 1963). In reaction to perceived limitations in the overly general strategies, many researchers began to work on narrowly defined application problems.

By the mid-1970s several expert systems had begun to emerge. A few investigators who recognized the central role of knowledge in these systems then initiated efforts to develop comprehensive knowledge representation theories and associated general-purpose systems (Bobrow and Winograd 1977; Minsky 1975; Brachman 1977; Szolovits, Hawkinson, and Martin 1977). Within a few years it became apparent that these efforts had limited success for reasons similar to those that doomed the first overly general problem-solvers. "Knowledge" as a target of study is too broad and diverse; efforts to solve knowledge-based problems in general are premature. On the other hand several different approaches to knowledge representation proved sufficient for the expert systems that employed them. The lesson learned from these experiences was, finally, what Feigenbaum expressed: the expert's knowledge provides the key to expert performance, while knowledge representation and inference schemes provide the mechanisms for its use. The search for powerful or general knowledge representations, although apparently intuitively desirable, has no empirical justification.

In short, an expert's knowledge per se seems both necessary and nearly sufficient for developing an expert system. This observation is empirical, not tautological.

Figure 1.1 displays some of the developmental lines within the expert systems field. The field spans two decades, and, because most projects continue for many years, the temporal positions shown in the figure are approximate. Many expert systems do not appear in the figure. Those that do appear are briefly described in the following paragraphs.

The DENDRAL project at Stanford recently entered its sixteenth year. This project produced two systems, DENDRAL and META-DENDRAL (Buchanan and Mitchell 1977, 1978; Buchanan and Feigenbaum 1978; Feigenbaum, Buchanan, and Lederberg 1971; Lindsay et al. 1980). DENDRAL analyzes mass spectrographic, nuclear magnetic resonance, and other chemical experiment data to infer the plausible structures of an unknown compound. DENDRAL employs an efficient variant of generate-and-test in its problem-solving. Its generator can enumerate every possible organic structure that satisfies the constraints apparent in the data by systematically government. A partial list of its accomplishments to date includes the following:

- PROSPECTOR has discovered a molybdenum deposit whose ultimate value will probably exceed $100,000,000. (Personal correspondence, John Gaschnig, SRI International).
- R1 configures customer requests for VAX computer systems at Digital Equipment Corporation, despite the fact that even the resident experts thought it could not be done (McDermott 1981).
- DENDRAL, which years ago demonstrated its superhuman performance, supports hundreds of international users daily in chemical structure elucidation (Lindsay et al. 1980).
- CADUCEUS embodies more knowledge of internal medicine than any human and can correctly diagnose complex test cases that stymie human experts (Pople, Myers, and Miller 1975; Pople 1981; Miller, Pople, and Myers 1982).
- PUFF integrated knowledge of pulmonary function disease with a previously developed domain-independent expert system for diagnostic consultations and now provides expert analyses at a California medical center (Feigenbaum 1977).

These and other accomplishments indicate that the field of expert systems is maturing rapidly. The scientific and technical bases that support this field, however, have achieved only limited development. Each new application requires creative and challenging work, although some principles and systematizations have emerged. At this point expert systems is a highly experimental field with little in the way of general theory. Nevertheless, core problems have surfaced and numerous tools and techniques now exist that transfer from one application to the next.

1.1 History

At the International Joint Conference on Artificial Intelligence in 1977, Feigenbaum, in an invited paper, presented the key insight into expert systems paraphrased here: The power of an expert system derives from the knowledge it possesses, not from the particular formalisms and inference schemes it employs. This insight summarizes a major change in the perspective of many workers in AI. Briefly reviewing the mind-set of the earlier periods helps us to appreciate the significance of this new perspective. The first period of AI research

1980; Pauker et al. 1976; Pople, Myers and Miller 1975; Pople 1981; Shortliffe 1976; Weiss, Kulikowski, and Safir 1978a, b; Weiss and Kulikowski 1979), and electronics analysis (Stallman and Sussman 1977; Sussman 1977).

The third reason for focusing on knowledge recognizes its intrinsic value. Knowledge is a scarce resource whose refinement and reproduction creates wealth. Traditionally the transmission of knowledge from human expert to trainee has required education and internship years long. Extracting knowledge from humans and putting it in computable forms can greatly reduce the costs of knowledge reproduction and exploitation. At the same time the process of knowledge refinement can be speeded up by making private knowledge available for public test and evaluation.

In short, expert performance depends critically on expert knowledge. Because knowledge is the key ingredient in solving important problems, it has features characteristic of a rare element: justifying possibly expensive mining operations; requiring efficient and effective technologies to be fashioned into products; and making the means to reproduce it synthetically a dream come true.

Expert systems differ in important ways from both conventional data processing systems and systems developed in other branches of AI. In contrast to traditional data processing systems, AI applications generally involve several distinguishing features, which include symbolic representation, symbolic inference, and heuristic search. In fact, each of these corresponds to a well-studied core topic within AI, and a simple AI task often yields to one of the formal approaches developed for these core problems. But expert systems differ from the broad class of AI tasks in several respects. First, they perform difficult tasks at expert levels of performance. Second, they emphasize domain-specific problem-solving strategies over the more general "weak methods" of AI (Newell 1969). Third, they employ self-knowledge to reason about their own inference processes and provide explanations or justifications for conclusions reached. And, last, they solve problems that generally fall into one of the following categories: interpretation, prediction, diagnosis, debugging, design, planning, monitoring, repair, instruction, and control. As a result of these distinctions, expert systems represent an area of AI research that involves paradigms, tools, and system development strategies.

The motivation for this book derives from the great current interest in expert systems (Feigenbaum 1977; Duda and Gaschnig 1981; Michie 1979; Yasaki 1981; F. Hayes-Roth 1981; Webster and Miner 1982; Edelson 1982). It is the one area within the young field of AI that has a record of successful applications and is consequently the area with the most immediate significance for industry and for constructing man-machine systems with specialized problem-solving expertise. Expertise consists of knowledge about a particular domain, understanding of domain problems, and skill at solving some of these problems. Knowledge in any specialty is usually of two sorts: public and private. Public knowledge includes the published definitions, facts, and theories of which textbooks and references in the domain of study are typically composed. But expertise usually involves more than just this public knowledge. Human experts generally possess private knowledge that has not found its way into the published literature. This private knowledge consists largely of rules of thumb that have come to be called *heuristics*. Heuristics enable the human expert to make educated guesses when necessary, to recognize promising approaches to problems, and to deal effectively with errorful or incomplete data. Elucidating and reproducing such knowledge is the central task in building expert systems.

Researchers in this field suggest several reasons for their emphasis on knowledge itself rather than on formal reasoning methods. First, most of the difficult and interesting problems do not have tractable algorithmic solutions since many important tasks originate in complex social or physical contexts, which generally resist precise description and rigorous analysis. Planning, legal reasoning, medical diagnosis, geological exploration, and military situation analysis exemplify these problems. Furthermore, contemporary methods of symbolic and mathematical reasoning, which have limited applicability to the area of expert systems, do not provide means for representing knowledge, describing problems at multiple levels of abstraction, allocating problem-solving resources, controlling cooperative processes, and integrating diverse sources of knowledge in inference. These functions depend primarily on the capacity to manipulate problem descriptions and to apply relevant pieces of knowledge selectively. Current mathematics offers little help in such tasks.

The second reason for emphasizing knowledge rather than formal reasoning methods is pragmatic: human experts achieve outstanding performance because they are knowledgeable. If computer programs embody and use this knowledge, then, they too should attain high levels of performance. This has proved to be true repeatedly in the short history of expert systems. Systems have attained expert levels in several tasks: mineral prospecting (Duda et al. 1979, Gaschnig 1980a), computer configuration (McDermott 1980c, b), chemical structure elucidation (Buchanan and Feigenbaum 1978; Feigenbaum, Buchanan, and Lederberg 1971; Feigenbaum 1977; Lindsay et al. 1980), symbolic mathematics (Martin and Fateman 1971), chess (Wilkins 1979, 1980), medical diagnosis and therapy (Clancey 1979; Clancey, Shortliffe, and Buchanan 1979; Fagan et al. 1979; Kulikowski

1

An Overview of Expert Systems

Frederick Hayes-Roth, Donald A. Waterman, and Douglas B. Lenat

This chapter traces the principal developments in artificial intelligence that have led to the current emphasis on knowledge-based expert systems and the corresponding field of knowledge engineering. Machines that lack knowledge seem doomed to perform intellectually trivial tasks. Those that embody knowledge and apply it skillfully seem capable of equaling or surpassing the best performance of human experts. Knowledge provides the power to do work; knowledge engineering is the technology that promises to make knowledge a valuable industrial commodity.

Artificial intelligence (AI) has achieved considerable success in the development of expert systems since the mid-1960s. This area of AI has concentrated on the construction of high-performance programs in specialized professional domains, a pursuit that has encouraged an emphasis on the knowledge that underlies human expertise and has simultaneously decreased the apparent significance of domain-independent problem-solving theory. A new set of principles, tools, and techniques has emerged that forms the basis of knowledge engineering.

The area of expert systems investigates methods and techniques

3

Introduction

Building Expert Systems

provide a comprehensive picture of the state of the art. Many specific approaches to problems are presented; more unresolved, but central questions are raised. The field will move forward from here, and this book will provide a firm foundation for such progress.

In rereading the book during final editing, I was struck by the sheer number of important ideas it contains. This reflects the scope of the task the contributors undertook: to clarify the nature of knowledge and its relationship to machine embodiments of expertise. Eventually, I expect that many additional books will focus specifically on a good many of the important ideas introduced here.

The authors have created a valuable work, synthesizing the state of the understanding at the present time, providing a basic textbook for students of knowledge engineering, and laying out the territory for future research. Their work also provides an impetus for the adventurous to travel further into the realm of knowledge-based expert systems, wherein knowledge is a natural source of power and knowledge engineers convert this potential into accomplishment.

Weaknesses

This book is overambitious, its authors apparently attempting, all at once, to survey, teach, and advance the field of knowledge engineering. Any one of these goals would be difficult to achieve, but the three together strike me as impossible. So I interpret its objectives differently: what this book can and does accomplish is to establish the first homestead in a new land, in which all successive travelers can rest and sup before moving on to more distant settlements.

In striving for comprehensiveness we have sacrificed the narrow focus that would enhance cogency and terseness; but the new field of expert systems seems to resist reduction to a few simple, elegant ideas. In this book we do not, after all, tell the reader how to build an expert system. Nor should that be expected. Books with titles like *Remodeling Your Home Painlessly, Designing a Backyard Hydro-electric Plant,* and *Building an Expert System for Crisis Management* should raise eyebrows. The people who build expert systems have studied AI, experimented in knowledge engineering, and labored over their laboratory and field systems for many years. Perhaps this book will shorten by one or two years the time it takes the reader to acquire such expertise. That will satisfy all of us who have worked to produce it.

Frederick Hayes-Roth
Palo Alto, California

January 1983

The intent of this book is to convey what is known today about building expert systems. It identifies the many different things that an engineer or technical manager would want to know.

- An overview of the expert systems field that explains what it is, where it came from, and what it means (Chapter 1)
- An analysis of how expert systems differ from conventional software programs, laboratory artificial intelligence (AI) programs in particular, and human beings who perform tasks expertly (Chapter 2)
- An explanation of the basic concepts of AI and knowledge engineering that affect design and implementation (Chapter 3)
- An analysis of the architectural choices faced in building expert systems, including specific design prescriptions for tasks of different kinds (Chapter 4)
- An examination of the evolutionary process of knowledge acquisition needed to put expertise into a machine (Chapter 5)
- A comparative analysis of the strengths and weaknesses of existing knowledge engineering tools, based on experiences with using eight different techniques on an "identical" problem (Chapter 6)
- A discussion of the myriad important ways systems need to understand and apply knowledge in order to attain robustness, awareness, and extensibility (Chapter 7)
- A discussion of the pitfalls and opportunities that arise from the important need to evaluate artificial expertise (Chapter 8)
- An examination of the most widely used knowledge engineering tools that emphasizes their technical origins and capabilities (Chapter 9)
- A crisis-management problem statement that, in its complexity and requirements for knowledge processing, exemplifies a large class of potential applications that have created the need to build expert systems (Chapter 10)
- Samples of dialogues between a crisis manager and various prototype expert systems built by the knowledge engineers who tackled the workshop's Mystery Problem (Appendix)

Achievements

This book marks the adolescence of a major area of science and the birth of a new industry: knowledge engineering. The expert systems analyzed, the methodologies discussed, and the techniques presented

outline covering the current state of knowledge. We then organized
the workshop participants into groups associated with each subarea
of focus. Each of these groups accepted responsibility for elucidating
particular bodies of technical knowledge.

At the same time we needed a comparative evaluation of the software tools and methodologies of knowledge engineering. No one had
ever approached the same task with two different tools, so the field
lacked a basis for real comparison. To this end I covertly recruited and
brought to the workshop a Mystery Expert and his colleague (Carroll
Johnson and Sara Jordan), armed with an exceptionally well-prepared
statement of requirements for an expert system (abstracted in Chapter
10). By the time the workshop began I had persuaded every developer
of a significant knowledge engineering tool to attend, meet the Mystery
Expert, and participate in a week-long effort to develop primitive but
worthwhile experimental versions of expert systems to deal with the
Mystery Problem.

This book represents the primary accomplishment of the workshop. Many people played crucial parts in creating and producing the
workshop and the book itself, of course. Don Waterman valiantly
wrote, rewrote, and rewrote again the proposals for government funding of the workshop expenses. He deserves kudos for his persistence
and his expert performance at this demanding task. And heartfelt
thanks go to Eamon Barrett, then of the National Science Foundation,
and Bob Engelmore and Bob Kahn of the Defense Advanced Research
Projects Agency for ultimately shepherding those proposals through
the labyrinthine Washington funding process. Doug Lenat, who had
criticized our Hawaii conference arrangements so effectively, was co-
opted easily into the new workshop management team and helped us
throughout. The workshop also depended on significant cooperation
by many people, including the authors of the chapters, Lee Baumann
of SAI, and Mary Shannon, then of Rand.

Motivations

The contributors to this book set themselves several objectives. We
wanted to stimulate a synthesis of ideas in a field that often moves
too fast for extensive and effective scientific deliberations. We wanted
to provide a situation that would create tremendous incentives for
intellectual synthesis. We wanted to see the result of that synthesizing
effort aid the uptake of this new technology by the large numbers of
future knowledge engineers we anticipate. And we wanted to encourage cooperative, group efforts that cut across traditional regional,
institutional, and methodological boundaries.

Preface

As the first text in an explosive and exciting field, *Building Expert Systems* requires a special introduction.

Origins

Early in 1979 Don Waterman and I conceived the idea of holding a Workshop on Expert Systems, much in the spirit of our earlier Workshop on Production Systems held in 1977 in Hawaii. For that workshop, which brought together most of the leading researchers interested in rule-based systems, invitees had prepared and presented scholarly papers in a conventional way, and the best of these were collected in a book called *Pattern-Directed Inference Systems* (Waterman and Hayes-Roth, 1978). Although others considered the workshop important and the book valuable, I had some reservations about both, which reflected a general reaction to efforts of this sort: they generally collect an unbalanced assortment of contemporary ideas on a subject rather than catalyzing a deeper understanding of its scientific state.

When the topic of expert systems arose, I suggested that we organize the proposed workshop in a significantly different manner. Our Workshop on Expert Systems would convene all active researchers for the purpose of synthesizing the knowledge of the field. To do that, several tasks had to be performed. At the outset we had to develop an for solving important problems. We can foresee two beneficial effects. The first and most obvious will be the development of knowledge systems that replicate and autonomously apply human expertise. For these systems, knowledge engineering will provide the technology for converting human knowledge into industrial power. The second benefit may be less obvious. As an inevitable side effect, knowledge engineering will catalyze a global effort to collect, codify, exchange, and exploit applicable forms of human knowledge. In this way, knowledge engineering will accelerate the development, clarification, and expansion of human knowledge itself. If this series contributes to these exciting developments we will have achieved our aims.

Series Foreword

In recent years, research in the field of artificial intelligence has had many important successes. Among the most significant of these has been the development of powerful new computer systems known as "expert" or "knowledge-based" systems. These programs are designed to represent and apply factual knowledge of specific areas of expertise to solve problems. For example, collaborative efforts by human experts and system developers have resulted in systems which diagnose diseases, configure computer systems, and prospect for minerals at performance levels equal to or surpassing human expertise. The potential power of systems which can replicate expensive or rare human knowledge has led to a worldwide effort to extend and apply this technology.

The Teknowledge Series in Knowledge Engineering is a collaborative effort by Teknowledge Inc., an editorial board of knowledge system engineers, and Addison-Wesley to aid in this effort through book publication. Through this series we hope to provide an effective channel for informing and educating people interested in understanding and implementing this technology. We will be defining needed works, encouraging their development, and editorially managing their publication. Our intended audience includes practicing knowledge engineers, students and scientists in related disciplines, and technical managers assessing the potential of these systems. Readers with criticisms or suggestions for needed books are urged to contact the managing editor or a member of the editorial board.

Over time, the knowledge engineering field will have an impact on all areas of human activity where knowledge provides the power

Edward A. Feigenbaum, Computer Science Department, Stanford University

Charles Forgy, Department of Computer Science, Carnegie-Mellon University

John Gaschnig, late of SRI International

Michael Genesereth, Computer Science Department, Stanford University

Ira Goldstein, Hewlett-Packard Corporation

Daniel Gorlin, formerly of The Rand Corporation

Russell Greiner, Computer Science Department, Stanford University

Peter Hart, Fairchild Laboratory for Artificial Intelligence Research

Frederick Hayes-Roth, Teknowledge Inc.

Carroll K. Johnson, Chemistry Division, Oak Ridge National Laboratory

Sara R. Jordan, Chemistry Division, Oak Ridge National Laboratory

Philip Klahr, The Rand Corporation

Casimir Kulikowski, Department of Computer Science, Rutgers University

Douglas B. Lenat, Computer Science Department, Stanford University

Philip London, Teknowledge Inc.

John McDermott, Department of Computer Science, Carnegie-Mellon University

Tom Mitchell, Department of Computer Science, Rutgers University

H. Penny Nii, Computer Science Department, Stanford University

Peter Politakis, Computer Science Department, Rutgers University

Harry Pople, Decision Systems Laboratory, University of Pittsburgh

Rene Reboh, Computer Resources, SRI International

Stanley Rosenschein, Computer Resources, SRI International

Earl Sacerdoti, Machine Intelligence Corporation

Howard Schrobe, Artificial Intelligence Laboratory, Massachusetts Institute of Technology

A. Carlisle Scott, Teknowledge Inc.

Edward Shortliffe, Division of Clinical Pharmacology, Stanford University Medical Center

Mark Stefik, Xerox Palo Alto Research Center

Allan Terry, Teknowledge Inc.

William van Melle, Xerox Palo Alto Research Center

Donald A. Waterman, The Rand Corporation

Sholom M. Weiss, Department of Computer Science, Rutgers University

David E. Wilkins, SRI International

List of Contributors

Nelleke Aiello, Computer Science Department, Stanford University

Janice Aikens, IBM Palo Alto Scientific Center

Saul Amarel, Department of Computer Science, Rutgers University

Robert Balzer, Information Sciences Institute, University of Southern California

David R. Barstow, Schlumberger/Doll Research

Robert Bechtel, Naval Ocean Systems Center

James Bennett, Teknowledge Inc.

John Benoit, The MITRE Corporation

Lawrence Birnbaum, Department of Computer Science, Yale University

Ronald Brachman, Fairchild Laboratory for Artificial Intelligence Research

Bruce G. Buchanan, Computer Science Department, Stanford University

William Clancey, Computer Science Department, Stanford University

Randall Davis, Artificial Intelligence Laboratory, Massachusetts Institute of Technology

Jon Doyle, Department of Computer Science, Carnegie-Mellon University

Richard O. Duda, Fairchild Laboratory for Artificial Intelligence Research

Carl Engelman, The MITRE Corporation

Robert S. Engelmore, Teknowledge Inc.

Lee D. Erman, Teknowledge Inc.

ix

Contents

Chapter 4: Reprinted with permission granted by North Holland Publishing Company. This work appeared previously as "The Organization of Expert Systems: A Tutorial" in *Artificial Intelligence* Vol. 18, No. 2; March 1982. The material in "Basic Artificial Intelligence Concepts" and "The Architecture of Expert Systems" also appeared earlier as "The Organization of Expert Systems: A Prescriptive Tutorial" in Xerox Palo Alto Research Center Technical Report VLSI-82-1, January 1982.

Chapter 6: Reprinted with permission from Rand report R-2812-NSF, May 1982.

Library of Congress Cataloging in Publication Data

Main entry under title:

Building expert systems.

    (Teknowledge series in knowledge engineering ; v. 1)
    Bibliography: p.
    Includes indexes.
    1. Expert systems (Computer science) 2. System design. I. Hayes-Roth, Frederick. II. Waterman, D. A. (Donald Arthur), III. Lenat, Douglas B.   IV. Series.
QA76.9.E96B84 1983   001.64'2   82-24511
ISBN 0-201-10686-8

Building Expert Systems

Edited by

Frederick Hayes-Roth
Teknowledge Inc.
Palo Alto, California

Donald A. Waterman
The Rand Corporation
Santa Monica, California

Douglas B. Lenat
Department of Computer Science
Stanford University
Stanford, California

1983
ADDISON-WESLEY PUBLISHING COMPANY, INC.
Advanced Book Program
Reading, Massachusetts
London · Amsterdam · Don Mills, Ontario · Sydney · Tokyo

Teknowledge Series in Knowledge Engineering

Frederick Hayes-Roth, *Series Editor*

Volume
1
BUILDING EXPERT SYSTEMS
Frederick Hayes-Roth, Donald A. Waterman,
and Douglas B. Lenat (eds.), 1983

Other volumes in preparation